TIDES OF INNOVATION IN OCEANIA

VALUE, MATERIALITY AND PLACE

TIDES OF INNOVATION IN OCEANIA

VALUE, MATERIALITY AND PLACE

EDITED BY ELISABETTA GNECCHI-RUSCONE AND ANNA PAINI

MONOGRAPHS IN
ANTHROPOLOGY SERIES

Australian
National
University

PRESS

ANU PRESS

Published by ANU Press
The Australian National University
Acton ACT 2601, Australia
Email: anupress@anu.edu.au
This title is also available online at press.anu.edu.au

National Library of Australia Cataloguing-in-Publication entry

Title: Tides of innovation in Oceania : value, materiality and
            place / Elisabetta Gnecchi-Ruscone,
            Anna Paini, editors.

ISBN: 9781760460921 (paperback) 9781760460938 (ebook)

Series: Monographs in anthropology series.

Subjects: Hauʻofa, Epeli--Influence.
            Ethnology--Oceania.
            Oceania--Social conditions.
            Oceania--Economic conditions.

Other Creators/Contributors:
            Paini, Anna, editor.

Cover design and layout by ANU Press. Front cover photograph by Elisabetta Gnecchi-Ruscone. Back cover photograph by Anna Paini.

Contents

Part One. Mapping Materiality in Time and Place

Part Two. Value and Agency: Local Experiences in Expanded Narratives

List of Figures and Tables

Acronyms and Abbreviations

ADCK	Agency for the Development of Kanak Culture
ACP	African, Caribbean and Pacific Group of States
BTF	Bureau Technique des Femmes
CEDAW	Convention on the Elimination of All Forms of Discrimination against Women
CF.NC	Conseil des Femmes de Nouvelle Calédonie
CFM.NC	Council of Melanesian Women of New Caledonia
CFP	French Pacific Franc
CHD	coronary heart disease
CIRAD	Coopération Internationale en Recherche Agronomique pour le Développement
CMAA	Cambridge Museum of Archaeology and Anthropology
EC	expression of culture
EHESS	École des hautes études en sciences sociales
ESCAP	United Nations Economic and Social Commission for Asia and the Pacific
ESfO	European Society for Oceanists
ESK	Etudes des Sociétés Kanak
EU	European Union
FAFM-NC	Federation of Melanesian Women's Associations of New Caledonia

FAO	Food and Agriculture Organization of the United Nations
FF	French Franc
FIPO	Fiji Intellectual Property Office
FITE	Festival International des Textiles Extraordinaires
FJD	Fiji dollar
FLNKS	Front de Libération Nationale Kanak Socialiste
GSM	Global System for Mobile Communications
IMF	International Monetary Fund
INSEE	National Institute of Statistics and Economic Studies
IP	intellectual property
IR	international relations
ITALY	I Truly Always Love You
JARCF	Jeunesse Agricole et Rurale Catholique des Femmes
JBE	Jastis Blong Evriwan (Justice Belong Everyone)
KFC	Kentucky Fried Chicken
LMS	London Missionary Society
MDG	Millennium Development Goals
MEG	Musée d'ethnographie de Genève
MEN	Musée d'ethnographie de Neuchâtel
MET	Metropolitan Museum of Manila
mfSVM	mouvement féminin vers un Souriant Village Mélanésien
MNC	Musée de Nouvelle-Calédonie
MQB	Musée du Quai Branly
MSG	Melanesian Spearhead Group
MSME	micro, small and medium enterprise

NAGPRA	Native American Graves Protection and Repatriation Act
NCDs	non-communicable diseases
NGO	non-governmental organisation
NHO	Native Hawaiian organization
NLA	National Library of Australia
NMA	National Museum of Australia
PPE	Papuan Pidgin English
PIFS	Pacific Islands Forum Secretariat
PNG	Papua New Guinea
SPC	Secretariat of the Pacific Community (formerly South Pacific Commission)
SPREP	Secretariat of the Pacific Regional Environment Programme
SWIMMING	Sleep While I Move My Inter National Gear
TOM	French Overseas Territory
TK	traditional knowledge
TKS	Tafea Kaljoral Senta
UHM	University of Hawai'i at Mānoa
UNESCO	United Nations Educational, Scientific and Cultural Organization
VKS	Vanuatu Kaljoral Senta (Vanuatu Cultural Centre)
VP	Vanuaaku Pati
WCED	World Commission on Environment and Development
WHO	World Health Organization
WIPO	World Intellectual Property Organization
WTO	World Trade Organization

Acknowledgements

Our greatest thanks are due to the women and men of the Pacific for welcoming us, sharing their time, knowledge and food and entering in a long-lasting dialogue which continues across the ocean, of which this volume is just one outcome. We are also thankful to the two anonymous reviewers for their constructive advice and for stimulating us to make more explicit the interconnections among the different dimensions explored by the essays gathered in the book. We trust that all those who have helped us throughout these years know of our continuing gratitude.

We have been inspired to edit this work following the organisation of the European Society for Oceanists (ESfO) Conference in Verona, for which we received generous support from the Wenner-Gren Foundation for Anthropological Research. We also thank the Università di Verona for supporting the conference and this work. We are grateful to the Musée d'ethnographie de Genève (MEG) for permission to reproduce photographs from its archives and to Michelle Antoinette for the compilation, reproduction and permissions for the photographs in Margaret Jolly's chapter. Finally, we wish to thank Carolyn Brewer for the editorial efforts she applied to preparing our manuscript for publication.

Elisabetta Gnecchi-Ruscone and Anna Paini
August 2016

Prologue: Where is Anthropology Located in the Task of Putting People First?

Andrew Moutu

I would firstly like to acknowledge the whole-hearted support which the European Society for Oceanists (ESfO) organising committee gave towards me going to and participating in the conference in Verona. I participated in three sessions of the conference which included being a discussant on the session on 'Re-forming the Land'; a contributor on the session on 'Roy Wagner: Symbolic Anthropology and the Fate of New Melanesian Ethnography'; and a panellist on the 'Round Table' discussion on the theme of the conference.

My comments here are limited to my participation in the panel on the theme of 'Putting People First: Intercultural Dialogue and Imagining the Future in Oceania'. The panel featured me and three others who represented different parts of Pacific Island societies.[1] The appearance and involvement of Pacific Island scholars in such international gatherings are neither an accident nor merely politically correct. In this conference, there was a deliberate attempt to listen to and engage with Pacific Islanders not only on a common intellectual footing, but also on matters of mutual academic and practical concerns. The session was held early in the evening after the day's round of conferencing.

---

1   These included: Manuka Henare, Aotearoa New Zealand; Joe Lizama, Northern Mariana Islands; and Marie-Claire Beboko-Beccalossi, Kanaky New Caledonia, who could not be present in person but sent a paper to be read.

1

I adopted a particular moral stance about the public role or value of anthropology when I participated in the panel and my strategy involved telling some jokes, each of which I hoped carried its own moral. Here I will reproduce only one of those jokes.

In 1998, I was trying to find my way from the Victoria Coach Station to Piccadilly in Central London. This was my first time travelling into London by coach so I had to ask an Englishman, who was walking along the same street, for directions for the train station in Victoria so that I could find my way to Piccadilly Circus in Central London.

I asked, 'Excuse me, Sir, can you help me find my way to the train station from here?'

Then he answered, 'Oh that's simple but I could tell you this on one condition that you first tell me, where do you come from?'

When I told him my Papua New Guinean origin, he said, 'So what brings you to London then?'

I then replied 'I came here to study.'

I thought my responses were already sufficient to lift the conditions he had imposed on my initial request for information, but he pursued further and asked: 'What are you going to study?'

'Anthropology,' I replied.

'Interesting. Anthropology and New Guinea, so do you guys still practise cannibalism?'

I was taken aback momentarily with his exoticism but managed to lend him a blowing punchline: 'I wish we still did because I am looking at my first meal on the streets of London.'

The story above will ring familiar echoes with the experience of anthropological fieldwork. The joke revealed that we were engaged in a cross-cultural dialogue and the punch-line brought home some measure of common understanding which our dialogical interaction sought to resolve. Subsequently I was guided to the train station where I was given coffee and a crash course on reading the London Underground map before I set off on my first trip. Anyone familiar with the story of Balinese cockfights will recall how Clifford Geertz (1973) and his wife had to run for freedom when police officers arrived in their village to arrest villagers who were involved in illegally staging cockfights. When the police started harassing villagers, Geertz and his wife dashed after another villager. Running away from the police was a shared experience between the two anthropologists and the villager and it made the Balinese recognise, among other things, the common humanity that the anthropologists had with the villagers. After heading out into the fields they ended up with the villager who invited them into his home where they had coffee. That was the turning point that opened up access for a productive interaction that Geertz subsequently had with the villagers.

In the story that I have told, the arresting moral problem was the exoticisation of New Guinea and cannibalism, which was held up as a foil to inspire a line of conversation. It is nonetheless true that exoticisation has been part of the way in which anthropology has constructed its knowledge of the other (Fabian 1983; Peirano 1998). There have been other kinds of criticisms—one being its association with the western colonial project. Indeed, anthropological knowledge has been scrutinised because of the way it has been conceived and instrumentalised (see Asad 1973; Clifford and Marcus (eds) 1986). Leaving aside all such criticisms, I want to comment specifically on the theme of this conference.

The notional sense of 'putting people first' summons other kinds of pressing questions which revolve around the larger question of why we would want to put people first. Is this a concern about trying to restore subjectivity to where it has been de-subjectivised? Is it a concern with giving back voice to subjects who have been muted? Is it about incorporating cultural variables into the equations of development? If we want to put people first, where have they been located in yesteryears? If anthropology is to be involved in a putting people first project, where will it find itself and what will its values encompass?

I am from Papua New Guinea (PNG) and when I started studying anthropology in the early 1990s, it was considered one of the 'dumbest' subjects on campus by the student population. It was, nevertheless, considered slightly brighter than social work and library science. At least that was the mindset of the students during my years at the University of Papua New Guinea (UNPG) (1991–1996).

My teachers at UPNG at that time had to take decisive steps about the courses they could and should teach so that they could make their graduates competent enough to find decent jobs in the labour market.

So they committed their ingenuity to inventing courses such as Social Impact Studies, Social Mapping, Rural Sociology and Cultural Policy—some of which are still being taught with constant modification. However, a fertile field of some complexity was burgeoning in the discipline of applied anthropology. But this demanded that the only way for a Papua New Guinean to appreciate the complexity was to be trained to use and engage with the language involved.

My interest and curiosity in anthropology was sparked by lectures on Karl Marx and other sociologists such as Max Weber, Émile Durkheim, C. Wright Mills and Peter L. Berger. But these interests dwindled as my years at UPNG were brought to an end (1994–1995). These were the years when applied anthropology took on a particular relevance. Applied anthropology was a step removed from my earlier interests in the subject in the sense that, in order to appreciate and be able to do applied anthropology, one must not only know the basic grammar and lexicons of anthropology, but be equally competent in research methods as well as the art of analytical writing—writing that puts description into the service of explanation and explanation into the service of policy objectives.

The public relevance and perhaps respect for anthropology in PNG came with the onset of the Bougainville crisis in 1989. The PNG Government found an intellectual ally in anthropologists. Soon after that mines, logging and oil projects boomed in different parts of PNG and this made it necessary for the engagement and use of anthropological expertise to bring sociological variables into the mathematical equations of development. There is legislation in PNG now, such as the *Oil and Gas Act*, that legally mandates the employ of anthropologists in conducting social mapping and landowner identification studies. These are not just studies that serve to satisfy a bureaucratic checklist monitored by a clerk behind a desk. The studies are extremely rich and intellectually demanding and the problem is that there may be no one in the government who has the competence to understand what the studies are about and to be able to transform the insights into the pragmatics of governance. If the reasons for these studies have not yet been discovered, it means that the public value of anthropology awaits the discipline at large.

The second issue that attracted a public interest in anthropology was the theoretical crisis revealed in the intellectual property debate of the 1990s and subsequent years. These were the years when the World Trade Organization (WTO) and the International Monetary Fund (IMF) were sponsoring developments in intellectual property regimes and exporting them elsewhere, especially to the developing world. I do not intend to suggest a causal link here, but in PNG the debate found a moral sound bite in the now famous Hagahai saga case. Another case, that provided a supply of fuel to a glowing fire of moral and intellectual respect for anthropology in PNG, came from the Miriam Willingal case in the Waghi area of Western Highlands Province. Miriam was part of a compensation payment made to her father's mother's people. Non-governmental organisations (NGOs) and human rights activists stepped in and the case made its appearance in the press and in the National Court of PNG. I am mentioning these cases to highlight the fact that it is in the public arena that people come to marvel at and be dazzled by the insights of anthropological thinking. Maybe the public value of anthropology should be to make anthropology conscious of the shape and form in which it wishes to make itself accessible, persuasive, legitimate and relevant in the public imagination.

I was converted to anthropology about 11 years ago when I first met and witnessed first-hand conversations among some of the finest minds of anthropology at the 'Myths to Minerals' conference held at The Australian National University in Canberra.[2] It was also during that time that I met the esoteric Roy Wagner who after learning that I was working for the PNG National Museum, told me, 'your country has a huge intellectual capital to export'. Having heard and seen Roy perform his customary poetics in the conference the previous day, I was left astounded and returned to PNG wanting to explore the intellectual capital that he mentioned. I thought to myself, 'This is a man of considerable learning and wisdom. Through his anthropology, he has seen something about my people and country that I have taken for granted and which I would never have had reason to suppose existed'. Since then I have come to realise that anthropology is one of the most noble of all the inventions of western cultural rationalisation. However, the intellectual capital that Roy Wagner told me about, and of which I have now become a bit cognisant, is something that has yet to be converted into stock that can be exchanged for the legitimacy of our discipline in countries like PNG.

---

2   Two volumes came from this conference: Alan Rumsey and James F. Weiner (eds), *Mining and Indigenous Lifeworlds in Australia and Papua New Guinea*, Adelaide: Crawford Publishing House, 2001a; and Alan Rumsey and James F. Weiner (eds), *Emplaced Myth: Space, Narrative, and Knowledge in Aboriginal Australia and Papua New Guinea*, Honolulu: University of Hawai'i Press, 2001b.

At times, I am unsure what it is that I am not convinced about with anthropology. This has mainly to do with the public value of anthropological knowledge. Among other things I have learnt from reading Marilyn Strathern's *The Gender of the Gift* (1988), is that social knowledge is about creating the conditions for apprehending the world anew and that 'conversion' works to retain its own value but 'transformation' carries it to yet another dimension of reality. I am wondering what transformations might yet exist for the public value of anthropological knowledge and await the moment when anthropology can ensorcell me by a power akin to a positivist sanction such as is publicly commanded by lawyers and economists.

I feel that the theme of 'putting people first' must cause anthropology to ask where it might want to locate itself in such an undertaking. The general message of the plenary session was that anthropology must take itself more seriously than merely being a social science that stimulates the brain cells of academic production. By calling 'for a morally resolved intellectual action', the panel reiterated the ongoing and increasing value of anthropological intervention in matters of public debate and policy in the Pacific and beyond.

References

Asad, Talal (ed.). 1973. *Anthropology & the Colonial Encounter*. New York: Humanities Press.

Clifford, James and George Marcus (eds). 1986. *Writing Culture: The Poetics and Politics of Ethnography*. Berkeley: University of California Press.

Fabian, Johannes. 1983. *Time and the Other: How Anthropology Makes Its Object*. New York: Columbia University Press.

Geertz, Clifford. 1973. *The Interpretation of Cultures: Selected Essays*. New York: Basic Books.

Peirano, Mariza G.S. 1998. 'When anthropology is at home: The different contexts of a single discipline'. *Annual Review of Anthropology* 27: 105–28. doi.org/10.1146/annurev.anthro.27.1.105.

Rumsey, Alan and James F. Weiner (eds). 2001a. *Mining and Indigenous Lifeworlds in Australia and Papua New Guinea*. Adelaide: Crawford Publishing House.

Rumsey, Alan and James F. Weiner (eds). 2001b. *Emplaced Myth: Space, Narrative, and Knowledge in Aboriginal Australia and Papua New Guinea*. Honolulu: University of Hawai'i Press.

Strathern, Marilyn. 1988. *The Gender of the Gift: Problems with Women and Problems with Society in Melanesia*. Berkeley: University of California Press. doi.org/10.1525/california/9780520064232.001.0001.

Introduction: Tides of Innovation in Oceania

Anna Paini and Elisabetta Gnecchi-Ruscone

The title of our collection, *Tides of Innovation in Oceania*, is directly inspired by Epeli Hauʻofaʻs vision of the Pacific as a 'Sea of Islands' in which seawater is an element that has always favoured connections between people rather than acting as a barrier between them (1993).[1] The image of tides refers to the ocean as a medium of communication and transformation through interactions recalling the cyclical movement of waves, which may have unpredictable consequences: some objects are carried by the outgoing tides entering into wider flows of communication, others are deposited on the shore where they move along local routes acquiring new life and value in specific cultural contexts associated to contingent situations and calling for the creative responses of Pacific islanders. This framework allows us to propose innovation as a fluid concept, unbound and open to many directions, and at the same time allows us to address the resulting unexpected cultural forms as a combination of new, old and creole elements.

In turn, the subtitle *Value, Materiality and Place* focuses on three intersecting dimensions informing the ethnographic contributions to this volume, providing some comparative terms useful for foregrounding innovative lines of thinking within the anthropological debate. At the core of these three themes is our commitment to the notion of agency as 'the socio-culturally mediated capacity to act' (Ahearn 2001: 109). All the chapters hinge on deeply elaborated analyses of locally inflected agencies

---

1   This introduction, 'Tides of Innovation in Oceania', and the editing of this volume, *Tides of Innovation in Oceania: Value, Materiality and Place*, are the product of the joint effort of Anna Paini and Elisabetta Gnecchi-Ruscone. Each one has contributed 50 per cent.

involved in confronting different transforming contexts. Although each paper engages with more than one of these dimensions, and we are aware of their continuous interconnections, we present each theme separately before considering the ways in which they feed into each other within the expanded theme of 'tides of innovation'. Early versions of all essays in this collection, with the exception of those by Pigliasco, Tabani and Paini, were originally presented at the European Society for Oceanists (ESfO) conference in Verona 'Putting People First': Intercultural Dialogue and Imagining the Future in Oceania.

Value

Value is a very dense and complex notion, which in social sciences has different connotations. Within anthropological thinking a great variety of meanings have been attributed to the term, depending on whether the focus is on economic, social or religious phenomena. Value in any case is a relevant issue if we share David Graeber's perspective on 'social worlds not just as a collection of persons and things but rather as a project of mutual creation, as something collectively made and remade' (Graeber 2013: 222).

The wide range of approaches to the question of value has been a central and controversial theme in the anthropological debate going back to Bronislaw Malinowski (1922), Marcel Mauss (1924), Karl Polanyi (1944), Claude Lévi-Strauss (1949) and Marshall Sahlins (1972), among others;[2] more recently it has been taken up in the 2013 double issue of *HAU Journal of Ethnographic Theory*, devoted to exploring the possibility and usefulness of developing an anthropological theory of value. However, the two guest editors, Ton Otto and Rane Willerslev, admit that despite the interesting and innovative contributions to the volumes they were unable to integrate their diverging positions into an encompassing

---

2   Chris Gregory provides an overview of the paradigmatic turns in economic anthropology that he considers to fall into three major phases: pre-1970s, 1970s and post-1970s (2009: 286). The keyword for the first period was reciprocity in the context of exchange theories, such as Sahlins's lasting contribution (1972); during the 1970s the dominant paradigm centred around articulation, and the focus shifted from exchange to production (288). In the post-Vietnam war period, Gregory singles out a new shift of paradigm in which '*consumption* replace[d] *production* as the privileged economic concept and the rise of the "spirit" of the commodity as the new problem of global value to be investigated'; agency becomes the new keyword (289). He further points to the recent flourishing of works relating to different regional sub-fields and underscores that the issue that is shared by such diverse ethnographic and theoretic approaches is money (291).

theory (2013: 3). We share the concern for the conundrum they expose, which looms large in anthropology as a whole: is the recurrent need for anthropology to develop grand theories compatible with the discipline's position at the margins? How can anthropology contribute to an overarching theory while maintaining its habitual peripheral position, from which stems its capacity of bringing into the picture the experience of other world views and thus offering alternative viewpoints? Otto and Willerslev express it thus: 'As ethnographers, we enter into other realities and find striking kinds of thought and practice that can potentially subvert the dominating theories by confronting them with new understandings of what human life entails' (2013: 5). At the same time we are very well aware that value intended as moral standard casts light on another fundamental issue in anthropology, which is the comparability or incomparability of cultural worlds; in other words it brings to the fore the issue of relativism. Graeber (2001), among others, exemplifies the case of authors who are endeavouring to lay the grounds for a grand theory of value transcending geocultural boundaries. Others, such as Marilyn Strathern (1987), are more concerned with an analysis that keeps at the centre elements specific to a regional context. Similarly, we propose a reflection on these issues as articulated in the South Pacific. Without aiming at grand theory, we maintain the importance of comparative work for its ability to bring to the fore both unique histories and commonalities.

This ongoing debate provides an extended reflection on the varied use and relevance of the concept of value throughout the history of the discipline. Graeber maintains that the field of anthropological value theory since the 1980s has been shaped by the value/values issue: 'The fact that we use the same word to describe the benefits and virtues of a commodity for sale on the market … and our ideas about what is ultimately important in life … is not a coincidence. There is some hidden level where both come down to the same thing' (2013: 224). Nevertheless, the equivalence that is so fundamental in the economic dimension of value is absent when the term is applied in the moral and ethical field. Graeber (2001) has proposed that current research has engaged with this issue from three broad perspectives: the moral standards shared by a community; the worth attributed to a given object, good or practice; and the linguistic category referring to meaningful difference.

These different dimensions are reflected in a number of contributions to this volume, which draw out the entanglements between the value of things or practices and the words that are associated to them.

Sahlins (Chapter 1), for example, brings to the fore the significance that can be attributed to both material and immaterial things in his description of voyagers returning to their islands, when he says: 'The social value that Tikopia men acquired from voyages in the transcendental world was expressed in the tales they told, in the objects they brought back, even in the talismanic virtues of English phrases they had learned'. Margaret Jolly's (Chapter 2) analysis of the return of valuable objects from Europe to Oceania, by discussing the two different titles chosen by the curators of the same exhibition held in the two venues, Honolulu and Canberra, reveals the value of words in the flow of historical processes. Susanne Kuehling (Chapter 6) demonstrates the power of words to signify transformations and convey new meanings and values associated with goods and practices, in dealing with changes in everyday life on Dobu. Guido Carlo Pigliasco (Chapter 9), instead, highlights the value that can be attributed by islander communities to information, not so much for how it can be exploited in the market place, as for its contribution to 'the group's cultural capital and its sustenance'. We thus propose 'value' as a fruitful analytical key for reading this volume, spotlighting *its* value in terms of richness of ethnographic narrative, fluidity and dynamicity. As Jonathan Friedman wrote, 'Questions of value, of ethos, are important, but [they] need not be seen as free-floating texts since ethos and values are active forces, embedded in social relations and strategies' (1996: 7).

There are a number of dimensions of value that we wish to foreground here: first of all, value is not an essential dimension of things, practices, or words; things can have value, can lose or gain value, can change value in different contexts and mean different things to different people in the same context; objects may thus be recontextualised and 'move in and out of a commodity state' (Thomas 1991: 28). Nicholas Thomas's insistence on 'the mutability of things in recontextualisation' (28) clearly applies to both tangible and intangible domains. From an Oceanic perspective, the intangible dimension of value is strongly present in the entangled relation between narrative, secrecy, public knowledge and the control of power among different groups. The worth attributed to a thing is socially created by its very inclusion within a process of exchange, be it formal or informal. Value thus emerges in action, since it results from the intentional action of someone, but this intention must be recognised and shared in order for something to take on value (see Munn 1986).

All these considerations lead us to focus on the polysemic nature of the concept of 'value'. We believe that this concept can provide insights for understanding complex social situations in the present as well as in the colonial period. One of the more lasting influences of *Entangled Objects* (1991) is Thomas's application of Arjun Appadurai's innovative argument to cross-cultural exchanges in colonial encounters, in which 'the discrepancies between estimations of value are one of the crucial sources of conflict' (31), or, in Sahlins's terms (1981), 'working misunderstandings' are often the result of attribution of different values to the same object, practice or event by indigenous people and colonials. Jean-François Baré's analysis (1985) of the encounter between the Protestant missionaries in Tahiti and Pomare II, leading to exchanges that allowed both sides to reinforce their authority reciprocally despite the ambiguity in estimation of value and the resulting *malentendu*,[3] is an emblematic case. From this perspective, therefore, value is not an intrinsic property of goods and objects, in as much as it is attributed by actions and processes entailed in local – national – global flows of relationships, or in the 'creative action' involved in the shifting meaning of value in expanded social contexts (Graeber 2001: 249). As Nancy Pollock reminds us (Chapter 8), in local/global relations the value of goods and practices can also acquire a negative sign: despite the outside health experts' rhetoric of encouraging the consumption of local produce, their recognition (or not) of the nutritional value of local foods cannot be disassociated from the (negative) moral value attributed by the same outside observers to local practices of feasting.

The attribution of value can be relative or absolute. The attention to actions and processes not only shows us that 'few objects are simply one thing or another' (Graeber 2001:104), but also brings to the fore the gendering of goods, words and practices. Several intersecting elements participate in such an analysis; following Tatiana Benfoughal (2012), we suggest the importance of the gender of the producer and the context of use of an object for understanding its value or worth. Thus, the gendering of an object is a reflection of multiple intersecting elements, such as the transformations of social and gender divisions. These processes are clearly exemplified in a number of researches presented in the volume edited by Élisabeth Anstett and Marie-Luce Gélard (2012); among these Bjarne Rogan's study is telling. Rogan's research on collections and collecting

---

3   Misunderstanding.

of stamps and colour postcards in Europe from 1840 to 2000 shows 'that it is not the nature of the object that is sexed, but an object acquires a male or female connotation depending on social practices' (2012: 17).[4]

Value is thus pertinent to social and gender relations. A telling example is illustrated by Karen Sykes (2013: 98) when she considers the links between brothers and sisters as 'valuable relations' that are challenged by contemporaneity. She emphasises that it is not sufficient to account for value in terms of creative ways of living together, since transformations of social and cultural realities have consequences for the question of value, which therefore must be 'reposed' in ethnographic accounts. Hence the question of value becomes more complex insofar as new concerns such as women's esteem and dignity come to the fore. By emphasising how value is generated in embodied practice, Anna-Karina Hermkens and Katherine Lepani's forthcoming edited volume looks beyond economic theories of value to focus on the agency of people who create and attribute value as a way to 'make sense of their own social practice' (see Paini 2013; and Gnecchi-Ruscone forthcoming). In particular, they concentrate on dynamics of gender, power and change in considering women's objects as part of the processes of materialisation through which social relations, desires and values are activated (see Bell and Geismar 2009). The forthcoming edited volume by Hermkens and Lepani shares with ours a focus on ethnographic contributions in order to appreciate the peculiar dynamics of 'what value means and does in particular societies and particular people' rather than 'conceiving of value as *a priori* based on labour, or looking for a foundational basis for value' (Hermkens and Lepani forthcoming).

Materiality

A further useful dimension in approaching the contents of this volume is that of materiality. We maintain that in order to understand social dynamics in the contemporary Pacific and beyond it is necessary to bring to the foreground the relationships between people and things. A focus on these interrelations enables us to deepen our understanding of cultural, social, economic and political relations in each place considered. The term

---

4   Though this study does not concern the Pacific, we find it useful insofar as it focuses on objects that have become virtually universal.

materiality opens up complex issues broached by the anthropology of objects and its reflections on the tension between 'how people make objects' and 'how objects make people', thus transcending the subject/object dualism (Gell 1998; Latour 1997; Miller 2005; see also Bell and Geismar 2009 for a review of the specifically Oceanic ethnography contributing to this line of thought). Engaging with Miller's discussion of objectification, Joshua A. Bell and Haidy Geismar argue for a shift in perspective from the static concepts of material culture and materiality to the more dynamic one of materialisation as 'an ongoing lived *process* whereby concepts, beliefs and desires are given *form* that are then *transformed* and *transforming* in their social deployment' (2009: 4–6).

This shift in the debate, in all its inflections, continues to be indebted to Appadurai's (1986) emphasis on the social life of things and Igor Kopytoff's stress on the biography of objects (in the same volume, 1986). Another essential challenge to material cultural studies is offered by Fred Myer's edited collection (2001), resulting from a seminar held at the School of American Research in 1996, which stressed 'the existence of multiple, coexisting and variously related "regimes of value"' (Myers 2001: 6). As Janet Hoskins has pointed out, both these ground-breaking collections 'emphasise commerce and external constraints over local meanings and internal configurations, in keeping with the broader disciplinary change from "local" levels to "global" ones, and from single-sited field projects to multi-sited ones in order to trace persons and things as they move through space and time' (Hoskins 2006: 75). However, she underscores that the risk inherent in this approach is that of losing sight of the relationships between 'objects and individual subjectivity' and 'objects and gender or personality' (ibid).

The terms of the debate have, over time, become more complex and articulated, encompassing new perspectives and providing new insights into the relevance of things; from the point of view of economic anthropology, Chris Gregory considers the current dominant paradigm of agency as 'committed to a theory of value that turns the labour theory of value on its head: things as agents give value to people rather than the other way around' (Gregory 2009: 290). The central question remains the relationship between subjects and objects. Moving beyond this distinction is necessary, nevertheless we believe that it is *as* important not to attribute the same kind of agency to objects as to subjects (see, for example, Hoskins 1998); taken to its extreme, the idea that an object is a *thing plus agency* can become slippery and may lead to studying objects outside of their social and historical contexts. Though Kopytoff's contribution had an enormous impact in anthropology and beyond, too often his aim has been misinterpreted by over emphasising the agency of things: as Christopher Steiner has clearly expressed, 'the point is not that "things" are any more animated than we used to believe, but rather that they are infinitely malleable to the shifting and contested meanings constructed *for them* through human agency' (2001: 210). Highlighting the dimension of malleability, Steiner encourages us to address the tension between subject and object while avoiding the danger of reification that is involved when an object is considered to embody an essence. This perspective circumvents over-stressing the vision of an object as a *thing plus agency*. On this point we agree with Steiner's analysis on the recent agentive turn in anthropology as having loaded excessive weight on objects as the locus of agency, disregarding the relationship between the meaning of things and the wider cultural signification through which they are interpreted and used.

Mindful of the limits and risks on both sides of the argument (things plus agency vs. malleability of things) we are persuaded that analysis of the material aspects of life should be grounded in historically contextualised ethnography. The recent interest for intangible heritage has moreover contributed to reshaping the concept of material culture itself,[5] another factor to be taken into consideration in discussing the agency of objects, which thus takes on further complex dimensions. Authors like Pierre Lemonnier insist on grounding their theoretical contributions on the immaterial dimensions of material culture in ethnographically rich accounts; he argues that objects 'are situated at the heart both of a way of living together and of doing anthropology' (2013: 24). Another author who has engaged with the question of materiality is Ludovic Coupaye: in his very thorough analysis of the life of Abelam long yams, he considers the complexity condensed within an object without going as far as attributing sole agency to the yam: '*L'objet fini est donc un condensé de relations (sociales, matérielles, symboliques) réalisées au cours de la chaîne opératoire et concrétisées sous la forme d'un seul artefact ... qui doit impérativement*

---

5   See for example the rich documentation following from UNESCO's Convention for the Safeguarding of the Intangible Cultural Heritage, 2003 (www.unesco.org) and the lively academic debate that ensued (icom.museum/programmes/intangible-heritage/), as well as the extraordinary interest by local communities to be included in UNESCO's list. Following the Faro Convention, drafted between 2003 and 2005 and entered into force in 2011, the term 'heritage community' has given further impulse to the rush to apply for inscription.

être donné à voir' (The completed object is thus a distillation of (social, material, symbolic) relationships, accomplished in the course of the operative chain and made concrete in the shape of a single artefact ... which must imperatively be made visible) (2009: 15).

Important observations from fieldwork centred upon material objects reveal the potential for things' capacity to start social processes in which human agency remains significant.[6] Following in this well-established tradition of Oceania-based research on materiality and materialisation (see Bell and Geismar 2009) all the contributors to this volume differently engage with theoretical issues in important ways, and by keeping ethnography at the core of their work, they avoid the risk of sliding into ideologically biased theory. For instance Colombo Dougoud (Chapter 3), describing the exhibition on Kanak engraved bamboos—which opened at the Musée d'ethnographie de Genève (MEG) in 2008 and was shown for the first time in Nouméa in 2010—reflects on a key notion developed by Kanak elders engaging with their dispersed material heritage: the bamboos 'were far away because they had been sent in order to accomplish a specific task, that of becoming messengers, ambassadors who create connections and open paths'.[7] Such connections are made possible by the history of relationships created by Kanak ancestors through objects; of course this vision does not deny the violence of the colonial past but emphasises those encounters that are still alive in native memory as important transformations marked by the handing over of gifts (Kasarhérou 2005). The messages carried by objects are not necessarily conflict-free, as Jolly (Chapter 2) reminds us in her comparison between the different curatorial strategies adopted in two exhibitions (in Honolulu and Canberra) on the Cook/Forster collection travelling temporarily from Göttingen to Oceania in 2006: 'I ponder the affective responses such objects elicit, how they move living human subjects, variously stimulating curiosity, respect, awe, terror or rage in spectators, some of whom are genealogically connected to the original creators, but most of whom are not'. To return to New Caledonia, in Anna Paini's chapter the relationship between people and things is analysed through a case study on an object that for a long time

---

6   Going beyond the context of Oceania, Anna's own students' ethnographic research on the relationship between people and things, in particular a current study by Francesca Nicalini in an old people's home near Verona ('Oggetti residenzializzati. Anziane e cose in casa di riposo') shows the power of objects in eliciting memories, feelings and desires in the old women who live there, and the resulting changes that the people working in the institution brought about to improve the guests' lives.
7   For an in-depth analysis of the concept of *objets ambassadeurs*, see Kasarhérou, 2014.

was ignored in ethnographic studies, namely the *robe mission*: a garment of colonial origin which has been reappropriated through time by Kanak women; by focusing on this dress, the analysis reveals its malleability and emphasises the agency of women. All these examples, though dealing with different kinds of things and relating to different Pacific histories, engage with the idea 'that persons cannot be understood apart from things' (Tilley 2006: 2).

A focus on transcending the dualism between objects and subjects hence permits a better understanding of historical and contemporary social processes at work in Oceania. As Maureen MacKenzie (1991) has brilliantly demonstrated in her classic work *Androgynous Objects* on the string bags made by Telefol women of New Guinea, interest in material culture should connect objects to the social and cultural construction of things and people, incorporating different levels of social and symbolic value. The value of things, she argues, is not inherent in the material object per se, 'but multivalent and variously realised' (MacKenzie 1991: 27). Remarkably, the same issue was taken up in the same year by Nicholas Thomas in his influential work on 'entangled objects', where he argued that value and meaning are contextually elaborated, and thus 'it must be appreciated that the estimations people make draw upon a range of historical and sentimental considerations' (Thomas 1991: 21). More recently, similar concerns are developed by Anna-Karina Hermkens, in her work on the female production of bark cloth among Maisin people, in which she stresses that 'things are dynamic entities: their meanings change for the participants in different contexts depending on the specific values that come into play' (Hermkens 2013: 339). For her this implies that the meaning of things do not reside only in objects: 'Objects such as tapa have to be contextualized and reconfigured within performances and networks of people and things' (ibid).

This take on object-subject relations also raises a question about whether objects should be seen as neutral, as male or female, or whether their gender affiliation should be considered as shifting according to their collocation in a wider scene including the historical, social and performative contexts of their production and use. Useful insights come from the above-mentioned work by Hermkens on engendering objects: 'The reproduction of clan identity through a material transmission of knowledge elucidates the significant position of women. Although clan membership flows through male lines and heirlooms are passed from one male generation to another, one of the most visual displays of clan identity is guarded and created by women' (2013: 116).

In our own research we have begun to reflect upon the issue of material production, the social uses of objects and the processes of engendering. The woven pandanus mats made by Lifou women (New Caledonia), which are no longer an item of customary exchange but continue to have a role in ceremonial events, are a case in point.[8] Until a couple of decades ago pandanus mats were laid over woven coconut leaves on the ground to welcome groups of visitors in both formal and informal settings; for example, wedding ceremonies were organised in spaces within the groom's village covered by such layers with pandanus mats on the top. These mats, essential for creating a welcoming ceremonial space, were recognised by everyone as products of female work, even though they were used by both men and women.[9] In the last 10 years, however, as locally handmade mats have become rare for several reasons, including the loss of interest in weaving by young women, they have come to be reserved for ceremonial occasions. An object that was previously widely made and used, the pandanus mat, over time has become scarce: not only has its value increased with the decrease of production, but it has also circulated in local networks, seldom reaching the market. Further, within such contexts the scarcity of mats has resulted in the social strategy of reserving pandanus mats for selected participants only. This practice has produced a new social experience which people in Lifou explained by stressing that the mats are reserved for the family of the chief, but since he sits on a bench on one side of the ceremonial ground, sided by other high-ranking men, the area covered by pandanus mats has effectively become reserved for high status women. Thus to an external observer, pandanus mats in Lifou are becoming associated with women, both as makers and as users. This fieldwork experience and analysis echo Lissant Bolton's work on objects and bodies in Vanuatu, in which she argues that a focus on

---

8   Anna Paini, 'Un art des femmes à explorer, le tressage à Lifou', Conférence-ethno, Musée de Nouvelle-Calédonie, Nouméa, 25 June 2010.

9   The pandanus mats manufactured by Korafe women (PNG) can also be said to create safe spaces for daily family activities such as eating and resting, as well as for ritual moments in ceremonies connected to the life cycle (Gnecchi-Ruscone forthcoming).

engendering must not neglect 'the intersection in relationships between gender, status and clothing as an embodiment of difference' (2003a: 120, see also Bolton 2001 and Bolton 2003b).[10]

We can analyse this kind of ethnographic data by stressing the value given to an object that has become scarce. In some cases an object that has become rare can be marginalised in ceremonial contexts to the extent that it becomes obsolete, in other cases a scarce object becomes more valued and thus reserved for specific situations in which it is considered to be irreplaceable; in any case the ethnographic data reveal that not all changes, incorporations or substitutions are acceptable. A telling example, to remain on the theme of pandanus mats, comes from the visit to New Caledonia by the then French prime minister Jean-Marc Ayrault at the end of July 2013. The objects he presented to the Jean-Marie Tjibaou Cultural Center in Nouméa in the course of the customary exchanges were arranged on an imported plastic mat, to the indignation of a Kanak woman friend who thought this to be an undignified replacement (email from Lifou, 29 July 2013).[11] So an object's itinerary can follow multiple paths, ranging from the re-attribution of value and function, to the realisation that its use has become too cumbersome for practicality resulting in its obsolescence, to defining it as inalienable (see Weiner 1992; Godelier 1999). Such outcomes may be considered as mutually exclusive alternatives as well as different stages in the social life of an object, which is attributed different social values in different historical contexts.

Place

The relation between value and materiality leads us to the third major theme of this collection, namely that of place. Like Aletta Biersack we ask what makes a place, subscribing to her suggestion that 'the answer is clearly both locational *and* relational' (Biersack 2006: 16). We do not conceive of place as a naturally bounded, isolated and confining locality; rather we prefer to think in terms of place-making as embodied practices involved in cultural, social and political processes situated within expanded arenas (Gupta and Ferguson 1997a). As Akhil Gupta and James Ferguson

---

10   Among the many texts addressing the intersections between gender, status, race and clothing in colonial times, see Margaret Jolly's 'A saturated history of Christianity and cloth in Oceania' (2014).
11   See also the photographs in Franceinfo, la1ere.francetvinfo.fr/nouvellecaledonie/2013/07/29/jean-marc-ayrault-visite-du-centre-culturel-tjibaou-51349.html (accessed 1 March 2017).

warned, 'It is fundamentally mistaken to conceptualize different kinds of non- or supralocal identities (diasporic, refugee, migrant, national, and so forth) as spatial and temporal extensions of a prior, natural identity rooted in locality and community' (1997c: 7); only by overcoming such deep-rooted anthropological approaches is it possible to reconfigure the local, avoiding the trap of the quest for originality and authenticity. It is noteworthy that a series of critical works on the concepts of boundaries, localities, place-making and the construction of identity, growing out of different anthropological conferences and meetings, were all published in the same year (Clifford 1997a; Gupta and Ferguson 1997a, 1997b). In particular Gupta and Ferguson, in *Anthropological Locations*, apply this critique to problematise place in constructing the 'field', underscoring that the 'the distinction between "field" and "home" leads directly to what we call a hierarchy of purity of field sites' (1997d: 13).[12]

Clifford's metaphor of 'roots and routes' (1997a), motivates us to focus on places as increasingly interconnected and entangled through time and space, and to articulate local belonging with processes of contemporaneity, be they fluid or, in Anna Tsing's words, sticky. In considering interactions between global and local she focuses on 'friction'—'the awkward, unequal, unstable, and creative qualities of interconnection across difference' (Tsing 2004: 4)—and she also calls into question the concept of 'universals'. She argues that it is important to decentre our focus from locality to universals, which are always to some extent local knowledge, insofar as they can only be understood in terms of 'historically specific cultural assumptions' (2004: 7). Thus rootedness and movement are interpreted from a contextual and relational perspective, as Teresia Teaiwa stressed in the preface to *Searching for Nei Nim' anoa*, 'to search for roots is to discover routes' (1995: ix). Such routes are preferential channels for 'knowledge that moves – mobile and mobilising – across locality and cultures' (Tsing 2004: 7). This vision represents an antidote to the common sense notion that constructs and opposes authenticity as centred in the local and modernity as connected to mobility.

To make a brief detour back to materiality, it is worth remembering Appadurai's contention that the production of locality cannot succeed 'unless hard and regular work is undertaken to produce and maintain its materiality' (1996: 180–81). However, materiality should not be

---

12　Clifford's essay 'Spatial Practices' (1997b) was also published in the volume edited by Gupta and Ferguson (1997b).

considered as an end in itself, but as connected to processes of place-making. Grounding in locality is an implied feature shared by most papers in this volume. Nancy Pollock's analysis of changing 'ethnographic practices of food use' in Oceania is a case in point, in so far as 'foodscapes are a depiction of an imagined bridge over space and time'. Further, Pigliasco's (Chapter 9) work on intellectual property is inextricably tied to notions of local cultural production. The boundaries between local and global are fluid and porous, indeed he writes: 'While cultural policies and cultural industries might stress local priorities, needs, and place-based cultural values, their activities are shaped by the activities of external actors, States and corporations, NGOs, UN bodies, and development aid institutions'. Similarly, Marc Tabani (Chapter 7) focuses on the importance of relations with one's place and, at the same time, warns that such relations may be drastically changed by the incorporation of external influences leading to the commodification of *kastom* and the resulting land grab in Vanuatu.

Our choice to highlight place as a thread running through these papers stems from our wish not to lose track of elements of continuity within the undeniable transformations of contemporary cultural worlds: such elements of continuity are expressed in living cultures rooted in changing local realities. For instance, as Strathern observed, the economic concept of value in the South Western Pacific cannot be understood if the comparison of entities is considered only in terms of ratio or rank equivalence (like and unlike items); a third relation of comparison must be taken into account in dealing with gift exchange: that 'between an entity and its source of origin. Value is thus constructed in the identity of a thing or person with various sets of social relations in which it is embedded, and its simultaneous detachability from them' (1987: 286).

In present time Oceania local to global dynamics are intertwined with an ongoing sense of belonging as people accommodate to expanded social processes. As a consequence of the resulting reconfiguration of localities, also the objects associated to a specific place may be re-signified as people, goods and ideas move faster and more frequently around the world, without breaking the connection with their place of origin, as 'local populations are integrated into the world system at the same time as they assimilate aspects of the latter to their own project' (Friedman 1996: 3). Place-making takes into account social change and cultural transformation as revealed in practices embodied locally, yet actively involved in wider contemporary networks of ideas, objects and people.[13] The recent volume *Belonging in Oceania* edited by Elfriede Hermann, Wolfgang Kempf and Toon van Meijl analyses the links between three dimensions: movement, identification and place-making by stressing the 'dynamic configuration crafted by history in a unique melding of practices, linkages and powerful relationships' (Hermann, Kempf and van Meijl 2014: 6). Seeing places as open-ended processes enables them to address localities as 'interfaces, as points where relationships and interactions meet' (ibid.: 8), where the local and extra-local cross paths (Biersack 2006: 16). We like to think of all these creative assemblages,[14] movements, flows, reconfigurations, articulations and creolisations in terms of 'tides of innovation'.

From 'Putting People First' to 'Tides of Innovation'

This collection of essays originally arose out of discussions and critical engagement with imagining 'Putting People First', a notion inspired by the motto adopted in 1993 by the Pacific Forum in the 'Suva Declaration', and which was chosen as the main theme of the ESfO conference in Verona 2008.[15] This vision emphasises the pivotal role of intersubjective relations at all levels of sociality for contemporary islanders in their daily efforts to imagine desirable futures and means to achieve them that reflect the ways in which value and values blend, giving rise to unpredictable social and cultural configurations. Dynamics involving processes of rupture and continuity, connection and rejection, resistance and domestication, overlapping and distancing, forsaking and revisiting: all processes reflecting islanders' engagement in contemporary Oceania. Thus an emphasis on artefacts, engraved bamboos, *robes mission*, returning

13 There exists a growing body of literature on mining and deforestation for this part of the world. Although this subject involves themes connected to people's livelihoods, the transformations of place, and place-making, this literature goes beyond the scope of our volume. However, we wish to mention, among others: Bell, West and Filer 2015; Hirsch and O'Hanlon 1995; Jacka 2015; Leach 2003; Stewart and Srathern 2003; Weiner 1991.

14 Tim Ingold contrasts two views of creativity: one, which he calls the 'combinatory view', focuses on the ongoing rearticulation of specific, discrete old and new elements; the other 'is rather a movement, or flow in which every element we might identify is but a moment' (2007: 47).

15 'Putting People First' Intercultural Dialogue and Imagining the Future in Oceania (with the support of the Wenner-Gren Foundation for Anthropological Research, Inc.) of which we were the conveners. The theme was inspired by the classic economic anthropology text by Michael Cernea (1985), which marked and fuelled the beginning of the Participatory Development policies of the 1990s, sponsored by the World Bank and other international agencies.

treasures, marvellous valuables from overseas, never transcends 'Putting People First'. We deem 'Tides of Innovation' to be an appropriate title for this volume, which opens with Andrew Moutu's reflections on the value of anthropology and his plea that anthropologists keep people first in daily practice. Early versions of all but three essays (Paini, Pigliasco and Tabani) in this collection were initially presented at the conference in Verona and have subsequently been substantially revised; they all differently engage with the dimensions condensed in the subtitle: value, materiality and place. Although the chapters are joined by several connecting threads, we have arranged them in two parts: Mapping Materiality in Time and Place, and Value and Agency: Local Experiences in Expanded Narratives.

In Part 1, Mapping Materiality in Time and Place, the emphasis is on the movement of objects, persons, ideas and meanings through interactions in networks at different scales and through time. The chapters take up a complex set of dynamics reflecting upon the toing and froing of people and objects today and in the past, considering the experiences, purposes and actions of the different parties involved, charting the processes of negotiation, readjustment and emotional involvement implicated in interpreting and making use of things whose biographies and trajectories are reviewed from the perspective of tides of innovation. Marshall Sahlins's wide-ranging excursus in time and space keeps people first by placing them on the forefront of his accounts of movements of people and goods, emphasising the aesthetics and values associated to alterity in autochthonous narratives and politics of encounters, extending well beyond the seas of Oceania. Starting from a discussion of the opposition of alterity and autochthony in Raymond Firth's remarkable Tikopia corpus, together with some general reflections on stranger-kingship, this essay reviews the marvellous Austronesian conceptions of Others opened by contact with various foreigner powers. Margaret Jolly, reflecting on the aesthetics and cultural politics of travelling Oceanic collections, leads us on a voyage from Göttingen to Honolulu, to Canberra. In her perspective, objects move in three dimensions: in the physical sense, in the affective response they elicit and in purposes of their display. She introduces the Göttingen's Cook/Forster collection, exhibited for the first time outside Europe in 2006, and moving to the Pacific, she elaborates on the intriguing differences between the two exhibitions, exemplified in the different titles that were given to them: in Honolulu, *Hele Mai: Life in the Pacific of the 1700s*; in Canberra, *Cook's Pacific Encounters*. In her analysis she reviews the diverse institutional engagements with Pacific peoples in the setting up of such exhibitions in different places, highlighting the conflicting emotional and political tussles provoked by the returning objects.

A further case study considering materiality from the point of view of museum collections is Roberta Colombo Dougoud's contribution on an exhibition at the MEG in 2008. The exhibition's aspirations were twofold: to valorise the museum's collection of Kanak engraved bamboos, while at the same time divulging part of the museum's history. The close collaboration with the Musée de Nouvelle-Calédonie then resulted in a more elaborate exhibition in Nouméa in 2010, an important opportunity for curators to experiment with innovative forms of cooperation and knowledge sharing, for people from New Caledonia to see for the first time such a rich presentation of engraved bamboos, and also for the MEG's bamboos to acquire new strength and power, to become revitalised in their original home before continuing to play their role as Kanak ambassadors. Moving on from exhibitions to the use of objects in everyday life, Anna Paini explores the complexity of ongoing changes in the meanings and values expressed by the *robe mission*. A once imposed dress, the *robe mission* has gone through cultural reformulation not only in its materiality but also in the linguistic labels attached to it; in time the *robe mission* has become a valued indigenised dress that can be worn to manifest local belonging, and at the same time can be drawn upon to express a wider Kanak identity. Paini's chapter brings to the fore the creative energies manifested by Kanak women by establishing dress-making ateliers, an unprecedented case of female entrepreneurship in Lifou.

In Part 2, Value and Agency: Local Experiences in Expanded Narratives, the chapters bear witness to different forms of enactment and transformation of specific cultural practices to accommodate old and new, inside and outside elements. The complexities involved in these interactions yield quite different outcomes and interpretations in terms of value, yet all involve strong elements of agency, as reflected in the five essays. The section opens with the voice of a female Pacific Islander, the late Marie-Claire Beboko-Beccalossi's, reflecting on the crucial passages of indigenous women's struggle in New Caledonia, from early colonial days to the present. In particular, it underlines the role of the younger generation of women of the 1960s and '70s in establishing women's groups, giving rise to networks which would enable Kanak women to overcome the pervasive tensions and conflicts of the *Événements* in the 1980s, thus effectively creating a constructive way to participate in the contemporary social and political life of Kanaky New Caledonia. Beboko-Beccalossi's contribution focuses on Kanak women's engagement and their assigning a central value to the pursuit of their own well-being together with that of the wider community. The narrative of her own experience as a female Kanak activist, almost anticipating Andrew Moutu's appeal for political involvement, illustrates the action of New Caledonia's women's groups which not only provide women with a space for sociality, but embrace the wider perspective of local engagement by dealing on a daily basis with problems of contemporary life in ways that empower them as women and as Kanak. Unfortunately, Marie-Claire Bekobo-Beccalossi sent us only the first draft of her text, which she was unable to revise because she became gravely ill, and a few months later passed away. We want to remember and to convey to our readers her abilities as a fine analyst and her standing as a grassroots activist, who was able to dialogue with local politicians and French ministers, but was also ready to soil her hands working with a concrete mixer while participating in a women's group's project to build toilets and ovens for local groups in Kouergoa, on the main island of New Caledonia.

Local ways of coming to terms with new values and social expectations in everyday life sometimes give rise to innovative solutions with unexpected implications. Susanne Kuehling explores this in her chapter that considers the dynamics of transformations starting from words for valuable objects and practices. She focuses on contemporary economic behaviour in Dobu and on a dilemma that can be solved through strategic choices of vocabulary. Through a case of not-giving, she shows the value and adaptability of the knowledge surrounding old exchange principles, and how they change according to new demands emerging from the ever intensifying contact with the global economy. Language needs frequent updating in terminology and as words are assigned more or less value they reflect dynamics of moral and economic aspects of life that help us to contextualise specific local instances of the 'tides of innovation'. Certainly one of the most pervasive innovations throughout the Pacific area is the use of money in the different aspects of life, not only in the economic domain but also in ceremonial contexts. The increased requirement for cash in many instances stimulates people's interest for tourism as a sustainable form of business or development. However, this strategy for contributing to the local economy brings with it a number of shortcomings. Marc Tabani's essay deals with the increasing commodification of the lifestyle, environments and ceremonial events of rural people in Vanuatu resulting from their involvement with the tourist industry, and emphasises the contemporary paradox in which the daily practices and national ideology centred on the rhetoric attributing value to *kastom* comes into conflict with the economic value of *kastom,* resulting in the exploitation of cultural heritage. An account of the development of tourism on the island of Tanna examines the intricate question of different agencies that interact or clash in locally managed tourist activities, resulting in local division, instability and wealth inequality. Further, the commercial exploitation of traditional ceremonies in Pentecost and the consequent disruption of their yearly occurrence in the local calendar, contribute to changing the value of rituals for the participants, and to the transformation of traditions into commercial products. Such monetisation of rural communities encourages wage employment, but it also leads to the phenomenon of land-grabbing, transforming peasants into poor workers in exile on their own lands.

Innovations in values and lifestyles are also entailed in the expanded horizons of dietary choices. Nancy Pollock's chapter reflects on the values inscribed in well-being through an excursus of the processes of diversification of foodscapes across the Pacific, showing a variety of different influences on household food consumption. Highlighting the relevance of notions such as 'good and healthy food' and showing how these values cannot be separated from that of sharing food, this contribution, through its contemporary ethnographic snapshots, underlines how despite changing practices and growing health-related concerns, the well-being of each person remains connected to social and cultural webs of relations. The final chapter of the volume focuses on the importance of shared values within relational networks. In Fiji and in contemporary Oceania, culture and policy are indicated as a strategic binomial artefact to structure collective action and community values. This model is sought to mobilise rules and government decision-making towards explicit guidelines for the regulation of intellectual property and the management of cultural heritage in the service of positive nation-building and development of cultural and creative industries. Beginning from the recent debate on the trademarking of *masi* designs by Air Pacific, Guido Carlo Pigliasco analyses the problematic issue of cultural heritage protection policies, raising a series of questions such as the distinction between cultural and intellectual property, owning and using a cultural product or practice, ownership and custodianship. In this context, he emphasises the implications of a crucial distinction: 'Whereas western intellectual property seeks to define products of human creativity that can be alienated from their creators ... across the Pacific, the ownership of intangibles does not include the possibility of alienation', thus stressing that like culture, legal acts and property relations should also be considered in a processual perspective.

The thoughtful Epilogue by Christian Kaufmann draws out intersecting paths from the different chapters. We hope that this volume will encourage further discussion on these interrelated themes and on the ways in which tides of innovation reach the Pacific Islands and the possible local responses of continuity, transformation and recurrence, and at the same time carry elements of Pacific creativity to other shores, engendering new stories.

References

Ahearn, Laura. 2001. 'Language and agency'. *Annual Review of Anthropology* 30: 109–37. doi.org/10.1146/annurev.anthro.30.1.109.

Anstett, Élisabeth and Marie-Luce Gélard (eds). 2012. *Les objets ont-ils un genre? Culture matérielle et production sociale des identités sexuées.* Paris: Armand Colin.

Appadurai, Arjun. 1996. *Modernity at Large: Cultural Dimensions of Globalization.* Minneapolis: University of Minnesota Press.

Appadurai, Arjun (ed.). 1986. *The Social Life of Things: Commodities in Cultural Perspective.* Cambridge: Cambridge University Press.

Baré, Jean-François. 1985. 'Les conversions tahitiennes au protestantisme comme malentendu productif (1800–1820)'. *Série Sciences Humaines, Cahiers de l'Orstom* 21(1): 125–36.

Bell, Joshua A. and Haidy Geismar. 2009. 'Materialising Oceania: New ethnographies of things in Melanesia and Polynesia'. *The Australian Journal of Anthropology* 20: 3–27. doi.org/10.1111/j.1757-6547.2009.00001.x.

Bell, Joshua A., Paige West and Colin Filer (eds). 2015. *Tropical Forests of Oceania: Anthropological Perspectives.* Canberra: ANU Press. Online: press.anu.edu.au/publications/series/asia-pacific-environment-monographs/tropical-forests-of%C2%A0oceania (accessed 4 August 2016).

Benfoughal, Tatiana. 2012. 'La dichotomie homme/femme à l'épreuve de la modernité. Le tressage des vanneries dans les oasis du Sahara maghrébin'. In *Les objets ont-ils un genre? Culture materielle et production sociale des identites sexuees*, ed. Élisabeth Anstett, and Marie-Luce Gélard, pp. 207–22. Paris: Armand Colin. doi.org/10.3917/arco. gela.2012.01.0207.

Biersack, Aletta. 2006. 'Reimagining political ecology: Culture/power/ history/nature'. In *Reimagining Political Ecology*, ed. Aletta Biersack and James B. Greenberg, pp. 1–40. Durham and London: Duke Unversity Press. doi.org/10.1215/9780822388142-001.

Bolton, Lissant. 2003a. 'Gender, status and introduced clothing in Vanuatu'. In *Clothing the Pacific*, ed. Chloë Colchester, pp. 119–39. Oxford: Berg.

———. 2003b. *Unfolding the Moon: Enacting Women's Kastom in Vanuatu*. Honolulu: University of Hawai'i Press.

———. 2001. 'Classifying the material. Food, textiles and status in north Vanuatu'. *Journal of Material Culture* 6(3): 251–68. doi. org/10.1177/135918350100600301.

Cernea, Michael. 1985. *Putting People First: Sociological Variables in Rural Development*. New York: Oxford University Press.

Clifford, James. 1997a. *Routes: Travel and Translation in the Late Twentieth Century*. Cambridge MA: Harvard University Press.

———. 1997b. 'Spatial practices: Fieldwork, travel, and the disciplining of anthropology'. In *Anthropological Locations. Boundaries and Grounds of a Field Science*, ed. Akhil Gupta and James Ferguson, pp. 185–222. Berkeley and Los Angeles: University of California Press.

Coupaye, Ludovic. 2009. 'Décrire des objets hybrides. Les grandes ignames décorées du village de Nyamikum, province de l'East Sepik, Papuasie-Nouvelle-Guinée'. *Techniques & Culture* 52–53. Online: tc.revues.org/4730 (accessed 26 May 2016).

Friedman, Jonathan. 1996. 'Introduction'. In *Melanesian Modernities*, ed. Jonathan J. Friedman and James Carrier, pp. 1–9. Lund: Lund University Press. doi.org/10.1017/cbo9780511584732.002.

Gell, Alfred. 1998. *Art and Agency: An Anthropological Theory*. Oxford: Oxford University Press.

Gnecchi-Ruscone, Elisabetta. forthcoming. 'The extraordinary values of ordinary objects: Stringbags and pandanus mats as Korafe women's wealth?' In *Sinuous Objects: Revaluing Women's Wealth in the Contemporary Pacific*, ed. Anna-Karina Hermkens and Katherine Lepani. Canberra: ANU Press.

Godelier, Maurice, 1999. *The Enigma of the Gift*. Cambridge: Polity Press.

Graeber, David. 2013. 'It is value that brings universes into being'. *HAU: Journal of Ethnographic Theory* 3(2): 219–43. doi.org/10.14318/hau3.2.012.

——. 2001. *Toward an Anthropological Theory of Value. The False Coin of Our Own Dreams*. New York: Palgrave.

Gregory, Chris. 2009. 'Whatever happened to economic anthropology?' *The Australian Journal of Anthropology* 20(3): 285–300. doi.org/10.1111/j.1757-6547.2009.00037.x.

Gupta, Akhil and James Ferguson (eds). 1997a. *Culture, Power, Place: Explorations in Critical Anthropology*. Durham: Duke University Press.

——. 1997b. *Anthropological Locations. Boundaries and Grounds of a Field Science*. Berkeley and Los Angeles: University of California Press.

——. 1997c. 'Culture, power, place: ethnography at the end of an era'. In *Culture, Power, Place: Explorations in Critical Anthropology*, ed. Akhil Gupta and James Ferguson, pp. 1–29. Durham: Duke University Press.

——. 1997d. 'Discipline and practice: "The field" as site, method, and location in anthropology'. In *Anthropological Locations. Boundaries and Grounds of a Field Science*, ed. Akhil Gupta and James Ferguson, pp. 1–46. Berkeley and Los Angeles: University of California Press.

Hau'ofa, Epeli. 1993, 'Our sea of islands'. In *A New Oceania: Rediscovering Our Sea of Islands*, ed. Eric Waddell, Vijay Naidu and Epeli Hau'ofa, pp. 2–16. Suva: School of Social and Economic Development, The University of the South Pacific.

Hermann, Elfriede, Wolfgang Kempf and Toon van Meijl (eds). 2014. *Belonging in Oceania. Movement, Place-Making and Multiple Identifications*. New York and London: Berghahn.

Hermkens, Anna-Karina. 2013. *Engendering Objects: Dynamics of Barkcloth and Gender among the Maisin of Papua New Guinea*. Leiden: Sidestone Press.

Hermkens, Anna-Karina and Katherine Lepani (eds). forthcoming. *Sinuous Objects: Revaluing Women's Worth in the Contemporary Pacific*. Canberra: ANU Press.

Hermkens, Anna-Karina and Katherine Lepani. forthcoming. 'Women's wealth in the contemporary Pacific'. In *Sinuous Objects: Revaluing Women's Wealth in the Contemporary Pacific*, ed. Anna-Karina Hermkens and Katherine Lepani. Canberra: ANU Press.

Hirsch, Eric and Michael O'Hanlon (eds). 1995. *The Anthropology of Landscape: Perspectives on Place and Space*. Oxford: Clarendon Press.

Hoskins, Janet. 2006. 'Agency, biography and objects'. In *Handbook of Material Culture*, ed. Christopher Tilley, Webb Keane, Susanne Kuechler, Mike Rowlands and Patricia Spyer, pp. 74–85. London: Sage. doi.org/10.4135/9781848607972.n6.

———. 1998. *Biographical Objects: How Things Tell the Stories of People's Lives*. London: Routledge.

Ingold, Tim. 2007. 'Introduction'. In *Creativity and Cultural Improvisation*, ed. Elizabeth Hallam and Tim Ingold, pp. 1–24. Oxford: Berg.

Jacka, Jerry. 2015. *Alchemy in the Rain Forest: Politics, Ecology, and Resilience in a New Guinea Mining Area*. Durham: Duke University Press. doi.org/10.1215/9780822375012.

Jolly, Margaret. 2014. 'A saturated history of Christianity and cloth in Oceania'. In *Divine Domesticities: Christian Paradoxes in Asia and the Pacific*, ed. Hyaeweol Choi and Margaret Jolly, pp. 429–54. Canberra: ANU Press. Online: press.anu.edu.au/publications/divine-domesticities (accessed 4 August 2016).

Kasarhérou, Emmanuel. 2014. 'Un caso di patrimonializzazione condivisa: gli oggetti ambasciatori della cultural kanak'. In *La densità delle cose. Oggetti Ambasciatori tra Oceania e Europa*, ed. Anna Paini and Matteo Arìa, pp. 207–17. Pisa: Pacini.

———. 2005. 'L'ambassadeur du brouillard blanc'. In *Cent ans d'ethnographie sur la colline de Saint-Nicolas*, ed. Marc Olivier Gonseth, Jacques Hainard and Roland Kaehr, pp. 285–86. Neuchâtel: Musée d'ethnographie.

Kopytoff, Igor. 1986. 'The cultural biography of things: Commoditization as process'. In *The Social Life of Things: Commodities in Cultural Perspective*, ed. Arjun Appadurai, pp. 62–91. Cambridge: Cambridge University Press. doi.org/10.1017/CBO9780511819582.004.

Latour, Bruno. 1997. *Nous n'avons jamais été modernes*. Paris: La Découverte.

Leach, James. 2003. *Creative Land: Place and Procreation on the Rai Coast of Papua New Guinea*. New York and Oxford: Berghahn Books.

Lemonnier, Pierre. 2013. 'De l'immateriél dans le materiél et réciproquement! Techniques et communication non verbale'. *Journal de la Société des Océanistes* 136–37: 15–26. doi.org/10.4000/jso.6959.

Lévi-Strauss. Claude. 1969 [1949]. *The Elementary Structures of Kinship*. London: Eyre & Spottiswoode.

MacKenzie, Maureen. 1991. *Androgynous Objects: String Bags and Gender in Central New Guinea*. Chur and Melbourne: Harwood Academic Press.

Malinowski, Bronislaw. 1922. *Argonauts of the Western Pacific: An Account of Native Enterprise and Adventure in the Archipelagoes of Melanesian New Guinea*. London: Routledge and Kegan Paul.

Mauss, Marcel. 1924. *Essai sur le don. Forme et raison de l'échange dans les sociétés archaïques*. Paris: Année Sociologique.

Miller, Daniel (ed.). 2005. *Materiality*. Durham: Duke University Press.

Munn, Nancy. 1986. *The Fame of Gawa: A Symbolic Study of Value Transformation in a Massim (Papua New Guinea) Society*. Cambridge: Cambridge University Press.

Myers, Fred (ed.). 2001. *The Empire of Things: Regimes of Value and Material Culture*. Santa Fe, NM: School of American Research Press.

Otto, Ton and Rane Willerslev. 2013. 'Introduction. Value *as* theory: Comparison, cultural critique, and guerrilla ethnographic theory'. *HAU: Journal of Ethnographic Theory* 3(1): 1–20. doi.org/10.14318/hau3.1.002.

Paini, Anna. 2014. 'Relocaliser les pratiques culturelles autour du tressage à Lifou'. In *Hèritage d'une mission, James et Emma Hatfield, îles Loyauté (1878–1920)*, pp. 44–55. Nouméa: Musée de Nouvelle-Calédonie.

———. 2013. 'Le "chemin des richesses" des femmes'. In *Kanak. L'art est une parole*, ed. Roger Boulay and Emmanuel Kasarhérou, pp. 314–17. Paris: Musée du Quai Branly, Actes Sud.

———. 2010. 'Un art des femmes à explorer, le tressage à Lifou'. Conférence-ethno, Musée de Nouvelle-Calédonie, Nouméa, 25 June.

Polanyi, Karl. 1944. *The Great Transformation*. New York: Rinehart.

Rogan, Bjarne. 2012. 'Objets de collection et modes de collectionner. À propos de la sexualisation des objets'. In *Les objets ont-ils un genre? Culture materielle et production sociale des identites sexuees,* ed. Élisabeth Anstett and Marie-Luce Gélard, pp. 17–34. Paris: Armand Colin. doi.org/10.3917/arco.gela.2012.01.0017.

Sahlins, Marshall. 1981. *Historical Metaphors and Mythical Realities: Structure in the Early History of the Sandwich Islands Kingdom*. Ann Arbor: University of Michigan Press. doi.org/10.3998/mpub.6773.

———. 1972. *Stone Age Economics*. Chicago: Aldine.

Steiner, Christopher. 2001. 'Rights of passage: On the liminal identity of art in the border zone'. In *The Empire of Things: Regimes of Value and Material Culture*, ed. Fred Myers, pp. 207–31. Santa Fe, NM: School of American Research Press.

Stewart, Pamela J. and Andrew Strathern (eds). 2003. *Landscape, Memory and History: Anthropological Perspectives,* Anthropology, Culture, and Society Series. London: Pluto.

Strathern, Marilyn (ed.). 1987. *Dealing with Inequality: Analysing Gender Relations in Melanesia and Beyond*. Cambridge: University of Cambridge Press.

Sykes, Karen. 2013. 'Mortgaging the bridewealth: Problems with brothers and problems with value'. *HAU: Journal of Ethnographic Theory* 3(2): 97–117. doi.org/10.14318/hau3.2.007.

Teaiwa, Teresia. 1995. 'Preface'. In *Searching for Nei Nim'anoa*. Suva: Mana Publications.

Thomas, Nicholas. 1991. *Entangled Objects. Exchange, Material Culture, and Colonialism in the Pacific*. Cambridge: Harvard University Press.

Tilley, Christopher. 2006. 'Introduction'. In *Handbook of Material Culture*, ed. Christopher Tilley, Webb Keane, Susanne Kuechler, Mike Rowlands and Patricia Spyer, pp. 1–6. London: Sage. doi.org/10.1177/1359183506062990.

Tsing, Anna Lowenhaupt. 2004. *Friction: An Ethnography of Global Connection*. Princeton, NJ: Princeton University Press.

Weiner, Annette. 1992. *Inalienable Possessions: The Paradox of Keeping-While-Giving*. Berkeley: University of California Press. doi.org/10.1525/california/9780520076037.001.0001.

Weiner, James F. 1991. *The Empty Place: Poetry, Space, and Being among the Foi of Papua New Guinea*. Bloomington: Indiana University Press.

Part One. Mapping Materiality in Time and Place

1

Alterity and Autochthony: Austronesian Cosmographies of the Marvellous[1]

Marshall Sahlins

Raymond Firth's Tikopia corpus is a treasure for all time. 'A treasure for all time' was Thucydides's modest assessment of his own *History of the Peloponnesian War*, no doubt intended as an invidious contrast to Herodotus, since it followed from the observation that *he* was not one to pander to a credulous public by relating fanciful tales of the marvellous. Indeed, Thucydides's invocations of a universal, interest-driven rationality based on supposed natural desires of power and gain—of the kind that led to the spectacularly irrational debacle of the Sicilian campaign—have made him the darling of contemporary IR realists. All the same, the ethnographically-informed history of Herodotus, rich in its accounts of local legends and unusual customs, turned out to be the real intellectual gold. And in the same way as Herodotus's sustained excursus on the marvellous of the peoples involved in the Greco-Persian

1   Marshall Sahlins originally delivered this text as the Raymond Firth Lecture in Verona, at the 2008 European Society for Oceanists (ESfO) conference. We subsequently translated it into Italian for publication in *La Ricerca Folklorica* 63 (2011). In agreement with the author and the editors of *HAU*, the paper was first published in English in volume 2(2) 2012 of the journal, with the understanding that it would also be included in this volume.

Wars, Raymond Firth's incredibly rich ethnography will be an enduring source of anthropological reflections on the cultural ordering of practice and history.

Here I proffer an example of Firth's legacy by taking up certain anomalies that he repeatedly observed in the Tikopian politics of autochthony and alterity. They offer insight into the phenomenon of stranger-kingship so widely distributed among Austronesian peoples and others the world over. Beyond that, Firth's ethnography of alterity opens the way to an anthropological appreciation of the politically marvellous, such as the descent of certain Malay sultans from Alexander the Great or the self-identification of Polynesian chiefs with British royalty. For all the great value the Tikopians attached to autochthony of lineage, they were literally dying to participate in the wonders and powers of overseas lands—'strolling around the sky', they called it—even as most gave no credence to the claim of the paramount Ariki Kafika that his original ancestors sprang from the Tikopian earth (Firth 1961: 53ff). In the opinion of most, the ruling chiefs came from lands in the foreign skies.

One of the differences between historians and anthropologists, most of them anyhow, is that the former are inclined to debunk such narratives in their pursuit of historical fact, while for anthropologists the issue is how, as cultural facts, they truly make history. For anthropologists the credence given to the seemingly marvellous opens questions of the distinct cultural logic these narratives entail and their efficacy as significant conditions of world order and practical action. The historians want to know 'what actually happened', the anthropologists, rather, what it meant to the people concerned—what it is that happened—from which actually follows the course of events.

Alterity and autochthony in Tikopia

For Firth, the striking 'anomaly' in the narratives of chiefly legitimacy was that, despite a near-obsessional concern for priority and indigeneity of lineage, and more particularly for autochthony, neither the ruling Kafika people nor any other *ariki* lineage had an indisputable claim to such status. A bare table of the relation between the rank of major lineages and the antiquity of their appearance in Tikopia was enough to show there was 'no close coincidence' between these attributes (Firth 1961: 178). On the other hand, several of the leading *matapure*, or ritual elders, although inferior in rank to *ariki*, could claim derivation from autochthonous peoples, such as the Nga Faea; or else, as in the case of one elder of Kafika (Pa Porima), his ancestor was senior and his god older than the chief's own ancients. Since, as Firth reported, the 'immense importance' of lineage priority is that it gives title to land, while at the same time the seniority of their ancestors gave the ritual elders certain ceremonial privileges, the relations of native elders to immigrant chiefs is much like that of 'owners' to rulers in many Austronesian stranger-kingships (Firth 1970: 55–57; 1967: 62ff; cf. Sahlins 2008). Recall the classic case of the ruling Tabalu subclan of the Trobriands, whose immigrant status in many villages Malinowski likewise found 'anomalous' in light of the privilege otherwise accorded to local, earth-born origins (1948: 94). (The 'anomalies' of alterity and autochthony are piling up: we are approaching a Kuhnian moment of paradigm shift, to which I hope to give further impetus here.)

Actually, the claim of the Ariki Kafika family was that they were ancestral strangers, the descendants of immigrant heroes who were human forms of the Pu Ma twins, autochthonous gods who had left Tikopia long before. The gods went away and came back as humans (like Captain Cook at Hawai'i, for example). The Kafika ruling house would thus have it both ways, adding the values of the transcendental to the legitimacy of the local—had they been believed. However, even the so-called 'Sacred Tale' of Tikopia betrayed them. For it told that when the native Pu Ma gods returned as men to Tikopia—when they 'came hither from foreign skies'—it was not as older and younger brother but as mother's brother and sister's son; and while the Kafika chief claimed descent from the latter, the sacred nephew, in this strictly patrilineal society it would leave him with unspecified lineage origins—he would still be a stranger. Indeed the mother's brother cum older brother of the original Pu Ma twins was rather the ancestor of a principal ritual-elder line. Here is the Tikopian version of the Austronesian relation between indigenous native elders and *parvenu* kings, with the transfer of sovereignty to the latter marked by a union of the original stranger with a daughter of the former.

In any event, the general body of the people knew the Kafika chiefs as canoe-borne immigrants rather than earth-born Tikopia, the principal matter in contention being whether they came from Pukapuka, Somosomo, or, more vaguely, Fiji. (The tradition of Somosomo origins, incidentally, strengthens the case for a settlement from the Fijian island of Cikobia, off Vanua Levu, as Somosomo in Taveuni was the ruling town of the Cakaudrove confederacy, the dominant polity in that area at least since the eighteenth century.) In the matter of chiefly origins, however, Tikopia shared more with Fiji than a few place names. Recall A.M. Hocart's report of the Lau man's observation that the ruling chiefs 'came from overseas; it is so in all countries of Fiji' (Hocart 1929: 27). Just so, the son of a former Ariki Kafika told Firth that whereas the traditional autochthonous peoples of Tikopia, the Nga Faea and Nga Ravenga, 'have their roots in the earth; we came here, we voyaged from overseas' (1961: 59).

Not that their immigrant origins had to be a slur on the status of Tikopian chiefs or a detriment to their authority. Only that, as we have seen, it put them on the transcendental side of the dual system of values, the opposition of foreign chiefs from the sky or sea and native people of the earth, that orders so many Austronesian polities. If Tikopians were almost obsessively concerned with autochthony, they were equally interested in entering into relations with the vital forces, beings and things in the celestial realms beyond the horizon. For as Firth observed, the European presence greatly expanded this cosmography of the marvellous, providing unparalleled opportunities for enhancing local authority by acquiring external agency.

In the few generations before Firth's 1929 fieldwork, well over 100 men undertook overseas voyages—the 1929 population was 1298—including one period when fleets of canoes set off in 'almost a frenzy … and if they were not scattered by storms and lost, no sooner did their captains return to Tikopia than they set forth again' (ibid.: 152). More than half died at sea. And in another spate of 30 voyages after 1929, about 80 men were lost. Firth cites a stanza from a well-known song:

> We here, great is the greed of our eyes
> For valuables from abroad
> Which come with disaster (1957: 36).

Were not the dangers of the foreign a sign of its powers? And would not overcoming these risks endow value and prestige on the successful voyagers? Probably this was what Firth meant in speaking of the spirit of adventure animating these men, and the meaning also of the little ritual attending their return (1957: 18–21). The successful voyager was smeared with turmeric by his mother's brother as 'a mark of distinction', and the family of the mother's brother carried a basket of food to him. The ceremonial welcome is structurally isomorphic with the advent of the Ariki Kafika's human ancestor from abroad in the Sacred Tale of Tikopian chieftainship. According to the Sacred Tale, the rule and the resources of the island—political analogues of the mark of distinction and the basket of food in the welcome ritual—were accorded the immigrant sister's son or 'sacred child' (*tama tapu*), the avatar of the younger of the foundational twin gods (Pu Ma). The turmeric makes the connection between the structural registers of kingship and kinship. Produced in a highly ritualised manner and stored as an object of great value, turmeric was the perfume of the great culture hero and Kafika ancestor, the Atua i Kafika. Turmeric attracted the sacred hero and, as applied to the principal persons and objects of important ceremonies, in effect consecrated them (Firth 1950, 1957).

The social value that Tikopia men acquired from voyages in the transcendental world was expressed in the tales they told, in the objects they bought back, even in the talismanic virtues of English phrases they had learned. These powerful words might be solicited from them with gifts by stay-at-homes; or else, the returning voyagers kept their English to themselves for the advantages it gave them in dealing with European visitors. Most tellingly, successful voyagers came back with foreign names for themselves and their houses. Consider that, apart from members of the immediate family, Tikopians know each other by the names of their dwellings: as 'Pa' (husband) and 'Nau' (wife) prefixed to the house-name. So if the house was known as Niukaso or Melipani, the inhabitants were 'the Newcastles' or 'the Melbournes'. Moreover, other relatives might solicit or inherit such foreign names from their voyaging kinfolk. It follows that alterity is a widespread condition of Tikopians' native identity.

The complement of the acquisition of status from abroad is the power that important foreign visitors were thought to exercise, for better or for worse. Firth noted that although in the island the title of *ariki* was exclusively used for the four clan chiefs (and in certain ritual formulas, for the gods), it was liberally accorded to distinguished members of other societies, particularly Europeans such as ship captains, senior government officials, the Bishop of Melanesia, and their like (1970: 39–40). Some of these outsiders might even be the subjects of avoidance taboos. Firth considered such practices as courtesies for the most part, although the question remains why the foreigners merited such deference; and more significantly, why they were specifically considered political figures, sometimes as the rivals of Tikopian *ariki*; and still more significantly, why some at least were attributed divine powers capable of bringing down natural disasters on the local people—and were inclined to do so. Regarding native Christian mission teachers (from other islands), it was held by prominent converts and 'heathens' alike that the teachers' object was 'to depreciate the status of chiefs' by taking away their rights to first fruits and other offerings. 'A general opinion was that the mission teachers, especially their leader, from another island, wish to exalt themselves at the expense of traditional authority' (1957: 46). Most notable were the powers of a former Bishop of Melanesia who resigned from his position for reasons of ill health. Although he had been generous to the Tikopians, they aver that on his departure he cursed the islands of his charge, causing a tidal wave from which Tikopia suffered in common with other places. He also sent grubs that devoured the taro (ibid.: 35).

The would-be good Bishop was hardly the first foreign person to be credited by Malayo-Polynesian people with divine powers akin to those of indigenous gods, or even the status of one of them now returned. In a seminal article, Ward Goodenough made the case that the famous Micronesian homeland Kachaw (Katau, Achau, etc.) referred to a spirit land in the sky, which helps explain why the Trukese always described the beings who came from there as énúúyaramas (i.e. spirits that can take fully human form). Besides Truk, the Sandeleur rulers of Nan Madol in Ponape claimed Kachaw origins, as did the dynasty that replaced them; while Belau and even atolls in the Carolines and Marshalls knew similar distinctions between immigrant rulers from the spirit world and the subordinate indigenous peoples. Goodenough (1986: 559) suggests that this can be a structure without an actual event, without an historical migration, insofar as local people 'who wish to bolster their political power with magical power' will claim ancestry from the transcendent spiritual realm. On the other hand, in certain real-historical metaphors of such mythical realities, 'Europeans, on their first arrival at Pacific islands were often greeted as if they were from the spirit world' (ibid.). By their own folkloric conceits, the Europeans attributed this status to their superior technology and firepower, but as Goodenough notes, in the islanders' 'viewpoint, they were simply the latest in a long succession of arrivals from the spirit world' (ibid.). Standing Marx on his head—hence back to Hegel right side up—by the islanders' lights, superior technology would be a function of the outsider's divinity rather than the other way around. If the Trukese assigned marvellous powers to their early European visitors, it was no more than they accorded the Master of Kachaw (Sowerkachaw), spirit-ancestor of their ruling chiefs, who made several trips to Truk by sea and air, riding a frigate bird, a banana, a scorpion fish and a whale, to mark his claim to the islands by names and deeds.[2]

---

2   On stranger-kings and stranger-chiefs of Micronesia see, among others: Parmentier (1987); Hanlon (1988); Bernart (1977); Petersen (1990); Lingenfelter (1975).

On stranger-kings in general[3]

Stranger-kings or stranger-chiefs ruled indigenous peoples throughout much of the Austronesian world, from the Malay Peninsula to Hawai'i. James Fox (1995a, 1995b, 2006) has made a careful analysis of the variant forms of these dualistic polities in Timor, Roti, Palembang (Sumatra), Gayo, Fiji, Bali and the Trobriands (cf. van Wouden 1968). In addition to the classic ethnographies of Firth, Malinowski, Goodenough and Hocart, Jukka Siikala has studied the like in the Cook Islands, Engseng Ho in Malaya, Janet Hoskins in Sumba, Glenn Petersen in Ponape, John Bowen in Gayo (Sumatra), Schulte Nordholt in Atoni (Timor), Josselin de Jong in Negri Sembilan (Malaya), Danilyn Rutherford in Biak, Thomas Gibson in South Sulawesi, R.H. Barnes in Lembata (Lesser Sundas), and Catarina Krizancic in the Society Islands, among others; while historians such as Anthony Reid, Jeyamalar Kathirithamby-Wells, Leonard Andaya, B. Schrieke, J.H. Walker, and O.W. Wolters have documented such polities in various Indonesian locations. I will not rehearse these findings in detail here. (Besides, I left out a lot of people.) Rather, I call attention to the larger planetary distribution of stranger-kingships in premodern societies, with a view toward a general description of their constitution and some reflections on the dynamics of their formation.[4]

If I called this description 'ideal-typical', would I be exonerated from the crime of essentialising? In any case, to generalise, if at some risk: by their dynastic origins, as rehearsed in ongoing traditions and enacted in royal rituals, the rulers of a remarkable number of societies around the world have been strangers to the places and peoples they rule. East, South and Southeast Asia have been breeding grounds of such outsider-kings from early times: not only in major centres such as the Cambodian kingdoms of Brahmin ancestry, the Ayudhya dynasty in Siam founded by a Chinese merchant prince, or the Lanka realm established by the princely descendant of a lion from India; but also in adjacent lowlands such as those occupied by Shan, Yi, or Malay principalities; and into the more peripheral areas

---

3   Parts of this section of the essay are rehearsed from an earlier article (Sahlins 2008)—the documentation of which leaves something to be desired. A fuller treatment of stranger-kingship is in preparation in book form: provisional title, *The Stranger-King; or, the Powers of Otherness*.
4   Aside from works previously cited, those noted in this paragraph are: Siikala (1990; 1991; 1996); Ho (1999; 2002); Hoskins (1993); Schulte Nordholt (1971); Josselin de Jong (1975); Rutherford (2002); Gibson (2005); Barnes (1974); Krizancic (2006); Reid (1994; 2008); Kathirithamby-Wells (2006); L. Andaya (1975; cf. 2006); Schrieke (1957); Walker (2002); Wolters (1970; 1986). On Fijian analogues, see Sahlins (1981a; 2004).

where hill peoples more or less willingly acknowledge the authority of lowland rulers, and their own leaders are known to have 'become Shan', Burmese, or Chinese in genealogy, attire and other attributes.[5]

Elsewhere I have noted similar structures among the Indo-European ancients (Sahlins 1981a, 2004). The early kings of the Peloponnesus down to Agamemnon and the Heraclid rulers of Sparta were Zeus-descended strangers. Aeneas was from Troy; while Romulus, warrior-prince of Alba, founded Rome—by killing his brother and subsuming the indigenous Sabines through the slaughter of their men and marriage with their women. Sir James Frazer provided an early description of the phenomenon in the Indo-European family:

> Thus it would seem that among some Aryan peoples, at a certain stage of their social evolution, it has been customary to regard women and not men as the channels in which royal blood flows, and to bestow the kingdom in each successive generation on a man of another family, and often of another country, who marries one of the princesses and reigns over his wife's people. A common type of popular tale which relates how an adventurer, coming to a strange land, wins the hand of the king's daughter and half or the whole of the kingdom, may well be the reminiscence of a real custom (Frazer 2006: 86; cf. Preaux 1962).

In something like the abduction of the Sabine women or the draconian usurpations of native rulers in the Peloponnesus, Africa too has been the site of conflictual-cum-contractual syntheses of indigenous 'owners' of the land and stranger-rulers of different ethnic origins, violent dispositions, and cosmic powers. Referring broadly to West and Central Africa, Luc de Heusch writes: 'Everything happens as if the very structure of a lineage-based society is not capable of engendering dialectical development on the political plane without the intervention of a new political structure. The sovereignty, the magical source of power, always comes from elsewhere, from a claimed original place, exterior to society' (1982a: 26).

---

5   See especially: Leach (1954); Strathern (2009); Li (2001); Lehman (1963); Horstmann and Wadley (2006); Turton (2000); Kasetsiri (1976); Robinne and Sadan (2007); Glahn (1987); Sprenger (2006); Fiskesjö (1999); Taylor (1983, 1999); Wyatt (1984); Backus (1981); Giersch (2006); Took (2005); Wang (1981).

Well-known examples include Alur, Benin, Shilluk, Nupe, Mossi, Kongo, Luba, Lunda, Ruwanda, Nyoro, Burgo—not to mention the many lesser kingdoms and chiefdoms that are effectively satellites of the greater ones.[6]

The major American empires of the Aztecs and Inkas were ruled by immigrant strangers. Likewise, 'the arrival of strangers' initiated the Mayan dynasties of Tikal and Copan, according to the classic-period inscriptions, and similar kingly origins were known in post-classic cities of the Quiche, Mayapan and others.[7]

A common permutation—found in Japan, Korea, Natchez, Tonga— involves kings who originally came from the heavens, always a good address for persons of royal pretensions. Still another variant is the return of the ancestral stranger, such as we saw in Tikopia, where the dominant newcomers (sometimes) allege their descent from primordial local ancestors. Such is also the derivation of certain East African rulers and of many colonising Whitemen the world over, who were initially conceived by the indigenous people as long-lost brothers of their own legendary progenitors—if they were not the embodiments of their original gods.

Still generalising (and risking): in these stranger-kingdoms, two forms of authority and legitimacy coexist in a state of mutual dependence and reciprocal incorporation. The native people and the foreign rulers claim precedence on different grounds. For the underlying people, it is the founder principle, the right of first occupancy, or in the maximal case, the claim of autochthony. In many Austronesian as well as African societies the native people are the 'owners', which reflects their belonging to the land as much as the land belonging to them, and entails a special relation to the ancestral sources of its productivity. (I like what Sather (1990: 30) says about Iban in this connection, that the rice they raise is the transubstantiation of their ancestors.) Within the dualistic state, then, the indigenous people are not only the main subsistence producers, they also retain a preeminent spiritual authority over the land and corresponding ritual functions. But the stranger-kings trump the native people's original rights by aggressive and transgressive demonstrations of superior might and thus claim the sovereignty. The claim is also a promise

---

6   See among others: Heusch (1962, 1982a, 1982b); Kopytoff (1989); Balandier (1968a, 1968b); Ekholm (1978); Cunnison (1951); Forde and Kaberry (1967); Skinner (1964); Oberg (1970); Evans-Pritchard (1962); Southall (2004); Lombard (1965); Richards (1960).
7   Sabloff (2003); Carrrasco, Jones, and Sessions (2000); Gillespie (1989); and Stuart (2000), among others.

of order and prosperity, for these stranger-heroes are ambiguous figures, both draconian and beneficent, whose untoward irruption into the native society in time becomes a civilising mission.

In traditions common in Africa and East Asia, the immigrant hero is the son of a powerful foreign king who fails to obtain the succession, perhaps for some fault that results in banishment from his native land. Or else, if he is not already marked by an antisocial past, his advent on the local scene is attended by incest, murder or other such crimes against kinship and morality. This 'exploit' as Luc de Heusch (1962) called it, by its transcendence of the local society, is a sign of the foreigner's power to organise it. In the ensuing time, the stranger-ruler is domesticated by the indigenous people, and his violence is turned outward toward the expansion of the realm; while internally, he bestows cultural benefits on the original owners that lift them from an initially rudimentary state.

The stranger-king is a rain-maker, both in the local sense that he fertilises the bearing earth of the native people and in our colloquial sense that, in contrast to their possession of land, he is the source of the society's riches, particularly in the form of life-enhancing foreign valuables. It is not for nothing that a number of Southeast Asian kingdoms were established by merchant princes, or that some of these were at the same time powerful religious figures, such as the rich Brahmin who founded the ancient Cambodian kingdom of Funan or the *sayid* traders who became prominent in Malay sultanates. As it is said in the *Malay Annals* (*Sejarah Melayu*), 'Where there is sovereignty, there is gold' (Brown 1952: 187). Providing foreign wealth and fertilising the land are of course parallel functions, insofar as both represent the vitality of alterity and comprise a necessary complement of external movable means for realising the fixed earthly powers of the indigenous people. This mutually beneficial conjunction is almost invariably accompanied by the union of the immigrant prince with a daughter of the indigenous ruler. Besides representing the reproductive synthesis of the foreign and the native directly in marriage, this union in the common case of patrilineal orders, by installing the stranger's lineage in power, is also a usurpation, thus making the formation of the polity an interesting mix of conflict and contract.

Typically, then, there is some continuing tension between the foreign-derived royals and the native people. Invidious disagreements about legitimacy and superiority may surface in conflicting versions of the founding traditions, depending on which party for what purpose is telling the tale. (Hence the disputes about chiefly origins in Tikopia.) More than political, however, the synthesis of the foreign and the indigenous is cosmological, which is what helps it endure. Corresponding to the conjunction of an external masculinity and an internal femininity, the foreign rulers are to the native people in some such encompassing relation as the Celestial is to the Terrestrial, the Sea to the Land, the Wild to the Settled; or, in abstract terms, as the Universal is to the Particular, a ratio that also holds for their respective gods. We see, then, why the narratives of the advent of the stranger-hero function as all-round cultural constitutions. The union with the Other gives rise to the society as a self-producing totality—and the permanent contradiction that this autonomy is a function of heteronymy.

A parenthetical note to place Tikopia in this general scheme, in addition to the aspects of stranger-kingship already mentioned: The devolution of rule on the immigrant Kafika ancestors, whether in divine or human form, rehearses the founding union of the foreign hero with a ranking woman of the indigenous people—in this case, several times over (Firth 1971). In the sequel to a liaison with a daughter of the Tafua lineage, a chiefly group that claims autochthonous origin, the Kafika usurp the Tafua as paramount chiefs. Another key Kafika marriage, this with a daughter of the autochthonous Faea people, is by all appearances (although no explicit statement) incestuous, as the woman had been married to her husband's father. The offspring of this transgressive marriage is the famous Atua I Kafika, the principal god and culture-hero of Tikopia, founder of its main institutions, including the ritual protocols of its prosperity. So in the event, the godly powers of the immigrant and incestuous strangers who marry the daughters and usurp the authority of the native rulers are domesticated and provide civilising benefits to the original Tikopia people. End of parenthesis.

The politics of alterity

Of course in a way, and as they say, all politics is local. But paradoxically the resources of political power in Austronesian societies and numerous others are generally foreign. I take Viveiros de Castro's point that, 'If humans were immortal, perhaps society would be confounded with the cosmos. Since death exists, it is necessary for society to be linked with something that is outside itself—and that it be linked *socially* to this exterior' (1992: 190–91). Ranging from beasts, spirits and gods to ineffable forces, by the way of the generic dead or the ancestors, and of other peoples with their remarkable gifts, the extraordinary agents that control the human fate live outside the space of human control. More precisely, the lack of control translates as being-in-other-space. I am speaking of the so-called and misnamed 'supernatural'. I say misnamed because the term supposes ethnocentric concepts of 'nature' and 'natural'—an autonomous world of soulless material things, of Cartesian *res extensa*—that are not pertinent to peoples who are engaged in a cosmic society of interacting subjects, including a variety of non-human beings with consciousness, soul, intentionality and other qualities of human persons.

Admittedly, my notions of the so-called 'supernatural' rest on simple-minded and old-fashioned premises. I take the rather positivist and Malinowskian view that people must in reality depend for their existence on external conditions not of their own making—hence and whence the spirits. Recall Malinowski's observation that magic comes into fishing in the Trobriands when one ventures beyond the reef. The going anthropological alternatives argue that divinity is some misrecognition of humanity. For Émile Durkheim, god is the misplaced apprehension of the power of society, a power people surely experience but know not wherefrom it comes. For a certain Marxist anthropology, god is an alienated projection of people's own powers of production and reproduction, an unhappy consciousness that has transferred human self-fashioning to the deity. Such theories may address the morphology of divinity, whether as reflection or mystification, but they do not tell us why society is set in a cosmos of beings invested with powers of vitality and mortality beyond any that humans themselves know or control, produce or reproduce. Neither sense of false consciousness takes sufficient account of the generic predicament of the human condition: this dependence on *sui generis* forces of life and death, forces not created by human science or governed by human intentionality.

If people really were in control of their own existence, they would not die. Or fall ill. Nor do they control the biology of sexual or agricultural generation. Or the weather on which their prosperity depends. Or, notably, the other peoples of their ken: peoples whose cultural existence may be enviable or scandalous to them. But in either case, by the very difference from themselves, ken are strangers who thus offer proof of a transcendent capacity for life. It is as if nothing foreign were merely human to them. Endowed with transcendent powers of life and death, the foreign becomes an ambiguous object of desire and danger. Hence the ubiquity—and ambiguity—of the aforementioned stranger-king formations. Dare one suggest that the much-maligned cargo cults are derived from the same general structures of alterity, except that they feature the people's own agency in appropriating the enriching powers of foreign subjects, by way of resistance, as it were, to a sovereign imposition.

In a way Josselin de Jong made the same point when he likened the initiation rites of the Toradja of Sulawesi, which entail taking an enemy head, to the foundation legend of the Negri Sembilan kingdom of Malaya by a Minangkabau stranger-prince from Sumatra (1969: 302–03; cf. Downs 1955). As famously reported for many Southeast Asian hinterland societies, these enemy heads, when ritually installed in the warrior's home community, become sources of the people's well-being, notably of the fertility of their crops—'for you', as Ifugao say to the enshrined head, 'have become one of us' (McKinley 1976: 115; cf. Hoskins 1996). Hence in respect of their beneficial effects as well as their initially hostile status, enemy heads are analogous to stranger-kings. Moreover, like the Minangkabau hero who successfully overcame dangerous adversaries on his way to seizing the kingship in Malaya, the young Toradja warrior acquires an exalted local status by his adventures in the realms of external-cum-cosmic powers. In the charter narrative of the headhunting complex, the warrior-hero first undertakes an arduous trip to the Upperworld to exact revenge on the killers of his parents, and then descends to the Underworld to take the heads of his victims' ghosts. Corollary Toradja traditions tell that the village of the headhunter had been dead during his absence but revives upon his triumphal return, and that the hero also brings home the magical daughter of his victim and marries her after the head-feast—thus transforming enemies into affines and marking their equivalence as reproductive agents. In sum, the Toradja warrior returns from a cosmic exploit with a foreign subject (the head) and enhanced reproductive virtue (the wife) in order to give life to (revive) the whole society. Allowance made for the inversions of stranger-king formations—the local hero who captures foreign power as opposed to the foreign prince whose power is captured locally—here is another modality of the same relationships.

Indeed one could say, at least in our colloquial terms, that the Iban of Borneo, in their raiding heyday, treated the heads of their victims royally, as something like stranger-kings. (For that matter, the symbolic killing of the royal heir as an outsider and his rebirth as a domestic ruler is a common feature of kingly installation rights in Oceania and elsewhere.) Consider, then, this nineteenth-century account of the Ibans' ritual regard for the enemy head, beginning with its debarkation from abroad:

> The fleet, returning from a successful cruise, on approaching the village, announce to the inhabitants their fortunes by a horrid yell, which is soon imitated and prolonged by the men, women and children, who have stayed at home. The head is brought on shore with much ceremony, wrapped in the curiously folded and plaited leaves of the nipah palm, and frequently emitting the disgusting odour peculiar to decaying mortality; this, the Dyaks have frequently told me, is particularly grateful to their senses, and surpasses the odorous durian, their favorite fruit. On shore and in the village, the head, for months after its arrival, is treated with the greatest consideration, and all the names and terms of endearment of which their language is capable are abundantly lavished on it: the most dainty morsels … is [*sic*] thrust into its mouth, and it is instructed to hate its former friends, and that, having been adopted into the tribe of its captors, its spirit must always be with them; sirih leaves and betel-nut are given it—and finally, a cigar is frequently placed between its ghastly and pallid lips. None of this disgusting mockery is performed with the intention of ridicule, but all to propitiate the spirit by kindness, and to procure its good wishes for the tribe, of whom it is now supposed to have become a member (Low 1848: 207).

Hugh Low and others writing of Iban at the time note that, like the Toradja, procuring a head was a necessary condition for obtaining a bride, although it appears that, even then, amassing heirloom wealth in a journey abroad (*bejalai*) was an alternative means.

Given that the rule of the stranger-king is not simply an imposition of foreign power but its beneficial integration on the part of the indigenous people, claims of external identity and potency are oft-used tactics of domestic political competition in Austronesian societies. Where foreign rulers become natives, so may natives become foreigners. I am not speaking simply of the estrangement of power: some sort of Clastrian contradiction between political authority and the common morality, the effect of which would be the ideological exile of the prince to the status of a foreigner. More fundamental is the structural dynamic that makes foreign identity a condition of indigenous authority. This can be a decisive move in the competitive process that Gregory Bateson (1958: 175ff) called symmetrical schismogenesis.

Bateson sometimes likened symmetrical schismogenesis to an arms race in which each side tries to outdo the other by doing more of the same, on the principle of 'anything you can do I can do better'. At the extreme, however, competition in quantity is exchanged for competition in quality: one goes outside the box, trumping the adversary by shifting the terms of contention to means of another kind and a superior value, like introducing a new, devastating weapon into the arms race. So analogously in cultural politics—and not only among Austronesian peoples—the play is to outdo rival others by engaging transcendent powers in one's own cause, powers above and beyond the society and its customary bases of authority. Speaking of the Cook Islands, Jukka Siikala succinctly states the principle: 'The internal chiefly rivalry constantly seeks a means of legitimation outside its borders' (1996: 51).

Reported from all over the Austronesian world as the 'status rivalry' between older and younger brothers or senior and junior lines, and celebrated in tradition by conflicts that reverse their rank order, this politics of transcendence seem to be built into genealogically-ranked lineage systems. The effect of the inscribed 'principle of sinking status' is a structural disposition of junior kinsmen to transgress the established order, fated as they and their descendants are to decline in rank as their senior kinsmen increase in number (Geertz and Geertz 1975: 124ff). Hence the well-known opposition between inherited rank and demonstrated *mana*: between the ascribed and restrained dignity of the firstborn and the boundary-crossing, derring-do of the younger brother. The same appears in other registers as the triumph of the warrior (*toa*) over the chief (*ariki*) and the trickster over the greater gods (e.g. Smith 1974–75).

Gregory Schrempp (1992) brilliantly analysed this politics of transcendence as it appears in the well-known cosmogonic narrative of the Māori concerning the conflicts among the divine sons of Rangi (Heaven) and Papa (Earth). The younger-brother god Tū, ancestor of mankind, is able to defeat his elder sibling and celestial enemy Tawhiri, and by his victory Tū gains superiority over all his older brothers as well as control of the earthly species descended from them. Tawhiri was the only one of his siblings to join the Sky Father when the others forcefully separated their heavenly parent from the Earth Mother. In retaliation for this crime, Tawhiri let loose devastating squalls, whirlwinds and hurricanes on the earth, scattering the brothers hither and yon—which accounts for the distribution of natural species respectively sprung from them. Only Tū stood up to Tawhiri, battling him to a standstill. 'Tū alone was brave,'

Māori say. And because his siblings had fled before Tawhiri, Tū then turned upon them, defeated and consumed them, rendering them inferior to himself. He became their senior brother. As Schrempp concluded, bravery is thus able to dominate as a political value, not merely as a physical force, because it is expressed and legitimated on a cosmic plane. Because Tū was victorious on this transcendent, heavenly plane, his human descendants are able to control the earthly species, including the staple foods, that instantiate his defeated brothers. The earthly privileges of the Māori are backed ultimately by higher cosmic values.

The real-politics of the marvellous

Recall, in this connection, Firth's correlation of an outburst of Tikopian overseas voyaging 'with the increasing realisation of the new worlds that lay beyond the horizon and the exciting experiences offered by contact with Europeans there' (1961: 152). Conversely, the early European visitors to Polynesian islands as it were brought heavenly power to earth, giving the people's traffic with them the character of ritual exchanges with ancient divinities. The records of Captain Cook's visits to Hawai'i offer several islander testimonies to this effect, such as Lt James King's notice of the common surmise that the great royal gods lived with the British:

> As they certainly regarded us as a superior race of people to themselves, they would often say, that the great Eatooa [god] liv'd with us. The little Image … they called *Koonooe akai'a* [Kunuiakea, principal god of the Hawai'i island paramount] & said it was Tereeoboos [King Kalaniopu'u's] God & that he also liv'd with us (Beaglehole 1967: 621).

The same cosmography was in play in the assumption of foreign identities by ruling chiefs in several Polynesian societies, especially British identities and particularly that of 'King George' (III or IV), as though they were themselves stranger-kings. This tactic was practised notably by ambitious chiefs who could not claim by ancestry the authority to which they now aspired by force and wealth—with means largely acquired in trade with the Europeans they were pleased to take as models of their own power. The paramounts of three Hawaiian islands who named their sons and heirs 'King George', Iotete of the Marquesas who declared himself an Englishman, King George Tupou of Tonga, Hongi Hika of New Zealand, the Pomares of Tahiti: all these *parvenu* rulers sought to legitimate their sovereignty by assuming the trappings of foreign royalty (Sahlins 1994).

The great Kamehameha, who usurped and sacrificed his senior royal kinsman (father's brother's son), the king of Hawai'i Island, and then went on to conquer the archipelago, considered George III his 'older brother' and addressed him so by letter. (I am repeating notices of Hawaiian chiefs' relations to Europeans that I have recorded elsewhere (Sahlins 1981b, 1992, 1995), begging your indulgence on grounds that the present context offers new insights into the meaning of these chiefly aspirations of alterity.) Kamehameha was flying the Union Jack from his house and canoe even before he ceded the Hawaiian Islands to 'King George', and he still considered himself under the British monarch's protection after the offer had been refused. In 1794, at the time he was campaigning to defeat the other Hawaiian rulers, Kamehameha lavishly hosted the British expedition captained by George Vancouver. As was his custom with passing European visitors, the Hawai'i Island king was curious to know their manner of doing things, and he even posted a man to the galley of one of Vancouver's ships for the purpose of learning how to cook (a rare instance indeed of foreign regard for English cuisine). When Vancouver was preparing to leave, Kamehameha made several requests of the British to supply him with domestic furnishings and cooking utensils. Master's Mate Thomas Manby commented in his journal: 'and now that he was in possession of the requisites for the table, a tolerable cook and every kind of implement for culinary purposes, the monarch boasted with evident pride and satisfaction that he should now live like King George' (Manby 1929: 46).

Manby had already heard from a high priest that the Hawaiian ruling family traced their descent to Whitemen who had come to the islands some generations before—a story of ultimate connection to colonising Europeans of a kind told by indigenous peoples the world over. As if in confirmation, during the last years of Kamehameha's reign, John Adams Kuakini was governor of Hawai'i Island, Cox Ke'eamuoku ruled Maui, and Billy Pitt Kalaimoku was the 'Prime Minister' of the kingdom. These were not just sobriquets bestowed on Hawaiians by Europeans for their own amusement. Kalaimoku insisted on being called 'Pitt', and the casket in which Ke'eamuoku was buried in 1824 was simply inscribed 'Cox'. Also to be seen in Honolulu in those days were Billy Cobbett, George Washington, Charley Fox, Thomas Jefferson, James Madison and Napoleon Bonaparte. In 1819 when Kamehameha's widow and effective ruler of the Islands, Ka'ahumanu, declared the abolition of the traditional religion, she said that she and her people intended 'to live as the White people do'. The short story of the ensuing transformation of Hawaiian culture is that the ruling chiefs became Haole and the Haole, ruling chiefs—except for the American missionaries, such as Hiram Bingham; they became the chiefs' big kahunas.

Still, the greatest Haole success as an Austronesian ruler was that achieved by James Brooke, the 'White Rajah of Sarawak', who was ceded that position in 1841 by the rulers of Brunei and founded a British royal house in Borneo that lasted until World War II.[8] By adroit diplomacy, the timely support of British warships, the encouragement of commerce and a certain divine potency, Rajah Brooke was able to gain complete independence from the Sultan of Brunei and to enlarge his own dominion over the indigenous Land and Sea Dayaks (Bidayuh and Iban). Brooke was, in effect, a foreign subject of marvellous powers that Malay aristocrats knew how to respect, if not how to resist, and native Borneo peoples vied one way or another to appropriate. Indeed there were probably many more than the one Iban who, according to the missionary wife Harriette McDougall, came to Kuching with the intention of taking the Rajah's head. Brooke's political manipulations and shows of force exacerbated the existing cleavages among Dayak groups, thus making his own enemies among the enemies of his friends. But those who opposed him would then have to fear the kind of calamities the Tikopia people attributed to the Bishop of Melanesia. Report has it that a powerful Iban chief, shortly before he died, gathered his people around him and exhorted them to give up 'piracy' because the failure of a recent raid as well as his approaching death, 'were all brought about by the supernatural powers of the Rajah of Sarawak, whom he said it was impossible to withstand' (Low 1848: 224).

On the positive side, Brooke was able to exploit the widespread reports of his beneficent spiritual powers in the *Realpolitik* of the marvellous by means of which he partly fashioned, largely extended, and regularly sustained his Sarawak kingdom. In fact, the reports of his extraordinary powers were spread far wider than his kingdom, let alone any empirical demonstration of his force or benevolence. Speaking of his own experience in the Borneo uplands in the early period of Brooke rule, Alfred Russel Wallace observed: 'Many of the distant tribes think that the Rajah cannot be a man. They ask all sorts of curious questions about him, whether

---

8   Brooke's ascent to power in Sarawak has been documented by many, both contemporaries and later historians, including: Low (1848); Keppel (1848); Mundy (1848); St. John (1879); Pringle (1970); and Walker (1998, 2002).

or not he is as old as the mountains, whether he can bring the dead to life' (in Walker 1998: 98). But the indigenous people who knew Brooke personally could quiet any such curiosity by drawing directly on this life-giving potency. Power could more or less literally be rubbed off him.

At a ceremony in which he installed a Bidayuh headman, Rajah Brooke noted that his own *simungi* and that of his ancestors were particularly invoked when spiritual presences were called upon, as well as the *simungi* of Malay notables, their ancestors, and the ancestors of the local people (Keppel 1848: 194). *Simungi* is the Bidayuh version of the Malay *semangat*, a soul-power particularly intense in high-ranking people, whence it can act in a *mana*-like way on the vitality of other persons (Endicott 1970; Skeat 1900). (Not to forget that in this highly animistic region, such other 'persons' include rice, pigs, fruit trees, celestial bodies, even some artefacts; hence the effects of the ruler's *semangat* may extend into what we call 'nature' or consider to be 'things'.) Under these circumstances, political submission is mediated by desires to acquire or participate in the ruler's *semangat*, which is why J.H. Walker can argue that Brooke's *semangat* was fundamental to his sovereignty. 'James Brooke was Rajah', he wrote, 'because so many in Sarawak recognized the intensity and expansiveness of his *semangat* and sought opportunities to engage it. This has been a fundamental process in state formation in Southeast Asia' (2002: 207)—notably, one might add, in connection with the installation of stranger-kings.

Brooke knew how to use his soul-power to political advantage. He found it 'highly gratifying' when the leaders of hinterland communities came to Kuching to obtain some of his bodily fluids, like the Bidayuh headman who 'brought me a young cocoa-nut for me to spit into, as usual; and after receiving a little gold dust and white cloth returned home to cultivate his fields' (Walker 2002: 116). Somewhat as a matter of course, Brooke noted that when he visited them, Dayak people would wash his hands and feet, and afterward sprinkle the bathwater on their houses and gardens.[9] Likewise for the gold and white cloth he presented—gifts they particularly desired of him—these too they planted in their gardens (Mundy 1848, v.2: 43). Several of Brooke's European companions and officials were treated in the same way, at least sometimes in virtue of their association with the Rajah.

---

9   A distant echo of Indian Buddhist practice?

I rehearse a couple of these incidents here, leaving reference to others to a footnote.

Harriette McDougall's description (1854: 56–57) of the reception given to her husband Bishop McDougall and Rajah Brooke on the occasion of a visit to the Suntah Dyaks was apparently taken from the former's journal. The Englishmen were boisterously welcomed by the elaborately costumed old women of the group, who proceeded to stroke the visitors' arms and legs, 'for they fancy there is some goodness or virtue to be rubbed out of white people'. The women then washed McDougall's and Brooke's feet in coconut water, and set it aside 'to steep their paddy in, imagining it would help it to grow'. At night, some women stood over the sleeping Bishop, whom they knew to be a doctor, and repeatedly woke him by stroking his limbs and swaying their arms close to his face. The next day they 'brought portions of cooked rice on leaves, and begged the Englishmen to spit into them, after which they ate them up, thinking they should be the better for it' (cf. Walker 2002: 115–16).

In 1845, Hugh Low, the first European to visit the Land Dayak village of Sebongoh, was escorted from his boat on fine mats, and soon enough solicited by the headman (*orang kaya*) for a small piece of cloth and a silver coin that could be hung up in the longhouse to 'preserve the village from evil influence'. Later the headman, holding aloft a saucer of turmeric-dyed rice, required Low to repeat after him a prayer addressed to a major deity, the sun and the moon, and Rajah Brooke. The prayer requested 'that the next Padi harvest might be abundant, that their families might be increased with male children, and that their pigs and fowl might be very prolific: it was, in fact, a prayer for general prosperity to the country and tribe'. Low noted that when Brooke visited Bidayuh groups, they could achieve similar effects more directly by bringing rice seed into contact with him. Moreover, tribes too distant for Brooke to get to 'send down to him for a small piece of white cloth and a little gold or silver, which they bury in the earth of their farms, to attain the same result' (Low 1848: 254–59).[10]

---

10   For similar treatments of Brooke and other Europeans, see Low (1848: 224, 246–47, 251); St. John (1879: 230); Morris (1905: 166); and the notices compiled by Walker (1998, 2002) and Pringle (1970). In *Malay Magic* W.W. Skeat noted a like conflation of the powers of indigenous rulers and European colonial agents (1900: 36–37).

Among other classic features of stranger-kingship, note in these descriptions that 'where there is sovereignty, there is gold'. Rajah Brooke & Co. are solicited for the mobile wealth that potentiates the reproductive capacities of the native people—such as the gold dust that could be showered like rain on the swidden fields of the indigenous owners. Implying direct contact with his person, the gifts of cloth would have the same fertilising virtue. Brooke was also known to present Malay officials and Dayak leaders with costumes of office, sometimes including decorated loincloths. The nakedness of the native rulers was thus encompassed and sublimated by the foreign king, they were at once civilised and empowered. In a related cosmic register, that of the founding union of the stranger-king with the daughter of his native predecessor, stories circulated about the liaisons of Rajah Brooke with important Malay and Dayak women. According to one (unconfirmed) report, Brooke married the niece (brother's daughter) of the Malay noble who originally ceded Sarawak to him (D.E. Brown 1970). The Iban had even less-verifiable and more marvellous stories of Brooke's relations to their own cosmogonic deities. Some comprehended him by the topos of the returning ancestral-stranger (like the Pu Ma twins of Tikopia), saying he was the son of their primordial mother and father, Kumang and Keling. Others said Brooke was not Kumang's son but her lover, and that he was in the habit of climbing Mt Santugong to make love to her—a magnified feat of union with the ranking woman of the people. Yet, for all that the structures of stranger-kingship order such narratives, Brooke's history suggests that they did so not in some necessary or predetermined way, but only through the particular agencies and contingencies they empowered.

Structure on one hand, agency and contingency on the other, are not here (or anywhere) opposed historical determinants in the sense that they exclude one another. On the contrary, each is the condition of the historical possibility of the other. In authorising particular persons and circumstances as historical difference-makers, the structural order is a sine qua non of their efficacy, though it is not responsible for their particularities, nor then for the difference they will make. In Sartrian terms, particularity is an irreducible way of living universality or the structure of the collectivity; and accordingly the collectivity must live through the attributes of the persons and things on which it has made itself dependent (Sartre 1963: 130). Hence the possibility of historical outcomes that are structurally consistent and evenementially variable. Between the structural order of the historical situation and what actually happens there is no necessary relation. Rather, the structure is realised in a particular historical form by the mediation of the contingencies it has empowered. So while one may justly conclude that the transcendent potencies ascribed to James Brooke allowed him to become the Rajah of Sarawak, *he could have just as easily been assassinated for the same reason—* by a rival Malay leader, for example, or some Dayak headhunter. (Perhaps nowhere more than in Dayakland, uneasy lies the head that wears the kingly crown.) Brooke's death would have followed from, and realised, the same concepts of the potency of alterity that had made him the rajah—for they also defined his enemies.

A certain Scotsman, Erskine Murray, came to just such an untimely end in 1843 when he tried to duplicate Brooke's feat by entrenching himself in the Sultanate of Kutei in south Borneo. Murray had not reckoned on the powerful Bugis sea-warriors who were already established there, nor on the Sultan's capacity for armed resistance. Compounding this unfavourable correlation of forces by his own maladroit diplomacy, Murray was killed as he tried to flee downriver—on one of the two heavily-armed trading vessels by means of which he had hoped to back his ambitions of rajahdom (Low 1848: 103; Saunders 1980).

Murray was not the only would-be European rajah on the Borneo coasts during the mid-nineteenth century, nor was Brooke the only foreigner to successfully rule there. Graham Saunders (1980) and J.H. Walker (2002) described a number of such western adventurers, most of whom failed badly although their projects were similar to the one James Brooke brought off. Nor were these men the first to try. Borneo had a considerable history of stranger-kings: mainly Malay, Javanese and Sumatran traders or aristocrats, as well as a number of Arabian-derived *sharifs* or *sayids,* who took over or carved out principalities of their own.[11] Sharif Abdul Rahman, who with Dutch support and a title bestowed by the Rajah of Riau founded the Sultanate of Pontianak south of Brunei, became known to historians as 'an Arab James Brooke' from the similarity of their royal careers. 'With the substitution of Dutch for English and Abdul Rahman for Brooke [and the Raja of Riau for the Sultan of Brunei], this is essentially the story of Sarawak, set only seventy years earlier' (Pringle 1970: 61).

---

11   On merchant-princes in coastal Southeast Asia, see Manguin (1991). Although not ruling kingdoms of their own, a considerable number of European merchant-adventurers, as also Chinese, Indians and other foreigners, held high offices in traditional Southeast Asian and Indonesian principalities (Reid 1994, 2008).

Again, the legendary charter of the Brunei Sultanate, from which Brooke
wrested his Sarawak kingdom, tells of a series of stranger-king dynasties—
in terms that by now should be quite familiar (D.E. Brown 1970, 1973;
Hughes-Hallett 1981). According to the traditions recorded by D.E.
Brown, Brunei was founded by 14 brothers, born of a celestial father—
who descended in an egg from Kayangan, the heaven of old Indonesian
gods—and autochthonous mothers, women from the various riverine
districts the heavenly hero visited. One of the brothers became the first
Sultan of Brunei by virtue of a union with the daughter of the powerful
Sultan of Johor, apparently a hypogamous marriage that differentiated
this Borneo line by its prestigious affinal connections. The successor
of the first Brunei Sultan was either Chinese himself or else married
a Chinese woman, according to the version. (In either case, taking the
same principle of affinally derived prestige into account, the Brunei ruler
would be endowed with extraordinary foreign powers.) Finally, in what
seems a foreshortened version of a longer royal narrative, the third Sultan
of Brunei was an Arabic *sharif* who 'married the daughter of the second
Sultan and strengthened Islam in Borneo' (D.E. Brown 1973: 114).[12]

With regard to the attempts of other Europeans to win kingdoms in the
manner of Rajah Brooke, there were of course differences among them
in character, knowledge and judgement that contributed to the various
political results. The historians also speak to certain long-term and
short-term contingencies that came into play in connection with these
individual expressions of the European *libido dominandi*. For example,
the hiatus in collective imperial enterprises—in the period between the
entrepôt colonialism that ended around 1819 (with the termination of
the Napoleonic wars) and the territorial imperialism of the 1870s and
80s—was a period of relative neglect by western powers that offered the
space for individual ambitions the likes of Rajah Brooke's. Yet Brooke
himself would have gone down in the 1840s or 50s were he not rescued
by British gunboats that had only lately come into the region because of
the Chinese opium wars. Call it 'timing' or 'luck', the point is that certain

---

12   Something like the rise and fall of the Chinese dynasty of Brunei is told in the legend of the
mountain, Kina Bulou, 'Chinese Widow' in North Borneo. Hugh Low (1848: 6–7) related the story,
as he had it from 'the Rajahs of Borneo'. In the time before the conversion to Islam, the summit
of Kina Bulou was the home of a beautiful spirit woman of whom a Chinese prince of Brunei was
enamoured. But on his attempt to reach the summit and marry her, the prince fell off the mountain
and was killed. Thereafter the spirit woman was called the 'Widow of the Chinese' and the mountain
was named after her. Compare the Brunei traditions with the 'China, White Malaya' stranger-kings
of the Southern Tetuns (van Wouden 1968: 46–47).

systemic relations of alterity and autochthony were realised in a unique way because of their engagement with circumstances whose own causes lay elsewhere.

The deaths of Captain Cook (aka 'Lono') at Hawai'i and the Reverend John Williams (aka 'Nobu') at Erromanga are perhaps more familiar instances of the same interaction of structure and contingency (Sahlins 2000: 415, 456). Both of these powerful foreigners were identified in stranger-king terms as the returning forms of original native gods and— talk of *timing*!—both arrived at the annual rituals of the god's fertilising passage through the land, which is also his temporary repossession of it. In Cook's case we know for sure that this involved a certain rivalry with King Kalaniopu'u of Hawai'i Island—their opposition was built into the *Makahiki* (New Year) rituals—and that rivalry became fateful for Cook the morning he tried to take the king hostage against the return of a stolen ship's cutter. Yet of all the myriad contingent factors that contributed to the fatal outcome, including Cook's irascibility and his practised hubris with Polynesian chiefs, they would have been irrelevant were it not for the storm that damaged the *Resolution's* mast and forced him to return structurally out-of-season. And that in turn would have had a different and more benign sequel if Cook had known how to swim, and thus escape from the confrontation with the defenders of the king, as had most of the marines who were ashore with him (Sahlins 1995). Again, the big argument I am making is that Cook was a god-figure who died as a function of the same kind of structural relations that allowed Brooke to be the man who became king.

Finally, speaking of 'The Man Who Would Be King', Kipling's short story of the Englishman who became an Asian potentate because the local people took him to be a descendant of Alexander the Great turns out to be a genre of romantic non-fiction in the Malay Peninsula, Sumatra and Borneo, where ruling Islamic sultans did actually claim Alexandrian ancestry.[13] But to back-track a bit: the historical Alexander III of Macedonia had already been a stranger-king in his own realm. According to their own royal traditions, the Argead rulers of Macedonia descended from the Heraclid kings of the Peloponnesus; and Alexander,

---

13   On Alexander the Great and the many Alexandrian Romances see: Arrian (1991); Curtius (1946); Diodorus of Sicily (1963); Plutarch (1915, 1936); Stoneham (1991); Leeuwen (1937); Polignac (1982); Southgate (1978); Pseudo-Callisthenes (1969); Winstedt (1938); Cartledge (2004); Burn (1962); Green (1991); Mossé (2004); Anderson (1932); Thomas (2007).

moreover, doubled his exalted derivation from Heracles on his father's side by his reputed descent from Achilles on his mother's. Alexander's father, Phillip, had greatly enlarged Macedonia by successful wars against neighbouring kings—whose daughters he regularly took to wife. And to fill out the stranger-king topos, the Argeads were civilisers. At a time during his Asian campaigns when Alexander had occasion to rebuke his Macedonian soldiers for ingratitude, he reminded them that his royal father had transformed them from a weak bunch of nomads wandering the mountains with their pitiful herds of sheep into trained warriors and properly clad, well-ordered city-dwellers of the Macedonian plains. Literally, he civilised them: 'He defined you as residents of cities and arranged good laws and customs' (Arrian 1991, VII.9: 2–3). But at the moment Alexander made this speech, he was on his way to becoming a stranger-king of world-historical proportions.

For by building cities from Egypt to Afghanistan, Hellenising the local populations, adopting the customs and costumes of defeated rulers, and marrying their daughters, Alexander reproduced the stranger-king scheme on a grand scale—leaving in his wake foreign dynasties of the same character, notably the Ptolemys and Seleucids. Tradition has it that Alexander carried a copy of the *Iliad* annotated by his tutor Aristotle on his campaigns, and according to Plutarch, he made it common reading among Asians, as well as setting their sons to reciting the tragedies of Sophocles and Euripides. Bringing Asians into such civilised community with Greeks could not have pleased Aristotle, who held Barbarians to be natural slaves. On the other hand, in constructing cities, making laws and otherwise taming the 'savagery' of Asian peoples, Alexander would be following Aristotelian prescriptions for repressing the appetitive soul by good education and legislation. In a work that perhaps should be placed with the many romances of Alexander, Plutarch says the Macedonian hero persuaded the Sogdians to support their parents instead of killing them, the Persians to respect their mothers instead of marrying them, and the Scythians to bury their dead instead of eating them. And this, said Plutarch, made him a great philosopher in his own right. For if philosophers take the greatest pride in civilising the untutored elements in human character, 'and if Alexander has been shown to have changed the savage natures of countless tribes, it is with good reason that he should be regarded as a very great philosopher' (Plutarch *Fortuna I.5*).

In the Islamic Romances of Alexander—Persian, Turkish and Arabic as well as Malay—the hero was identified with Iskandar Dzu'l-karnian of Koranic fame, a militant propagator of the Faith from the setting to the rising sun. Iskandar's conquests were not only of the same scope and direction as Alexander's, but he was likewise a civiliser, if in this case by Islamicising the Infidels rather than Hellenising the Barbarians. According to the Malay Romance (Winstedt 1938; Leeuwen 1937), Iskandar had been taught the Koran by Aristotle of Istanbul, a figure who generally appears in the Islamic versions as the conqueror's political adviser or vizier. As was then documented in local chronicles and traditions of the classic stranger-king form, the descendents of Alexander/Iskandar become the sultans of various states in the Malay Peninsula, Sumatra and coastal Borneo.

A key account of the Iskandar tradition appears in the *Malay Annals* (*Sejarah Melayu*), a text formulated on behalf of the rulers of the once flourishing commercial state of Melaka, apparently compiled shortly after the fall of that city to the Portuguese in 1511 (C.C.E. Brown 1952). O.W. Wolters (1970, 1986) persuasively argues that the adoption of the Alexandrian tradition functioned to legitimate Melaka as true successor of the ancient kingdom of Srivijaya in Sumatra, as against the claims of the trading centre of Malayu-Jambi. Srivijaya had in fact declined in the eleventh century and lost supremacy on the southern Sumatran coast to the rajas of Malayu-Jambi. But the *Malay Annals* would effectively erase Malayu-Jambi from historical memory by making the founder of Melaka a descendant in the fifth generation of one Sri Tri Buana, a heroic prince of Alexandrian lineage who miraculously appeared near the Srivijaya capital and became its ruler. Besides this direct genealogical connection to Srivijaya, by their privileged descent from the Islamic world-conqueror Iskandar/Alexander, the Sultans of Melaka would also trump Malayu-Jambi on a cosmic religious plane. Here is a clear example of transcendental schismogenesis on an interstate level.

To summarise the Melaka charter narrative in a radically abbreviated form. Three handsome youths in stunning royal garb appear on a mountain above Palembang, the ancient capital of Srivijaya. As in many traditions of stranger-kings, the youths miraculously bestow great wealth on the native people, here represented by the two widowed women who discover them, by turning the mountain top into gold and the rice fields to gold and silver.[14] When it is learned that the youths are descended from Alexander the Great, people come from various Malay states to take them as their king. The youngest, Sri Tri Buana, is so acknowledged by the Raja of Palembang. (Commenting on traditions of royal succession in Western Indonesia, Josselin de Jong (1980) observes that the junior son usually takes precedence.) But Sri Tri Buana is not formally installed as ruler in Palembang until the native Raja is able to neutralise a certain malevolent power manifested by the godly stranger. All of the 39 princesses who are brought to Sri Tri Buana as wives come down with a disfiguring skin condition (chloasma) upon sleeping with him. When Sri Tri Buana then asks for the hand of the Raja's beautiful daughter, the native ruler imposes the condition that the stranger will never shame or disrespect his subjects, in return for which the Raja promises eternal loyalty. This contract concluded, the marriage takes place without ill effect, Sri Tri Buana is installed as ruler, and the Raja becomes his chief minister.[15]

In a few generations the lineal successors of Sri Tri Buana would found Melaka, convert to Islam, and become sultans of a prosperous commercial kingdom. They and the other rulers tracing descent to Alexander the Great thereby inherited powers of global dimensions, world-dominating powers, originating in the great centre of 'Rum'—referring usually to Istanbul and the Ottoman emperors, but sometimes to Rome or Macedonia. On an edict issued in the late eighteenth century by a Sultan of Minankabau were affixed three seals representing three sons of Alexander/Iskandar: the Sultan of Rum, the oldest; the Sultan of China, the second; and himself, Sultan of Minankabau, the youngest and 'king of kings ... lord of the air and clouds ... possessed of the crown of heaven brought by the prophet Adam' (Marsden 1811: 339).[16]

---

14 Note the recurrent Indonesian form of the greeting of the stranger-king by older women, widowed or post-menopausal—for reasons I do not know.

15 This sort of diarchy consisting of an immigrant sacred ruler and an active second king from the indigenous people is also found in ethnographies of eastern Indonesia and as far off as Fiji. Permutations in Indonesia include immigrant warrior second kings such as the Bugis in the Straits area and sacred *sayid* second kings in Malaya and Sumatra.

16 Anthony Reid (2008: 254) points out that 'almost all rulers of [Sumatran] coastal port states proudly traced their origin to a mighty foreign ruler, of whom the epitome for Muslims was the world-conqueror Iskandar Zulkarnain (Alexander the Great). Malay rulers sought to trace their descent from this ultimate source, though often mixed with more probable antecedents associated with the Middle East (Raja Rum) or India (Raja Kalinga or Vijaynagar)'.

The Alexandrian tradition in Indonesia is linked to many more narratives of the marvellous, some of epic proportions; I will only mention a couple by way of conclusion. Sri Tri Buana's mother was the daughter of the King of the Sea, whom his father had married when he went under the ocean and thereby succeeded to the rule of that underwater realm. One is reminded of the Queen of the South Sea, the mystical bride of legitimate Javanese kings, herself descended in the ruling line of the ancient Sundanese kingdom of Pajajaran. Another Javanese hero, Baron Iskandar—whose moniker, as Anthony Reid (1994: 92) points out, combines a European title with the Javanese name for Alexander the Great—had a brother who also married a Pajajaran princess, and among their offspring was J.P. Coen, the Governor General of the Dutch East India Company, who established its headquarters at Batavia in 1619. Baron Iskandar himself, who in his career was a stranger-king of Spain before conquering the lands from Arabia to China, eventually winds up in the service of the Islamic ruler of Mataram—thus proving the superiority of that Javanese state to the intruding Dutchmen (Ricklefs 1974: 373ff).

It seems that these are so many more instances of a structure without an event, an unmotivated history, since none of this was 'what actually happened'. Yet not exactly, for as Raymond Firth observed of the new vistas of wealth and power opened to Tikopians by the advent of Europeans, or as the Hawaiian chiefs who identified with the likes of King George, John Adams, and Billy Pitt, so did people of the Malay archipelago enter into an expanded cosmography of the marvellous, centred in Rum, by virtue of Ottoman, Persian and Arabian commerce. Taken together, these examples show that modern European imperialism has not been the only source of the local desires of alterity. Nor are such desires ever a simple function of outside domination. Here is a further proof, if one is now needed, that in speaking of 'acculturation' we must consider from the beginning the role of indigenous agency. The Austronesian peoples have always known their own internal dynamics of transcendence: desires of alterity and quests of potency that in all probability led to their remarkable feats of voyaging and their settlement of distant islands—as far into the sky beyond the horizon as Madagascar and Easter Island. So far could their real-politics of the marvellous take them.

References

Andaya, Leonard. 2006. 'The stranger-king complex in Bugis-Makassar society'. Paper presented at conference on 'Stranger-Kings in Southeast Asia and Elsewhere', Jakarta, 5–7 June 2006.

——. 1975. 'The nature of kingship in Bone'. In *Pre-colonial State Systems in Southeast Asia: The Malay Peninsula, Sumatra, Bali-Lombok, South Celebes*, Monographs of the Malaysian Branch of the Royal Asiatic Society No. 6, ed. Anthony Reid and Lance Castles, pp. 115–125. Kuala Lumpur: Malaysian Branch of the Royal Asiatic Society.

Anderson, Andrew Runni. 1932. *Alexander's Gate, Gog and Magog, and the Inclosed Nations*. Cambridge, MA: Medieval Academy of America.

Arrian. 1991. *Anabasis of Alexander*, 2 vols. Loeb Classical Library. Cambridge, MA: Harvard University Press.

Backus, Charles. 1981. *The Nan-chao Kingdom and T'ang China's Southwestern Frontier*. Cambridge: Cambridge University Press.

Balandier, Georges. 1968a. *Daily Life in the Kingdom of Kongo: From the Sixteenth to the Eighteenth Century*. New York: Pantheon Books.

——. 1968b. *Anthropologie Politique*. Paris: Presses Universitaires de France.

Barnes, R.H. 1974. *Kedang: A Study of the Collective Thought of an Eastern Indonesian People*. Oxford: Clarendon Press.

Bateson, Gregory. 1958. *Naven*, 2nd edition. Stanford: Stanford University Press.

Beaglehole, J.C. (ed.). 1967. *The Journals of Captain James Cook on his Voyages of Discovery, Vol III: The Voyage of the* Resolution *and* Discovery, *1776–1780*. Cambridge: Cambridge University Press for the Hakluyt Society.

Bernart, Luelen. 1977. *The Book of Luelen*. Canberra: The Australian National University Press.

Bowen, John R. 1991. *Sumatran Politics and Poetics: Gayo History, 1900–1989*. New Haven: Yale University Press.

Briggs, Lawrence Palmer. 1951. *The Ancient Khmer Empire*. Philadelphia: Transactions of the American Philosophical Society. doi. org/10.2307/1005620.

Brown, C.C.E. 1952. 'The Sejarah Melayu or "Malay Annals": A translation of Raffles MS 18'. *Journal of the Malayan Branch of the Royal Asiatic Society* 25: 7–276.

Brown, D.E. 1973. 'Hereditary rank and ethnic history: An analysis of Brunei historiography'. *Journal of Anthropological Research* 29(2): 113–22. doi.org/10.1086/jar.29.2.3629986.

———. 1970. *Brunei: The Structure and History of a Bornean Malay Sultanate*. Brunei: Brunei Museum.

Burn, A.R. 1962. *Alexander the Great and the Hellenistic World*. New York: Collier Books.

Carrasco, David, Lindsay Jones and Scott Sessions (eds). 2000. *Mesoamerica's Classic Heritage: From Teotihuacan to the Aztecs*. Boulder: University Press of Colorado.

Cartledge, Paul. 2004. *Alexander the Great: The Hunt for a New Past*. New York: Vintage Books.

Coedès, George. 1968. *The Indianized States of Southeast Asia*. Honolulu: University of Hawai'i Press.

Cunnison, Ian. 1951. *History on the Luapula: An Essay on the Historical Notions of a Central African Tribe*. Capetown: Rhodes Livingstone Institute.

Curtius. 1946. *Histories*. Loeb Classical Library. Cambridge MA: Harvard University Press.

Diodorus of Sicily. 1963. *Library of History*, Book XVII. Loeb Classical Library. Cambridge MA: Harvard University Press.

Downs, R.E. 1955. 'Headhunting in Indonesia'. *Bijdragen tot de Taal-, Land- en Volkerkunde* 111: 40–70.

Ekholm, Kajsa. 1978. 'External exchange and the transformation of central African social systems'. In *The Evolution of Social Systems*, ed, J. Friedman and M.J. Rowlands, pp. 115–36. Pittsburgh: University of Pittsburgh Press.

Endicott, Kirk. 1970. *An Analysis of Malay Magic*. Oxford: Clarendon Press.

Evans-Pritchard, E.E. 1962. 'The divine kingship of the Shilluk of the Nilotic Sudan'. In *Essays in Social Anthropology*, ed. E.E. Evans-Pritchard, pp. 66–86. London: Faber and Faber.

Firth, Raymond. 1970. *Rank and Religion in Tikopia: A Study in Polynesian Paganism and Conversion to Christianity*. London: Allen & Unwin.

———. 1967. *The Work of the Gods in Tikopia*, 2nd edition. London: Athlone Press.

———. 1961. *History and Traditions of Tikopia*. Wellington: Polynesian Society.

———. 1957. *We, the Tikopia: A Sociological Study of Kinship in Primitive Polynesia*, 2nd edition. London: George Allen & Unwin.

———. 1950. *Primitive Polynesian Economy*. New York: Humanities Press.

Fiskesjö, Magnus. 1999. 'On the "raw" and the "cooked" barbarians of imperial China'. *Inner Asia* 1: 139–68. doi. org/10.1163/146481799793648004.

Forde, Daryll and P.M. Kaberry (eds). 1967. *West African Kingdoms in the Nineteenth Century*. London: Oxford University Press.

Fox, James J. 2006. 'Precedence, diarchy and stranger-kings in the Timor area'. Paper presented at conference on 'Stranger-Kings in Southeast Asia and Elsewhere', Jakarta, 5–7 June 2006.

———. 1995a. 'Instituting the "outside" inside: The exploration of an epistemic Austronesian cultural theme and its social significance'. Revised and extended draft of a paper presented at the first European Association for Southeast Asia Studies Conference, Leiden, 29 June– 1 July 1995.

———. 1995b. 'Austronesian societies and their transformations'. In *The Austronesians: Historical and Comparative Perspectives*, ed. Peter Bellwood, James J. Fox and Darrell Tryon, pp. 214–28. Canberra: Department of Anthropology, Research School of Pacific and Asian Studies, The Australian National University.

Frazer, James George. 2006. *The Golden Bough*. Sioux Falls, SD: New Vista Publications.

Geertz, Hilda and Clifford Geertz. 1975. *Kinship in Bali*. Chicago: University of Chicago Press.

Gibson, Thomas. 2005. *And the Sun Pursued the Moon: Symbolic Knowledge and Traditional Authority Among the Makassar*. Honolulu: University of Hawai'i Press.

Giersch, C. Patterson. 2006. *Asian Borderlands: The Transformation of Qing China's Yunnan Frontier*. Cambridge MA: Harvard University Press.

Gillespie, Susan D. 1989. *The Aztec Kings: The Construction of Rulership in Mexica History*. Tucson: University of Arizona Press.

Glahn, Richard von. 1987. *The Country of Streams and Grottoes: Expansion, Settlement and the Civilizing of the Sichuan Frontier in Song Times*. Cambridge, MA: Council on East Asian Studies, Harvard University.

Goodenough, Ward H. 1986. 'Sky world and this world: The place of Kachaw in Micronesian cosmology'. *American Anthropologist* 88: 551–68. doi.org/10.1525/aa.1986.88.3.02a00010.

Green, Peter. 1991. *Alexander of Macedon 356–323 B.C.: A Historical Biography*. Berkeley: University of California Press.

Hanlon, David. 1988. *Upon a Stone Altar: A History of the Island of Pohnpei to 1890*. Pacific Island Monographic Series No. 5. Honolulu: University of Hawai'i Press.

Heine-Geldern, Robert von. 1956. 'Conceptions of State and Kingship in Southeast Asia'. Southeast Asia Program Data Paper No. 18. Ithaca: Cornell University Press.

Heusch, Luc de. 1982a. *Rois nes d'un couer de vache*. Paris: Gallimard.

——. 1982b. *The Drunken King, or the Origin of the State*. Bloomington: Indiana University Press.

——. 1962. 'Aspects de la sacralité du pouvoir en Afrique'. In *Le pouvoir et le sacré*, ed. Luc de Heusch et al., pp. 139–58. Bruxelles: Institut de Sociologie, Université Libre de Bruxelles.

Ho, Engseng. 2002. 'Before parochialization: Diaspora Arabs cast in Creole waters'. In *Transcending Borders: Arabs, Politics, Trade and Islam in Southeast Asia*, ed. Huub de Jonge and Nico Kaptein, pp. 11–35. Leiden: KITLV Press.

——. 1999. 'Transformation and reformation of Malay polity and identity'. MA thesis, Department of Anthropology, Division of the Social Sciences, University of Chicago.

Hocart, A.M. 1929. *Lau Islands, Fiji*. Bernice P. Bishop Museum Bulletin No. 62. Honolulu: Bishop Museum.

Horstmann, Alexander and Reed L. Wadley. 2006. *Centering the Margin: Agency and Narrative in Southeast Asian Borderlands*. New York: Berghahn Books.

Hoskins, Janet. 1996. *Headhunting and the Social Imagination in Southeast Asia*. Stanford: Stanford University Press.

——. 1993. *The Play of Time: Kodi Perspectives on Calendars, History, and Exchange*. Berkeley: University of California Press.

Hughes-Hallett, H.R. 1981. 'A sketch of the history of Brunei'. *Brunei Museum Journal* 5(1): 1–18.

Josselin de Jong, P.E. de. 1980. 'Ruler and realm: Political myths in western Indonesia'. *Mededelingen der Koninklijke Nederlandse Akademie van Wetenschappen, Afd. Letterkunde* 43(1): 1–19.

——. 1975. 'The dynastic myth of Negri Sembilan (Malaya)'. *Bijdragen tot de Taal-, Land- en Volkerkunde* 131: 277–308.

——. 1969. *Contact der Continenten*, Leiden: Leiden Univeristy Press.

Kasetsiri, Charnvit. 1976. *The Rise of Ayudhya: A study of Siam in the Fourteenth and Fifteenth Centuries*. Kuala Lumpur: Oxford University Press.

Kathirithamby-Wells, Jeyamalar. 2006. 'Stranger-kinsmen as stranger-kings in eighteenth- and nineteenth-century, Perak, Siak, and Pontianak'. Paper presented at conference on 'Stranger-Kings in Southeast Asia and Elsewhere', Jakarta, 5–7 June 2006.

Keppel, Henry. 1848. *The Expedition to Borneo of H.M.S.* Dido *for the Suppression of Piracy; with Extracts from the Journal of James Brooke, Esq., of Sarawak*. New York: Harper & Bros.

Kopytoff, Igor. 1989. 'The internal African frontier: The making of African political culture'. In *The African Frontier: The Reproduction of Traditional African Societies*, ed. Igor Kopytoff, pp. 3–84. Bloomington: Indiana University Press.

Krizancic, Catarina. 2006. 'The rise of the House of Salmon: Before and beyond French Tahiti, 1842–present'. PhD dissertation draft, Department of Anthropology, University of Chicago.

Leach, Edmund. 1954. *Political Systems of Highland Burma*. Cambridge, MA: Harvard University Press.

Leeuwen, P.J. 1937. *De malaische Alexanderroman*. Meppel: B. Ten Brink.

Lehman, F.K. 1963. *The Structure of Chin Society: A Tribal People of Burma Adapted to a Non-western Civilization*. Urbana: University of Illinois Press.

Li, Tania Murray. 2001. 'Relational histories and the production of differences in Sulawesi's upland frontier'. *The Journal of Asian Studies* 60(1): 41–66. doi.org/10.2307/2659504.

Lingenfelter, Sherwood. 1975. *Yap, Political Leadership and Culture Change in an Island Society*. Honolulu: University of Hawai'i Press.

Lombard, Jacques. 1965. *Structures de type 'féodal' en Afrique noire: étude des dynamismes internes et des relations sociales chez les Bariba du Dahomey*. Paris: Mouton.

Low, Hugh. 1848. *Sarawak; its Inhabitants and Productions: Being Notes during a Residence in that Country with H.H. the Rajah Brooke*. London: Richard Bentley.

Malinowski, Bronislaw. 1948. *Magic, Science and Religion and other Essays*. Boston: Beacon Press.

Manby, Thomas. 1929. 'Journal of *Vancouver's* voyage to the Pacific Ocean'. *Honolulu Mercury* 1(3): 39–55.

Manguin, Pierre-Yves. 1991. 'The merchant and the king: Political myths of Southeast Asian coastal polities'. *Indonesia* 52: 41–54. doi.org/10.2307/3351154.

Marsden, William. 1811. *The History of Sumatra*, 3rd edition. London: Printed for the author by J. McCreery, Black-Horse Court.

McDougall, Harriette. 1992. *Sketches of our Life at Sarawak*. Singapore: Oxford University Press.

———. 1854. *Letters from Sarawak: Addressed to a Child*. Norwich: Thomas Priest.

McKinley, Robert. 1976. 'Human and proud of it! A structural treatment of headhunting rites and the social definition of enemies'. In *Studies in Borneo Societies: Social Process and Anthropological Explanation*, ed. G.N. Appell, pp. 92–126. DeKalb: Center for Southeast Asian Studies, Northern Illinois University.

Morris, Margaretta. 1905. 'Harvest gods of the Land Dayaks of Borneo'. *Journal of the American Oriental Society* 26: 165–75. doi.org/10.2307/592888.

Mossé, Claude. 2004. *Alexander: Destiny and Myth*, trans. Janet Lloyd. Baltimore: Johns Hopkins University Press.

Mundy, Rodney. 1848. *Narrative of Events in Borneo and Celebes … From the Journals of James Brooke, Esq, Rajah of Sarawak and Governor of Labuan*. London: John Murray.

Oberg, K. 1970. 'The kingdom of Ankole in Uganda'. In *African Political Systems*, ed. Meyer Fortes and E.E. Evans-Pritchard, pp. 121–64. London: Oxford University Press for the International African Institute.

Parmentier, Richard. 1987. *The Sacred Remains: Myth, History, and Polity in Belau*. Chicago: University of Chicago Press.

Petersen, Glenn. 1990. *Lost in the Weeds: Theme and Variation in Pohnpei Political Mythology*. Honolulu: Center of Pacific Studies, University of Hawai'i at Mānoa.

Plutarch. 1936. *Moralia*, vol. 4. Loeb Classical Library. Cambridge, MA: Harvard University Press.

——. 1915. *Lives: The Dryden Plutarch*, vol. 2, revised by Arthur Hugh Clough. London: Everyman.

——. *Fortuna I* (On the fortune of Alexander). Alexander Sources. Online: www.sites.google.com/site/alexandersources/plutarch/ (accessed 1 March 2017).

Polignac, François de. 1982. 'L'image d'Alexandre dans la littérature Arabe. L'Orient face à l'Hellénisme?' *Arabica* 29(2): 296–306. doi.org/10.1163/157005882X00310.

Preaux, Jean-G. 1962. 'La sacralité du pouvoir royal à Rome'. In *Le pouvoir et le sacré*, ed. Luc de Heusch et al., pp. 103–122. Bruxelles: Institut de Sociologie, Université Libre de Bruxelles.

Pringle, Robert. 1970. *Rajahs and Rebels: The Ibans of Sarawak under Brooke Rule, 1841–1941*. Ithaca: Cornell University Press.

Pseudo-Callisthenes. 1969. *The Romance of Alexander the Great by Pseudo-Callisthenes*, trans. and ed. Albert Mugrdich Wolohojian. New York: Columbia University Press.

Reid, Anthony. 2008. 'Merchant princes and magic mediators'. *Indonesia and the Malay World* 36(105): 253–67. doi.org/10.1080/13639810802268007.

——. 1994. 'Early Southeast Asian categorizations of Europeans'. In *Implicit Understandings: Observing, Reporting and Reflecting on the Encounters Between Europeans and Other Peoples in the Early Modern Era*, ed. Stuart B. Schwartz, pp. 268–94. Cambridge: Cambridge University Press.

Richards, A.I. (ed.). 1960. *East African Chiefs: A Study of Political Development in some Uganda and Tanganyika Tribes*. New York: Praeger.

Ricklefs, Merle. 1974. *Jogjakarta under Sultan Mangkubumi, 1749–1792*. London: Oxford University Press.

Robinne, François and Mandy Sadan (eds). 2007. *Social Dynamics in the Highlands of Southeast Asia*. Leiden: Brill.

Rutherford, Danilyn. 2002. *Raiding the Land of the Foreigners*. Princeton: Princeton University Press.

Sabloff, Jeremy A. (ed.). 2003. *Tikal: Dynasties, Foreigners and Affairs of State*. Santa Fe: School of American Research Press.

Sahlins, Marshall. 2008. 'The stranger-king: Or, elementary forms of the politics of life'. *Indonesia and the Malay World* 36(105): 177–99. doi. org/10.1080/13639810802267918.

———. 2004. *Apologies to Thucydides: Understanding History as Culture and Vice Versa*. Chicago: University of Chicago Press.

———. 2000. *Culture in Practice: Selected Essays*. New York: Zone Books.

———. 1995. *How 'Natives' Think: About Captain Cook, for Example*. Chicago: University of Chicago Press.

———. 1994. 'The discovery of the true savage'. In *Dangerous Liaisons: Essays in Honour of Greg Dening*, ed. Donna Merwick, pp. 41–94. Melbourne: History Department, University of Melbourne.

———. 1992. *Historical Ethnography*. Vol. 1 of Patrick V. Kirch and Marshall Sahlins, *Anahulu: The Anthropology of History in the Kingdom of Hawaii*. Chicago: University of Chicago Press.

———. 1981a. 'The stranger-king; or, Dumézil among the Fijians'. *Journal of Pacific History* 16: 107–32. doi.org/10.1080/00223348108572419.

———. 1981b. *Historical Metaphors and Mythical Realities: Structure in the Early History of the Sandwich Islands Kingdom*. Association for Social Anthropology in Oceania, special publication, no. 1. Ann Arbor: University of Michigan Press.

St John, Spenser. 1879. *The Life of Sir James Brooke, Rajah of Sarawak*. Edinburgh: Blackwood and Sons.

Sartre, Jean-Paul. 1963. *Search for a Method*, trans. Hazel E. Barnes. New York: Vintage Books.

Sather, Clifford. 1990. Trees and tree tenure in Paku Iban society: the management of secondary forestry resources in a long-established Iban community. *Borneo Review* 1: 16–40.

Saunders, Graham. 1980. 'Seekers of kingdoms: British adventurers in the Malay archipelago'. *Brunei Museum Journal* 4(4): 137–54.

Schrempp, Gregory. 1992. *Magical Arrows: The Maori, the Greeks and the Folklore of the Universe*. Madison: University of Wisconsin Press.

Schrieke, B. 1957. *Ruler and Realm in Early Java*. Indonesian Sociological Studies, Part Two. The Hague: W. van Hoeve.

Schulte Nordholt, H.G. 1971. *The Political System of the Atoni of Timor*. The Hague: Martinus Nijhoff. doi.org/10.1007/978-94-015-1013-4.

Siikala, Jukka. 1996. 'The elder and the younger—foreign and autochthonous origin and hierarchy in the Cook Islands'. In *Origins, Ancestry and Alliance: Explorations in Austronesian Ethnography*, ed. James J. Fox and Clifford Sather, pp. 41–54. Canberra: Comparative Austronesian Project, Department of Anthropology, Research School of Pacific and Asian Studies, The Australian National University.

——. 1991. *'Akatokamanava: Myth, History and Society in the Southern Cook Islands*. Auckland: Polynesian Society.

——. 1990. 'Chiefs, gender and hierarchy in Ngaputoru'. In *Culture and History in the Pacific*, ed. Jukka Siikala, pp. 107–38. Helsinki: Suomen Antrpolinen Society Transactions No. 27.

Skeat, W.W. 1900. *Malay Magic: An Introduction to the Folklore and Popular Religion of the Malay Peninsula*. New York: Dover.

Skinner, Elliott P. 1964. *The Mossi of the Upper Volta: The Political Development of a Sudanese People*. Stanford: Stanford University Press.

Smith, Jean. 1974–75. 'Tapu removal in Maori religion'. *Journal of the Polynesian Society (Memoirs of the Polynesian Society)* 40(83): 1–43; 40(84): 44–96.

Southall, Adrian W. 2004 [1956]. *Alur Society: A Study in Processes and Types of Domination*. Munster: LIT with the International African Institute.

Southgate, Minoo S. (trans.). 1978. *Iskandarnamah: A Persian Medieval Alexander-Romance*. New York: Columbia University Press.

Sprenger, Guido. 2006. Out of Ashes: Swidden cultivation in highland Laos. *Anthropology Today* 22(4) August: 9–13.

Stoneham, Richard (ed.). 1991. *The Greek Alexander Romance*. London: Penguin.

Strathern, Alan. 2009. 'The Vijaya origin myth of Sri Lanka and the strangeness of kingship'. *Past and Present* 203(1): 3–28. doi. org/10.1093/pastj/gtp019.

Stuart, David. 2000. 'The arrival of strangers: Teotihuacan and Tollan in classic Maya history'. In *Mesoamerica's Classic Heritage: From Teotihuacan to the Aztecs*, ed. David Carrasco, Lindsay Jones and Scott Sessions, pp. 465–514. Boulder: University of Colorado Press.

Taylor, Keith. 1999. 'The early kingdoms'. In *The Cambridge History of Southeast Asia, Vol. 2*, ed. Nicholas Tarling, pp. 137–82. Cambridge: Cambridge University Press.

——. 1983. *The Birth of Vietnam*. Berkeley: University of California Press.

Thomas, Carol. 2007. *Alexander the Great in his World*. Malden, MA: Blackwell. doi.org/10.1002/9780470774236.

Took, Jennifer. 2005. *A Native Chieftaincy in Southwest China: Franchising a Tai Chieftaincy under the Tusi System of Late Imperial China*. Leiden: Brill.

Turton, Andrew (ed). 2000. *Civility and Savagery: Social Identity in Tai States*. Richmond: Curzon Press.

van Wouden, F.A.E. 1968. *Types of Social Structure in Eastern Indonesia*. The Hague: Martinus Nijhoff. doi.org/10.1007/978-94-015-1076-9.

Viveiros de Castro, Eduardo. 1992. *From the Enemy's Point of View: Humanity and Divinity in an Amazonian Society*. Chicago: University of Chicago Press.

Walker, J.H. 2002. *Power and Prowess: The Origins of Brooke Kingship in Sarawak*. Asian Studies Association of Australia, Allen & Unwin. Honolulu: University of Hawai'i Press.

——. 1998. 'James Brooke and the Bidayuh: Some ritual dimensions of dependency and resistance in nineteenth-century Sarawak'. *Modern Asian Studies* 32(1): 91–115. doi.org/10.1017/S0026749X98002984.

Wang Gungwu. 1981. *Community and Nation: Essays on Southeast Asia and the Chinese*. Singapore: Heinemann.

Winstedt, R.O. 1938. 'The date, authorship, contents and some new Mss. of the Malay romance of Alexander the Great'. *Journal of the Malayan Branch of the Royal Asiatic Society* 16(2): 1–23.

Wolters, O.W. 1986. 'Restudying some Chinese writings on Sriwijaya'. *Indonesia* 42: 1–41. doi.org/10.2307/3351186.

——. 1970. *The Fall of Srivijaya in Malay History*. Ithaca: Cornell University Press.

Wyatt, David K. 1984. *Thailand: A Short History*. New Haven: Yale University Press.

2

Moving Objects: Reflections on Oceanic Collections

Margaret Jolly

In memory of Epeli Hau'ofa, Oceanic visionary

Prologue

In a conference dedicated to 'Putting People First' it may seem perverse to deliver an opening keynote talk about 'things'. But, as we all know, in the place we call Oceania the dichotomy between persons and things, subjects and objects is often refused as an imposition of the West, not just in the theory talk of anthropologists (Gell 1998; Strathern 1988; Thomas 1995; see also Paini and Gnecchi-Ruscone, and Pigliasco this volume) but in the quotidian conversations of Pacific people.[1] Valued objects of human creation are rather animated, embodying the presence of divine gods, ancestors, dead and living persons, sometimes in the midst of swirling

---

1   I am here of course alluding not just to Marilyn Strathern's hugely influential book *The Gender of the Gift* (1988), which refuses the dichotomies of persons and things, subjects and objects in Melanesia but to the theory of art developed by Alfred Gell (1998; cf. Thomas 1995) which suggested art was to be found not in beauty but efficacy, and that an art object is an agent intended to change the world; rather than images or idols representing gods they are embodiments of them, 'physical instantiation[s] of divinity' (Hooper 2006: 28). See also the influence of Bruno Latour (1993) in these debates and his discussions of modernity and the work of 'purification' in distinguishing human from nonhuman and agency from natural determinism. Webb Keane (2007) offers a scintillating exploration of cognate problems in the context of mission encounters, in the particular context of Calvinism in Sumba, Eastern Indonesia.

bodies in indigenous ritual practices, sometimes surrounded by curious spectators in galleries and museums, sometimes lying lonely in the vaults of institutional storage.[2]

In this lecture, I reflect on the aesthetics and the cultural politics of *moving* objects in Oceanic collections. I consider these objects as 'moving' in three dimensions. First, I look at Oceanic objects as moving in the physical sense, from their origins in Pacific places, across land and ocean, to resting places in museums and galleries within and beyond the region, in Europe, North America and Australia. Second, I ponder the affective responses such objects elicit, how they move living human subjects, variously stimulating curiosity, respect, awe, terror or rage in spectators, some of whom are genealogically connected to the original creators, but most of whom are not. Third, I trace how objects move in the sense of the changing purposes or curatorial contexts of their display between different periods and different places. 'Objects are never static' (Kimmelman 2006: 1); they accumulate the meanings invested in them in different times and places. I too will be moving, between Göttingen, Honolulu and Canberra. But three questions anchor my Oceanic passage.

First, I situate these reflections in earlier conversations about the 'new museum' (see Message 2006). The 'newness' claimed for the new museum is far more than recent creation or renovation. Some suggest that new museums reside in a novel cultural and political terrain, with newly configured, even 'postcolonial', relations between creators, collectors, objects, curators and spectators. These allegedly eclipse the earlier colonial character of Enlightenment knowledge, preoccupied as it was with distantiated classification and presumptuous evolutionary typologies of 'others' and the objects they created. Some consider this has been superseded by more open and dialogical relations of knowing, more interactive collaborations, more egalitarian curatorial postures. This claim bears critical scrutiny in its representation of pasts, presents and futures (see Jolly 2011a; MacDonald 2007).

Second, I ask how far contemporary curatorial practice has transcended the clichéd polarities between aesthetic and ethnographic frames, between art and anthropology, formalism and history? One side vaunts the spotlit isolation of the beautiful object, devoid of distracting captions, ethnographic and historical contextualisation, stunningly 'nude' in the

---

2   See my review article on *Atua: Sacred Gods from Polynesia*, an exhibition curated by Michael Gunn at the National Gallery of Australia in 2014 (Jolly 2014).

words of Stéphane Martin, director of the Musée du Quai Branly (MQB) (Naumann 2006: 122). This approach conceives curatorial work as like making theatre, as a performance art. The other side finds the beauty and potency of objects in ethnographic and historical context, celebrates tougher processes of cultural translation and digs deeper in painful excavation through the colonial sediment which clings to the histories connecting Oceanic objects and human persons.[3]

Third, I consider the relation between the creators, the objects in Oceanic collections and their descendants living in the islands of the Pacific and in the diaspora. At the opening of Musée du Quai Branly in June 2005, Ralph Regenvanu enjoined overseas curators to follow the precedent of the Vanuatu Cultural Centre in its stress on 'living culture' (Clifford 2007), animating objects from the past in relation to contemporary practices and novel artistic traditions. Such calls have been heeded by some institutions. How are museum directors and curators responding to such indigenous calls in Europe as well as that expanded region the late Epeli Hau'ofa reimagined and revalorised as Oceania (see Hau'ofa 2008; Jolly 2007a, 2008)?

In Göttingen: The Cook/Forster collection

The modest cloisters of the Institute of Social and Cultural Anthropology at the Georg-August University of Göttingen is the usual home of about 400 Oceanic objects collected during the three voyages of Captain James Cook. These objects come from diverse Pacific places: Tonga, Tahiti and the Society Islands, Hawai'i, the Marquesas, Easter Island (now Rapanui), Aotearoa New Zealand, New Hebrides (now Vanuatu) and New Caledonia, and from Alaska and Tierra del Fuego on the Pacific coasts of North and South America. During the course of the voyages, these Oceanic objects were variously given to or exchanged with Cook, scientists, officers, and crew for nails, iron tools, pins, buttons, beads and cloth, or exchanged for other Oceanic objects earlier collected, such as fine white tapa from Tahiti or red feathers from Tonga. They include objects of daily apparel and use: clothing, ornaments, combs, tattooing tools, fishhooks, bowls, baskets, musical instruments, weapons, barkcloth, sumptuous ritual regalia (see Figure 1)

---

3   James Clifford (2007) has suggested a truce between these opposing positions in the context of the MQB. To me such a truce, though desirable, seems rather fragile since the ethnographic mode is portrayed by the MQB as old-fashioned and colonial while the aesthetic mode allegedly transcends that past (see also Clifford 2014). But, as Sally Price has argued, seeing such Oceanic objects as 'art' rather than artefact is equally implicated in genealogies of 'primitivism' (2007; see Jolly 2011a for an extended discussion).

and images of gods. Yet, any distinction between practical use and ritual potency is fraught, since fishhooks, weapons of war, baskets and cloth were often also imbued with divine efficacy (see Hooper 2006: 41, 46).

Figure 1. A *heva tūpāpa'u*, or chief mourner's costume, from the Society Islands

Source. Reproduced courtesy of the National Museum of Australia from *Cook's Pacific Encounters: The Cook/Forster Collection of the Georg-August University of Göttingen* (National Museum of Australia 2006: 59)

The location of these objects in Göttingen reflects the late eighteenth-century connection between Britain and Germany. In part, this was a scholarly genealogy since two German naturalists Johann Reinhold Forster and his son George accompanied Cook on his second voyage, but it equally mirrored royal genealogical connections between England and Hanover. Johann Friedrich Blumenbach (1752–1840) was the major catalyst in this congregation of objects from the 'South Seas' in the Academic Museum he established in 1773 at the Georg-August University (founded in 1737). A few objects were donated by Johann and George Forster after the second voyage, but the initial nucleus was the result of Blumenbach's close contacts with Joseph Banks and a petition to King George III, then both ruler of Britain and Elector of Hanover, to donate something of 'the surplus of natural curiosities … collected in large quantities on the recently completed voyages around the world on Your Majesty's command' (cited in Hauser-Schäublin and Krüger 2006c: 21). His appeal succeeded and a 'regal gift' of 349 objects obtained from several London art dealers, and in particular the forced sale of the private collection of George Humphrey, arrived in Göttingen on 15 July 1782. (They were worth 105 pounds sterling, twice the annual income of a Göttingen professor at the time (Hauser-Schäublin and Krüger 2006c: 23).) A few objects had earlier been donated by the Forsters and then, after the death of Johann in 1798, his entire remaining private collection, his 'South Seas estate', was acquired by the Museum in 1799. As Adrienne Kaeppler has consummately shown, Cook voyage artefacts, including those collected by the Forsters are widely dispersed: in the Pitt Rivers Museum and Christ Church in Oxford (see Coote 2004), the British Museum, the Cambridge University Museum of Anthropology and Archaeology, in Scotland, Vienna, Bern, Wörlitz, Florence and Saint Petersburg. But the Göttingen collection is a very significant, well-preserved and relatively well-provenanced collection.[4] It has long been a source for study by scholars.

---

4   The complicated history of the dispersal and congregation of Cook voyage artefacts has been long investigated by Adrienne Kaeppler, and more recently she considered the collection of Joseph Bank's arch rival, Ashton Lever (Kaeppler 2008, 2009a). He amassed the largest collection of Cook voyage artefacts, first in Elkington Hall and then in the Leverian Museum in London. His museum displays stressed the singularity of the objects rather than plotting them in an evolutionary narrative: e.g. the chief mourner's costume from Tahiti was proximate to Oliver Cromwell's dress and a Turkish costume. Like many eighteenth-century collectors, including Johann Reinhold Forster and George Humphrey, Lever was forced to sell his collection to defray large debts. It was offered to the British Museum but Banks campaigned successfully to have them refuse it. It went to auction in 1806 and was dispersed in several

Johann Friedrich Blumenbach used the collection for both research and teaching, famously arguing that all peoples are 'true humans', mere varieties (*Spierlarten*) of the same species (Blumenbach 1775) and using artefacts in his lectures on comparative *Völkerkunde* (ethnology; a habit extended by Heren into the nineteenth century). Both Johann Wolfgang von Goethe and Alexander von Humboldt drew inspiration from the collection. But, after Blumenbach's death, the Museum was dissolved and the Oceanic objects (together with those from other regions) languished in storage for decades. Then in 1935–36, they were recongegrated and displayed in their present location at the Theatreplatz in Göttingen, under the direction of the new Chair of Ethnology, Hans Plischke, whose anthropology was confidently conjugated with colonial history and the less generous view of the 'varieties' of the human race associated with National Socialism. This rather austere building, described by the then Director[5] as 'unspectacular, rather neglected' (Hauser-Schäublin and Krüger 2006c: 18) is their home to this day, despite strenuous efforts to use the public relations potential of the collection to renovate and extend both museum and teaching facilities.[6]

The collection has been studied by several anthropologists more recently: Adrienne Kaeppler's pioneering work on 'artificial curiosities' and on the Göttingen collection in the international context of Cook voyage artefacts

---

private collections in Russia and Austria and several British museums. Of 26,000 objects, 1,859 came from the Pacific and 1,784 from the Cook voyages. Most of these were bought for the collection of the Austro-Hungarian Empire in 1821–26 and displayed in the Museum für Völkerkunde in Vienna from 1928.

5   Brigitta Hauser-Schäublin was director at the time of the exhibitions and the writing and delivery of my 2008 lecture; she has since retired.

6   It was built in the 1930s under the then director Hans Plischke (1890–1972), whose work on anthropology and colonialism is situated, on a board in the foyer, in the context of National Socialism. During her appointment as Professor and Director, Brigitta Hauser-Schäublin put tremendous effort into a plan to restore and expand the building, creating new spaces for the collections and the teaching. These plans were far advanced and approved by the Labor government of the state of Lower Saxony in 2001, but the decision was reversed by the incoming Conservative government. The architectural plans are displayed on the walls of the Institute, but the efforts at rehousing are now directed towards private donations, through the brochure *A New House for Gods and Shamans: World Famous Treasures of Göttingen University Endangered.* The architectural plans developed for the new building are still displayed in the old building, perhaps in both lament and hope. The travels of the Cook/Forster collection to Honolulu, Canberra and Paris, and subsequently to an exhibition in Bonn which opened in August 2009, *James Cook und die Entdeckung der Südsee* (and then travelled to Vienna and Bern) were clearly a way of raising the local profile and securing the future condition of the collection. See the book catalogue of the latter exhibition published in German and English in sumptuous illustrated editions (Fleck and Kaeppler 2009).

(1978a, 1978b, 1979, 1988, 1998, 2006, 2008, 2009a, 2009b); Brigitta Hauser-Schäublin and Gundolf Krüger's edited collection on these 'gifts and treasures from the South Seas' (1998) and cognate publications in recent catalogues (2006a, 2006b, 2006c); and Nicholas Thomas's critical reflections on collecting, the projects of Enlightenment anthropology, and especially Cook, Johann Reinhold and George Forster (1994, 1996, 1997, 2003, cf. J.R. Forster 1996 [1778], G. Forster 2000 [1777]).

In 2006, the objects of the Cook/Forster collection temporarily moved back to Oceania: first to Honolulu and then to Canberra.

To Honolulu

First, the words of the contemporaneous custodians of this collection, Brigitta Hauser-Schäublin and Gundolf Krüger on the passage of these objects:

> After more than 200 years, the world's largest collection of artefacts assembled during the three voyages of James Cook (1768–1771, 1772–1775, 1776–1979/1780) has travelled back to the Southern Hemisphere where most of the items were made, used and finally traded to crew members of ships of the British Admirality ... Exploration of the Pacific – an endeavour with primarily scientific goals – had unpredictable consequences for many of the peoples 'discovered' in the course of the voyages: illness, suffering and European colonisation. After long, painful decades and even centuries of oppression, growing claims of self-determination across the Pacific in the twentieth century resulted in the realisation of cultural and political autonomy ... When we look at the beautifully preserved artefacts ... we can ponder the changes that have taken place in the world over the past two centuries. The seemingly unchanging character of the artefacts suggests a journey back in time (Brigitta Hauser-Schäublin and Gundolf Krüger 2006a: 15).

As Hauser-Schäublin and Krüger noted, it was two centuries before the objects in the Göttingen collection moved back to the Pacific, in two widely publicised exhibitions in two locales, first from 23 February to 14 May at the Honolulu Academy of Arts (now Honolulu Museum of Art) and then from 1 July to 10 September 2006 at the National Museum of Australia (NMA) in Canberra. As Hauser-Schäublin and Krüger have emphasised (1998, 2006a, 2006b, 2006c), the 'seemingly unchanging character' of the objects is an illusion: they move with the changing perspectives of time and place. This was no less true for the movement from Honolulu to Canberra. There were significant affinities between the two exhibitions[7] but I here focus on the intriguing differences, differences distilled in their divergent titles: in Honolulu, *Life in the Pacific of the 1700s*; in Canberra, *Cook's Pacific Encounters*. As the objects moved, the curatorial objects and the frames for their display also shifted. But were the spectators of these objects moved in different ways? And were the relations constructed between these Oceanic objects and living Pacific peoples different in the two sites?

Stephen Little, then director of the Honolulu Academy of Arts, was very clear about *their* collective curatorial purpose.[8] In his letter of invitation to conference participants, he enthused: 'These amazing works, made largely before Cook's contact with the indigenous cultures, are extraordinary for their inherent beauty, craftsmanship and unique *mana* (spiritual power)' (Little 2006a). In a press release he elaborated:

> We recognize that the legacy of Cook's voyages in the Pacific included disease and death for many cultures of the Pacific – a fact Cook himself recognized. The purpose of this exhibition however is not to glorify Cook, but on the contrary to celebrate the brilliant cultural and spiritual lives of the indigenous peoples of the Pacific, as they existed prior to the first contact with Westerners. As such the exhibition represents a rare opportunity for cross-cultural understanding that may not come to Hawai'i again for many years. In a world that is still dealing with the aftermath and ongoing realities of colonialism, I hope this exhibition will shed new light on life in the Pacific in the 1700s. The Academy is working closely with members of the Hawaiian, Maori, and Tongan communities,

---

7   Alongside the Oceanic objects, the Honolulu exhibition included paintings by Sydney Parkinson from the first voyage, William Hodges from the second voyage, and John Webber's images of Hawai'i from the third voyage. The Canberra exhibition included additional objects from Australian collections: Hodges's *View from Point Venus, Island of Otaheiti*, 1774 (National Library of Australia); the *Portrait of Captain James Cook RN*, 1782 (National Portrait Gallery, Australia); first editions of voyage accounts held by the National Library of Australia; and various objects attributed to Cook: a station pointer and case, a 'gunner's quadrant', a sextant and an ivory scale rule, held by the State Library of New South Wales (NMA 2006:103–5).

8   I should note that the idea for the exhibition to travel to Hawai'i came from Peter Ruthenberg who is described in the catalogue (Little and Ruthenberg 2006b) as an art historian, collector and designer. Of German descent, he had long lived on the island of Kauai and was instrumental in engaging the curator Gerry Barton, from New Zealand, who had previously worked in Germany. Ruthenberg was appointed Special Advisor on the project, and Stephen Little delegated most decisions about it to him. According to Elfriede Hermann, he routinely desired the 'best' for the exhibition and publications, from the scale and quality of the catalogue to the expertise of the scholars invited (pers. comm., 1 July 2008, Nicolasberg).

as well as other Pacific Islands cultural specialists, to develop the interpretive and educational programs that will accompany the exhibition (Little, 26 January 2006b: 3).[9]

The exhibition justified the hype. It was stunning. There were several masterpieces: a *heva tūpāpaʻu*, the famous chief mourner's costume from the Society Islands, Tahiti; three *taumi* (breast ornaments or gorgets) also from the Society Islands; valuable baskets from Tonga and in the privileged centre of the exhibition the grimacing head of *kiʻi akua hulu manu* (made of wickerwork: red, yellow and black birds' feathers: dogs' teeth; mother of pearl: and wood), an image or rather an embodiment of Kukaʻilimoku (Kū) the Hawaiian 'war god', which was the focus of Hawaiian attention (Tengan 2016; see Figure 2). An extraordinary range of barkcloth, baskets, ornaments, musical instruments, weapons, and a huge array of fishhooks were displayed. The simplicity of the glass cases lined with pale blue felt evoked the ocean and the objects were brightly lit, amplifying the iridescence of shells, greenstone and feathers.[10] Because they were grouped not by country but by type, deep Oceanic connections and underlying cultural affinities were highlighted (see Figure 3). But deeper questions about the relation between form and function and the transformations in the manufacture of similar objects across the Pacific were not developed (Drake 2007: 343). Moreover, it meant that visitors, especially Pacific people, who sought to engage with the cultural heritage of particular places or specific countries, for example Hawaiʻi or Tonga, were unable to do so (see Andrade 2007 and Drake 2007). Labels were minimal—with name, origin and inventory number (e.g. 'club *patu meremere*, wood, New Zealand, Inv. Oz 275')—and devoid of any cultural contextual information which would illuminate use or meaning.

---

9   In elaboration, Little advanced four major reasons for the exhibition. 'First the museum has always represented the indigenous cultures of the Pacific in its collections and has supported these cultures (particularly native Hawaiian culture), ever since the museum opened in 1927' (2006a: 5), this was central to its primary mission of education through works of art. 'Second, these artifacts were for the most part created *before* Cook encountered these indigenous peoples. Their condition is largely pristine' (2006a: 5 emphasis in the original. He stressed that experiencing the 'visual and spiritual power' of the original works 'could not be duplicated in a book or electronic image'. 'Third, this exhibition demonstrates the close connection between ancient cultures in the Pacific—cultures that were often separated by great distances across the ocean' (2006a: 5). This was highlighted by the genre of display: works of similar function and manufacture were displayed together. 'Finally, the exhibition poses the question: what is the role and relevance of the indigenous cultures of the Pacific today?' The works in the exhibition, both mundane and sacred, are windows into the past, present and future' (2006a: 6).

10   Karen Kosasa (2007) also commented positively on the display, which she thought enabled that close aesthetic attention, which Svetlana Alpers has described as 'the museum effect' (1991).

This 'text-free' curatorial strategy was widely applauded by some of the 65,000 people who visited and by some reviewers in the Honolulu daily press, for letting 'objects tell Pacific peoples' stories' (Carvalho 2006). Others suggested that the lack of such interpretive material left spectators frustrated and craving more information and that the presentation of objects as 'art' without indigenous perspectives was, in the view of Tongan cultural practitioner and Bishop Museum curator, Maile Drake like seeing a 'body without a soul' (Drake 2007: 343). Ivy Hali'imaile Andrade, echoed this critique, finding the presentation of the objects as artefacts or art as 'cold': 'As a Hawaiian I am linked genealogically to the pieces from Hawai'i lying behind the glass cases; they are my ancestors. The lack of interpretive materials in the galleries relegated the works to mere historic "objects"' (Andrade 2007: 342).

Figure 2. A Hawaiian *ki'i akua hulu manu* in a glass case on a pedestal in *Life in the Pacific of the 1700s: The Cook/Forster Collection of the Georg-August University of Göttingen*, 23 February–14 May 2006, Honolulu Academy of Arts

Source. Photograph by Shuzo Uemoto, reproduced courtesy of the Honolulu Museum of Art

Figure 3. Barkcloth from many different Pacific places on display in *Life in the Pacific of the 1700s: The Cook/Forster Collection of the Georg-August University of Göttingen*, 23 February–14 May 2006, Honolulu Academy of Arts

Source. Photograph by Shuzo Uemoto, reproduced courtesy of the Honolulu Museum of Art

Still, comments in the visitors' book suggested that many indigenous Hawaiians were moved by the Hawaiian objects in the exhibition, particularly by the presence of Kū, since offerings were left in front of the high pedestal where he was elevated.[11] But some thought, having come home, Kū should remain. Jonathan Osorio, then director of the Kamakakūokalani Center for Hawaiian Studies at the University of Hawai'i at Mānoa (UHM) observed that since the objects were not stolen their ownership belonged with the Göttingen Museum, but that it would be a 'wonderful gesture' if the Hawaiian objects could be housed permanently in Hawai'i. The decision to make such a donation, he said, 'is something left up to the conscience of the people in the museum in Germany' (Pang 2006: 2). One Hawaiian visitor to the museum even asked 'When can we rebury them'? (Ulrich Menter, pers. comm., 30 June 2008, Göttingen). Moreover, several Hawaiians

11   Ivy Hali'imaile Andrade's critique of its display is revealing. 'I found the altar-like setting perplexing and there was no explanation for it. It seemed overly dramatic, and I feel encouraged people to leave *ho'okupu* (offerings), not understanding how this particular Kū (ancestral deity associated with politics and war) may have functioned as a private god for designated followers rather than a public god for all to worship' (2007: 342).

and other Pacific Islanders, including several scholars at the University of Hawai'i at Mānoa complained that the absence of indigenous voices and perspectives which would have enabled deeper processes of cross-cultural translation (Andrade 2007: 341–42; Drake 2007: 343; Kosasa 2007: 344), also suppressed the vaunted link between past and present.[12] Isolating the pristine beautiful objects and letting *them* speak seemed in danger of silencing contemporary indigenous interpretations and perhaps the political tensions and impurities of the present.

Both the title of the exhibition *Hele Mai: Life in the Pacific of the 1700s* and the form of display stressed the ancient, pristine, pre-contact character of the objects. Curators emphasised that there were no introduced fibres or dyes, no beads, no glass, no metal. Though often exchanged for European things, these Oceanic objects showed no 'traces of such imported material' (Hauser-Schäublin and Krüger 2006c: 16). Analysis of the context of European voyaging and of collecting in the late 1700s was thus rather muted in the exhibition, though not in the exhibition guide and the huge three volume catalogue which appeared later that year (Little and Ruthenberg 2006a, 2006b). Some well-known voyage portraits and landscapes by William Hodges, Sydney Parkinson's drawings of Pacific plants and John Webber's images of Hawai'i were mounted proximate to the main exhibition, but these seemed like an annex rather than integral to the show.

Little's invitation stressed the comprehensive educational program that accompanied the exhibition: a scholarly conference, lectures, films and cultural performances. He highlighted the indigenous presence in the opening events of *Voyage to the South Pacific* in ARTafter DARK on 24 February 2006. There were welcoming performances of hula by La'akea Suganuma and his daughters, Kawena, Pele and Kuhilani, great granddaughters of Mary Kawena Puku'i who introduced public hula performances to the Honolulu Academy of Arts in the late 1930s and 1940s (see Figure 4). Hawaiian chants were sung, a Tongan *tapu* lifted, and Māori, Tahitian and Tongan dancers performed. The Cook/Forster exhibition was accompanied by a photographic exhibition on *Life in the Pacific of the 21st Century*, which aspired to make 'connections between

---

12   Ulrich Menter stressed the varying Hawaiian responses as recorded in the exhibition's visitor books. His colleagues at the UHM Center for Hawaiian Studies were in general critical, probably because of the interaction with the simultaneous Kawaihae dispute (personal communication, 30 June 2008, Göttingen).

past and present' and drew school students, parents, *kūpuna* (elders), community leaders and scholars into discussions about the eighteenth-century objects. The Academy's Education Department provided digital cameras, with which participants shot nearly 7,000 images, of which 80 were selected to hang in the central courtyard of the Academy and in the foyer of the Outrigger Waikiki at Diamond Head. Still, despite these efforts to engage local people in the educational and interpretive programs, the broader involvement of Pacific Island curators and communities in planning and decisions about the exhibition, conference and educational programs was seen by many as insufficient (Andrade 2007: 142).

Figure 4. Kawena, Pele, and Kuhilani, daughters of La'akea Suganuma, perform hula as part of the opening ceremonies for *Life in the Pacific of the 1700s*, Honolulu Academy of Arts, 24 February 2006

Source. Photograph by Shuzo Uemoto, reproduced courtesy of the Honolulu Museum of Art

Moreover, the efforts to engage local Hawaiian and Pacific communities were vitiated by two major problems surrounding the exhibition's opening and the accompanying scholarly conference (see Kosasa 2007: 344). La'akea Suganuma, then president of the Royal Hawaiian Academy of Traditional Arts, who was chosen to enact the sacred protocols, the blessing in Göttingen on 23 January 2006, as part of the homecoming for the Hawaiian treasures and to perform the welcoming hula with his three daughters on the opening night, had been involved in a bitter dispute with other Hawaiians about the reburial of human remains and ancient funerary objects on loan from the Bishop Museum. The details of this controversy, the Kawaihae Caves case, are complex and difficult to distill (but see Johnson 2007 and note 13). Suganuma and Abigail Kawananakoa had brought a lawsuit against another group of Hawaiians, Hui Mālama i Na Kupuna o Hawai'i Nei and the Bishop Museum whom they alleged had violated a repatriation process authorised through NAGPRA (the Native American Graves Protection and Repatriation Act, a federal law of 1990). In 2001 Hui Mālama reburied human remains (bones or *iwi*) and then proceeded to rebury 83 objects which had been loaned to them by then Museum director, Donald Duckworth.[13] The law

---

13 This repatriation dispute is variously referred to as the Kawaihae Caves or 'Forbes Cave' dispute in the Honolulu press (see Office of Hawaiian Affairs Newsletter 2006; and Wong 2006a, 2006b, 2006c). It was enabled by the passing of NAGPRA (the Native American Graves Protection and Repatriation Act) by the federal legislature in 1990. Hui Mālama were one of four original claimants, registered as 'Native Hawaiian organizations' or NHO, who made a claim for repatriation of both human remains (bones, *iwi*) and burial objects taken from Kawaihae Caves in 1905. An amateur archaeologist, David Forbes, had removed both bones and 83 artefacts and sold them to the Bishop Museum. Later 'explorations' of the same 'Forbes Cave' and adjacent caves resulted in the removal of more bones and objects to the Bishop Museum and Volcanoes National Park during the 1930s. Repatriation processes were commenced and in the late 1990s human remains were given and then in February 2000, 83 'priceless objects' were loaned to members of Hui Mālama. Soon after they sealed both objects and remains in the caves, with rebar and concrete at the mouth of the lava tube. At this point the four claimants all agreed to bury the bones *and* the objects which had been loaned by Donald Duckworth, then director of the Museum because repatriation was not technically completed and a loan was the most expeditious form of transfer while the legal process was ongoing. But subsequently other claimants came forward to suggest that the repatriation was flawed since not all NHO were consulted. Amongst these were the Royal Hawaiian Academy of Traditional Arts, led by its president La'akea Suganuma (a grandson of Mary Kawena Puku'i), and much later in 2005, Na Le'i Ali'i Kawananakoa, led by Abigail Kawananakoa, with links to Prince Kūhiō. Of the 13 claimants by 2001, some were for and others against the reburial of the objects. In August 2001 a 'Document of Truth' was signed by all, including Suganuma that they would 'agree to disagree'. But, shortly after, Suganuma filed a complaint with the NAGPRA review committee who ruled in his favour. Then in 2004 a lawsuit was filed by both the Royal Hawaiian Academy of Traditional Arts and Na Le'i Ali'i Kawananakoa against both Hui Mālama and the Bishop Museum. Eventually, District Court Judge David Ezra ordered Hui Mālama to retrieve the objects or disclose their exact location. Hui Mālama responded with the GPS co-ordinates and an inventory but refused to divulge more and Edward Halealoha Ayau, as head of the board, was imprisoned for contempt of court for three weeks in a federal detention centre between December 2005 and January 2006. Ayau was released (but still subject to home detention and a monitoring device, Wong 2006b). Hawaiian mediation, *ho'oponopono*, was tried and failed and eventually Judge Ezra had the objects removed about August–September 2006 and returned to the Bishop Museum.

As Greg Johnson observes (2007, 2009) this is a poignant and telling case of making meaning in the present through laying claim to the dead and of how culture is animated by contestation. On the one hand, Hui Mālama and the other claimants who supported reburial of the objects, insisted that they were *moepu* or 'buried with the dead', because of the disposition of the objects in front of the bones (*Ka Wai Ola* September 2005: 7). *Moepu*, they argued, were invested with the *mana kupuna* (ancestral spiritual power) of the deities, and were there to guard the dead, in this case high-ranking *ali'i* (chiefs) from this area of the Big Island of Hawai'i. Those who opposed their reburial suggested they were not funerary objects, that *moepu* was only a word in the context of *ho'omoepu* (to place with the dead,

suit resulted in the prosecution of Hui Mālama for contempt of court
in failing to return the objects or divulge their exact location, and the
imprisonment of its leader Edward Halealoha Ayau for several weeks in
December 2005–January 2006. So, just as the exhibition was opening
at the Honolulu Academy of Arts, the protagonists were engaged in
sensitive negotiations using Hawaiian mediation techniques. These failed
and subsequently the objects were recovered and returned to the Bishop
Museum around August 2006.

This dispute which Greg Johnson has depicted as 'Hawaiian to its very
marrow' (2009: 6) engaged profound cultural questions about the rival
claims of the living to look after the dead. As Johnson shows, there is an
intimate link between this dispute and an earlier controversy about the
1994 theft from the Bishop Museum of 'royal caskets' or *kā'ai*, which had
been deposited on loan by Kawananakoa's ancestor, Prince Kūhiō. These

---

lit. to put to sleep with). La'akea Suganuma wrote, 'An object placed is still an object'. He claimed
they were rather precious objects which had been placed in this cave for safe-keeping at a time of
conversion to Christianity with the end of *ai kapu* (taboos) restrictions in 1816 and the destruction
or desecration of many sacred objects. He further suggested that it was ancestral intention that once
the *kapu* was lifted that the cave be 'found' and the objects preserved to be a living lesson on Hawaiian
life for descendants, that the return of the objects to the museum was thus the will of the ancestors.

This disagreement dates back to the early twentieth century, as attested by documents in the museum.
In 1906 its then director Brigham said there was no evidence to support the theory they were hidden
from being destroyed and that the objects were 'personal keepsakes' and 'household deities of the
dead'. But later documents, relying on oral traditions, claim one of the figures was buried 'at the
time of the destruction of the idols'. Both sides in the current dispute lay claim to acting in the best
interests of the *kūpuna* (ancestors/elders) and Hawaiian culture. But in these contesting claims to
authority there are also genealogical differences. Both Suganuma and Abigail Kawananakoa claimed
aristocratic pedigree: he is descended from Mary Kawena Puku'i, while she is a direct descendant of
Prince Kūhiō. As Johnson observes 'In contrast to her purportedly royal status, she has declared that
others, and especially members of Hui Mālama are *maka'ainana*—commoners—who have no right
to speak for the dead and their things' (Johnson 2009: 23), and especially not for dead *ali'i*, it seems.
Johnson analyses the crucial links between this dispute and a former controversy over the theft of
kā'ai, royal caskets, from the Bishop Museum in 1994. These caskets and their uncertain remains
(perhaps of two kings of the fifteenth and sixteenth centuries) had been moved many times before
in a series of struggles between Hawaiians for control over their *mana* (spiritual power), including
one between Queen Lili'uokalani and Prince Kūhiō. After her death he placed them in the Bishop
Museum on a loan. Abigail Kawananakoa makes an explicit link between the Kawaihae Caves case
and the theft of the *kā'ai*, as a way of acting in defence of her ancestors. But the link is broader as
Johnson suggests, since both pertain to the same area of the Big Island between the Waipi'o Valley
in the north and Kealakekua Bay in the south, homeland of King Kamehameha, who sacrificed at
Pu'a Kohala to accomplish his goal of uniting the islands. The Kawaihae Caves are just above. The
struggle between the ancient Hawaiian religion and Christianity was most intense in this region.
Struggles about both the *kā'ai* and Kawaihae objects are 'about reconstituting the power of the past
in the present' (Johnson 2009: 24). These repatriation disputes are neither 'merely political', nor a
sign of the 'decayed state of Hawaiian culture' but a sign that through invoking cultural and religious
arguments in contests of responsibility towards and authority over the dead, 'the dispute is Hawaiian
to its very marrow' (Johnson 2009: 6). As with the Jesus of Christianity there is no pure origin
story, no unifying harmonious culture, but rival traditions which in their very contestation, animate
'culture'.

kāʻai had been 'moving objects' for over a century; they were constantly relocated in struggles over the claims of rival royal pasts in the present, for example, between Prince Kūhiō and Queen Liliʻuokalani. Both these disputes were grounded in the turbulent political landscape of the Big Island, from Kealakekua Bay, where Cook was killed, to Waipiʻo Valley, the homeland of King Kamehameha who unified the islands. Some Hawaiians and other locals thought the intimate involvement of both Suganuma and Kawananakoa in the opening ceremonies on 24 February 2006 was insensitive at best and provocative at worst and chose to boycott both the opening and the exhibition. Yet, in an interview in the *Honolulu Advertiser* on 4 February, Little declared that he did not anticipate criticism of the exhibition and stressed that the exhibited items were not stolen but given to Cook and 'should not be confused with or associated with the high-profile court case [i.e. the Kawaihae Caves case]' (Pang 2006: 2). But although the objects might have been so differentiated, the claims of living subjects were connected and associations were made. This rather compromised the 'rare opportunity for cross-cultural understanding' that Stephen Little had envisaged.[14]

Second, despite the best efforts of the conference organisers and especially of Elfriede Hermann who issued many invitations,[15] Pacific Islander scholars were sparsely represented, as speakers, chairs, or participants at the conference *Changing Contexts – Shifting Meanings: Transformations of Cultural Traditions in Oceania* (Hermann 2011). Scholars from Europe, North America, Australia and New Zealand predominated. After Jacob Simmet from Papua New Guinea and Ropate Qalo from Fiji belatedly withdrew, the sole Pacific Islander speaker was Amy Kuʻuleialoha Stillman from Michigan who spoke consummately, as always, on modern hula as a

---

14   Elfriede Hermann insisted that Little was keen to have active engagement by many Hawaiians and solicited their communication with the image of Kū during the exhibition: some spoke to Kū, others surrounded him with leaves in blessing (Elfriede Hermann, pers. comm., 1 July 2008, Nicolasberg). Some of the difficulties which emerged may have been ameliorated if the Academy had earlier sought advice and assistance from colleagues at the University of Hawaiʻi at Mānoa who were strikingly few as speakers at the conference. I am uncertain how far the Kawaihae Caves dispute led to a call for a boycott of both exhibition and conference. Little tried to downplay the connection in interviews with the press. 'The Germans are legally the owners of the Cook artifacts … Everything in the show is either a gift to Cook or traded with Cook for something he had. So there's nothing in the show that was stolen; there's nothing in the show that was a burial object. These are all things that were above ground' (Pang 2006: 2).

15   Elfriede Hermann had invited Ralph Regenvanu, Lilikalā Kameʻeleihiwa, J. Kēhaulani Kauanui, Epeli Hauʻofa, Jacob Simmet and Ropate Qalo amongst a list of about 12 Islander scholars. All had to decline because of prior commitments. The invitations were issued rather late by the Honolulu Academy of Arts so this might also have been a factor.

crucible of Hawaiian tradition. The unfortunate absence of Pacific Islander scholars finally surfaced in the closing plenary when the discussants, Aletta Biersack and Peter Hempenstall suggested that the presence of more Pacific Islanders would have enriched our debates. A number of us echoed these sentiments and Amy Kuʻuleialoha Stillman stood up and passionately lamented her sense of discomfort and isolation.[16] In the midst of this fraught plenary discussion, Stephen Little invited us to listen to the eloquent ancestors, those loquacious objects, speaking upstairs in the galleries. This appeal to a mythical past of harmony and wisdom to ameliorate the present tensions seemed to parallel how a curatorial stress on the pristine had rendered contemporary cultural politics unseemly (see Johnson 2009).

To Canberra: Cook as hook

Life in the Pacific in the 1700s in Honolulu transmuted into *Cook's Pacific Encounters* in Canberra six weeks later. *Cook's Pacific Encounters* at the NMA in Canberra was widely promoted as the only chance 'in the Southern Hemisphere' to see these extraordinary objects Cook had collected. Cook was the hook to lure visitors to this show. Expensively advertised on television and in the print media, generously sponsored by Singapore Airlines, Prime Television, Art Exhibitions Australia, and the Australian government's Art Indemnity Australia, it proved rather popular with visitors.

Although the same objects were displayed in rather similar ensembles to Honolulu, some in more alluring ways with subdued lighting (such as the cases of fishhooks and jewellery, see Figure 5), the show in Canberra emphasised far more the European context of collecting. Instead of European maps, engravings and paintings being located as an annex to the main display of Oceanic objects, they were rather situated as the direct introit, as a narrative precursor to them. On first entering the gallery the spectator was confronted with two giant maps. One showed the 'probable migration routes' of Pacific peoples (a justified tentativeness since my

---

16 Amy Kuʻuleialoha Stillman subsequently wrote a reflective essay 'On academic voyages of encounter' (n.d.) comparing her experience of this conference with that of *Culture Moves*, held at Te Papa Tongarewa in November 2005. She shared this essay with me but it remains unpublished. I thank her for permission to mention it here.

colleague, eminent ANU Pacific archaeologist Matthew Spriggs, declared it so out of date he felt his entire career had been in vain). The other showed Cook's rather more certain tracks on his three voyages.

Figure 5. Fishhooks from many Pacific Islands on display in a glass case in *Cook's Pacific Encounters*, National Museum of Australia, 2006

Source. Photograph by George Serras, reproduced courtesy of the National Museum of Australia

Besides the vitrines encasing the objects were banners with quotes from the voyage texts, highlighting the exchange processes in which objects were traded with or 'gifted' to the Europeans. The central focus was thus on exchange and the privileged figure was Cook and *his* Pacific encounters (rather than the German naturalists Johann Reinhold and his son George Forster who are, in Australia, far more obscure figures, known mainly to scholars). Contemporary German-Australian cultural exchange was celebrated at the opening of the exhibition, at which the German ambassador and then director of the Institute for Ethnology at the Georg-August University of Göttingen, Brigitta Hauser-Schäublin, were present. In the accompanying catalogue, the then director of the NMA, Craddock Morton, readily acknowledged that in the Australian context it was irresistible and justifiable to highlight the Cook connection. Perhaps the curators in Honolulu had desired rather to downplay that connection, given Cook's rather different 'posthumous reputation' there (see Smith 1992).[17]

I am not suggesting that *Cook's Pacific Encounters* was innocently hagiographic. Like Little, Morton acknowledged that Cook's Pacific encounters were both 'benign and hostile' (Morton 2006: xi) but he came to the conclusion, echoing Sahlins (1982, 1985, 1989, 1995) and Salmond (2003), that Cook was revered by Pacific people too, and that the man killed in Hawai'i was 'certainly James Cook, but also Tute, Kuki and Orono. A god as well as a man' (Morton 2006: xiii). Whether Cook was perceived as a manifestation of the god Lono by indigenous Hawaiians has of course been the subject of passionate debate between Marshall Sahlins and Gananath Obeyesekere (Obeyesekere 1992; Sahlins 1995). Although Sahlins likely won the intellectual argument about the eighteenth century, Cook's deification is clearly not perpetuated by most twenty-first century Hawaiians; indeed many Hawaiian nationalists rather gleefully celebrate the fact that Hawaiians killed him. Still, Morton ultimately adjudged Cook a heroic discoverer: 'a man of the Enlightenment, bringing the new world to the old' (Morton 2006: xiv). The frame for the Canberra exhibition was thus, far more than in Honolulu, *European* discoveries: how the collection of objects was as crucial as the recorded observations of peoples and places in text and images, the meticulous collection of flora and fauna, and the attempts, especially by the Forsters on the second

---

17   As Chris Ballard (2006) has suggested, Cook is still 'fissile material' in Hawai'i.

voyage, to record the languages of the peoples of the Pacific, with the help of interpreters like Tupaia on the first voyage and Omai on the second (see Jolly 2011b).

The NMA exhibition texts and especially the catalogue constantly reiterated that the collection of objects were *not* acts of imperial appropriation but were for the most part traded or 'gifted' to the strangers. In a catalogue essay, Jenny Newell, then a curator at the British Museum, stressed: 'The passion to acquire exotic objects was mutual' (Newell 2006: 45). Islanders were collecting, not just European things but highly valued Oceanic objects, especially fine white tapa from Tahiti and red feathers from Tonga, which were enthusiastically traded between different islands of the Pacific through the conduit of the voyages. Following Greg Dening and Nicholas Thomas, Newell highlighted how European artefacts— painted portraits, bed sheets, and brass casts—became powerful Oceanic objects, enhancing local power and status. Islanders, she claimed, retained the 'upper hand' in such exchanges (in implicit contradistinction to the imperial trophies of later missionaries, travellers and other collectors. See Hooper 2006: 24–27).

Thus, there was an overwhelming focus on mutual exchange in the Canberra exhibition, and, like much writing on Cook, it tended to mist over the violence which was, as George Forster stressed at the time, an inherent part, and not just an unfortunate corollary, of these acts of 'discovery' (see Jolly 1992, 2007b, 2009a, 2009b, 2009c; Jolly with Tcherkézoff 2009). Such violence was often mutual too, but although the reciprocal allure of objects may have been roughly equal or even balanced towards Islanders because of the Europeans' vulnerability in needing fresh food, water and wood, it is hard to claim such parity for weapons of war. Bows and arrows, spears, sling stones and clubs were usually no match for iron weapons, muskets and cannons. In a poignant irony, although Cook was downed with Hawaiian clubs he was finished off with an iron dagger which had been traded for Hawaiian artefacts (see Hauser-Schäublin and Krüger 2006c). Yet, as Bernard Smith (1992: 232–40) long ago observed, in the creation of Cook's image in the European visions of the late eighteenth century and since, there has been a tendency to portray him primarily as a peacemaker. Unlike the more multivalent representation in *Cook's Sites* (by Mark Adams and Nicholas Thomas), remounted at the National Library of Australia earlier in 2006, which acknowledged Cook's 'dark side' (see Jolly 2007b), Cook was represented at the National Museum of Australia in a light as gleaming as the wintry atmosphere of Canberra outside.

Curators were perhaps in part responding to pressure coming from the then prime minister John Howard to tell a more positive story of the 'discovery' of Australia and white settlement and to eschew a 'black arm-band history' of colonialism.[18] Craddock Morton acknowledged the popular lure of Cook for visitors, a national icon of British settler colonial history (see Bolton 2006, 2009). Although the lure of that hook has sometimes been overestimated, this exhibition drew around 26,700 visitors.[19] There were more critical views of Cook offered at an associated symposium, *Discovering Cook's Collections,* but these were, for the most part, sequestered there.

As in Honolulu, there was a lone Pacific scholar and curator who spoke at that symposium, Paul Tapsell from the Auckland Museum, along with the Indigenous Australian scholar Doreen Mellor from the National Library of Australia. Pacific curators and scholars from museums in the islands from which the objects originated—Hawai'i, Tahiti, the Marquesas, Rapanui, Tonga, New Caledonia and Vanuatu—were not invited, and the main commentary thus came from experts from Australia, North America and Britain: the late Greg Dening, Paul Turnbull, Nigel Erskine, Adrienne Kaeppler and Lissant Bolton. Questions about the relationship between Cook's voyages, colonial power and knowledge were addressed, especially in presentations by the late Greg Dening (2009), Paul Tapsell (2009) and Doreen Mellor (2009).

Paul Tapsell spoke of how academic and museological practice still fixates on the figure of Cook. He rather celebrated the role of the Polynesian priest and navigator Tupaia, who remains 'near invisible' in 'official voyage writings' and Eurocentric history, despite his pivotal contribution to Cook's first voyage (2009: 103). He was more than a 'convenient translator who died en route while hitching a ride to England' (2009: 105); without him 'Cook's first footsteps on New Zealand's shores may have been his last' (2009: 103, 105, 93). Tupaia directly facilitated the European exploration

---

18 This phrase, coined by one of then prime minister John Howard's speechwriters, refers to the dark, funereal laments about colonialism and especially to white settler guilt about extreme violence enacted on Indigenous Australians. The decade or more of Howard's government was marked by passionate scholarly and public debates about the extent of this violence, debates which became known as the 'history wars' (see Macintyre and Clark 2004).

19 Susan Tonkin, then assistant manager of NMA Audience Development & Public Programs, reported that '*Cook's Pacific Encounters* attracted a total of 26,700 visitors during its July to September 2006 season at the National Museum' (pers. comm. by email, 6 November 2009). Bolton (2009) reflected on how Cook's fame can be seen as a kind of celebrity status which attracts visitors to museum exhibitions.

of the Pacific, through his extensive navigational knowledge, the graphic arts he learnt and in the collecting of Māori *taonga* (treasured objects), likely given to him as a sign of genealogical connection and trust. Though he died in Batavia, Tupaia's wisdom and assistance ensured that Cook and his compatriots arrived safely home with 'their precious cargo of scientific evidence' (2009: 92). As Tapsell notes, the *taonga* collected on Cook's first voyage, though likely prestations to Tupaia, have 'remained stratospherically detached' from the new museum practices which have allowed such objects to become 'rehumanised and approachable in a way that enables the customary system of kin-belonging to be positively expressed' (2009: 92). Yet 'like an uncharted rock just below the surface, his [Tupaia's] unrecognised influence continues to ripple and shape our maps, history books and museums' (2009: 107). And in Aotearoa New Zealand Tupaia is still known and cherished by contemporary Māori, seen as their own ancestor, and remembered through those many boys who are named after him.[20]

Doreen Mellor, who comes from the Atherton Tablelands of North Queensland, honoured the 'custodians of this land for millennia before James Cook appeared on the horizon in 1770' (2006) and addressed the 'life-changing consequences for Australian Indigenous peoples of James Cook's first Pacific journey and subsequent European settlement' (2009: 113). While acknowledging the achievements of Cook's first voyage in the *Endeavour* and Cook's status as a 'powerful symbol of the age of Enlightenment' (2009: 113) Mellor saw the science of exploration as perforce connected to the building of empire. Cook had only fleeting connections with Indigenous Australians on that voyage. The Eora people of Botany Bay refused his beads and nails. Said Cook, 'all they seem'd to want was for us to be gone' (Mellor 2009: 115; see also Nugent 2009). Later in North Queensland, after the *Endeavour* was holed by the coral

---

20 Tapsell noted that Māori today remember Tupaia as Tupaea (lit *tu*: stand, *paea*: cast ashore; 2009:109). In the language of his homeland Raiatea, it rather means 'beaten', in reference to a military defeat. Māori ancestors recognised him as a man of high rank, emanating from a sacred *marae* (a communal and sacred meeting ground) in the eastern Pacific who exercised great authority (even over the strangers) and spoke the *tapu* dialect of the priestly elite. He thinks it highly likely that the treasured dog-skin cloaks (*kahi kurī*) and greenstone (*pounamu*) in the collections from Cook's first voyage were prestations to Tupaia (2009: 102–104). Tupaia is now acknowledged as the creator of several watercolours previously attributed to Joseph Banks and has long been recognised as the author of Tupaia's chart. But, as Tapsell argued, after Di Piazza and Pearthree (2007), the original from which several copies were made was not a conventional European map plotted on the co-ordinates of longitude and latitude but a graphic expression of traditional Oceanic wayfinding frames of reference (2009: 95). See Jolly 2011b for a fuller discussion.

reef at Cape Tribulation and repairs were in process, Cook and his crew encountered the peoples of Gangarr (now Cooktown) and more friendly relations ensued. But when the British refused to share the spoils of their abundant catch of turtles, local people were angered and lit a grass fire around the ship's camp.

Mellor juxtaposed two treasured objects in the collection of the National Library of Australia (NLA), Cook's *Endeavour* journal with the papers of Eddi Mabo a 'record of his long and ultimately successful endeavour to reclaim as native title the land annexed by Cook' (2009: 116). She stressed how the colonial appropriation of Indigenous land and the dissemination of a racist evolutionary ideology separated and divided white and Indigenous Australians. Such separations culminated in the forcible separation of Aboriginal and Torres Strait Islander children from their families in the period from 1918 to 1970—'the story of the Stolen Generations'—which Mellor suggests can be best accessed through the poignant stories told in the audiotape collection of the NLA. The bicentenary of the arrival of the First Fleet in 1988 was thus more an occasion for Indigenous mourning than celebration. But, concluding with the famous Indigenous motto from that year—'White Australia has a Black History'—she suggests that this signifies not just anger and resistance but the need for mutual understanding and the recognition of the prior presence of Indigenous Australians (2009: 125).

There was thus a powerful and poignant dialogue between the situation of Māori and Indigenous Australians in these two proximate settler colonies. But alas, perhaps because of time and funding constraints, there was no broader conversation with curators and scholars from the broader region of Oceania as represented in the objects of the exhibition or in the diversity of peoples from Oceania who are migrants to Australia.

A later weekend of community activities included a dialogue between Ralph Regenvanu from the Vanuatu Cultural Centre and Lissant Bolton from the British Museum. But, compared to Honolulu, not much was done to engage local Pacific communities nor to foster a dialogue about the relation between these ancient objects and the living culture of Pacific peoples in Australia. Māori and Tongan dance groups were invited as part of the lavish opening night performances, but Islanders were not included in projects or conversations around the objects, as was attempted with Pacific communities in Hawai'i. There was thus little to link the objects with the 'living cultures' of Pacific migrants in Australia. In September 2006, most objects from the exhibition returned to Göttingen, while a few moved on to Paris, to be exhibited at the Musée du Quai Branly in late 2006.

A difficult passage

How then might we see the passage of these moving objects of the Cook/ Forster collection to Honolulu and Canberra in relation to the three questions I posed at the outset?

First, did these exhibitions evince more open and dialogical relations of knowing, more interactive collaborations and more egalitarian curatorial postures, which proponents of the 'new' museum avow? In Honolulu, Stephen Little spoke of celebrating 'the brilliant cultural and spiritual lives of the indigenous peoples of the Pacific, as they existed prior to the first contact with Westerners', addressing the 'aftermath and ongoing realities' of colonialism and promoting 'cross-cultural understanding' (2006b: 3) As we have seen, although there were attempts to make connections with the living cultures of Hawaiians and other Pacific Islanders through performance events, photographic exhibitions and community consultations, there was far less engagement in the foundational curatorial processes, and a significant number of Hawaiians boycotted both exhibition and conference. With only one Pacific scholar ultimately presenting, the conference disappointed high hopes of cross-cultural dialogue. Moreover, the curatorial emphasis on the 'pristine', pre-contact nature of the objects tended to sequester them in a distant past, removed from the mixtures and impurities of cultural exchange, remote from the realm of contemporary indigenous knowledge and the politics of the present.

The curatorial intentions in Canberra were less a celebration of indigenous Oceanic creativity and connectivity, and more yet another celebration of the contested figure of Cook, not so much in his usual garb as simultaneously 'hero and villain', but rather as both a 'founding father' of Australia and an Oceanic ancestor. This twinning in the genealogy of Cook and the overwhelming emphasis on mutuality in material and cultural exchanges on his voyages blurred many of the hard questions about the reverberations of colonial power and knowledge in the present. These were addressed by some speakers in the associated symposium, *Discovering Cook's Collections*, but such critical views were barely evident in the exhibition itself. Moreover, the singular chance not only to see these objects in the 'Southern Hemisphere' but also to animate them through conversations with curators, scholars and cultural experts across the vastness of Oceania, including Pacific peoples resident in Australia, was, for the most part, missed.

Second, as we have seen, although the objects exhibited were almost identical in the exhibitions at the Honolulu Academy of Arts and the National Museum of Australia, the curatorial frames dramatically diverged.[21] In Honolulu, the pristine Oceanic materiality of the objects was highlighted, devoid of both ethnographic and historical context. They were in Stéphane Martin's words 'nude' (Naumann 2006: 122). Bare of explanatory captions either about their indigenous creation or the context of their collection, they were thus more open to focused aesthetic attention, that effect cultivated by curators in most art galleries and some museums. But, despite being seen in an elite art gallery they were framed less as 'high art' and more as cultural treasures from the Pacific, and especially from Hawai'i, 'coming home'. This framing was patent in the promotional and publicity materials produced and in most of the newspaper and magazine articles about the exhibition (see, e.g. Carvalho 2006; Pang 2006). Many Hawaiian visitors were visibly moved, especially by the presence of Kū and there was much speculation in both the press and the electronic media that he might remain.

In Canberra, by contrast, the Oceanic creativity and connectivity of the objects was de-emphasised in favour of a focus on the European exploratory voyages. The exhibition space was rather darker and more crowded than the Honolulu venue. Although here the exhibition was mounted in a museum it did not display the objects as 'artefacts', nor surround them with copious ethnographic information. Rather, large pennants alongside the vitrines reproduced resounding phrases from the journals of Banks, Cook and the Forsters, describing the objects we were seeing, the peoples who made them and the contexts of their being collected or 'gifted' to the Europeans. The glass cases were often so engulfed by the English words of the voyagers that it was hard for the objects to speak to the viewer with their own Oceanic inflections.

---

21 Note, however, that the institutional appellation does not always mould curatorial style since although a 'museum', the MQB adopts a predominantly 'aesthetic' approach (see Jolly 2011a).

Moreover, both in the exhibition texts and in the catalogue there was a recurrent emphasis on the *mutuality* evinced in exchanges. Mutuality in the exchange of objects transmuted into the mutuality of unfamiliar peoples. Ultimately a warm bath of mutual cross-cultural exploration was brewed rather than a more critical sense of how such voyages of European exploration heralded the later colonisation of Oceania. A stress on the agency of Pacific peoples in the face of persisting narratives of colonialism as a fatal impact and of indigenous victimhood is welcome. But an opposite danger beckons when we prefer to see symmetry rather than asymmetry, parity rather than inequality and harmony rather than escalating violence in the wake of Cook's voyages. Rather than a sense of these objects coming 'home', as in Hawai'i, cosmopolitan cultural exchange between Europe and Oceania was highlighted and an optimistic genealogy for Australian multiculturalism plotted. This was most obvious in the transfiguration of Cook not just as an Enlightenment hero and founding father to the white nation of Australia but as an Oceanic ancestor: 'Tute, Kuki, Orono'.

Third, how far did these exhibitions succeed in reconnecting Oceanic objects with living Oceanic peoples, with their 'living culture' and with contemporary artistic traditions, as Ralph Regenvanu called for at the opening of the MQB in May 2005? Three years later at a conference in June 2008 in association with the *Pacific Encounters* exhibition at the MQB, Arapata Hakiwai, Māori curator at Te Papa Tongarewa, suggested that the real treasures of Oceanic collections reside not in the objects themselves but in how they become subjects engendering new relationships. He stressed that this does not necessarily entail the repatriation of objects to establish reconnections with the descendants of their creators. Indeed, in some instances Māori *iwi* have rather decided that overseas museums are the 'custodians of choice' for their *taonga* and have seen virtual electronic repatriation as sufficient. Oceanic objects are thus better seen as subjects, reanimated as good cultural ambassadors (see Jolly 2011a).

Significantly at that same conference the Hawaiian curator from the Bishop Museum, Noelle Kahanu, and other delegates from Hawai'i did not speak with such equanimity about Hawaiian objects as cultural ambassadors. Indeed, on seeing another manifestation of Kū, exhibited as part of the *Pacific Encounters* show at the MQB, Noelle Kahanu and Lilikalā Kame'eleihiwa wept and expressed a hope that all the overseas images of Kū might be united back in Hawai'i. But Kame'eleihiwa elaborated, she did not want them to come back home only to leave again soon after—likely a pointed reference to the evanescent passage of Kū through

Honolulu in 2006.[22] Thus, the way in which Oceanic peoples relate to the Oceanic 'objects' made by their ancestors is diverse and signals not just their past efficacy but their efficacy in the present, especially in contexts where they are animated subjects in political struggles. The relevant Māori *iwi* who are its custodians have decided that a valuable ancestral house, a *whare tupuna* embodying the ancestor Ruatepupuke should remain in the Field Museum in Chicago, but curators at Te Papa were equally adamant that the several *mokomōkai* (heads chiselled with moko designs) in overseas museum collections, many collected in the context of the New Zealand land wars, should, as ancestral remains, come home for reburial.[23] This was finally been agreed to by the French government in 2011, but other nations, institutions and individuals have yet to agree to such repatriations (see Jolly 2011a).

Yet, as we have seen, the moving of Oceanic objects 'back home' is no simple matter, and can animate not only the differences created across the beach of colonialism but differences between Oceanic peoples. The celebrated passage of the moving objects of the Cook/Forster collection back to Oceania was a grand act of cross-cultural diplomacy between Europe and Oceania. But their passage proved difficult in both Oceanic locations, of Honolulu and Canberra. In Hawai'i, some objects were clearly reanimated as subjects in the present, but in a way which reopened painful divisions between Hawaiian people. Their display articulated with other protracted and poignant disputes (notably the Kawaihae Caves case) and the broader conversations between all Hawaiians as to how best to look after the dead in the service of the living and how best to be custodians of the past in the service of the present. By contrast in Australia, no similar

---

22   The three images of Kū held by Göttingen, the Peabody and the Bishop Museum were briefly united at an exhibition at the Bishop Museum in Honolulu from 5 June–4 October 2010. But this was, as envisaged, an evanescent reunion (see Tengan 2016).

23   I thank the anonymous reviewers for *The Contemporary Pacific* for corrections and elaborations here. The *whare tupuna* (ancestral house) at the Field Museum embodying the ancestor Ruatepupuke is connected with the closely related *hapu* of Te Whānau a Ruataupare and Te Whānaua Te Aotawarirangi from Tokomaru Bay. Māori curators at Te Papa liaise with the appropriate Māori *iwi* over such policy decisions. Moreover, there is a designated team of Māori curators at Te Papa that deals with repatriation issues. It is important to see *mokomōkai* not just as individual ancestral remains but as embodying the ancestry of an entire *iwi*. *Mokomōkai* were usually collected by private individuals such as Horatio Robley (a British army officer and artist), often appropriated in the context of brutal land wars and traded with museum curators overseas. After the New Zealand government declined to buy Robley's collection, he sold it to the American Museum of Natural History. Hundreds of *mokomōkai* still remain in public and private collections overseas and are the subject of ongoing demands for repatriation.

passions were raised, perhaps because little was done to reconnect these objects with Oceanic peoples either in the islands or the diaspora, to reanimate them as subjects, as living presences in the present.

The project to create 'new' museums and galleries that realise postcolonial aspirations and truly respect the vital connections between living descendants and ancestral Oceanic creations is ongoing. This is not just the work of single exhibitions or solo curators but must be a foundational part of institutional curatorial practice. Te Papa Tongarewa, the National Museum of New Zealand, which opened in 1998, has long been at the forefront of this project, not just articulating but practising an ethos of partnership with Māori, Pacific Islanders and diverse communities. In Hawai'i there have been important advances over the last decade with the recreation of the Hawaiian and Pacific Halls at the Bishop Museum under the inspired vision of Noelle Kahanu and in 2012 the merger of the Honolulu Academy of Arts with the Contemporary Museum to form the Honolulu Museum of Art and the appointment of Healoaha Johnson as its first indigenous Hawaiian curator in 2015. There are also hopeful signs in Australia, Europe and North America.[24] So perhaps we are witnessing an acceleration in reenvisioning the moving objects of Oceania as rather Oceanic subjects, propelling the practices of contemporary museums and galleries forward, toward a better future, not just in the region but globally.

Acknowledgements

This derives from the opening keynote lecture for the European Society for Oceanists' biennial conference held in Verona, Italy 10–12 July 2008. My heartfelt thanks to Anna Paini and Elisabetta Gnecchi-Ruscone for their welcome invitation to deliver this in Verona and for their hard work in translation for the Italian version published in Paini and Gnecchi-Ruscone 2011. In editing that spoken lecture I have tried to retain some of the

---

24   In a similar period to the exhibitions discussed here were two exhibitions curated in the UK—*Pasifika Styles* at the Cambridge Museum of Archaeology and Anthropology (CMAA) from 2006–2008 (Raymond and Salmond 2008) and *Pacific Encounters* at the Sainsbury Centre at the University of East Anglia and then MQB in 2008 (Hooper 2006; Jacobs 2009). These were distinctive in that the former focused on contemporary Pacific artists, while the latter incorporated contemporary art alongside earlier Oceanic creations. The animation of objects through the presence of Pacific peoples and artists in museum contexts and community collaborations has been pursued by Nicholas Thomas, currently director of CMMA, and Lissant Bolton, keeper at the British Museum. Similar hopes are foregrounded in the current *Pacific Presences* project at CMAA.

voice of the oral original, but this final English text differs in significant ways. The section on the MQB became the subject of a related paper (Jolly 2011a) and a written but unread section on the Australian Museum in Sydney has been omitted to enhance the focus on the exhibitions of the Cook/Forster collection. The final epilogue on the artist Fiona Hall which proved popular in the oral presentation has been deleted, hopefully to re-emerge in future writing on her work and especially her presentation at the Australian Pavilion in the Venice Biennale of 2015, restaged at the National Gallery of Australia from May to July 2016. The very extensive footnotes have been pared back, but are more extensive than in the journal version. Given the time elapsed since that lecture, I have updated and revised a little. Many thanks to James Clifford, Robert Foster, Elfriede Hermann, Chris Ballard, Geremie Barmé and Michelle Antoinette for comments and criticisms at several stages of writing and revision. I warmly thank Michelle for superb assistance with proofreading and with the compilation, reproduction and permissions for images both for the conference presentation and for the Italian publication. More recently many thanks to Carolyn Brewer for stellar editing assistance, and Nicholas Mortimer for checks for continuing online references and image permissions. A shorter English version has recently appeared in *The Contemporary Pacific* 28(2): 281–314 and I thank the editors of that journal for permission to republish this slightly longer version here. All remaining errors and infelicities are mine.

References

Alpers, Svetlana. 1991. 'The museum as a way of seeing'. In *Exhibiting Cultures: The Poetics and Politics of Museum Display*, ed. Ivan Karp and Steven D. Lavine, pp. 25–42. Washington DC: Smithsonian Institution Press.

Andrade, Ivy Hali'imaile. 2007. 'Review of *Life in the Pacific of the 1700s*'. *The Contemporary Pacific* 19(1): 341–42.

Ballard, Chris. 2006. 'Tied to the cabinet of curiosities'. *The Times Literary Supplement*, 15 September, 5938: 20.

Blumenbach, Johann Friedrich. 1775. *De Generis Humani Varietate Nativa*. Goettingae: Frid. Andr. Rosenbuschii.

Bolton, Lissant. 2009. 'Brushed with fame: Museological investments in the Cook voyage collections'. In *Discovering Cook's Collections*, ed. Michelle Hetherington and Howard Morphy, pp. 78–91. Canberra: National Museum of Australia.

——. 2006. 'The museum as cultural agent: The Vanuatu Cultural Centre extension worker program'. In *South Pacific Museums: Experiments in Culture*, ed. Chris Healy and Andrea Witcomb, pp. 13.1–13.13. Melbourne: Monash University ePress.

Carvalho, Marie. 2006. 'Objects tell Pacific peoples' stories'. *Honolulu Advertiser*, 9 April.

Clifford, James. 2014. 'Art and ethnography'. Paper presented at Macquarie University Anthropology Seminar, Sydney. 23 October.

——. 2007. 'Quai Branly in process'. *October* 120 (Spring): 3–23. Republished in edited form in *Le debat: Le moment du Quai Branly* 147: 29–39.

Coote, Jeremy. 2004. *Curiosities from the* Endeavour: *A Forgotten Collection – Pacific Artefacts given by Joseph Banks to Christ Church, Oxford, after the First Voyage.* Whitby: Captain Cook Memorial Museum.

Dening, Greg. 2009. 'Looking across the beach – both ways'. In *Discovering Cook's Collections*, ed. Michelle Hetherington and Howard Morphy, pp. 11–24. Canberra: National Museum of Australia.

Di Piazza Anne and Erik Pearthree. 2007. 'A new reading of Tupaia's chart'. *Journal of the Polynesian Society* 116(3): 321–40.

Drake, Maile T. 2007. 'Review of *Life in the Pacific of the 1700s*'. *The Contemporary Pacific* 19(1): 342–43. doi.org/10.1353/cp.2007.0009.

Fleck, Robert and Adrienne L. Kaeppler (eds). 2009. *James Cook und die Entdeckung der Südsee/James Cook and the Exploration of the Pacific.* Bonn: Kunst-und Ausstellungshalle der Bundesrepublik Deutchsland; English version, London: Thames and Hudson.

Forster, George. 1777. *A Voyage Round the World in His Britannic Majesty's Sloop Resolution.* London: B. White.

Forster, George. 2000 [1777]. *A Voyage Round the World*, vols 1 and 2, ed. Nicholas Thomas and Oliver Berghof. Honolulu: University of Hawai'i Press.

Forster, Johann Reinhold. 1778. *Observations Made During a Voyage Round the World on Physical Geography, Natural History and Ethic Philosophy*. London: G. Robinson.

———. 1996 [1778]. *Observations Made During a Voyage Round the World, on Physical Geography, Natural History and Ethic Philosophy*, new edition, ed. Nicholas Thomas, Harriet Guest and Michael Dettelbach. Honolulu: University of Hawai'i Press.

Gell, Alfred. 1998. *Art and Agency: An Anthropological Theory*. Oxford: Clarendon Press.

Hau'ofa, Epeli. 2008. *We Are the Ocean: Selected Works*. Honolulu: University of Hawai'i Press.

Hauser-Schäublin, Brigitta and Gundolf Krüger. 2006a. *Cook's Pacific Encounters*, Cook/Forster Collection: Pacific Cultural Heritage. National Museum of Australia website. Online: www.nma.gov.au/online_features/cook_forster (accessed 5 August 2016).

———. 2006b. 'Introduction'. In *Life in the Pacific in the 1700s: The Cook/Forster Collection of the Georg-August University of Göttingen*, ed. Stephen Little and Peter Ruthenberg. Vol. 2, *European Research, Traditions and Perspectives*, co-ed. Brigitta Hauser-Schäublin and Gundolf Krüger, pp. 21–35. Honolulu: Honolulu Academy of Arts.

———. 2006c. 'Pacific cultural heritage: The Göttingen Cook Forster collection'. In *Cook's Pacific Encounters: The Cook/Forster Collection of the Georg-August University of Göttingen*, pp. 15–27. Canberra: National Museum of Australia.

Hauser-Schäublin, Brigitta and Gundolf Krüger (eds). 1998. *James Cook: Gifts and Treasures from the South Seas*. Munich and New York: Prestel.

Hermann, Elfriede (ed.). 2011. *Changing Contexts, Shifting Meanings: Transformations of Cultural Traditions in Oceania*. Honolulu: University of Hawai'i Press and Honolulu Academy of Arts.

Hetherington, Michelle and Howard Morphy (eds). 2009. *Discovering Cook's Collections*. Canberra: National Museum of Australia.

Hooper, Steven. 2006. *Pacific Encounters: Art & Divinity in Polynesia 1760–1860*. Norwich: Sainsbury Centre for Visual Arts and British Museum Press.

Jacobs, Karen (ed.). 2009. *Encounters with Polynesia: Exhibiting the Past in the Present*. Special issue of *The Journal of Museum Ethnography*, 21.

Johnson, Greg. 2009. 'Social lives of the dead: Contestation and continuities in the Hawaiian repatriation context'. In *Culture and Belonging in Divided Societies: Contestation and Symbolic Landscapes*, ed. Marc Ross, pp. 45–67. Philadelphia: University of Pennsylvania Press. doi.org/10.9783/9780812203509.45.

——. 2007. *Sacred Claims: Repatriation and Living Tradition*. Charlottesville and London: University of Virginia Press.

Jolly, Margaret. 2014. 'Animatimg *Atua*: In the presence of Polynesian gods'. *Art Monthly Australia* April: 34–39.

——. 2011a. 'Becoming a "new" Museum: Contesting Oceanic visions at Musée du Quai Branly'. *The Contemporary Pacific* 23(1):108–39.

——. 2011b. 'Beyond the beach: Re-articulating the limen in Oceanic pasts, presents and futures'. In *Changing Contexts, Shifting Meanings: Transformations of Cultural Traditions in Oceania*, ed. Elfriede Hermann, pp. 56–73. Honolulu: University of Hawai'i Press and Honolulu Academy of Arts.

——. 2009a. 'Revisioning gender and sexuality on Cook's voyages in the Pacific'. In *James Cook und die Entdeckung der Sudsee/ James Cook and the Exploration of the Pacific*, ed. Robert Fleck and Adrienne L. Kaeppler, pp. 98–102. Bonn: Kunst-und Ausstellungshalle der Bundesrepublik Deutchsland; English version, London: Thames and Hudson.

——. 2009b. 'The sediment of voyages: Re-membering Quirós, Bougainville and Cook in Vanuatu'. In *Oceanic Encounters: Exchange, Desire, Violence*, ed. Margaret Jolly, Serge Tcherkézoff and Darrell Tryon, pp. 57–111. Canberra: ANU E-Press. Online: press.anu.edu. au/publications/oceanic-encounters (accessed 5 August 2016).

——. 2009c. 'Revisioning gender and sexuality on Cook's voyages in the Pacific'. In *James Cook und die Entdeckung der Sudsee/ James Cook and the Exploration of the Pacific*, ed. Robert Fleck and Adrienne L. Kaeppler, pp. 98–102. Bonn: Kunst-und Ausstellungshalle der Bundesrepublik Deutchsland; English version, London: Thames and Hudson.

——. 2008. 'The south in *Southern Theory*: Antipodean reflections on the Pacific'. *Australian Humanities Review* 44(March): 75–100.

——. 2007a. 'Imagining Oceania: Indigenous and foreign representations of a sea of islands'. *The Contemporary Pacific* 19(2): 508–45. doi.org/10.1353/cp.2007.0054.

——. 2007b. 'Unsettling memories: Commemorating "discoverers" in Australia and Vanuatu in 2006'. In *Fernández de Quirós et le Vanuatu. Découverte mutuelle et historiographie d'un acte fondateur 1606*, ed. Frédéric Angleviel, pp. 197–219. GROCH Nouméa with assistance of the European Union, République Française, Vanuatu Government and Vanuatu National Cultural Council. Port Vila: Sun Productions.

——. 1992. '"Ill-natured comparisons": Racism and relativism in European representations of ni-Vanuatu from Cook's second voyage'. *History and Anthropology* 5(3-4): 331–64.

Jolly, Margaret with Serge Tcherkézoff. 2009. 'Oceanic encounters: A prelude'. In *Oceanic Encounters: Exchange, Desire, Violence*, ed. Margaret Jolly, Serge Tcherkézoff and Darrell Tryon, pp. 1–36. Canberra: ANU E Press. Online: press.anu.edu.au/publications/oceanic-encounters (accessed 5 August 2016).

Kaeppler, Adrienne L. 2009a. '"To attempt some new discoveries in that vast unknown tract": Rediscovering the Forster collections from Cook's Second Pacific voyage'. In *Discovering Cook's Collections*, ed. Michelle Hetherington and Howard Morphy, pp. 58–77. Canberra: National Museum of Australia.

——. 2009b. 'Enlightened encounters in the unknown Pacific'. In *James Cook und die Entdeckung der Sudsee/James Cook and the Exploration of the Pacific*, ed. Robert Fleck and Adrienne L. Kaeppler, pp. 88–92. Bonn: Kunst-und Ausstellungshalle der Bundesrepublik Deutchsland; English version London: Thames and Hudson.

———. 2008. 'Exhibiting Cook's voyages in the Leverian Museum and today'. Paper presented to symposium Exhibiting Polynesia: Past, Present and Future, 17–18 June, Musée du Quai Branly, Paris.

———. 2006. 'Life in the Pacific in the 1700s and today'. In *Life in the Pacific in the 1700s: The Cook/Forster Collection of the Georg-August University of Göttingen*, ed. Stephen Little and Peter Ruthenberg. Vol. 2, *European Research, Traditions and Perspectives*, co-ed. Brigitta Hauser-Schäublin and Gundolf Krüger, pp. 8–19. Honolulu: Honolulu Academy of Arts.

———. 1998. 'The Göttingen collection in an international context'. In *James Cook: Gifts and Treasures from the South Seas*, ed. Brigitta Hauser-Schäublin and Gundolf Krüger, pp. 86–93. Munich and New York: Prestel.

———. 1988. 'Pacific culture history and European voyages'. In *Terra Australis: The Furthest Shore*, ed. William Eisler and Bernard Smith, pp. 141–46. Sydney: Art Gallery of New South Wales.

———. 1979. 'Tracing the history of Cook voyage artifacts in the Museum of Mankind'. *The British Museum Yearbook.* British Museum London, vol 3: 167–97.

———. 1978a. *Artificial Curiosities: An Exposition of Native Manufactures Collected on the Three Pacific Voyages of Captain James Cook, RN.* Bernice P. Bishop Museum Special Publication 65. Honolulu: Bishop Museum Press.

———. 1978b. *Cook Voyage Artifacts in Leningrad, Berne and Florence Museums.* Honolulu: Bishop Museum Press.

Keane, Webb. 2007. *Christian Moderns: Freedom and Fetish in the Mission Encounters.* Berkeley: University of California Press.

Kimmelman, Michael. 2006. 'A heart of darkness in the city of light'. *New York Times*, 2 July. Online: nytimes.com/2006/07/02/arts/design/02kimm.html (accessed 4 April 2013).

Kosasa, Karen. 2007. 'Review of *Life in the Pacific of the 1700s*'. *The Contemporary Pacific* 19(1): 344–45. doi.org/10.1353/cp.2007.0020.

Latour, Bruno. 1993 [1991]. *We Have Never Been Modern*, trans. Catherine Porter. Cambridge, MA: Harvard University Press.

Little, Stephen. 2006a. Press Release for exhibition *Life in the Pacific of the 1700s, Exhibition Guide*. Honolulu: Honolulu Academy of Arts, 26 January.

———. 2006b. 'Foreword'. In *Life in the Pacific of the 1700s, Exhibition Guide*, ed. Stephen Little and Peter Ruthenberg. Honolulu: Honolulu Academy of Arts.

Little, Stephen and Peter Ruthenberg (eds). 2006a. *Life in the Pacific of the 1700s, Exhibition Guide*. Honolulu: Honolulu Academy of Arts.

—— (eds). 2006b. *Life in the Pacific in the 1700s: The Cook/Forster Collection of the Georg-August University of Göttingen*, vol. 1. In *Artifacts from Life in the Pacific in the 1700s: The Cook/Forster Collection of the Georg-August University of Göttingen*, ed. Stephen Little and Peter Ruthenberg. Honolulu: Honolulu Academy of Arts.

MacDonald, Sharon. 2007. 'Review of Kylie Message 2006. *New Museums and the Making of Culture*. In *reCollections, Journal of the National Museum of Australia* 2(2). Online: recollections.nma.gov.au/issues/vol_2_no2/book_reviews/new_museums_and_the_making_of_culture/ (accessed 4 April 2013).

Macintyre, Stuart and Anna Clark. 2004. *The History Wars*, 2nd edition. Melbourne: Melbourne University Press.

Mellor, Doreen. 2009. 'Cook, his mission and Indigenous Australia: A perspective on consequence'. In *Discovering Cook's Collections*, ed. Michelle Hetherington and Howard Morphy, pp. 112–26. Canberra: National Museum of Australia.

Message, Kylie. 2006. *New Museums and the Making of Culture*. Oxford: Berg.

Morton, Craddock. 2006. 'Introduction'. In *Cook's Pacific Encounters: The Cook/Forster Collection of the Georg-August University of Göttingen*, pp. xi–xiv. Canberra: National Museum of Australia. doi.org/10.1017/ccol0521826047.001.

National Museum of Australia (NMA). 2006. *Cook's Pacific Encounters: The Cook/Forster Collection of the Georg-August University of Göttingen.* Canberra: National Museum of Australia.

Naumann, Peter. 2006. 'Making a museum: "It is making theater, not writing theory"'. An interview with Stéphane Martin, Président-Directeur General, Musée du Quai Branly. *Journal of Museum Anthropology* 29(2): 118–27. doi.org/10.1525/mua.2006.29.2.118.

Newell, Jennifer. 2010. *Trading Nature: Tahitians, Europeans and Ecological Exchange.* Honolulu: University of Hawai'i Press. doi.org/10.21313/ hawaii/9780824832810.001.0001.

——. 2006. 'Collecting from the collectors: Pacific islanders and the spoils of Europe'. In *Cook's Pacific Encounters: The Cook/Forster Collection of the Georg-August University of Göttingen*, pp. 29–45. Canberra: National Museum of Australia.

Nugent, Maria. 2009. *Captain Cook Was Here.* Cambridge: Cambridge University Press.

Obeyesekere, Gananath. 1992. *The Apotheosis of Captain Cook: European Mythmaking in the Pacific.* Princeton, NJ: Princeton University Press; Honolulu: Bishop Museum Press.

Office of Hawaiian Affairs Newsletter. 2006. Discussion Forum – Perspectives on the Kawaihae burial controversy. January 2006: 7.

Paini, Anna and Elisabetta Gnecchi-Ruscone (eds). 2011. *Putting People First: Dialogo interculturale immaginado il futuro in Oceania.* Special issue of *La Ricerca Folklorica* 63 (April).

Pang, Gordon Y.K. 2006. 'Gifts to Cook come back to Pacific'. *Honolulu Advertiser*, 4 February. Online: the.honoluluadvertiser.com/ article/2006/Feb/04/In/FP602040330.html (accessed 1 March 2016).

Price, Sally. 2007. *Paris Primitive: Jacques Chirac's Museum on the Quai Branly.* Chicago: University of Chicago Press.

Raymond, Rosanna and Amiria Salmond (eds). 2008. *Pasifika Styles: Artists inside the Museum.* Cambridge: University of Cambridge Museum of Archaeology and Anthropology.

Sahlins, Marshall. 1995. *How 'Natives' Think. About Captain Cook, For Example*. Chicago: University of Chicago Press. doi.org/10.7208/chicago/9780226733715.001.0001.

———. 1989. 'Captain Cook at Hawaii'. *Journal of the Polynesian Society* 98(4): 371–423.

———. 1985. *Islands of History*. Chicago: University of Chicago Press.

———. 1982. 'The apotheosis of Captain Cook'. In *Between Belief and Transgression: Structuralist Essays in Religion, History and Myth*, ed. Michel Izard and Pierre Smith, pp. 73–102. Chicago: University of Chicago Press.

Salmond, Anne. 2003. *The Trial of the Cannibal Dog: Captain Cook in the South Seas*. London: Allen Lane, Penguin Books.

Smith, Bernard. 1992. 'Cook's posthumous reputation'. In *Imagining the Pacific: In the Wake of the Cook Voyages*, pp. 225–40. Carlton: Melbourne University Press at the Miegunyah Press.

———. 1985 [1960]. *European Vision and the South Pacific, 1768–1850*, 2nd edition. Sydney: Harper & Row.

Stillman, Amy Kuʻuleialoha. n.d. 'On academic voyages of encounter'. Ms in author's collection.

Strathern, Marilyn. 1988. *The Gender of the Gift: Problems with Women and Problems with Society in Melanesia*. Berkeley: University of California Press. doi.org/10.1525/california/9780520064232.001.0001.

Tapsell, Paul. 2009. 'Footprints in the sand: Banks's Māori collection, Cook's first voyage 1768–71'. In *Discovering Cook's Collections*, ed. Michelle Hetherington and Howard Morphy, pp. 92–111. Canberra: National Museum of Australia.

Tengan, Ty P Kāwika. 2016. 'The mana of Kū: Indigenous nationhood, masculinity and authority in Hawaiʻi'. In *New Mana: Transformations of a Classic Concept in Pacific Languages and Cultures*, ed. Matt Tomlinson and Ty P Kāwika Tengan, pp. 55–75. Canberra: ANU Press. Online: press-files.anu.edu.au/downloads/press/p343683/pdf/ch02.pdf (accessed 5 August 2016).

Thomas, Nicholas. 2003. *Discoveries: the Voyages of Captain Cook*. London: Allen Lane, Penguin Books.

——. 1997. 'Liberty and license: New Zealand societies in Cook voyage anthropology'. In *In Oceania. Visions, Artifacts, Histories*, pp. 71–92. Durham and London: Duke University Press.

——. 1996. '"On the varieties of the human species": Forster's comparative ethnology'. Introduction to new edition of J.R. Forster, *Observations Made During a Voyage Round the World on Physical Geography, Natural History and Ethic Philosophy*, pp. xxiii–xl. Honolulu: University of Hawai'i Press.

——. 1995. *Oceanic Art*. London: Thames and Hudson.

——. 1994. 'Licensed curiosity: Cook's Pacific voyages'. In *The Cultures of Collecting*, ed. John Elsner and Roger Cardinal, pp. 116–36, 281–82. London: Reaktion Books.

Wong, Sterling Kini. 2006a. 'Burial group resists court order'. In *Office of Hawaiian Affairs Newsletter*, January 2006: 6.

——. 2006b. 'Burial dispute goes to mediation'. In *Office of Hawaiian Affairs Newsletter*, February 2006: 9.

——. 2006c. 'Forbes Cave objects reportedly returned to Bishop Museum'. In *Office of Hawaiian Affairs Newsletter*, October 2006: 8.

3

Kanak Engraved Bamboos: Stories of the Past, Stories of the Present

Roberta Colombo Dougoud

Introduction

A few months after being appointed curator of the Oceanic department at the Musée d'ethnographie de Genève (MEG) in September 1999, I was called in by Dr Louis Necker, the museum director. He took me to a tiny room adjacent to his office, a kind of dark back stage where things were kept out of sight, but not away from memory. With the serious voice of someone leaving his will, he handed me nine large dusty boxes, pronouncing solemnly the following words: 'Dear Madam, I am entrusting to your care these boxes that I myself received when I became director. Inside is the entire work of Marguerite Lobsiger-Dellenbach on the engraved bamboos of New Caledonia. I hope that you will do something. Unfortunately, I myself have not had the time.'

Being the curious woman I am, I eagerly opened the cartons, one after the other. I still remember very clearly how I felt: like a child in front of a box full of toys. As I opened the containers, I was submerged by books, letters, articles, but particularly by dozens and dozens of rolls of tracing paper reproducing bizarre motifs. I woke up from this state of confusion with some vague ideas of a story that might be staged and told through artefacts: a type of object (the engraved bamboos), a woman (Marguerite Lobsiger-Dellenbach, former MEG director), and a people (the Kanak). This was the beginning of an extraordinary journey, an intellectual, professional and personal experience which took me from Geneva to Nouméa, from a small country surrounded by mountains to a land cradled by the waves of the ocean, from a past when Kanak artists fixed important events on bamboos, to a present where contemporary artists reconnected with this ancient tradition, renewing it in order to vehicle messages to the new generations.

Some years later, in February 2008, the exhibition *Bambous kanak. Une passion de Marguerite Lobsiger-Dellenbach* (Kanak bamboos: Marguerite Lobsiger-Dellenbach's great passion) was inaugurated in Geneva, showing the MEG's important collection of Kanak engraved bamboos and the pioneering work of Marguerite Lobsiger-Dellenbach.[1]

Kanak engraved bamboos

The engraved bamboos (Figure 6) are among the most original works of Kanak art. As the name itself indicates, these are bamboo tubes of varying length and diameter that are engraved or pyrographed. Their entire surface covered with geometric and figurative etchings, they depict with impressive precision and skill many aspects of Kanak life and of the European irruption since the nineteenth century. According to French missionary and anthropologist Maurice Leenhardt (1937: 110), whenever Kanak ventured outside their villages they carried with them an engraved bamboo to ward off danger along the way. The bamboos were sometimes filled with magical herbs for protection. Father Pierre Lambert reported that the old people carried an engraved bamboo like a cane and recounted the exploits and mishaps of their ancestors by referring to the engraved designs (1900: 67–68). To their owners, these objects were at the same time visual prompts, memory aids for speakers in storytelling, devices to remember important events (Vieillard and Deplanche 1862–1863), rollers on which to inscribe their most vivid impressions in order to share them with others (Leenhardt 1937: 111).

---

1   For a presentation of the exhibition see Cousteau 2008b and Paini 2010.

Figure 6. Kanak engraved bamboos

Source. Used with permission of Musée d'ethnographie de Genève © MEG, photographed by Johnathan Watts

In the inventories of museums engraved bamboo have often been registered as chief's staff (*bâton de chef*), magician's stick (*bâton de magicien*), walking stick (*bâton de voyage*) or ceremonial staff (*bâton de cérémonie*). However, these designations are inexact, because these items were not used as canes and did not belong to a single leader or magician. They were then called 'engraved bamboos' which according to Maurice Leenhardt is the only name given by Kanak (Leenhardt 1937: 109) or, in the Ajië language, *kārè e tā*, as reported in the myth 'Les deux sœurs Moaxa' (Leenhardt 1932: 90).

The bamboo tube was carved while it was still green because, once cut, it begins to dry out very quickly and becomes very difficult to engrave. In some cases it was pyrographed. The etchings were done using quartz crystals, claws of crustaceans, seashells, and more recently metal blades or improvised knives. The tube was then either rubbed with oil extracted from the bankul nut tree or with lampblack, or it was held over a fire, allowing the soot to deposit into the incised parts. In this way, the engraved patterns emerged starkly in black on the clear golden yellow surface of the bamboo.

Collected between 1850 and 1920, the Kanak engraved bamboos date mainly from the nineteenth century. Their production ceased around 1917, the date of one of the major anti-colonial revolts in New Caledonia (Boulay 1993: 27). We do not know the exact causes of this abandonment, but we could suggest the destruction of the chiefs' huts as well as the breakdown of Kanak society under pressure from colonisation and evangelisation. The disappearance of this practice went together with the spread of writing. Paper would have progressively replaced bamboo as a support for memorisation. This would confirm the hypothesis that engraved bamboos' principal function was to fix the most important events in an oral culture (Ohlen 1999: 197). Nevertheless, despite interruption in the practice of engraving bamboos, their graphic expression continues to be an emblematic dimension of Kanak identity to this day.

In order to understand the language of this art form, we must plunge back into the New Caledonia of the nineteenth century. These true 'comic strips' (Métais-Daudré 1973) allow us to reconstruct Kanak material and ceremonial activities as well as their encounter with colonial oppression. Very seldom are Kanak traditional life scenes depicted on their own. In most cases they are represented on the same tube together with motifs inspired by colonisation. In her remarkable work on Kanak engraved bamboos, Carole Ohlen (1987) has classified the incised motifs into two groups: the first includes figurative scenes depicting either Kanak traditional life or the life of Europeans, the second group comprises geometric patterns (Figure 7).[2] By observing the engravings carefully we can recognise scenes of everyday life: fishing, hunting, yam and taro

---

2   Carole Ohlen (1987) analysed 84 bamboos, which she numbered and classified by topic. Each item is accompanied by a series of relevant information such as the name given in the register, the museum where the bamboo is stored, its inventory number, the donor's name, the date of entry into the museum, its dimension, a general description, its tracing, and the related bibliography.

cultivations (Figure 8), villages with the cleared avenue leading to the chief's hut (Figure 9), but also the myths, rituals, *pilou*,[3] and mourning (Figure 10). The engravers represented what they saw and, as the main centres of missionary and colonial occupation were close to Kanak villages, they also described colonial life in its numerous aspects: European houses with four-sided roofs, horses mounted or harnessed to a buggy, sailing vessels or steamboats, agricultural and carpentry tools, punitive expeditions, soldiers (Figures 11 and 12) and of course military uniforms. As related by Roger Boulay (1993: 70) the uniforms of the colonial infantry played an important role in Kanak social life. Associated with the military supremacy of the occupant, tunics with stripes were used by the French administrators as insignia of authority, and were offered to the Kanak leaders allied with them.

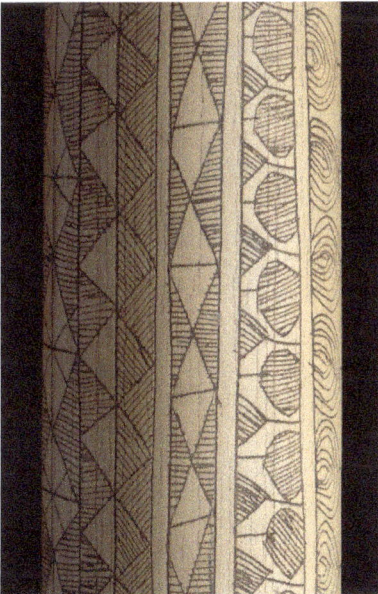

Figure 7. Kanak engraved bamboo with geometric patterns

Source. Used with permission of Musée d'ethnographie de Genève Inv. ETHOC 011682 © MEG, photographed by Johnathan Watts

Figure 8. Detail of Kanak engraved bamboo illustrating taro cultivation

Source. Used with permission of Musée d'ethnographie de Genève Inv. ETHOC 020507 © MEG, photographed by Johnathan Watts

---

3   *Pilou* is a generic term for various Kanak ritualised exchanges and ceremonies.

Figure 9. Detail of Kanak engraved bamboo illustrating the chief's hut

Source. Used with permission of Musée d'ethnographie de Genève Inv. ETHOC 012938 © MEG, photographed by Johnathan Watts

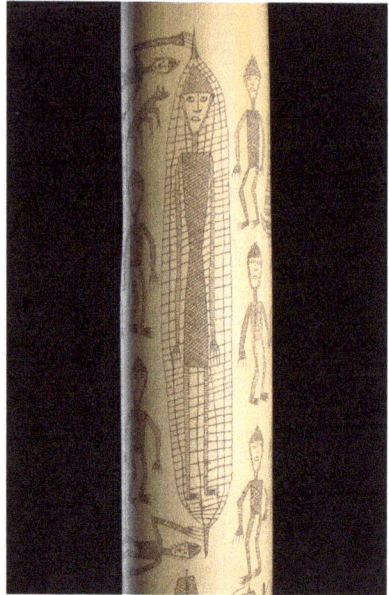

Figure 10. Detail of Kanak engraved bamboo illustrating mourning

Source. Used with permission of Musée d'ethnographie de Genève Inv. ETHOC 022862 © MEG, photographed by Johnathan Watts

But engraved bamboos can also be seen as indicators of how the Kanak perceived and judged European colonisation. With extraordinary lucidity and a meticulous attention to detail, the engraver of a bamboo held at MEG has shown the vices introduced by Europeans. This piece constitutes a severe criticism and a mockery of western customs, particularly its immorality, including first of all alcoholism, hitherto unknown in New Caledonia. On the tube, we can see four soldiers in a state of evident drunkenness displaying symbols of their status, bottle, cigar, rifle and money in a parade that we imagine to be noisy and pathetic. Nearby a man is sitting at a table covered with five bottles, one of which is already partly empty (Figure 13).

Figure 11. Detail of Kanak engraved bamboo illustrating a soldier
on a horse

Source. Used with permission of Musée d'ethnographie de Genève Inv. ETHOC 031759
© MEG, photographed by Johnathan Watts

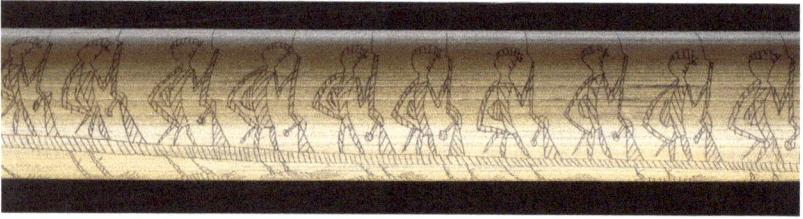

Figure 12. Detail of Kanak engraved bamboo illustrating soldiers with rifles

Source. Used with permission of Musée d'ethnographie de Genève Inv. ETHOC 041749 © MEG, photographed by Johnathan Watts

Roger Boulay (1993: 24) raises the question of the origin of engraved bamboos. Could it be an ancient practice, already common before colonisation? Or could the motifs inspired by the European presence be a proof of their late emergence in response to the influence of westerners observed by Kanak in the act of filling their sketchbooks? It is interesting to mention here one of the oldest engraved bamboos, from the Île des Pins. This entirely geometric bamboo, now vanished, was collected in 1875 by Paul Tirat, a naval officer, and exposed in 1888 by the Geographical Society of Paris on the occasion of the commemoration of the centenary of La Pérouse's death. Extremely rare, the engravings were explicated in detail to the acquirer by one of the oldest Kanak chiefs of the Île des Pins, owner of the object. We learn that the entanglement of the engraved geometric figures related one of the first European landings on the island. The zigzag lines indicate the distress of the Kanak at the view of strangers, two sets of diamonds represented the Kanak tribes and the newcomers rushing to assault each other. A series of rifles pointed towards the diamonds symbolising the indigenous groups was placed between these two sets of patterns (Boulay 1993: 20–22). According to historian Georges Pisier (quoted by Ohlen 1987, vol. 1: 25), this story certainly refers to the arrival of *La Boussole* and of *L'Astrolabe*, La Pérouse's ships, on the shores of the Île des Pins in 1788. As soon as the crew had disembarked, their many riches and tools excited the envy of natives who attempted to seize them. The Europeans' reaction was immediate and brutal; three Kanak were killed by carbine bullets.

The example of this bamboo along with the old Kanak chief's explanation shows that the geometric patterns are far from being meaningless. This stylised iconographic vocabulary seems to have been a privileged mode of expression before the European arrival fostered a more figurative language. The latter style was apparently already employed, but it was developed further under the influence of newcomers and attests to the existence of an ancient tradition of geometric patterns that have gradually lost their significance in favour of figurative scenes (Ohlen 2008: 62). However, very little evidence confirms the existence of engraved bamboos before the colonial period. Therefore, as suggested by Patrice Godin in his article 'Le bambou gravé comme énigme' (2010: 5), the origin and function of engraved bamboos are still shrouded in mystery.

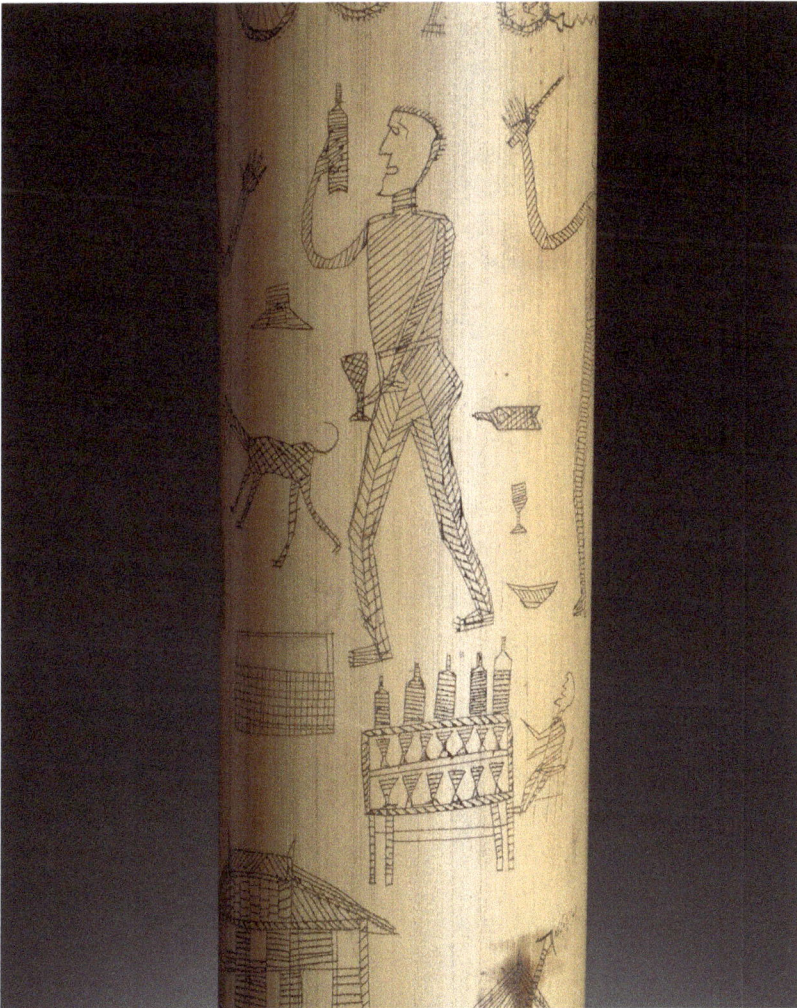

Figure 13. Detail of Kanak engraved bamboo illustrating drunken soldiers

Source. Used with permission of Musée d'ethnographie de Genève Inv. ETHOC 041750 © MEG, photographed by Johnathan Watts

Marguerite Lobsiger-Dellenbach

It is difficult to calculate the exact number of existing engraved bamboos from New Caledonia, however it is likely that around 300 specimens are stored in museums. If it is predictable that the largest collection is found in France, at the Musée du quai Branly (MQB) with its 64 bamboos, it may appear surprising that the second one, comprising 26 specimens, is in Switzerland, at the MEG. This is due to the fact that Marguerite Lobsiger-Dellenbach, who directed the MEG between 1952 and 1967, had such a strong passion for these objects to the point of becoming a world expert. But who was this woman?[4]

Marguerite-Elisabeth Dellenbach was born in Geneva on 9 July 1905. After training as a milliner and a shorthand typist, she was hired in 1922 as secretary to Professor Eugène Pittard, the MEG's founder. This modest woman became passionately interested in anthropology and decided to continue her studies, obtaining a PhD and a 'habilitation' after 13 years of hard work. Under Pittard's guidance she oversaw archaeological digs, undertook anthropological measurements and carried out field research in Europe, Western Africa, Nepal, China and the Middle East. Her thirst for discovery and her ambition led her to become first assistant and then deputy director of the MEG from 1947 to 1952. When Eugène Pittard retired, she took over the management of the museum from 1952 to 1967.

During her career, Marguerite Lobsiger-Dellenbach never ceased to explore the diversity of humankind. However, one theme accompanied her throughout her life: the engraved bamboos from New Caledonia. She was captivated by these objects to the point that she became the world's specialist on them, despite the fact that she had never visited New Caledonia. Other researchers had proposed interpretations before hers (Grünewald 1936; Luquet 1926), but she was the one who began their systematic study. Exercising the patience of a saint, alone or with Georges Lobsiger, whom she married in 1936, she copied all the details engraved on the tubes and puzzled out the meanings of the carvings of the MEG collection as well as of bamboos held by many other European museums.

---

4   For a more detailed biography of Marguerite Lobsiger-Dellenbach, see Colombo Dougoud and Wüscher 2008.

The two 'Champollion of Kanak writing', as they came to be known, saw in these works an Oceanian version of the Mesoamerican 'painted codex' recording major historical events.

From her earliest writings, Marguerite Lobsiger-Dellenbach distanced herself from a purely decorative analysis or interpretation. She complained that some authors may consider Kanak bamboos only as sketchily engraved, picturesque representations of daily life. For her they were precious ethnographic documents (Dellenbach and Lobsiger 1939: 336), a faithful translation of New Caledonian thought and a lucid vision on the encounter between two worlds. By understanding and interpreting bamboos motifs, it was possible to grasp entire chapters of the material and spiritual life of the Kanak.

When she retired, Marguerite Lobsiger-Dellenbach left the MEG an exceptional series of documents on 93 engraved bamboos. Her dream was to study the bamboos of the entire world and to write a comprehensive work on them.

Bambous kanak, a continuing tradition

In preparing the exhibition *Bambous kanak. Une passion de Marguerite Lobsiger-Dellenbach*, we faced some general difficulties and challenges, but in particular two issues were at the centre of our concerns. We wanted to underline that our interpretation of the engraved bamboos comes directly from Marguerite Lobsiger-Dellenbach's research. At the same time, presenting her research offered us an opportunity to explain to our visitors the work of an anthropologist who, through his/her assumptions, hypotheses and interpretations, makes artistic expressions intelligible to us, so that we can better appreciate their aesthetic qualities.

A second relevant issue was linked to contemporaneity. As mentioned above, the production of Kanak engraved bamboos stopped around 1917. Some of them had been collected and kept in the Musée de Nouvelle-Calédonie (MNC) in Nouméa. In recent years some contemporary artists such as Micheline Néporon, Yvette Bouquet and Paula Boi, inspired by the historical bamboos seen in museums and by publications, have revived this art form in order to express their modern-day concerns. Their remarkable artistic work assumes the same conceptual approach as that of the ancient bamboos. To these artists engraving bamboos does not mean looking back but looking ahead, towards the future. In fact, the aim of their project is not the artificial resuscitation of relics from the past, but to express contemporary identity issues. At the same time, the presence of motifs inspired by ancient engraved bamboos in the infrastructures of urban areas—such as the gate of the MNC, the patterns painted on the toll bar north of Nouméa, on the fuselages of Air Calédonie's aircraft as well as on the decorations of its travel agencies—indicate a willingness to reintegrate Kanak cultural elements into a highly westernised urban landscape (Cousteau 2008a: 70). As stated by Diane Cousteau (ibid.: 71), Kanak contemporary artists consider the old engraved bamboos as a source of inspiration, a tradition that they perpetuate, adapt and re-actualise.

Micheline Néporon and her bamboos

During the preparation of the exhibition *Bambous kanak. Une passion de Marguerite Lobsiger-Dellenbach*, we were able to acquire four bamboos engraved by Micheline Néporon. Born in the Unia tribe, in the Yaté region of New Caledonia on 8 October 1955, Micheline Néporon (Figure 14) is one of the most prominent contemporary Kanak artists, and one of the first Kanak women to devote herself to art. She currently lives in Nouméa where she unremittingly pursues her career as an artist.

As a little girl she wanted to become a nun following the example of Sister Caro,[5] her mother's sister, but once grown up, she found it difficult to make her own way. Two events were to leave a mark on her and determine the course of her life. In September 1975, she attended the Mélanésia 2000 festival organised by Jean-Marie Tjibaou, the first cultural manifestation in the country that aimed at demonstrating the strength and richness of Kanak culture to the Kanak themselves, while at the same time introducing Europeans to it. Gathering 2,000 Kanak and involving 50,000 spectators, this great celebration marked the beginning of a cultural renaissance for the Kanak people. For the first time Kanak culture was presented as living, as opposed to a culture doomed to disappearance. For Micheline Néporon, as for many other Kanak, Mélanésia 2000 was a revelation.

---

5   Caroline Newedou (1922–2008), better known as Sister Caro, was an emblematic figure in New Caledonia acknowledged for her engagement in different social activities.

Figure 14. Micheline Néporon

Source. Used with permission of © ADCK – centre culturel Jean-Marie Tjibaou, photographed by David Becker

But another event was going to change the direction of her life. After many odd jobs in catering, house-care and as a lady's companion, she fell ill, a heart disease that forced her to spend two months in hospital. During her convalescence, she kept drawing (Néporon and Bachelot 1991: 71–76), an activity that she has been practising since 1975. She discovered that this was her vocation, and decided to take painting classes. In 1983 she studied with Giovanni Righi at the Academy of Drawing and Painting and 1985 with Jean-Pierre (Jipé) Le Bars at the Office Culturel Scientifique et Technique Canaque in order to learn different techniques (oil, watercolour, Indian ink) and to diversify support. From 1984 to 1985 she ran some art workshops for children at the Centre Récréatif de la Jeunesse and began to exhibit and sell her work. She was noticed by the manager of the gallery Galéria, where her work has been exhibited regularly since 1987.

From 1985 she began drawing motifs inspired by the engraved bamboos she had first seen at the MNC. She adopted their engraving technique and extended it to other media: canvas, banyan bark, stones and scratchboard using watercolours, acrylics and Indian ink. She freely transposed the traditional technique and drew on different media in order to release the gesture and allow curved lines.

In 1990, she participated in the collective exhibition *Ko I Névâ. Sculpteurs et Peintres kanak d'aujourd'hui*, organised by the Agency for the Development of Kanak Culture (ADCK). Presented first at Nouméa at the MNC and then travelling throughout New Caledonia for three months, the exhibition was seen by more than 12,000 visitors. The aim was to celebrate and to present a clear picture of the status of contemporary Kanak art, to make an inventory of Kanak painters and sculptors, to present '"the soul of our country", conceived by the A.D.C.K. as a survey of the Kanak cultural reality of today' (Togna 1992: 12).

At the end of 1990, Micheline Néporon received a two-year scholarship (Bourse Territoriale de Formation) and left for France to pursue her studies at the Fine Arts Institute in Bordeaux. On the occasion of the exhibition, *De jade et de nacre. Patrimoine artistique kanak*,[6] in Paris, an exhibition on

---

6   The exhibition, *De jade et de nacre. Patrimoine artistique kanak* was first presented in Nouméa, at the Musée territorial de Nouvelle-Calédonie (today MNC) and then in Paris at the Musée national des arts d'Afrique et d'Océanie. For this occasion, 200 objects were borrowed mostly from the French provincial museums and from other European museums.

her work, *Micheline Neporon, artiste kanak,*[7] was presented at the Musée en Herbe de la Halle Saint-Pierre. In 1992, she continued her training at the Luminy Architectural Fine Arts Institute in Marseille. While in France she had the opportunity to meet many people and see several exhibitions, in a certain way widening her horizons, but she was always aware of the richness of her own cultural heritage. As she writes, 'By immersing myself in Western culture, I felt that I myself had a culture, the Kanak way of thinking and living, a very rich heritage' (Néporon 1993: n.p., my translation).

In 1992, she was part of the New Caledonia delegation to the Festival of Pacific Arts in Rarotonga, in the Cook Islands. The Festival of Pacific Arts is a travelling festival hosted every four years by a different country in Oceania. Following the success of the first festival held at Suva (Fiji) from 6–20 May 1972, it was decided to repeat the experience every four years, each time in a different South Pacific country. Since then, delegations from 27 Pacific Island countries and territories have come together to share and exchange their cultures. Conceived by the Conference of the South Pacific Commission (now the Pacific Community), this was meant as an attempt to combat the erosion of traditional cultural practices. Fearing that the younger generations might be tempted away from their cultural heritage by the introduction of western values, technologies and entertainment, it was established in order to help preserve and develop various local art forms, as well as to provide an occasion for Pacific Islanders to meet, share and celebrate their cultural heritage (Carell 1992; Stevenson 2002).

During the Festival of Pacific Arts in Rarotonga, Micheline Néporon was impressed by the work done by artists from other countries, by the variety of techniques used and by their way of combining their heritage with new technologies, medias and messages, in a word by their capacity to experiment. Back in New Caledonia, she spent a month in Unia with her people, and participated in all the daily and ritual activities such as mourning, weddings and everyday life. As she explained herself (Néporon 1993), this made her want to reproduce all these activities on bamboos. She had already thought of this possibility upon her return from France, and suddenly the penny dropped. She started to revive the traditional technique of engraving bamboos herself—rather than simply painting the motifs inspired by engraved bamboos with Indian ink on paper, as she had been doing since 1985. She restored Kanak bamboos to their primordial

---

7   A catalogue was published by Micheline Néporon and Roger Boulay (1990).

function as supports for narratives and memories. For her this was a way of renewing the work of the elders, updating their techniques to express the Kanak's changing world.

For the past 30 years, Micheline Néporon has exhibited widely throughout New Caledonia, France, New Zealand, Australia, Mali, Cook Islands and Vanuatu. Her work is represented in many private and public collections including the Kanak and Oceanian Contemporary Art Collection at the Jean-Marie Tjibaou Cultural Center in Nouméa, the MEG and the MQB. She has developed a personal style that aims to show the coexistence of tradition and modernity and their consequences on the lifestyles of contemporary Kanak. Inspired by models that are now kept in museums, her creations reflect a quest for her roots, but at the same time they testify to her need to look at reality from a contemporary perspective (Gama 2008: 93). She puts the people and culture of New Caledonia today at the centre of her art, and works to reconcile custom with western culture; in her works, scenes of indigenous women with their children and men, dancing in traditional dress, are combined with tokens of modernity and westernisation such as cell phones, radio, motorboats. In the catalogue to a personal exhibition presented at the Jean-Marie Tjibaou Cultural Center, *Gû te mâ, racines de banian*, she is descried thus: 'Sensitive and imaginative, she conveys the nostalgia she feels for the world of her childhood, and her desire to help today's young Kanak acquire a better understanding of their own culture, and thus of their identity' (Togna 2004: 4).

Micheline Néporon believes that art is a means of empowerment and emancipation for Kanak women. But at the same time art has a pedagogical capacity, a capacity to convey a message: 'As an artist, I must send a message. Each one of my paintings is a signpost' (cited in Togna 2004: 4). Her works bear witness to the enduring values that underpin Kanak society, but they also denounce the new scourges afflicting the Kanak settlements, the malaise of their young people, the ill effects of alcohol and violence (Tjibaou 2008: 9). She worries about the difficulties faced by young people, apathy towards alcohol, cannabis and traffic accidents.

One of her bamboos conserved at the MEG is particularly representative of her attitude. Engraved in 2005, it has been entitled *Halte à l'alcool* (Stop to alcohol) by Micheline herself. The story illustrated is a common one, which too often takes place on the roads not only in New Caledonia, but all over the world. It begins in a suburban area as suggested by public housing buildings whose rigid appearance contrasts with the nearby bucolic landscape and a traditional hut, reminding us that we are in New Caledonia. We also see large trees, one of which is filled with fruit. A cow is grazing (Figure 15). Below, next to a radio playing at high volume, a young couple is dancing with bottles, the girl is holding one in her mouth (Figure 16). At their feet, empty cans litter the ground. The story continues with a damaged minibus, crashed against a tree (Figure 17). An unconscious person is lying on the ground while someone is trying to assist him. Two rescuers are rushing with a stretcher while a policeman is already on site (Figure 18). But this drama is not isolated. Another vehicle has just had an accident by an embankment. Its distraught occupants are getting out while a rescue helicopter approaches.

Figure 15. *Halte à l'alcool* (Stop to alcohol). Detail of Kanak engraved bamboo by Micheline Néporon

Source. Used with permission of Musée d'ethnographie de Genève Inv. ETHOC 064815 © MEG, photographed by Johnathan Watts

Figure 16. A girl drinking from a bottle of alcohol. Detail of Kanak engraved bamboo by Micheline Néporon

Source. Used with permission of Musée d'ethnographie de Genève Inv. ETHOC 064815 © MEG, photographed by Johnathan Watts

Figure 17. A damaged minibus, crashed into a tree. Detail of Kanak engraved bamboo by Micheline Néporon

Source. Used with permission of Musée d'ethnographie de Genève Inv. ETHOC 064815 © MEG, photographed by Johnathan Watts

Figure 18. An unconscious person lying on the ground. Detail of Kanak engraved bamboo by Micheline Néporon

Source. Used with permission of Musée d'ethnographie de Genève MEG Inv. ETHOC 064815 © MEG, photographed by Johnathan Watts

From Geneva to Nouméa and back

It was between 1840 and 1890, during the so-called 'Museum Period' (Sturtevant 1969) that most ethnographic collections were built up with the purpose of gathering the material heritage of peoples of the colonised countries who were considered to be dying out. Museums as cultural institutions had the task of safeguarding their cultural expressions for the future. Collecting was a one-way relationship deriving from a principle of colonial inequality: artefacts and information about their origin, production, function and use went from people all over the world to the museums. Their curatorial and institutional authority consolidated the knowledge (Peers and Brown 2003: 1). Over the last 40 years, this relationship has deeply changed. Not only physical ownership of the objects but also the right of representing their meaning have become issues of contention (Stocking 1985). Shifts towards a more two-way type of relationship can be observed. Indigenous interests, values and perspectives are increasingly taken into account by museum curators and some source communities have started to cooperate with them in the context of the management of their ethnographic collections. In this changing power relation, museums are no longer the sole voice of authority and new paradigms for a critic and reflexive museography are discussed (Karp and Lavine 1991). Aware of the political, identity, cultural and social stakes involved in the representation of their culture in a museum, source communities wish to be no longer merely spectators, but active players, who claim the right to speak about themselves and their heritage. It is in this context of confrontation that the demands for retreat from display or for repatriation of human remains and of sensible objects must be understood (Edwards, Gosden and Phillips 2006; Fforde, Hubert and Turnbull 2002).

Noteworthy and inspiring is the perspective developed in New Caledonia which considers the Kanak objects stored abroad as ambassadors of Kanak culture. In the 1980s, at the bequest of Jean-Marie Tjibaou, French anthropologist Roger Boulay undertook an extensive project to locate the Kanak collections in Europe and metropolitan France. The aim was not to carry out an exhaustive inventory of what is known as 'dispersed Kanak heritage' but to build a database of the major museums holding Kanak artistic heritage (Boulay 2006: 36). This project led to the exhibition *De jade et de nacre. Patrimoine artistique kanak* first presented in Nouméa at the Musée Territorial de Nouvelle Calédonie from March to May 1990 and then in Paris at the Musée National des Arts Africains et Océaniens from October to December of the same year.[8] In order to prepare for the temporary return of dispersed heritage to New Caledonia, Roger Boulay and Emmanuel Kasarhérou, the exhibition curators, undertook a series of visits to different communities so that they could not only explain the exhibition aims and contents, but also understand people's expectations and anticipate their reactions. Emmanuel Kasarhérou (2005: 286) was willing to display a *gwâ mie*, a head of Kanak currency, held at the Musée d'ethnographie de Neuchâtel (MEN) that had been donated in 1910 by Maurice Leenhardt. He had received this extraordinary piece from the Misikoéo (Miyikwéö) clan, Kasarhérou's clan. When elders from Kasarhérou's family saw the object they were astonished by its artistic and cultural value. They did not ask for the final return of the object to New Caledonia because they did not know the reasons, or the conditions in which it had been offered. Given its symbolic importance, the elders thought it had been given to Maurice Leenhardt probably following a conversion to Christianity. They declared that they could not go back on a given word. Rather, they were grateful to Switzerland to have kept the *gwâ mie* and to have allowed them to see it. In the discussion between the Agency for the Development of Kanak Culture and the elders, it was determined not to actively seek the return of any of these objects, many of which have spent up to 150 years away from New Caledonia (and which, according to traditional beliefs, may be dangerous in cases in which the conditions of acquisition are unknown). As Emmanuel Kasarhérou explained in an interview to Anna Paini and Adriano Favole in 2007, these objects had indisputably left; nevertheless, they should not be considered as an absence, as something that was missing. They were far away because they had been sent in order to accomplish a specific task, that of becoming messengers, ambassadors who create connections and open paths. Having travelled and been exposed abroad, these objects should be considered as 'ambassadors' of Kanak culture, employed to let the rest of the world know that Kanak exist (Paini and Favole 2007: 10–11).

I think that these reflections will help us to understand the spirit of the exhibitions on the Kanak engraved bamboos held in 2008 at the MEG, but also the collaboration with the MNC, which gave birth to a more elaborate exhibition on engraved bamboos. *Entre-vues sur Bambous*

---

8   More than 20 years later the extensive and comprehensive research on the dispersed kanak heritage led to a major exhibition *Kanak, l'Art est une Parole* presented at the MQB from October 2013 to January 2014 and then in a reduced version at the Jean-Marie Tjibaou Cultural Center in Nouméa from March to June 2014.

kanak, de Genève à Nouméa opened in Nouméa in March 2010.[9] The title proposed by the MNC team underlines that it is an encounter, a dialogue, a collaboration around Kanak bamboos, a sharing of gazes and knowledge. And, indeed, the MNC didn't just host MEG's exhibition; together, in partnership, we created a new exhibition.

Entre-vues sur Bambous kanak, de Genève à Nouméa was a great chance for curators to experiment with forms of collaboration and knowledge sharing, for people from New Caledonia to see for the first time such a rich presentation of engraved bamboos, and also for the MEG bamboos, historical and contemporary, to acquire new strength and power, to revitalise themselves back home before continuing to play their role of ambassadors of Kanak existence.

References

Boulay, Roger. 2006. 'Les collections océaniennes dans les collections publiques françaises: état des lieux', *Mwà Véé* 54: 34–44.

——. 1993. *Le bambou gravé kanak*. Marseille: Éditions Parenthèses / Agence de développement de la culture kanak.

Carell, Victor. 1992. 'The purpose, origin and future of festivals of Pacific arts'. *Pacific Arts* 5: 1–5.

Colombo Dougoud, Roberta and Lorin Wüscher. 2008. 'Marguerite Lobsiger-Dellenbach et les bambous kanak: une femme, une passion, un peuple'. In *Bambous kanak. Une passion de Marguerite Lobsiger-Dellenbach*, ed. Roberta Colombo Dougoud, pp. 17–35. Gollion and Genève: Infolio and Musée d'ethnographie de Genève.

Cousteau, Diane. 2008a. 'Les bambous gravés dans la Nouvelle-Calédonie contemporaine'. In *Bambous kanak. Une passion de Marguerite Lobsiger-Dellenbach*, ed. Roberta Colombo Dougoud, pp. 69–79. Gollion and Genève: Infolio and Musée d'ethnographie de Genève.

——. 2008b. 'Scénographie et sensorialité'. *Totem* 51: 8–9.

---

9   For a presentation of the exhibition, see Paini 2010.

Dellenbach, Marguerite and Georges Lobsiger. 1939. 'Quelques scènes de la vie sociale, religieuse et matérielle des Néo-Calédoniens, gravées sur bambou'. *Archives suisse d'Anthropologie générale* VIII(3–4): 336–50.

Edwards, Elizabeth, Chris Gosden and Ruth Phillips (eds). 2006. *Sensible Objects: Colonialism, Museums and Material Culture*. London: Berg Publishers.

Fforde, Cressida, Jane Hubert and Paul Turnbull (eds). 2002. *The Dead and their Possessions: Repatriation in Principle, Policy and Practice*. London and New York: Routledge.

Gama, Henri. 2008. 'Micheline Néporon, la tresseuse d'histoires'. In *Bambous kanak. Une passion de Marguerite Lobsiger-Dellenbach*, ed. Roberta Colombo Dougoud, pp. 91–93. Gollion et Genève: Infolio et Musée d'ethnographie de Genève.

Godin, Patrice. 2010. 'Le bambou gravé comme énigme'. In *Entre-vues sur Bambous kanak, de Genève à Nouméa*, ed. Solange Néaoutyine, p. 5. Éditions du musée de Nouvelle-Calédonie, Nouméa: Service des Musées et du Patrimoine.

Grünewald, Roland. 1936. 'Trois bambous gravés néo-calédoniens inédits'. *L'Anthropologie* T. 46: 633–40.

Karp, Ivan and Steven D. Lavine (eds). 1991. *Exhibiting Cultures. The Poetics and Politics of Museum Display*. Washington D.C. and London: Smithsonian Institution Press.

Kasarhérou, Emmanuel. 2005. 'L'ambassadeur du brouillard blanc'. In *Cent ans d'ethnographie sur la colline de Saint-Nicolas*, ed. Marc-Olivier Gonseth, Jacques Hainard and Roland Kaehr, pp. 285–86. Neuchâtel, Musée d'ethnographie.

Lambert, Pierre. 1900. *Mœurs et superstitions des Néo-Calédoniens*. Nouméa: Nouvelle Imprimerie Nouméenne.

Leenhardt, Maurice. 1937. *Gens de la grande terre. Nouvelle-Calédonie*. Paris: Gallimard.

——. 1932. *Documents néo-calédoniens*. Paris: Institut d'Ethnologie.

Luquet, Georges-Henri. 1926. *L'art Néo-Calédonien. Documents recueillis par Marius Archambault, directeur du service des postes et télégraphes en Nouvelle-Calédonie*. Paris: Institut d'Ethnologie.

Métais-Daudré, Éliane. 1973. *Les Bandes dessinées des Canaques*. Paris: Mouton.

Néporon, Micheline. 1993. *Geïra. Le lieu d'où je suis*. Nouméa: Agence de développement de la culture kanak.

Néporon, Micheline and Suzanne Bachelot. 1991. '*Kungô Bré: 'Les racines de l'arbre nouveau'. Paroles de femmes kanak de la tribu d'Unia (Yat*é)'. Nouméa: Agence de développement de la culture kanak.

Néporon, Micheline and Roger Boulay. 1990. *Micheline Néporon, artiste kanak*. Paris: Halle Saint-Pierre.

Ohlen, Carole. 2008. 'L'art traditionnel du bambou gravé kanak'. In *Bambous kanak. Une passion de Marguerite Lobsiger-Dellenbach*, ed. Roberta Colombo Dougoud, pp. 47–66. Gollion and Genève: Infolio and Musée d'ethnographie de Genève.

——. 1999. 'Les bambous gravés'. In *Chroniques du pays kanak*, ed. Orso Filippi, pp. 196–207. Nouméa: Planète Mémo, III, éd.

——. 1987. *Iconographie des bambous gravés de Nouvelle-Calédonie. Objets et "décors"*, vols 1 et 2, Mémoire de Maîtrise en Esthétique et Sciences de l'Art, Paris I, Paris: Panthéon-Sorbonne.

Paini, Anna. 2010. 'Bambù kanak: objets de relation. Da Ginevra a Nouméa con una postilla genovese'. *Antropologia Museale* 27: 60–64.

Paini, Anna and Adriano Favole. 2007. 'Intervista a Emmanuel Kasarhérou'. *Antropologia Museale* 5(16): 7–16.

Peers, Laura and Alison K. Brown (eds). 2003. *Museums and Source Communities: A Routledge Reader*. New York: Routledge.

Stevenson, Karen. 2002. 'The Festival of Pacific Arts: Its past, its future'. *Pacific Arts* 25: 31–40.

Stocking, George W. Jr. (ed.). 1985. *Objects and Others: Essays on Museums and Material Culture*. Madison: University of Wisconsin Press.

Sturtevant, William C. 1969. 'Does anthropology need museums?' *Proceedings of the Biological Society of Washington* 82: 619–50.

Tjibaou, Marie-Claude. 2008. 'Avant-propos'. In *Bambous kanak. Une passion de Marguerite Lobsiger-Dellenbach*, ed. Roberta Colombo Dougoud, pp. 7–9. Gollion and Genève: Infolio and Musée d'ethnographie de Genève.

Togna, Octave. 1992. 'The kanak fiber. La fibre kanak'. In *Sculpteurs et Peintres Kanak contemporains. Ko i Névâ*, ed. Cristina D. Chaplain, pp. 12–13. Nouméa: Agence de développement de la culture kanak.

Togna, Octave (ed.). 2004. *Gû te mâ, racines de banian. Banyan Roots. Micheline Néporon*. Nouméa: Agence de développement de la culture kanak.

Vieillard, Eugène and Émile Deplanche. 1862–1863. 'Essais sur la Nouvelle-Calédonie'. *Revue Maritime et Coloniale* VII, Paris.

4

Re-dressing Materiality: *Robes Mission* from 'Colonial' to 'Cultural' Object, and Entrepreneurship of Kanak Women in Lifou

Anna Paini

'Colored textiles for Terra Madre' read the caption of a photograph of a Kanak woman from Lifou wearing a *robe mission* (mission dress) at the opening ceremony of Terra Madre 2008;[1] I had not expected that the Kanak delegation present at this international bi-annual event organised by Slow Food in Turin, where for the first time natural fibre producers were invited, would attract such interest and be one of the most photographed. Even women from Central Asian countries dressed in clothes made with precious, finely ornamented hand-woven fabrics wanted to be photographed with Kanak women, who wore *robes mission* tailored from an industrial printed cotton fabric with floral motifs, white on a red background. The choice of fabric (colour and floral motifs) was made by a member of the delegation. I later realised that it was the colour code of the village in Lifou, Loyalty Islands, where the woman and her husband (a pastor of the Evangelical Church) were living at the time.

---

1   See Terra Madre Salone del Gusto website 2008. The picture accompanying an article on natural fibres appeared in the supplement devoted to the event in the daily newspaper *la Repubblica* (Torino), October 24 2008: v.

One of the people eager to be photographed with the Kanak wanted to be reassured that it was their 'traditional costume'; her question brought home to me the reason beneath this fascination for the *robe mission*. It was perceived by other participants as the Kanak costume, a dress that is standardised not only in form but also in colours and motifs, and thus the red and white fabric with floral motifs was perceived as a conventional element of the traditional Kanak dress, rather than a choice related to the occasion.

I start from this vignette to look into the complex semantic and symbolic dimensions of the *robe mission*, an article of clothing of colonial origin worn by Kanak women in Lifou, and more generally in Kanaky New Caledonia. It is an introduced garment, which has been appropriated by Kanak women and incorporated into their customary and daily life as a versatile outfit: worn on important and formal occasions, its life continues as a garment for working in the fields and then, once old, crumpled and torn, finishes its life as a useful rag. In time its materiality, meanings and values have been transformed. As Igor Kopytoff has argued 'what is significant about the adoption of alien objects—as of alien ideas—is not the fact that they are adopted, but the way they are culturally redefined and put to use' (1986: 67). And as Nicholas Thomas has remarked concerning the introduction of clothing by missionaries in this part of the world, 'it is most evident that these garments have not been inflicted, but adopted by entirely dignified women' (2005: ix).

The dress of very light cotton gauze, which today reaches below the calf, in the 1980s and 1990s could be worn buttoned at the front or at the back.[2] The versatility of this article of clothing is such that it has also been adopted by cricket players. In this, the leading women's national sport, each team is identified by the colour code of its uniform. The styles vary from season to season with new colours, new fabrics and new patterns. In the twenty-first century the changes have been faster and even more innovative, concerning both the style of the dress—which has gone through changes in the fabrics, colours and motifs, and the design of certain parts of the dress such as the *carré* (yoke) and the sleeves—and its manufacturing, today often in the hands of Kanak women tailors. A flourishing entrepreneurship centred on the *robe mission* is growing.

---

2   The more recent models of *robe mission* do not have buttons.

Female sartorial entrepreneurship is unprecedented for Lifou, as in the past the production of the *robe* was the monopoly of Chinese tailoring workshops in Nouméa, the capital.

The mission dress is thus quite distant from the image of the monotonous garment and never-changing style which looms so large in the early writings from Lifou as well as in the rhetoric of researchers up to the 1990s, who have never shown interest in a garment that they assumed to be imposed by European colonial rules. I present a more articulated story, a story from the perspective of Lifouan women and a telling case of 'tides of innovation'. The *robe mission* is one of those exogenous elements that have been indigenised, showing local capacity to appropriate what comes from other contexts and at the same time that a variety of elements coalesced in the process of indigenisation (see Paini 2012). I consider this as a privileged arena for illustrating how agency is retained with local actors—women in particular.

Vilsoni Hereniko comments that 'the profound sense of belonging … is lost when what we wear ceremonially is not woven collectively with the blood, sweat and tears of our elders, but by cotton thread and needle pushed along by foreign machines' (2005: 108). This vision needs to be tweaked a little in order to fit the story of Kanak women and their *robe mission*, a story in which materiality-value-place are differently connected; a story and a vision which provide the focus for this article.

I looked into the complex and articulated story of this dress, a garment that has caught my attention since my doctoral fieldwork and which later became the subject matter of my research (Paini 2002, 2003a, 2009, 2012). My discussion of the *robe mission* as a multidimensional subject matter is based on data from my fieldwork and on archival material in order to show how the transition from colonial to cultural object was activated by Kanak women and stresses women's dynamism and protagonism in the setting in motion of these changes. Men until very recently have been less interested in the topic, and non-governmental organisations (NGOs), which are very seldom present in the country, have played no role.

A brief foray into the question of Kanak women's appraisal of a loose garment different from the *robe* as the uniform to wear on a couple of official occasions gives weight to my argument (see Paini 2003a). The episodes were recounted by a Kanak male interlocutor involved in both events. The choice of the uniform of women working in the

Jean-Marie Tjibaou Cultural Center in Nouméa (which opened in 1999) was not an easy one. The proposal of a different style of loose garment was debated during the working committee, and whereas men favoured the change, women preferred the *robe mission*. For the Festival of Pacific Arts held in Nouméa in 2000, the choice of a loose garment, designed by two young female stylists, as the uniform of the personnel escorting the guest delegations was contested by several Kanak women. The same male interlocutor from the Grande Terre (main island) favourably commented on this choice: 'It was the only time in which the mission dress was avoided', adding that 'it was important to break the habit of using the mission dress because it is the symbol of the church' (Boengkih, 23 August 2001).[3] This echoed the more ambiguous connotations associated with the mission dress in those years in some other parts of Melanesia.[4] Since then many works on cloth and clothing have taken another perspective, more articulated, well put forward in a recent article by Margaret Jolly: 'They were and are fabrics saturated with the values of indigenous sanctity and rank, anti-colonial resistance, cultural pride, women's collectivities, national identities and transnational connections in an increasingly globalised world'(2014: 433).

Nevertheless, I consider it is important to remember how the *robe* has been differently reclaimed in Lifou and in the Grande Terre through time and how this echoes different configurations of colonial history (among others, see Bensa and Leblic 2000; Bensa, Goromoedo, Muckle, 2015 (including a very detailed bibliography); Douglas 1998; Merle 2002; Shineberg 1999; Tijbaou 1996). Recall that Lifou unlike the main island was not converted into a penal colony in the second half of the nineteenth century nor invested by land alientation and the program of free colonisation through the policy of *cantonnement*, which confined Kanak to the reserves (see Paini 2007, forthcoming in French).[5]

---

3   References to interviews are followed by name of the interlocutor and date only when the information refers to one single interview; otherwise only the name of the interlocutor is given.
4   For instance, the artist Ellen José from the Torres Strait Islands regarded the mission dress as a strong symbol of colonial and religious intervention on Islander women's lives, and this became the conceptual frame for one of her art works in which lifeless black mannequins were shown wearing a mission dress (Jolly 2001, 2003).This contrasted with the work of Kanak artist Denise Tiavouane as revealed in her exhibition at the Jean-Marie Tjibaou Cultural Center in Nouméa in July 2001 (*Mwà Vëë*: 2001; see also Paini 2003a).
5   On forms of control over indigenous mobility by colonial authorities as well as freed convicts and indentured labourers in New Caledonia, see Muckle 2011. He also points out the 'preoccupation with controlling the movement of Kanak women' and 'the regulation of movement between the Loyalty Islands and Nouméa' (148).

Following Kopytoff's argument that 'biographies of things can make salient what might otherwise remain obscure' (1986: 67), this chapter is deliberately ethnographic in its emphasis in order to convey the multidimensional features condensed in the Kanak *robe mission* (see also Paini 2003a).

A versatile exogenous garment: An acceptable ethnographic subject?

Unlike other areas of the world, the literature on the Pacific region has marginalised the role of cloth and clothing in colonial and missionary history until the early 2000s.[6] As pointed out by Chloë Colchester (2003), although it has been recognised as a key area of intervention, particularly by the missionaries, only in the twenty-first century has research on cloth, clothing and the manufacture of dresses produced a number of publications, opening up a new and interesting field and making clothing an ethnographic subject that is 'good to think with'.

Clothing has been an area of relative little interest in ethnographic and historical studies on New Caledonia. The only publication of the past on the subject, to my knowledge, goes back to 1953. That year's monographic issue of *Journal de la Société des Océanistes,* dedicated to New Caledonia, presents an overview of the subject by Patrick O'Reilly and Jean Poirier. In 'L'évolution du costume', the two authors stressed that although prohibition of nudity was a joint objective of the agents of colonisation, government and missions, the French administration was more interested in dressing chiefs in gallooned uniforms. It was mainly the discourse of white missionaries that focused on the imposition of a conjugal moral, the valorisation of the domestic milieu[7] resulting in the imposition of moral restraint on bodies that so far were dressed according to local customs and now had to conform to western norms of decency. Although for most missionaries nudity had been emblematic of savagery, O'Reilly and Poirier argued that it was forbidden by pre-European indigenous morality, which imposed a strong sense of modesty, though regarding only the pubic area. Maurice Leenhardt (1978: 4) reflected on

6   But see Weiner (1989).
7   On Christian missionaries' intervention in Pacific women's daily life, see Douglas 2002, 2003; Jolly and Macintyre 1989; Jolly 1991; also Jolly 2012 and 2014, including a very extensive bibliography.

143

the 'false modesty' of western society, which is alien to many non-western peoples, as they 'distinguish the idea of nudity from that of decency. The misfortune of our culture has been that of mixing the two ideas, and to hold nudity, even that of a child, as indecent' (4). Further, Leenhardt's article, which was first published in 1932, stressed the importance for these populations of wearing ornaments because wearing them means 'being invested with the power they contain' (4).

As I have discussed in a previous essay (Paini 2003a), my older Lifouan female interlocutors in the 1990s acknowledged that the sense of modesty and shame vis-à-vis their body was recent, a post-European contact development. They also recalled that in the past women were bare breasted (see also Tcherkézoff 2003) and that female modesty required covering the pubic area. During my doctoral fieldwork, women breastfed in public and some of the older women at home still wore only a skirt (this was reported to me by some Protestant women referring to their elder relatives). Also, the advice given to me by local women in the first months of my fieldwork in 1989 as to how to wear a *robe mission* properly always concerned this part of the body. Women have developed bodily techniques which allow them to crouch or to sit with crossed legs taking advantage of the fullness of the dress, which is tucked in between the legs, an 'investment of existing indigenous preoccupations into new materials' (Küchler and Were 2005: xxi). Coming from a Catholic background, where girls were taught to keep their knees covered, I was intrigued by this indigenous solution in which thighs were not concealed. For Lifouan women it is simply a natural and comfortable style of sitting, though I have always found it awkward to adopt myself. Roberta Colombo Dougoud, writing about her fieldwork experience in Papua New Guinea, recounts a similar story (2002: 56)—women persisted in telling her how to sit properly, by folding the skirt between her legs.

The *robe mission* is not to be considered as a costume but rather as an item of clothing, although it has become included in customary exchanges (I'll return to this). Thus the dimensions of ordinariness, of creolisation, its colonial origin and its name meant that for a long time it was a very visible yet ambiguous object: although the windows of the shops in the Chinese quarter were filled with colourful mission dresses, they were invisible to researchers in the late 1980s and early 1990s. A dress too entangled with colonisation and considered only as an introduced garment inflicted on Kanak women, could not be taken into account by an ethnographic research which positioned itself as committed. Instead, I suspect that the idea that clothing was an irrelevant aspect of daily life was upheld by the binary logic of authenticity and inauthenticity, and thus the *robe mission*—perceived as an unauthentic, spurious, contaminated object—was not considered a proper ethnographic subject matter.

Figure 19. Poster of the second Fête de la Robe Mission, June 2010, Koohné

Source. Provided by the organisers

From a certain visual angle what works for other objects also applies to the *robe*. 'Commonplace things are worn to oblivion and replaced with new objects, or are viewed as too trivial in their own time to be removed from circulation … and saved for posterity' (Kirshenblatt-Gimblett 1998: 25). Indeed the *robes mission* are seldom preserved for posterity because as they grow older and worn they are used for working in the gardens, and finally they become household rugs or rags. This can explain why *robes mission*, until recently, were absent from museum collections.

However, the first years of the twenty-first century have seen a new wider interest in the subject, as revealed by some events organised in Nouméa: from the 2000 Festival des Arts du Pacifique (23 October–3 November) where a section was devoted to clothing, to a photographic exhibition on the *robe mission* in 2003 at the Jean-Marie Tjibaou Cultural Center (20 August–3 November). More recently, an issue of *Mwà Véé* (2010), the journal of the Cultural Centre, was entirely devoted to the mission dress. It featured several interviews, an account of the second Fête de la Robe Mission (Figure 19) and images and conversations with the artists who were involved in the exposition of contemporary art *Robes mission: un art de la rue?* which opened in June 2010 at the Cultural Center in Nouméa. The mission dress has at last been recognised as an artistic and ethnographic subject.[8]

A *nyipi* dress[9]

Following local usages which draws a rigid distinction between *fille* and *femme* (married and unmarried women) regardless of age (see Paini 2007), for this essay I draw mainly from the experiences and insights I shared throughout the years with married women. Let's take a closer look at this *robe*, starting with the 'three buttons model', which had been the mainstream model up to the end of the 1990s. I deliberately present a detailed description of it as this allows me to draw comparisons with later models and describe the innovations that occurred over time. A *tulu*, or yoke, is shaped and fitted around the neck, it is decorated in the front with lace or cotton braids, and has three buttons at the back. The rest of the garment is gathered and hangs loosely from it, with no indication

---

8 I do not explore here the use of the *robe mission* in the work of artists such as Stéphanie Wamytan. It is the focus of a forthcoming essay.
9 Literally, true/dress.

of a waistline. The neck—*hninawa*—is emphasised by a high neckline, the opening reaches the mid-back and closes with three buttons, usually white or clear, with two holes and sewn almost indifferently on the right or the left side, contrary to western custom which differentiates closure according to gender. The sleeves—*imen (à la raglan)*—are very wide and stop above the elbow. They have a border accentuated with bands of lace or ribbons matching the yoke, slightly gathered by a string on the inside to create a ruffle.

Younger women ignore the elements that in the past distinguished a Lifouan *robe* from one worn by a woman from the nearby island of Ouvéa. As Pohnimë Haluatr told me repeatedly over the years, in the first case three *galons*, or lace, delimited the yoke, in the second only two. I want to draw attention to this detail because it shows that women were able to invest local meanings in the *robe* by replicating in the acquired dresses elements that were present in other forms in their pre-European clothing. And this contradicts what is often argued: that the new imported clothes had replaced the local ones suppressing any difference in origin and status.

Isabelle Leblic, in an essay on technical changes in the fishery sector since the introduction of objects from outside, insisted that the substitutions made by the Kanak concern 'functionally equivalent objects' or items that are different from the traditional ones 'for the materials of which they are made: they already exist in the system in the equivalent form' (1998: 92). However, Lissant Bolton, in her writing about the introduction of European clothing in Vanuatu takes a different position: '[they] represented not just the substitution of one material form for another, but the importation of a different set of ideas and distinctions embodied in the specific material form of introduced clothing' (2003: 126). Yet, she stresses that if the adoption of clothing was viewed by missionaries as a sign of conversion, 'the specifics of how this was imposed and received varied greatly from place to place' (2003: 127). In the case of Vanuatu, Bolton argues that the distinctions of status previously associated with indigenous clothes were lost in the 'Mother Hubbard' dress, adding that 'the principal source of differentiation marked by clothes reflected missionary denomination' (129). Women's dress among the Anglicans consisted of a blouse (today a t-shirt) and skirt, whereas Presbyterians wore a dress, often called Mother Hubbard. Bolton further comments that this term was used only to refer to indigenous women's clothing, thus creating 'a specific distinction between expatriate and indigenous' (129). I find Bolton's delineation of the shift from old to new clothing very inspiring. In Lifou, though, the introduction of the mission dress has not produced the same dynamics, as certain regional differences in style and status have long been incorporated into the *robe*. Kanak women were able to reappropriate an exogenous garment transferring some elements of distinction based on status, age, as well as the village of belonging; distinctions which, however, have weakened over the years.[10]

Kanak women clearly show a yearning for *robes mission*. When the late Hnauleqatr spoke of the *robe* at the time the missionaries were a constant presence in Lifouans' life, she pointed to the lack of laces in those imported garments. The material was heavier and the dress touched the feet. When women describe the *robe* of the more recent past they specify that it was trimmed with more lace and folds. The dresses displaying more trimming were considered *nyipi ewekë la i heetre popine* (the dress of value for women).[11] In the words of Billy Wapotro, a Kanak interlocutor, *nyipi heetr* referred to Sunday best. The use of the term *nyipi* requires some clarification. It is a very dense term that points to the linguistic process through which a non-local object acquires 'authenticity' and thus becomes indigenised, particularly for the older generations. The recent origin of the dress is concealed by a linguistic label that allows Kanak to assign it a new status (Milie and Paini 1996), which also reveals an indigenous attribution of hierarchy upon categories of clothing. A once imposed dress, the *robe mission* has gone through cultural reformulation not only in its materiality but also in the linguistic label attached to it.[12]

The quality of the material and the manufacturing varies. The fabric comes from Asia,[13] mostly from Taiwan: relatively cheap, colourful, and printed mainly in bold floral designs. There is a wide choice of colours and colour combinations. The dress today covers the knee, but fashion has also affected this aspect and during the 1960s the dress was shorter. Pohnimë showed me a dress from that period, the only one that I was shown to

---

10   The aforementioned differences are not taken into account in the article by O'Reilly and Poirier (1953).

11   In the use of Drehu orthography I follow *Dictionnaire Drehu-Français* by Léonard Drïle Sam, 1995.

12   The notion of foreignness has been the focus of fieldwork carried out in 1996 with Imela Milie from Lifou thanks to an Etude des Sociétés Kanak (ESK), École des hautes études en sciences sociales (EHESS) grant. See the paper 'Ka xep qa hnagëje (everything that comes from the sea); or foreignness as articulated by Lifuans', presented by the two of us in December 1996 at the European Society for Oceanists (ESfO) conference in Copenhagen.

13   I have met a Kanak dressmaker who used to go to India to buy fabrics to stock her store. She had a few seamstresses working for her in Nouméa.

have been preserved from earlier times: it was shorter than present-day ones, made of nylon, and in gaudy colours. Photographs from Melanesia 2000, the first festival of Kanak arts held in Nouméa in September 1975, support this (Tjibaou and Missotte 1978).

The dress can be worn buttoned at the front or at the back. Dwelling on this is not simply to get hung up on ethnographic details, rather 'such biographical details reveal a tangled mass of aesthetic, historical, and even political judgments, and of convictions and values' (Kopytoff 1986: 67). If in the 1990s on important occasions the *robe* was buttoned at the back, in the past the dress was worn with the three buttons at the front. The narratives on this point differ: for some women the reason was practicality, the high neckline impedes movement when the dress is buttoned at the back; for others this practice was associated with Protestant women, especially the wives of pastors, who could thus follow the service at the same time as they were breastfeeding. However, some women suggested that it was not only for practical reasons as it distinguished a status, more generally a way 'to signal the status of a married woman' (Kacatr, We, 14 August 2001). A photograph taken at a Catholic women's gathering in July 1971 and given to me by Pohnimë Haluatr,[14] shows her, at the time married and with three children, with other women from Drueulu wearing the dress buttoned at the front. Yet one of them was not married (Figure 20). As undergarment, an underskirt—*iut*—made with cotton or synthetic material replaces that of the past made of thick and colourful fabric, laced at the waist. Women also used to wear a large camisole, *isimis*; after giving birth they also used a hidden belt to support the stomach. Some elderly women still use *isimis* and *iut* and they are still included in the customary gift made to the bride's family. There is also a standard way to store this garment. The locally appropriate way requires a woman to fold the dress vertically in half, then to fold in both sleeves and finally to fold it into thirds starting from the bottom and ending with the yoke on top.

---

14   The photograph was in bad condition, I took it back to The Australian National University, had a new negative and new copies made, and later I returned the original and a new copy of the photo to its owner.

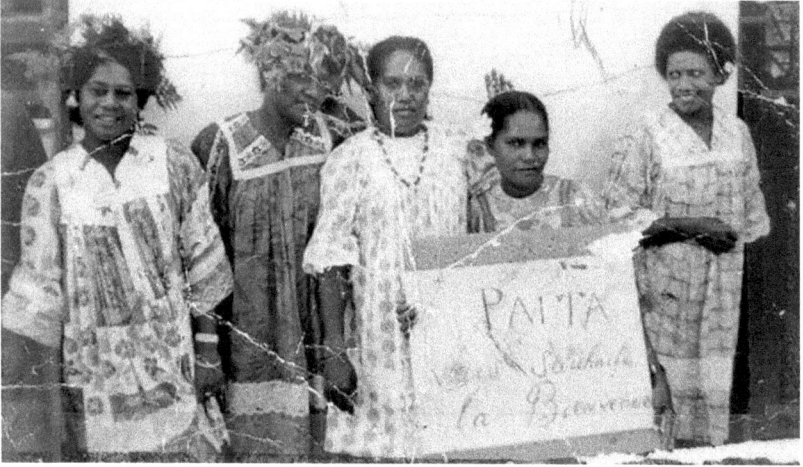

Figure 20. Pohnimë Haluatr (far left) and other Loyalty Islander women in Paita, near Nouméa, July 1971

Source. Photograph courtesy of Pohnimë Haluatr, Drueulu (Lifou)

Juxtaposing oral and written sources as I have attempted to do in my research on the *robe mission* (Paini 2003a, 2009), I am not aiming to reconstruct the history of this dress, but rather to evince the selective use of memories and the narratives deployed that reveal similarities and differences both between Catholics and Protestants and between the Grande Terre (main island) and the Loyalty Islands. Indeed, the distinction between Lifouans belonging to the two missions established on the island since the mid-1850s has always been strongly marked and visible (see Paini 1998). In the period between 1930 and 1950 Catholic Fathers imposed both dress and hairstyle 'norms' on church-going women to mark them apart from Protestant women. Nevertheless, it was mainly the hairstyle that expressed difference: Catholic women wore their hair short, reintroducing a local pre-European practice. During my fieldwork in the late 1980s to the early 1990s, while women expressed no regret concerning the differences in clothing, they harboured a deep grudge against the hairstyle rule imposed by a specific missionary.

The fact that both Catholic and Protestant women's narratives account for religious differences through the memories of the imposition of a different hairstyle and not of a different practice of clothing means that today the *robe mission* is perceived as the proper dress by Kanak women, regardless of their religious affiliation, quite a different situation from that analysed by Bolton in Vanuatu, where Presbyterian women 'see the dress as particularly their own' (2003: 134), whereas Anglican women do not. I'll return to this. Paradoxically during the 1990s the *robe* was locally considered as an indigenous item of clothing while short hair, which was worn by Lifouan women in the nineteenth century, was considered a European hairstyle; for elderly women short hair was reminiscent of the imposed missionary rule, while for younger women it was a mark of westernisation.[15] However, external differences between Catholic and Protestants are still present.[16] For instance, during religious services, Catholic women do not cover their heads while Protestant women, especially seniors, wear a hat; in the past this was often a colourful woven *basque*. On less formal occasions women shield their heads from the sun using a piece of cloth.

The *robe mission*, made of finely woven cotton, apparently very delicate to the touch, in practice was stronger than it appeared. The range of situations in which women used the 'three buttons *robe*' in the 1990s was wide: from sleeping to bathing in the sea. Ernesta Cerulli writes that the work dress 'often is quite different from the ceremonial and holiday costume' (1999: 104). In the case of Kanak women this distinction does not seem to be so rigid: in the gardens women dress in very informal ways; often they wear an old *robe*, no longer suitable in other contexts, buttoned in front for practical reasons. In the past this distinction was more marked, because missionaries imposed white *robes* as Sunday best; today the difference tends to lie more at the level of manufacturing. Women's dresses, which are part of daily life clothing, are also worn on important occasions (religious functions, weddings, funerals, yam feasts, women's gatherings), assuming a strong meaning of kanak-ness. As Pohnimë emphasises the *robe* is included in the gifts exchanged during wedding ceremonies. But when old, worn and torn, and no longer suitable as a garment, it is still put to use as a rag until there is nothing left. The long life of the *robe mission* thus goes from Sunday best to service as a rag.[17]

Whereas in nearby Vanuatu, Bolton explains that 'soon after Independence, island dresses were officially nominated as national dress for women' (2005: 26), in Lifou the adoption of the *robe mission* appears to be more

---

15 This has changed in the last decade; wearing short hair is no longer perceived as a missionary imposition.

16 On the articulated and complex relationship between Catholics and Protestants in Lifou, see Paini 1998.

17 I have also observed people taking off their sandals and using a rag from an old *robe mission* to clean their feet before entering a house.

rooted in women's choices and desires, as confirmed by women's pleasure in showing off their best dress on appropriate occasions, for instance when going to church.[18]

The missionary experience in Lifou

At the turn of the twenty-first century, cloth and clothing in the Pacific began to attract more attention. In her edited volume *Clothing the Pacific*, which inaugurates a welcome series of books on this subject,[19] Chlöe Colchester, referring to Jean Comaroff, stresses that

> a distinguishing feature of the Protestant mission to the Pacific, as to other parts of the colonial periphery, was the emphasis placed on defining ordinary everyday activity, a pursuit in which the imposition of foreign practices of domesticity, home-making, dress and deportment were regarded as being as central to conversion as translating the Holy Book (2003: 2).

Colchester contrasts this with what she considers to be the ways in which Catholic missionaries would become involved with local contexts:

> Catholic priests did not share this degree of concern with everyday material things since their approach to the place of objects in worship and religious practice was different, and moreover the impact of Roman Catholics was to remain small compared to that of the Protestant Evangelicals. For Protestant Evangelicals wanted the islanders' [sic] to accept not only their faith, but their way of life (2003: 2).

A caveat is required at this point before returning to clothing. Norman Etherington in the 'Afterword' to *In God's Empire: French Missionaries and the Modern World* (2012) supports the idea that not only British and French practices of colonial rule had more in common than was often thought, but that 'a comparable argument can be advanced for Christian

---

18   Nevertheless, I want to point out what could become a novel pattern of male control on female clothing, which I observed at the next-to-be Gaica's high chief's wedding in May 2011. It was a big event, which had been prepared for a long time and was extensively covered by the media. Almost 50 years separated the wedding of the present chief from that of his first-born son. Among the many rules established for the occasion, the council of elders had decided that Kanak women 'working' at the ceremony should all wear the *robe*. Most young women conformed to this requirement; however, I did observe exceptions. In any case I did not read into it a moral imperative but rather a way to present themselves to outsiders.

19   It was followed in 2005 by another edited volume by Susanne Küchler and Graeme Were— part of the same 'Clothing the Pacific' project of the British Museum.

missions in the modern colonial era. In the long run, underlying similarities outweighed eye-catching differences' (2012: 280). He points at 'striking contrasts' such as the fact that the British missionary movement was linked to a leadership imbued with faith in progress and commerce, whereas the nineteenth-century French Catholic missions recruited missionaries from rural areas and considered 'civilisation' to be part of an anticlerical agenda. But he also argues that 'the longevity and diversity of Christian missionary experience ensure that counterexamples abound' (280). Ethnographic and archival material from Lifou, as well as from other parts of the country offer one such counterexample regarding missionary activity.

In addition to the active role played in the imposition of a European dress code by the wives of Protestant pastors (see below), the Marists believed that the best way to reform Lifouans was through education. This view was voiced in their request for sisters to join them in the missions as revealed in a passage from a letter by Father Lubin Gaide to Father Victor Poupinel, *Visiteur* of the Société de Marie's Missions in Oceania:

> Without sisters we will never have Christian mothers; and without Christian mothers, we are building on kanakism, that is on the sand. We will never have Christians worthy of this name if they do not first become men. Now, they will become men only through maternal education (Gaide to Poupinel, 9 February 1872, APM/ONC 208).

The letter conveys Gaide's view on the decisive role he assigned to the presence of female missionaries; he believed that sisters could educate local women in what he considered to be good mothering practices, and that this process was essential for achieving the redemption of souls. Although Marist Fathers did not write in much detail about daily local life, a very telling example of their work, connecting specifically to the theme of this essay, comes from a letter that Father Xavier Montrouzier, who was in charge of opening the new mission in Lifou in 1858, wrote to his parents from Balade on the main island; this letter reveals unusual and unexpected details of life on the mission and shows the close link between spiritual and daily life that characterised the work of Catholic missionaries:

> I would not know how to tell you, my dear parents, the happiness which I felt when I saw my old parishioners again ... Magdeleine whom I so named in honour of my mother is an excellent catechist. She knows how to read and P[adre] Forestier teaches her to sew, to spin, etc. A small gift from you consisting of an assortment of needles, yarn and brightly colored fabrics,

would, I believe, sort a good effect. At the same time as we work on the conversion of the indigenous, we aim at ways to make their existence down here less miserable. P. Vigouroux, with admirable patience, trains ploughmen. P. Forestier, on his part, busies himself teaching the women to sew, to spin (Montrouzier to his family, 16 March 1853, APM/ONC 208).

Montrouzier clearly conveys the idea that the Catholic missionaries were indeed engaged in both converting and getting involved in local men and women's daily life. This account is very rich, and particularly relevant to this essay is the detail concerning a Father who teaches sewing, as well as Montrouzier's request for sewing material from home. The passage reveals an unusual practice for the time and points to the complexity of Marist attitudes to involvement in redefining indigenous daily life. Thus the claim that Catholic missionaries did not participate in rethinking local life is reductive; Catholic and Protestant missionaries were equally eager to save souls, as well as to harness the exotic and normalise it to a European order of things. Yet missionary projects had to face indigenous responses.

Clothing and agency

Continuing the dialogue with historical sources, I focus on local women's agency in connection with clothing. Missionaries, adhering to a specific moral code, made people cover themselves, trying to put an end to what they considered to be nudity (and many of their narratives refer to the indigenes' nakedness). Nine months after his arrival in Lifou, Montrouzier wrote that 'the most difficult obstacles to overcome were polygamy, nudity—of the most revolting kinds—superstitions' (Montrouzier to Favre, 1 January 1859, APM/ONC 208). Covering nakedness then become a priority and clothing became 'an icon of conversion' (Jolly 2014: 431). Both men and women seem to have willingly adopted new ways of concealing and adorning parts of their bodies. While the former wore western-style clothes, the latter adopted loose-fitting, calf-length dresses (O'Reilly and Poirier 1953). Kanak women came to consider the *robe mission* to be the proper dress for specific events (see Paini 2003a). I want to elucidate the complex issue of imposition/reappropriation by widening my analysis to include other written missionary sources.

The references found in the texts of missionary men—both Protestants and Catholics—regarding male and female clothes are vague, while the texts written by women contain detailed accounts of daily life on Lifou (see Paini 2003a, 2009). I rely on the observations of two women who spent approximately 30 years on the island, one following in the steps of the other: Emma Hadfield and Eugénie Péter. Emma Hadfield, who lived most of the years 1886–1920 in Lifou,[20] wrote about a local woman who 'from the husk of coconuts … made herself a skirt or fringe, from five to 15 inches in depth, which she wore round the waist'. She commented that 'fashions never changed; all dressed alike', although she observed differences in clothing associated to status, such as how chiefs 'fastened their girdles differently from others, and also wore more elaborated ornaments' (1920: 35). It's interesting to see that Emma Hadfield's comments on the persistence of dressing code and the absence of local imagination were echoed a few years later by Mademoiselle Péter, as the Protestant lay missionary is still called in Lifou. The writings of Eugénie Péter[21] provide an interesting source on this subject as she underlined an analogous lack of interest in changing style of clothing, but this time she is referring to the *robe mission*. In an unpublished letter dated 1923, she wrote:

> Women are all dressed in the same way, with a kind of a sheath dress with wide *carré* and puffed sleeves. This is probably still the fashion of the time of Mrs. Hadfield. I am surprised at this uniformity and that they prefer to make their dresses in this way rather than kimonos which would be nicer, cheaper, more easily made, but nothing can be done (Eugénie Péter to Mr et Mme Bergeret, 2 August 1923).

The Swiss missionary elaborated on what she perceived as Kanak women's insensitivity to innovation. Yet late nineteenth to early twenty-century photographs from the Archives in Nouméa show that change has always taken place. From these images one can infer that the materials used in the earlier dresses were woven with warps and wefts of different colours making plaid and checkered patterns, whereas the later materials were printed on solid white fabric. Still, today, many visitors to the area, in

---

20   Emma Hadfield came to the Loyalty Islands with her husband, the London Missionary Society (LMS) pastor James Hadfield. She became very involved in local life and published *Among the Natives of the Loyalty Group* (1920). Once the Hadfields left, the charge of the mission was passed on to the Bergeret couple.

21   Eugénie Péter-Contesse was born in Switzerland in 1889; she arrived in New Caledonia in 1923 as a missionary teacher for the Société des missions évangéliques of Paris.

a very simplistic way, believe that this dress has remained unchanged. In 2001, as I wrote in my fieldnotes, a new style of yoke and lace was introduced: unlike in the past, they were in a single colour that contrasted strongly with the rest of the dress.

The quote from Péter above reveals the tension between imposition/ reappropriation which characterised indigenous contexts and enables a deeper reflection on the issue of Kanak women's agency. It reveals that Lifouan women did not always seem interested in changing their dress style, thus they did not approach every kind of imported idea on clothing with the same attitude. They had already adopted a European garment that Péter believed to be impractical, as manufacturing it required excessive fabric and time; yet her proposals, centred on a logic of saving, did not meet the favour of local women. Her suggestion of adopting a kimono at first went unheard; however, during War World II the difficulties in finding fabric did produce some changes. In a time of lack of resources, rules and practices changed, so women were allowed to go to the Sunday service wearing clothes other than the *robe*. As Péter wrote, 'the large dresses with *carré* and lots of frills have long been the only ones accepted for worship. The kimono dresses were good for working and for young girls. It is changing!' (Péter, 15 June 1941).

The term 'kimono' has become part of the vernacular language to identify a specific category of clothing; in fact in Drehu a female dress can be called *kimonu* or *iheetr*. Asked to elaborate on this difference, women explained that the former is a straight dress, with a V-neck, buttoned up the front, with or without sleeves, that is unpopular today. In a post-World War II photograph portraying a family from Drueulu,[22] the wife is wearing a *kimonu*.[23] How this Japanese word came into Drehu and other languages of the country is an issue that is still unresolved. *Iheetr*, instead, is a term that refers both to the *robe mission* and to the *modèle*. The latter denotes the newly fashionable pattern: a yoke, sometimes replaced with a triangular shaped one-coloured piece, from which the rest of the plain garment hangs loosely (Jeanne, Hunëtë, 22 August 2001).[24]

---

22   The original is with the family; a copy is at the Drueulu registry office.
23   The 'kimono' category of clothing appears to be common both in Lifou and the Grande Terre (Emmanuel Kasarhérou, personal communication, 6 July 2002, Vienna).
24   During the time of Madame Bergeret the mission dress was called 'Madame' (Billy Wapotro, 23 August 2001).

Some women in the 1990s used this term to refer to the *robes* created by Madame Walenu's new atelier, La Perle Grise, one of the earliest Kanak sartorial enterprises.

Figure 21. New style *robe mission* by Eseka, showing details of the top part of the dress and sleeves
Source. © Photographed by Anna Paini, Lifou, November 2007

Agency is at issue also with naming things. The *robe mission* in Kanaky New Caledonia has followed an itinerary analogous to that of the term Kanak, which was initially used in a derogatory way by colonisers to refer to indigenous people. However, the latter have inverted this connotation, thus turning the word Kanak into a symbol of positive cultural identity. But metamorphoses of signs are selective. When years ago I asked Hnauleqatr to tell me about the *robe mission*, the elderly woman looked at Pohnimë for help; she explained that I was referring to the *robe popinée*. This kind of incomprehension occurred again with younger people. Invited to speak in the Primary School of Hnathalo (northern district of Lifou) about being an anthropologist and speaking in French, I referred to my research on the *robe mission*. The Kanak teacher kindly interrupted me, saying he had to clarify to the class that I was referring to the *robe popinée*, a term which is contested in the rest of the country. Returning to Nouméa from Lifou, I was sharing what my interlocutors had told me with a Kanak friend,

Marie-Claire Beboko-Beccalossi, while she was driving us to her home from the airport. On the threshold of her house, Marie-Claire corrected me very firmly saying that I should stop referring to the dress in such a way; it was a *'robe mission'* or *'robe mélanésienne'*. Other friends from the Grande Terre to whom I explained what I perceived as a misunderstanding had similar reactions. To them the term *popine*[25] still carries a highly negative connotation, as seniors still remember it being used by French colonialists to refer in denigratory terms to young Kanak women. Back in Drueulu one afternoon the well-known Kanak singer from Lifou, Edou (alias Edouard Wamai) was visiting my host family while I was puzzling over this question of naming with her, and Edou reminded me that in 'Océanie' he sang of *'vahine* popine *aux milles couleurs amour sans frontière'*. And this window, opened on the scene of naming, once again reveals that the experience of colonisation has marked Kanak from the two areas differently, and continues to influence contemporary practice, though for younger people this is mitigated as they have not lived the same experiences as their elders:[26] novel articulations of colonial pasts and presents are taking place.

Kanak remember a time when it was forbidden to wear the *robe mission*. Denise Kacatr recalls that when she was young, on the Grande Terre wearing the *robe* during the week was forbidden, and for her this rule was a way for French institutions to 'take possession of Kanak culture' (We, 14 August 2001). In 1966 three Kanak students at the Lycée Laperouse of Nouméa (Billy Wapotro, Fote Trolue and Jimmi Ounei) demonstrated against the school rules prohibiting girls from wearing the *robe* and boys from wearing open sandals (Wapotro, 23 August, 2001). Although I have not yet found a written record of this vestimentary code of conduct imposed by the principal, other witnesses confirm the story. The devaluing colonial gaze on Kanak women had first imposed the *robe*, but in some urban situations, in particularly those connected with schools, the colonial power preferred to deny any indigenous specificity. What were the implications of this colonial measure? It was a time when also vernacular languages were banned in public places and the French

---

25 *Popine* is the Drehu spelling.
26 When I published my first article in French on the *robe mission* (2003a) I puzzled over the title, and following Billy Wapotro's advice I decided not to include the word *popine* because of its loaded history.

colonial government was trying to stifle any outward symbol of local identity that might show an incomplete assimilation to a French order of things.

La robe et la coutume

I would like to expand on what was stressed by my interlocutors, namely that the *robe mission* is now part of customary exchanges by considering its role during marriage ceremonies. I'll briefly introduce the event though I do not intend to tackle all the issues involved in this complex ceremony. *Qene noj*, 'the way of land' and glossed in French as *la coutume* (custom), is opposed by Lifouans to *qene wi wi*, 'the way of the French'. *Faire la coutume* (making custom) refers to the rituals underlying daily social relations in which people exchange goods, marking these transactions of gifts and counter-gifts with speeches, that may be more or less elaborate depending on the occasion and on the setting. *La coutume* is considered as constituting the core of life and identity. Custom is, however, not perceived in opposition to modernity, as exemplified by the use of money in customary exchange. Significantly, *la coutume* in Lifou has not been widely appealed to in mounting a critique of the Christian religion (see Paini 1998).

To initiate marriage negotiations, the groom and his family make a visit to the family of the bride-to-be to take *kuië june hmala* (thanks for acceptance of a marriage proposal), a gift consisting of money. Unlike other exchanges, this transaction is made in private; the amount involved varies, depending on financial possibilities. In May 1990, I was able to attend such a ceremony in Drueulu, which involved partners from the same villlage. It took place in the evening and lasted half-an-hour. When the man's family entered the hut they first gave 3,000 French Pacific Francs (CFP) for *qëmek*;[27] opening the way to two transactions: 100,000 CFP for *kuië june hmala* and, as the unmarried couple had a child, a further 50,000 CFP as *otren hne la nekönatr* (literally, bond with the child) to legitimise the paternity: *hnöth la nekönatr* (literally, to tie the child). The woman's family accepted and presented its monetary counter-gift

---

27 A gift of money is required as an opening gesture in a wide range of contexts; the amount depends on the importance of the occasion. The French Pacific Franc (CFP) is the currency of the country. At the time the CFP and the French Franc (FF) had fixed parity: 100 CFP was equal to 5.5 FF. Today it has fixed parity with the Euro.

(20,000 CFP). Each customary gesture was accompanied by a very formal speech. The exchanges over, the date of the marriage was communicated to the bride's family, though unofficially it was already known. In Lifou at the time of my first fieldwork both women and men admitted that the amount of money circulating on these occasions was increasing and perceived contributions to weddings were becoming too competitive. Both criticised the high expectations and yet attempts by the customary authorities to set limits to the trend toward excessive commoditisation have not been too successful.[28]

The work done by the bridegroom's party for the bride's family was explained by Sipo as showing the importance of women within custom. Marriages are planned a year ahead of time allowing members of the kin group to plant yams and other crops for exchanging and for the wedding meals. For the two-week period of preparation, a large group of people will eat together every day, the women being responsible for organising the food. Both men and women of the kin group are also engaged in other tasks, such as determining the monetary contributions expected from each branch of the group, and preparing the contents of the *valise* (suitcase). Several days before the bride is accompanied by her family to the bridegroom's place, people arrive to bring their *tro* (customary marriage gifts), consisting of money, cloth, yams and other staple foods. Groups are welcomed one at a time, so if several groups arrive at the same time they have to wait their turn. After these gifts and counter-gifts have been made (accompanied by formal speeches from both parties), the group is invited to eat. These contributions, together with those of *mathin* (mother's brother) and *ifaxa* (real and classificatory married sisters), are assembled, and at the end of the ceremony they will be divided into three parts: *pua*, for the bride's family to be divided among the guests; *wenehleng*, for the parents of the bride (or, as some women say, for the mother of the bride); and *hna hetrenyin*, which goes to the newly wed couple. A further category of gift is *ihehe*; it consists of western goods for the household and some money and is given by guests of both sides to the couple. Generally at the end of a wedding, the organisers announce the amount of money that was contributed and how it was divided into the three categories. The success and the status of the ceremony (and thus of

---

28   In 2014 a new set of written regulations were codified in Lifou. It is too soon to determine their impact and long-term effects on wedding practices.

the family) tends to be judged on these terms. When people comment on how much money has been raised and thus on that particular wedding ceremony's importance, they will not include the *ihehe*.

If the bridegroom's family is responsible for raising the money and organising the ceremony, going to a marriage on their side, *lapa i trahmany*, entails 'work', the bride's group will instead be considered as honoured guests: they are invited to 'come and eat'. However, it will be up to that group to determine the number of *peleitr* (plates); that is, the number of formally invited guests. To be included in the guest list does not simply mean to be given precedence in eating on the day of the wedding *manger à la premierè table* (eating at the first table) . If the bride's lineage decides to distribute 60 'plates', it means that the *pua* will be divided into 60 parts. *Pua* consists of money, food, fabrics and clothes contained in the *valise* that the bride's family will receive at the end of the ceremony. The *valise* (today a large wheeled suitcase) is prepared by the women and filled with different kind of clothes, western and local; a certain number of *robes mission* is always included. The presence of the *robe* also characterises other exchanges of the wedding ceremony, such as the gifts brought by each party to the wedding. Further, when the bride arrives with her family to the groom's place, she sits in front of her mother-in-law wearing two mission dresses, she takes one off and gives it to her. The *robe mission* plays an important role also as the dress worn by women on the groom's side in specific parts of the event. In fact, a senior woman is appointed to decide months before on a specific style of robe—its colour, trim, type of sleeves—and commission an artisan to create the dress in different sizes to be bought by female relatives for the ceremony of welcoming the bride. The order often is for 50 or more dresses. It is evident that the *robe mission* mediates different phases of this very important life-cycle ceremony, and in this respect I have observed continuity since 1989.

New female entrepreneurship: A story

Chlöe Colchester introduces the edited volume *Clothing the Pacific* by stressing that Pacific women's contemporary dress, known as 'Mother Hubbards', 'seems stuck in the nineteenth century … an indication of the way that women's dress has lagged behind other social innovation' (2003: 1). Again, a counterargument can be shown from Lifou.

Up to the late 1990s the dress could be worn buttoned at the front or at the back. As I have already remarked, this article of clothing has never been conceived of in a rigid way. Aesthetics in the 1980s and 1990s favoured large floral prints, the new fashion prefers single colours often with a contrasting white design; frequently the dress is made with white cotton fabric dyed one colour with a stencilled design and buttons are no longer found on the back of the dress. The raglan sleeve attaches to the yoke and the fabric is slightly pleated and flows from it. A recent innovation is the addition of an invisible pocket on the right side that can be used to carry keys or a mobile phone. The *robe* persists as a mode of dress regardless of all these stylistic innovations (Figure 21).

The mission dress, as we have seen, leaves plenty of room for creativity, imagination and taste. I started doing fieldwork in Lifou in 1989, and between periods of fieldwork I saw new models, sometimes very popular for one season only. But in more recent years a new phenomenon relating to female creativity has arisen, making these changes increasingly visible. Some Kanak women have opened their own small tailoring ateliers, giving rise to a new trend which has rapidly spread; these have incentivised greater inventiveness than in the past, from the choice of fabrics (new materials and designs) to the sleeves and other stylistic details. These new creations have immediately aroused the interest of Islander women. I have pointed out how in the past differentiation tied to place or religious affiliation was signalled by clothing; in recent years a new element has come into play, the style of the atelier where the dress is made. This is a change that affects both urban and rural contexts.

In fact, until the second half of the 1990s, women would buy their *robes* mainly from Chinese shops in the capital. In recent years, Kanak women have become involved with tailoring, producing a good level of craftsmanship, with affordable prices for the local market, although higher than those charged in Chinese shops. A flourishing entrepreneurship has risen centred on the mission dress. Forerunner of this new involvement of Kanak women in dress-making has been the experience of the atelier La Perle Grise in Nouméa in the 1990s. Its impact was more limited, affecting primarily women in the capital.

Today, women have put forward their skills in tailoring by creating their own models, which quickly become very popular. Kanak women design, manufacture and market both locally and across islands. The new Kanak designers have indulged in designing and creating different models, whose originality is distinguished by certain elements such as the material utilised (from Indian fabrics to the yoke from Caribbean tissues), the type of sleeves, and the neckline.

In 2005, 2007 and again in 2009, I had long conversations with some of these dressmakers in Lifou and in Nouméa. When discussing the extent to which they could push to introduce creative changes on the dress while continuing to define it as a *robe mission*, I obtained different answers. The dress and sleeves must remain wide. One of the dressmakers, after some hesitation, clarified that an element that makes the difference are the pockets; if you put in pockets you 'ruin everything, it is the French' (Sélèké). Yet in those years some women wore *robes* with a single pocket; more recently a second pocket was added to some new models. Another element that is considered incompatible with a *robe* is the belt. A feature that has not been modified by the new dressmakers is the length of the *robe*. All in all, the sartorial code has changed and the dress has been revolutionised: different, wider necklines which do not require buttons and sleeves that may have openings to reveal one's shoulder or arm. I should add that these new *robes* do not have an interchangeable front and back like the old ones, an element which gave the wearer a further possibility of choice. In all cases, these contemporary outfits created and made by Kanak dressmakers continue to be recognised as a *robe*.

Agency is expressed both by the women who have taken a new direction in their work, through their creativity and inventiveness, and by those who have started to buy from them. There was a kind of contagious word of mouth: not only women from Lifou wore outfits made in these ateliers, especially on formal occasions. They began to be able to recognise the dressmaker who had designed the *robe* from its style; and some of these ateliers were struggling to keep up with orders, especially during the period of the marriage season.

Whereas in the 1990s in Lifou the French wedding dress was most popular, in the early twenty-first century a new fashion trend has emerged. Many brides to be choose to have their dress made by one of these ateliers because their style is considered to be more local and personal. The dresses chosen by each side of the wedding party to wear during the ceremony, clearly marking those belonging to the bride's or the groom's side, are also increasingly ordered from these dressmakers. These new ateliers have the advantage that clients in the rural areas can discuss with the tailor the colour and style of their choice.

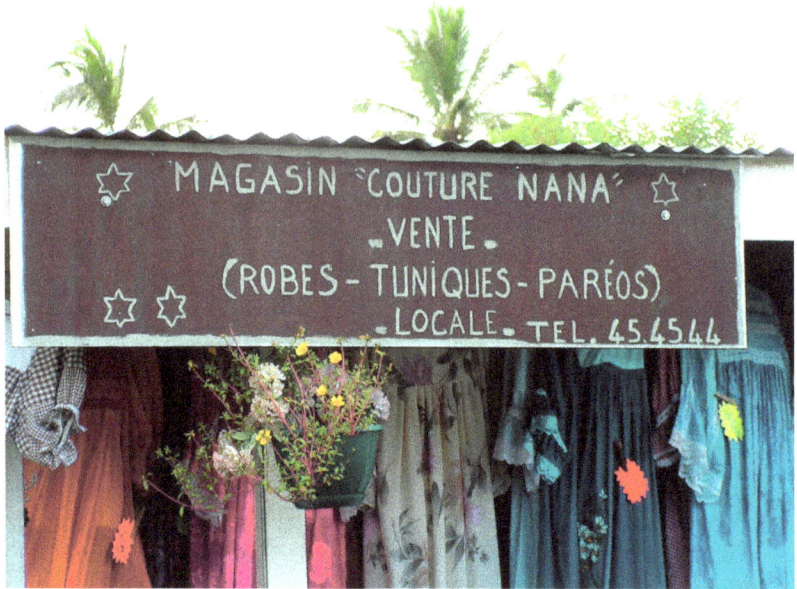

Figure 22. Magasin 'Couture Nana', Nang, Lifou
Source. © Photographed by Anna Paini, Lifou, 27 March 2005

To illustrate all these innovations, I present here a story collected in Lifou in March 2005. Two years earlier Sélékè[29] had opened 'Couture Nana' (Figure 22) after a successful request for assistance to the Province des îles in order to carry out a project she had had in the pipeline for some time. I interviewed her in her atelier in Nang, in the northern part of Lifou. She agreed to answer my questions at the same time as serving her customers. She had started to learn how to sew as a child, both at home and in school. Later she learned from her mother-in-law, who was a skilful seamstress. One of the walls of the room that she converted into her atelier was covered with photographs of her creations. She emphasised the choice of new fabrics, especially plaid and checked material, which she was inspired to use for *robes mission* after seeing them in a fabric store in Nouméa. She argued that it was a novelty: 'it was my idea' that soon became fashionable. Sélékè had started to make these *robes à carreaux* in June 2004; less than a year later she had already made and sold approximately 800 of them. Besides her husband, who helped her in the different phases of the hand dyeing process, she also had the help of a seamstress.

---

29   This story has already been introduced in Paini 2009.

The cotton and cotton-synthetic fabrics arrived from Nouméa. Most of the time she placed her orders by telephone; in cases of larger quantities they were shipped by sea, otherwise by air. 'I do not design, I look at the fabric and cut,' Sélékè recounted. And, speaking of the demands of some customers to make them a dress according to a certain style, she insisted: 'I do not like to copy but to create models'; she told me that she had refused to follow a customer's request because the idea was taken from another stylist. Her clients were from Lifou as well as from nearby Maré and also from the capital, where two shops were selling her *robes*. The path followed by her creations provides an interesting situation in which dresses are locally produced in a rural area and from there reach the capital to meet the urban demand. This reverses the traditional commercial route of the *robes* made in the capital and sold on the islands.

Sometimes clothes were hand dyed with stencilled patterns or embroidered designs. She would agree to dye *robes*, only if she received an order of 15–20. When choosing colours, ordered in Nouméa, Sélékè explained that she took into account the 'desires of women'. The designs were hand-made individually for each *robe*, but in the case of group orders for weddings she would use a pattern to ensure a more homogeneous outcome. Her spirit of innovation led her to experiment with new techniques for drying hand-dyed robes even in the absence of the sun. The price of a *robe* depended on the hours of work—the average price was around 5,000/6,000 CFP. 'The dresses for the *coutume* tear easily, mine are more expensive', however, she points out, they 'last longer'. Though she was busy that day, she was proud to tell me that 'women prefer to buy in Lifou. When they go to Nouméa, women know when a dress has come from Lifou. The Chinese have always the same model, with a narrow neck'. Sélékè relates an experience she had in town: 'The check material dress … I went into a shop in Nouméa and I was told: "Lady, this is a new model, it has just came out". And I retorted: 'That model comes from Lifou'. But then she added: "That's the way it is in commerce".' Sélékè claimed to have solved the problem of imitation by resorting to labels, which she had just ordered from Thailand.

Figure 23. Old and new *robes*, Protestant convention, Kumo, Lifou
Source. © Photographed by Anna Paini, 27 March 2005

Asked to indicate the terms she used to talk about the *robe*, Sélékè specified: '*Robe à carreaux*, plain simple robe, robe dyed with dentelle, double dress … You know "mission" is a bit …'. She left the sentence incomplete. *Robe popinée* instead returned several times during the conversation. A customer from Maré who followed part of the interview responded without hesitation that she preferred the expression *robe popinée* because 'it comes across as more related to Kanak women', while *robe mélanésienne* 'sounds too French'. She admitted, however, that she was aware that on the Grande Terre the term had a pejorative connotation, but insisted that this was not the case on the Loyalty Islands.

The use of the *robe mission* has expanded; even girls and young girls are increasingly wearing it on important occasions. Thus, alongside the standard sizes—1, 2, 3, i.e., small, medium, large[30]—the new dressmakers are beginning to make sizes for girls. Work is guaranteed throughout the year as there are plenty of opportunities to buy a new *robe*: before and during the Easter Protestant convention (Figure 23); on the occasion of

---

30   Lately also size 4.

marriages; and for various other celebrations. On funeral occasions, some women purchased from her both the garment they were intending to wear to the event and those for ceremonial exchanges. In this case women chose ready-made dresses, while for weddings the choice was more personalised.

Sélékè took part in three *defilés* (fashion shows), one in downtown Nouméa during a promotional event organised by the craft associations. Among the customers there were some tourists, but 'they do not choose the check materials because they view [them] as coming from the *métropole* [France], they prefer the dyed dresses, the pareos'.[31]

Figure 24. The worktable of Eseka's atelier, Lifou
Source. © Photographed by Anna Paini, 8 November 2007

---

31   When I returned to Lifou the atelier was closed. Sélékè had died after a long illness. Eseka, one of the most succesful business women from Lifou, who today runs a big atelier in town, told me that she was inspired by Sélékè's example. (Eseka, June 2015; see Figures 24 and 25).

Figure 25. Eseka Couture, Nouméa
Source. © Photographed by Anna Paini, 5 June 2015

Figure 26. Hand-dyed *robes* drying in the sun, Hapetra, Lifou
Source. © Photographed by Anna Paini, 11 November 2009

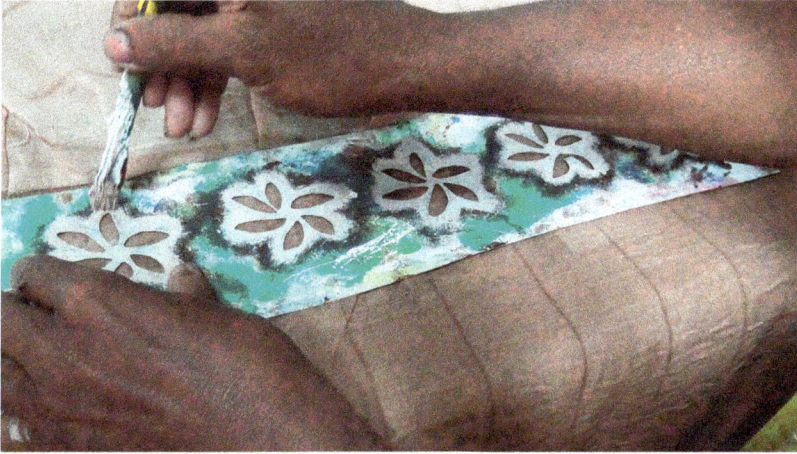

Figure 27. Hand painting flowers on a hand-dyed *robe mission,* 'Naji Couture' by Ijane, Hapetra, Lifou
Source. © Photographed by Anna Paini, 1 June 2015

Conclusion: '*De la robe mission à la robe kanak*'

The new interest in the *robe* has spread over to the Grande Terre. More and more Kanak women are choosing to sew not just for themselves but for other women, starting small businesses (see Figures 26 and 27). In 2010, I attended the second 'Fête de la Robe Mission' in Koohné, organised by the Northern Province. Waimalo Wapotro (2010) and I were invited to talk on the *robe mission*.[32] Kanak women determinately voiced their concern regarding the Nouméa shops' practice of imitating their models. They considered their handiwork as a 'creative endeavour' and asked the governmental officers present what could be done at the central level in order to defend what they perceived as their 'intellectual cultural propriety' rights (seé Pigliasco, Chapter 9, this volume), and to put in place a system enforcing the protection of the *robe* made by Kanak women. The government representatives were taken back by such an unexpected vehement request.

---

32   Waimalo Wapotro had given an important talk on the history of the dress at the Jean-Marie Tjibaou Cultural Center in 2003, in the same year my article on the *robe mission* was published in *Journal de la Société des Océanistes* (JSO). This conference in 2010 was the first occasion in which we were both involved (see *Mwà Véé* 2010).

The perception of the mission dress as a colonial garment, that for a long time connoted the Grande Terre where the colonial influences have been more intense, is giving way to a different one now that Kanak women are designing, manufacturing and marketing the dress themselves. Thus moving along 'tides of innovation', the *robe mission* has been accorded a novel local content and thus is becoming the kanak female dress across the country; both older and younger women acknowledge it as a symbol of pride.

I do not want to convey a false image that all Kanak women make the same choices. In the early 1990s I wrote that dress codes in Nouméa had changed, they were more relaxed, especially for young women who often wore trousers both at home and outside. Older women instead still wore the mission dress to go to work or to go out to places such as the post office or to bingo. They wore the same style of dress regardless of the public space they moved in. For important events, such as a wedding, however, even a Lifouan girl in Nouméa would wear a *robe mission* (Paini 2003a). Today, more adult women wear pants combined with a long, loose top, often in the style of a *robe mission* (see Cummings 2013; Jolly 2014). Yet, for important occasions adult Lifouan women will choose a *robe*, which they consider the proper way to dress. Nevertheless, the mission dress has been transformed by Kanak women into a versatile garment, worn on formal and informal occasions. Its versatility is such that it has been used by players of female cricket teams at all levels. Their official uniform above the sneakers is the mission dress in the colours of the village team they belong to: Drueulu, for instance, chose blue and white; the neighbouring villages of Hapetra and Wedrumel respectively yellow-green and green-white-red. The mission dress is thus associated with the most popular national sport among Kanak women and at the same time its colours distinguish the teams on the field, enabling players and fans to identify with their team.

The polysemic dimensions of this dress show that women can turn to it in articulating the tension between belonging and difference. Locally made, the *robe* is now considered as an element of belonging that, depending on the context and the strategies adopted, can emphasise either the place one comes from or a common feeling of being Kanak, or both. At the conclusion of the General Assembly celebrating 20 years of activity of the women's movement 'Smiling Melanesian Village',[33] which was held in Drueulu (Lifou) in February 1992, women organised a march through the village that saw 200 participants parading in *robes mission*: each group adopted a chosen colour code and pattern (see Paini 2003a and 2003b). Just like the Kanak delegation present at the international event Terra Madre in Turin chose a white and red floral fabric, in local, regional and international arenas, the fabric used is chosen for each occasion. However, if the fabric connects to a specific place and thus emphasises locality, the dress itself emphasises communality; thus multiple threads of meanings are woven into this garment.

Gradually Kanak women have transformed the *robe*, adapted it to their taste and made it their own 'traditional' dress in which they recognise themselves. Annamaria Rivera's assertion (2005) that the symbols and practices of clothing and the meanings that they take on depend on how they are acted out in a given historical situation, is relevant here; it helps us to understand the specific colonial experiences lived in different parts of the country, and the ways in which these experiences have been locally elaborated over time: a new rearticulation has taken place in the context of the new female creativity and entrepreneurship. In 2008 a project titled 'Popinée', centred on a dance by Kanak choreographer Richard Digoué, was performed at the Musée de Nouvelle-Calédonie. The subject of Kanak women's empowerment was explored through the history of the mission dress. On that occasion Marie-Solange Néaoutyne, director of the Museum, wrote a poem which she entitled 'Popinée'; it was published in the special issue of *Mwà Véé* (2010: 69) and dedicated to the *robe*. In her poem she emphasised the changing status of women wearing the dress: 'from submission to creation' and endorsed the switch '*de la robe mission à la robe kanak*'; her phrase was then borrowed as title for the special issue. Further, the *robe* has been included in the second Festival International des Textiles Extraordinaires (FITE); the textile exhibit *Renaissance* opened at the Bargoin Museum in Clermont Ferrand in 2014 (Athenor 2014) and moved to Manila at the Metropolitan Museum (MET) in 2015 (Figure 28).[34]

---

33 An association of Catholic Kanak women spread throughout the country.
34 I have kept the *robes mission* purchased or received as gifts through the years and I loaned them to the Bargoin Museum in Clermont Ferrand and to the Metropolitan Museum of Manila for the Festival International des Textiles Extraordinaires (FITE) in 2014/2015 (see Figure 28).

Figure 28. Festival International des Textiles Extraordinaires (FITE), Metropolitan Museum of Manila (MET), Manila
Source. © Photographed by Anna Paini, 9 July 2015

In recent years Kanak female agency has taken on new forms: on the one hand, seamstresses/dressmakers/artisans/artists have created a new female entrepreneurship, spreading from Lifou to the rest of the country; on the other hand, female customers have chosen clothes in the new styles, purchasing them from the Kanak dressmakers' ateliers, thus provoking a snowball effect. Symbols and practices in clothing were re-contextualised in the past and continue to be rearticulated in the present, even if the pace of innovation is faster in the twenty-first century.

It is still too early to predict if the successful ventures of these women will lead to more radical changes, for now they all say: 'It is always the robe' that is invested with local value. The notion of 'pragmatic creativity', defined by Heather E. Young Leslie and Ping-Ann Addo as 'a way of seeing, being in, and fashioning the world that is alert, flexible, pliable, open to modification, adaptation, re-adaptation' (2007: 12), surely applies to Kanak women who have resignified a colonial object turning into a cultural one by transforming it into an interisland and interconfessional cultural object, negotiating its meanings, turning it into something they appreciate in terms of value as well as of aesthetics. Re-dressing signs and designs, Kanak women consider the *robe mission* as an expression of a deep-rooted sense of place, but at the same time also an expression of routedness, of a mobile interplay with other times, places and people (Clifford 2001).

Acknowledgements

This essay relies on material collected during various periods of fieldwork in New Caledonia. I thank the Kanak women of Lifou, in particular of Drueulu, who once again have agreed to share with me their experience and their knowledge. I am particularly grateful to Sélékè, Eseka and Ijane for allowing me to learn from them. The *robe mission* has already been the focus of previous works (Paini 2002, 2003a) which only partially tackled the issues developed here, the result of further research on the topic. My long article in Italian (2009) begins to address Kanak women's recent engagement with entrepreneurship. A more recent contribution (Paini 2012) deals instead with the processes of naming the dress. Missionary correspondence was consulted in the Archives of the Marist Fathers in Rome. I thank archivist Padre Carlo Maria Schianchi for his invaluable help. I also thank the late Marie-Claire Beboko-Beccalossi, Bess Flores, Elisabetta Gnecchi-Ruscone, Giuliana Sellan, Vanessa Maher, and Gabriela Vargas-Cetina. Each of them knows what I owe them. I am also grateful to Billy Wapotro. A special thanks to Barbara Setsu Pickett for comments on clothing construction. Field research carried out in 2005, 2007, 2009, 2011 and 2015 was supported by the University of Verona.

References

Archival repositories

APM, Archives of the Marist Fathers, Rome, ONC 208, missionaries personal dossiers, Lifou.

Books and journals

Athenor, Christine. 2014. *Renaissance*, Catalogue HS Projets, Musée Bargoin and ville de Clermont-Ferrand, Aubière: Drouin.

Bensa, Alban and Isabelle Leblic (eds). 2000. *En pays kanak. Ethnologie, linguistique, archéologique, histoire de la Nouvelle-Calédonie*. Paris: Éditions de la Maison des sciences de l'homme.

Bensa, Alban, Kacué Yvon Goromoedo and Adrian Muckle (eds). 2015. *Les sanglots de l'aigle pêcheur. Nouvelle-Calédonie: la guerre kanak de 1917*. Toulouse: Anacharsis Éditions.

Bolton, Lissant. 2005. 'Dressing for transition: Weddings, clothing, and change in Vanuatu'. In *The Art of Clothing: A Pacific Experience*, ed. Susanne Küchler and Graeme Were, pp. 19–31. London: UCL Press.

———. 2003. 'Gender, status and introduced clothing in Vanuatu'. In *Clothing the Pacific*, ed. Chloë Colchester, pp. 119–39. Oxford: Berg.

Cerulli, Ernesta. 1999. *Vestirsi spogliarsi travestirsi: come quando perché*. Palermo: Sellerio.

Clifford, James. 2001. 'Indigenous articulations'. *The Contemporary Pacific* 13(2): 468–90. doi.org/10.1353/cp.2001.0046.

Colchester, Chloë. 2003. 'Introduction'. In *Clothing the Pacific*, ed. Chloë Colchester, pp. 1–22. Oxford: Berg.

Colchester, Chloë (ed.). 2003. *Clothing the Pacific*. Oxford: Berg.

Colombo Dougoud, Roberta. 2002. 'Ricerca sul campo. Istruzioni per l'uso'. In *La terra dei miei sogni. Esperienze di ricerca sul campo in Oceania*, ed. L. Brutti e Anna Paini, pp. 48–69. Roma: Meltemi.

Cummings, Maggie. 2013. 'Looking good: The cultural politics of island dress for young women in Vanuatu'. *The Contemporary Pacific* 25(1): 33–65. doi.org/10.1353/cp.2013.0007.

Douglas, Bronwen (ed.). 2003. *Women's Groups and Everyday Modernity in Melanesia*. Special issue of *Oceania* 74 (1–2).

———. 2002. 'Christian citizens: Women and negotiations of modernity in Vanuatu'. *Contemporary Pacific* 14(1): 1–38. doi.org/10.1353/cp.2002.0007.

———. 1998. *Across the Great Divide. Journey in History and Anthropology*. Amsterdam: Harwood Academic Publisher.

Etherington, Norman. 2012. 'Afterword'. In *In God's Empire: French Missionaries and the Modern World*, ed. Owen White and J.P. Daughton, pp. 279–301. New York: Oxford University Press. doi.org/10.1093/acprof:oso/9780195396447.003.0013.

Hadfield, Emma. 1920. *Among the Natives of the Loyalty Group*. London: Macmillan.

Hereniko, Vilsoni. 2005. 'Dressing and undressing the bride and groom at a Rotuman wedding'. In *The Art of Clothing: A Pacific Experience*, ed. Susanne Küchler and Graeme Were, pp. 103–109. London: UCL Press.

Jolly, Margaret. 2014. 'A saturated history of Christianity and cloth in Oceania. *Divine Domesticities: Christian Paradoxes in Asia and the Pacific*, ed. Hyaeweol Choi and Margaret Jolly, pp. 429–54. Canberra: ANU Press. Online: press.anu.edu.au/publications/divine-domesticities (accessed 29 August 2016).

——. 2012. 'Material and immaterial relations: Gender, rank and Christianity in Vanuatu'. In *The Scope of Anthropology: Maurice Godelier's Work in Context*, ed. Laurent Dousset and Serge Tcherkézoff, 110–54. Method and History in Anthropology 23. Oxford: Berghahn.

——. 2003. 'Epilogue'. In *Women's Groups and Everyday Modernity in Melanesia*. Special issue of *Oceania*, ed. Bronwen Douglas, 74(1–2): 134–47.

——. 2001. 'On the edge? Deserts, oceans, islands'. *The Contemporary Pacific* 13(2): 417–466. doi.org/10.1353/cp.2001.0055.

——. 1991. '"To save the girls for brighter and better lives": Presbyterian Missions and women in the south of Vanuatu'. *Journal of Pacific History* 26(1): 27–48. doi.org/10.1080/00223349108572645.

Jolly, Margaret and Martha Macintyre (eds). 1989. *Family and Gender in the Pacific*. Cambridge: Cambridge University Press.

Kirshenblatt-Gimblett, Barbara. 1998. *Destination Culture: Tourism, Museums and Heritage*. Berkeley: University of California Press.

Kopytoff, Igor. 1986. 'The cultural biography of things: Commoditization as process'. In *The Social Life of Things: Commodities in Cultural Perspective*, ed. Arjun Appadurai, pp. 64–91. Cambridge: Cambridge University Press. doi.org/10.1017/CBO9780511819582.004.

Küchler, Susanne and Graeme Were (eds). 2005. *The Art of Clothing: A Pacific Experience*. London: UCL Press.

Leblic, Isabelle. 1998. 'L'évolution des techniques de pêche en Nouvelle-Calédonie'. *Techniques et Cultures* 12: 81–119.

Leenhardt, Maurice. 1978. 'Pourquoi se vêtir?' *Journal de la Société des Océanistes* 34(58): 3–7. doi.org/10.3406/jso.1978.2960.

MacFarlane, Samuel. 1873. *The Story of the Lifu Mission*. London: Nisbet.

Merle, Isabelle. 2002. 'Retour sur le "Code de l'Indigénat": réflexions autour des principes répressifs dans l'Empire français'. *French Politics, Culture and Society* 20(2): 3–15. doi.org/10.3167/153763702782369803.

Milie, Imelda and Anna Paini. 1996. 'Ka xep qa hnagëje (everything that comes from the sea); or foreignness as articulated by Lifuans'. Paper presented at the European Society for Oceanists conference, Copenhagen, 13–15 December.

Muckle, Adrian. 2011. '"Native", "Immigrants" and "libéré": The Colonial Regulation of Mobility in New Caledonia'. *Law Text Culture* 15: 135–161.

Mwà Véé, Revue culturelle kanak. 2010. *De la robe mission à la robe kanak*. Special issue 69.

Mwà Véé, Revue culturelle kanak. 2001. *Vision poétique du monde. Écritures kanak, calédoniennes et océaniennes*. Special issue 33.

O'Reilly, Patrick and Jean Poirier. 1953. 'L'évolution du costume'. *Journal de la Société des Océanistes* 9: 151–69. doi.org/10.3406/jso.1953.1775.

Paini, Anna. 2012. 'I processi di indigenizzazione nelle pratiche culturali e linguistiche dei Kanak di Lifou'. *Ethnorêma* 8: 1–15. Online: www.ethnorema.it/pdf/numero%208/05%20Paini.pdf (accessed 29 August 2016).

——. 2010. 'Rhabiller les symboles: robes mission et femmes en pays Drehu'. *Mwà Véé* 69: 6–9.

——. 2009. 'Risemantizzare vecchi e nuovi simboli. Robe mission e imprenditorialità delle donne kanak (Nuova Caledonia)'. In *Antropologia dell'Oceania*, ed. Elisabetta Gnecchi-Ruscone and Anna Paini, pp. 237–63. Milano: Raffello Cortina Editore.

——. 2007. *Il filo e l'aquilone: I confini della differenza in una società kanak della Nuova Caledonia*. Torino: Le Nuove Muse.

——. 2003a. 'Rhabiller les symboles. Les femmes kanak et la robe mission à Lifou, Nouvelle-Calédonie'. In *Nouvelle-Calédonie 150 ans après la prise de possession*. Special issue of *Journal de la Société des Océanistes*, ed. Isabelle Leblic, 117(2): 233–53.

——. 2003b. '"The kite is tied to you". Custom, christianity and organization among Kanak women of Drueulu, Lifou'. in *Women's Groups and Everyday Modernity in Melanesia*. Special issue of *Oceania*, ed, Bronwen Douglas, 74(1–2): 81–97.

——. 2002. 'Ri-abitare il corpo. Le donne kanak e la "robe mission" a Lifou (Nuova Caledonia)'. *DiPAV Quadrimestrale di psicologia e antropologia culturale* 3: 79–92.

——. 1998. 'Praying Samoa and praying Oui-Oui. Making Christianity local in Lifu (Loyalty Islands)'. In *Common Worlds and Single Lives: Constituting Knowledge in Pacific Societies*, ed. Verena Keck, pp. 171–206. Oxford: Berg.

Péter-Contesse, Eugénie. (1923-1951) personal correspondence. PMB 1011. Pacific Manuscripts Bureau, Canberra.

Rivera, Annamaria. 2005. *La guerra dei simboli. Veli postcoloniali e retoriche sull'alterità*. Bari: Dedalo.

Sam, Léonard Drïle. 1995. *Dictionnaire Drehu-Français: (Lifou, Nouvelle-Calédonie): suivi d'un lexique français-drehu (pour débutants)*. Nouméa: Coédition du C.P.R.D.P. des Iles avec la participation du Vice-Rectorat.

Shineberg, Dorothy. 1999. *The People Trade: Pacific Island Laborers and New Caledonia, 1865-1930*. Honolulu: University of Hawai'i Press.

Tcherkézoff, Serge. 2003. 'On cloth, gifts and nudity: Regarding some European misunderstandings during early encounters in Polynesia'. In *Clothing the Pacific*, ed. Chloë Colchester, pp. 51–75. Oxford: Berg.

Terra Madre Salone del Gusto website. 2008. Turin. Online: www.salonedelgusto.com (accessed 16 September 2016).

Thomas, Nicholas. 2005. 'Preface'. In *The Art of Clothing: A Pacific Experience*, ed. Susanne Küchler and Graeme Were, pp. ix–xi. London: UCL Press.

Tjibaou, Jean-Marie. 1996. *La présence kanak*. Edition établie et présentée par Alban Bensa et Eric Wittersheim. Paris: Odile Jacob.

Tjibaou, Jean-Marie and Philippe Missotte. 1978. *Kanaké: The Melanesian Way*. Papeete: Les éditions du pacifique.

Wapotro, Waimalo. 2010. 'Robe histoire'. *Mwà Véé* 69: 10–11.

Weiner, Annette B. 1989. 'Why cloth? Wealth, gender, and power in Oceania'. In *Cloth and Human Experience*, ed. Annette B. Weiner and Jane Schneider, pp. 33–72. Washington: Smithsonian Books.

Young Leslie, Heather E. and Ping-Ann Addo. 2007. 'Introduction'. in *Hybrid Textiles: Pragmatic Creativity and Authentic Innovations in Pacific Cloth*. Special issue of *Pacific Arts* 3–5: 12–21.

Part Two. Value and Agency: Local Experiences in Expanded Narratives

5

Kanak Women on the Move in Contemporary New Caledonia

Marie-Claire Beboko-Beccalossi[1]

Les femmes ont une place importante
à prendre (dans la société),
elles sont une richesse dans l'évolution du pays.[2]

Marie-Claire Beccalossi

Editors' preface

This text was sent to us on occasion of the 7th ESfO conference in Verona, and was read by Christine Jourdan at the round table. It was accompanied by an email from Marie-Claire Beboko-Beccalossi, 'Alors que tu t'apprêtais à me recevoir à Vérone pour cette rencontre que tu fignoles depuis un moment déjà, voilà que je te fais faux bond; sois sûre que si ma santé était sans accros, je serais venue vous rejoindre là avec grand, grand plaisir. Bonne rencontre, Bonne conférence! Je suis de tout cœur avec vous'.[3]

---

1 This text is the translation of the Italian version that was assembled by Silvia Bernardi from the notes sent by Marie-Claire for the ESfO conference, 'Les femmes de Nouvelle-Calédonie', March 2008, Verona.

2 Women have an important place in society, they are wealth for the country's evolvement.

3 'Just as you were preparing to welcome me in Verona for this meeting which you have been nurturing for some time, I must let you down; rest assured that if my health were not problematic, I would have joined you there with great, great pleasure. Have a good meeting, a good conference! I'm with you with all my heart.'

Unfortunately, Marie-Claire's illness proved to be fatal, and when we published her notes in Italian in the journal *la Ricerca Folklorica* (Paini and Gnecchi-Ruscone 2011: 63) Anna Paini consulted with her husband, Ermenegildo Beccalossi, who commented on the translation in the following email:

> I have read through the original French text and the hand written corrections added by Marie-Claire. I find that the translator/s have done a commendable job of coordination and comprehension. To help capturing and understanding a text by Marie-Claire, I take the liberty of underlying some elements. Marie-Claire came from an oral culture, she had a great ease with speech, and her writings go through unforeseen changes and also repetitions which could have weighed down the translated and published text, especially for readers who are unfamiliar with the person and her country (31 October 2011).

Marie-Claire Beboko-Beccalossi was recognised as a prominent figure for Kanak women; she devoted her life to social justice and women's rights in the Pacific area. Her life history shows a record of commitment and struggles to give Pacific women a voice, a face and political representation. She was active on several fronts at both local and regional levels, but also internationally: as a young woman she militated in Jeunesse Agricole et Rurale Catholique des Femmes (JARCF), becoming its president, and later in life she participated in the Pontifical Council for Justice and Peace.

The notes that compose this chapter constitute Marie-Claire's personal account of the crucial passages of indigenous women's struggles in New Caledonia from early colonial days to the present. In particular, it underlines the role of the younger generation of women of the 1960s–70s in the establishment of women's groups (both confessional and secular organisations), to which older women participated only at a later stage, giving rise to networks which enabled Kanak women to endure the upheaval of the *Événements* in the 1980s, showing their resilience in the pervasive tensions and conflicts of the period.

This chapter focuses on issues that were close to her heart, placing Melanesian women at the centre; she held that Kanak women have been and still are agents of change and innovation and, above all, they 'hold their heads high'.

We believe these pages exemplify the passion, commitment and vision constituting her lasting legacy.

Before the Great War

A bird's-eye view over the traditional Kanak world during colonial times reveals the novelty represented by the space devoted to women's collective activities within the tribes and around places of worship, under the influences of Catholic and Protestant churches. Religion undoubtedly provided a stimulus for the formation of groups and collective moments. Away from their customary obligations and from habits and impositions of the male world, these new forms of encounters have helped women to understand and acquire new knowledge: they were able to satisfy their curiosities, to exchange and use new materials; they have diversified their cooking skills and their household management, they have learned to sew, mend and even a new language: the language of whites, the idiom that had kept them at a distance from many activities of colonial society.

Some girls were even able to engage in learning reading skills and 'French style' good manners: depending on their rank in traditional society, these young women have profited, by choice or imposition, from the teaching and education given by nuns and the wives of the pastors. The ecclesiastical communities have thus given rise to the formation of long-term learning groups for Kanak girls and boys. A sort of private school, still at the embryonic stage, yet complete with all the prohibitions brought by the new way of life: the prohibition to speak one's own language in favour of French, for example, was essential for moving from the 'savage' to the 'civilised' condition. Undoubtedly in this phase the assimilation of French culture was inflected almost exclusively through imitating white people's behaviour, that is 'acting like the white man', like the *kamadra* (Drehu).[4]

The event which gave a jolt to this way of thinking, based on a single model—the *kamadra* model—and that has deeply affected Kanak mentality, is World War II: many young Melanesian volunteers left for the front encountering unknown lands, radically different from their own, while the presence of Americans in New Caledonia produced an unprecedented situation of encounter with the *other*. The war was thus

---

4   This Drehu word, *kamadra*, is widely used throughout New Caledonia; it means 'white person' (editors' comments).

a situation of conflicts but also of encounters, as shown by the tales and memories of the young volunteers who returned: families and whole tribes listened with amazement to the incredible stories told by their sons, and learned of women's involvement on the battle ground.

Despite the blood, pain and losses, the war had multifaceted implications, it created the circumstances for recognising a new form of warrior with very different qualities from those that were traditionally known.

The steps leading to social changes are very slow; as I had the opportunity to recall during the International Women's Day celebration of 8 March 2007:

> The day before yesterday our great grandmothers moved from silence to speaking, within the family and among themselves within the different clans. Yesterday our grandmothers moved from speaking to representing, within the family and the clan.

The 1950s: From colonisation to participation

World War II thus marks an important moment for Melanesian society. New Caledonia is shaken by impulses that profoundly change the structure of society. New associations are formed which are organised according to religious and political leanings. Assemblies, increasingly characterised by a secular approach, involve groups of women, youths and intellectuals. At the same time, periods spent abroad for studying or to acquire an appropriate education for modern times become more common, and in the following decades many students, both girls and boys, leave to spend a length of time in France and other foreign countries.

If today education and training are a priority in the context of the *Cadres Avenir* project within the Matignon and Nouméa Accords, in the 1960s such an opportunity was an absolute novelty. It is not surprising that initially the establishment of new women's organisations was structured around the initiatives and spontaneity of the younger girls, often returning from a period of study abroad. Later they were flanked by women gathered in confessional associations and federations, as well as in secular NGOs. It is precisely in this lively historical moment that I had the opportunity to live my first experience within a great federation. In 1963 I was elected President of the Jeunesse Agricole et Rurale Catholique des Femmes (JARCF), a women's organisation which at the time had over 3,000 Kanak members. I held this position until my marriage, six years later.

It is true that, on the one hand, for two-thirds of last century the activities of Melanesian women's groups adopted the west as a model of civilisation, a partial heritage of colonial history. On the other hand, all the movements demonstrated the evident will of Kanak women to take a further step on the path towards their rights: a step towards representation and social participation. The mouvement féminin vers un Souriant Village Mélanésien (mfSVM), established in 1972, is a good example of such a gradual process of affirmation of Kanak women's groups in New Caledonia.

From social to political participation: The 1980s and 1990s

In the 1980s New Caledonia is a territory that lives neither in peace nor at war: tense, restless, lively, the island is crossed by a series of intense upheavals aiming at independence from the French government. At mid-decade, the FLNKS movement (Front de Libération Nationale Kanak et Socialiste) headed by Jean-Marie Tjibaou, leads the struggle for the autonomy of Melanesians[5] from the *caldoches*[6] living on Kanaky.[7]

---

5   The term Melanesians here is translated directly from Marie-Claire's French notes to reflect the practice, common in New Caledonia in the recent past, to label as *Mélanésiens* only Kanak (see, for example, Census (New Caledonia) 1989 and National Institute of Statistics and Economic Studies (INSEE) (1997) (eds comments).

6   *Caldoches* designates the descendants of European convicts and colonists settled in the country over several generations (eds comments).

7   *Kanaky* is the name given to New Caledonia by Kanak independentists and widely adopted in the country. Some people believe that once the country achieves a new political status it should be renamed Kanaky New Caledonia.

For a better contextualisation, we mention here the events of the tormented colonial history referred to in this chapter. New Caledonia, a French possession since 1853, was a penal colony before becoming a settlement colony. After World War II it became a French Overseas Territory (TOM). In the 1980s the country was traversed by deep-rooted political tensions between Kanak and *caldoches* (*les événements*). The Matignon Accords (1988) created the conditions for a new climate in the country. A process of decentralisation provided for by the Matignon Accords was initiated to balance the social and economic gap between the capital Nouméa, a prevalently white centre, and the rest of the country, mainly inhabited by Kanak, resulting in the institution of three provinces: the Loyalty Islands Province, the Southern Province and the Northern Province. The referendum on the political future of the country foreseen in the Accords for the end of the 1980s was made obsolete by the Nouméa Accord of May 1998, which gave more autonomy and a new denomination to the country, *collectivité sui generis*. The referendum on self-determination has now been rescheduled for 2018 (eds comments).

The Matignon Accords, at least partly, placate the revolts. This did not stop the achievements of women in government agencies, and thus their growing visibility in the political arena. A historical date is 1983: the first Bureau Technique des Femmes (BTF) was instituted at the SPC,[8] followed just a few months later by the Conseil des Femmes de Nouvelle Calédonie (CF.NC), an outcome of women's expectations and their growing autonomy. As the head of the BTF and as regional delegate to the Council of Ministers of the French government, I invested all my energies in a project calling for the establishment of the Office for Women's Rights in New Caledonia. With great satisfaction on the part of my colleagues and me, the project was approved by the government, and soon the office came to life. Once this service was created it recruited some women; they went on to form the New Caledonia Regional Delegation for Women's Rights. At last I was no longer alone, even when facing the Council of Ministers.

The early 90s were devoted to working towards further reforms in the wake of the previous successes. Most of the women's associations of all the provinces gathered in councils, thus gradually widening their sphere of competence. If, on the one hand, the new Nouméa Accord of 1998 has disappointed the expectations of most of the population by postponing the date of the pro-independence referendum to the fourth term of the Congress, on the other hand it has ratified a further strengthening of the country's prerogatives for autonomy, thus progressing towards a gradual hand over. Women's organisations wish to seize the opportunities offered by the Accord, working towards the best conditions for an administration that would respect every community in the country.

The significance of 3 June 1983

Following an invitation which I extended as head of the BTF for the Community of the South Pacific, more than 70 coordinators of religious and secular women's associations gathered in a large assembly on 3 June 1983. My aim was, first of all, to raise awareness of the Bureau Technique des Femmes, that had been established only three months before within the

---

8   SPC is the principal scientific and technical organisation in the Pacific region. It was founded in 1947 under the Canberra Agreement. Although the acronym has never changed given its widespread use across the Pacific Islands region, the name has changed over time from South Pacific Commission, to Secretariat of the Pacific Community, to Pacific Community (2016) (eds comment).

SPC regional service alongside its sister English-speaking section. Second, I wanted to encourage the different representatives to meet in order for them to equip themselves with a structure of dialogue, that should be at the same time representative of the entire female population of the Territory (New Caledonia), but also a means of mediation between the different local and central administrative powers. I should emphasise that these goals were undoubtedly in syntony with the requests of the United Nations, which were recommending to offices and structures such as the BTF and the SPC to promote and support women's organisations in each country, so that women could make their voice heard and cooperate in order to solve problems concerning education, health and employment.

Each of the coordinators attending the meeting took on the message of the conference, welcoming it with great enthusiasm; the atmosphere was one of conscious participation. All the women were aware of the importance of the decisions stemming from the meeting, to the point that on the following day, 3 June, they all agreed to give life to the Conseil des Femmes de Nouvelle Calédonie (CF.NC, Council of Women of New Caledonia), and they chose that day as the date of the first General Assembly. Mme. Léontine Ponga, a member of the Christian Women's Movement, was the first chairwoman to be appointed. Year after year the activities of the organisation proceeded with tenacity and determination, fulfilling its decisions, without ever resorting to having to applying for public subsidies.

The history of a name: From the Council of Melanesian Women to the Federation of Melanesian Women's Associations of New Caledonia

The tormented times of revolts and struggle, however, were just around the corner. Soon after the country was deep in rivalries and resentments, different ethnic groups regarded each other with suspicion, and the two main political alliances fought like bitter enemies. Such a climate of tension inflamed people's minds, and eventually it infiltrated within the women's council. Many among the association leaders ceased taking part in the meetings, and those who did attend brought with them proposals that were biased by their political sympathies.

At a time like that it would have been easy to lose heart and hope. However, among all the difficulties of that scene, my colleagues and I were motivated to move forwards by the awareness that Kanak women were still there: they resisted, and, for a long time they had been the only ones to do so. Realising that, we decided to rename the Assembly in order to highlight their constant presence and give it a 'a truer face', more congruent to the actual composition of the structure: a name that was in use from 1989 to 1995. Thus was born the Council of Melanesian Women of New Caledonia (CFM.NC), a transitional organisation before the establishment of the Federation.[9] According to many of us, we were still struggling to find an adequate way for our purposes to develop, and it appeared that the Council's orientation should change once more: the executive agreed that a single organisation was necessary to represent women from different ethnic groups living in the country, and to coordinate such groups among themselves and with others from other nations. We also aimed at creating a non-party, multi-confessional assembly with a clear ethnic identification of its membership—a membership that would be able to bring strength to the movement as a whole without discriminating against others in any way, allowing different ethnic groups to establish similar associations, and to bring their contribution within their own council.

The new organisation thus took the name of Federation of Melanesian Women's Associations of New Caledonia (FAFM-NC), a name that is still in use.

Developments of the new millennium

The Federation today is highly regarded in the panorama of international NGOs. Thanks to its longevity and extensive presence in the territory, it is recognised by other organisations as well as by the government offices relating to women's conditions and roles. Besides defending their rights and interests, today's goal is that of promoting economic, social and cultural exchanges with women from other associations, also beyond New Caledonia: because to build networks implies first of all creating potential alliances.

---

9   The Council of Women of New Caledonia was open to all women's organisations in the country, while the Council of Melanesian Women of New Caledonia gathered indigenous groups of women (eds comment).

Pivotal to the FAFM-NC's resolutions is the search for individual and collective autonomy within the groups that are active in the country and the promotion of forms of development centred on the human being—development that responds to real needs as expressed by the communities living in tribal settlements. Among the government structures responsible for the protection of these principles, today there is a new office: the Observatory for the Condition of Women, to which I belong as representative of the Federation. The main mission of this new body is aimed at the redefinition of Kanak women's roles within their society, at education and professional training for women. It includes also the elaboration of information and communication strategies for the empowerment of women (through the yearly event of the International Women's Day and the publication of the Federation's *Nouv'elles*), and the drawing up of a Convention on the Elimination of All Forms of Discrimination against Women (CEDAW) in New Caledonia.

Holding our heads high

We are living in an era in which each society must necessarily face up to deep changes, and New Caledonia is certainly no exception. Day after day we realise the complex implications of globalisation, transforming our way of thinking about history and of framing the flow of our lives. We are unavoidably faced by this challenge: in recent times our country has witnessed the spread of modernity and the advancement of women's movements. Kanak women have demonstrated a remarkable ability to adapt to social changes, often greater than that of Kanak men. Globalisation has drawn them into a tumultuous cross-cultural civilisation, which can enrich them if they take the time to appreciate it, analyse it, understand its potential, and absorb it without losing themselves. With few means but great fortitude, Kanak women are trying to make room for themselves in an ever-increasing number of professional and social sectors, proving their flexibility, pragmatism and resoluteness. One of the best-known examples, in this regard is their employment within the three large nickel plants on the main island.[10]

---

10 For a history of the nickel industry in New Caledonia, see Bencivengo (2014) (eds comments).

New Caledonia today is thus the image of its inhabitants, eight different ethnic groups that share and live on the same land.[11] Each feeds on the others' cultures: food, clothing, languages, places, feasts and so on, but each of them, independently from the others, claims its origins with firmness and dignity. All this is possible thanks to the processes of adaptation that the New Caledonian society has been able to engage in, seizing those valuable chances for growth that integration is always able to offer. Girls in particular have thrown themselves enthusiastically into the training opportunities arising from the new economic system and the development projects within the country (Paini 2007).

The women of New Caledonia are thus on the move, they move ahead at great speed, but most of all they hold their heads high.

Figure 29. Marie-Claire Beboko-Beccalossi (24 February 1942–
29 March 2009)
Source. Photographed by Anna Paini, Nouméa, 28 March 1992

---

11 'Ethnic groups' is a term commonly used in New Caledonia to refer to the different non-autochthonous communities living in the country (eds comments).

References

Bencivengo, Yann. 2014. *Nickel. La naissance de l'industrie calédonienne.* Tours: Presses universitaires François-Rabelais.

Census (New Caledonia). 1989. *Recensement de la population 1989.* Nouméa: Institut territorial de la statistique et des etudes economiques.

Convention on the Elimination of All Forms of Discrimination against Women (CEDAW). 1979. Online: www.un.org/womenwatch/daw/cedaw/cedaw.htm (accessed 30 December 2015).

National Institute of Statistics and Economic Studies (INSEE). 1997. *Images de la population de la Nouvelle-Calédonie. Principaux résultats du recensement 1996.* Paris: Imprimerie Nationale.

Paini, Anna. 2007. *Il filo e l'aquilone: i confini della differenza in una società kanak della Nuova Caledonia,* Torino: Le Nuove Muse.

Paini, Anna and Elisabetta Gnecchi-Ruscone (eds). 2011. *Putting People First. Dialogo interculturale immaginando il futuro in Oceania.* Special Issue of *La Ricerca Folklorica* 63 (April): 3–105.

6

A Fat Sow Named Skulfi: 'Expensive' Words in Dobu Island Society

Susanne Kuehling

Introduction

In this chapter, I argue that words for valuable objects and practices are a useful starting point to study the dynamics of change at the grassroots level. Innovative and creative strategies of dealing with globalisation do not seem to fit into categories like gift and commodity, old and new, individualistic and communal. I propose to focus here on the realisation of contemporary economic behaviour and the dilemmas that are confronted by strategic choices of vocabulary. My example explores a case of not-giving in order to demonstrate how Dobu Islanders assign value to certain words and the interactions that are associated with them.[1] Knowledge of old exchange principles remains valuable when it is adaptable to new demands, and new demands are continuously emerging from the ever-intensifying contact with the global economy. Language needs frequent

1   Fieldwork on Dobu Island was carried out from 1992–94 and in 1997. This text greatly profited from a presentation at the 2008 European Society for Oceanists (ESfO) conference in the session on 'Expensive words', organised by me. I am grateful for the participants' inspiring contributions and the discussion. I also want to thank Michael Young, Gediminas Lankauskas, and the reviewers for their 'expensive' comments.

updating in terminology and as words are assigned more or less value, they reflect dynamics of moral and economic aspects of life that help us understand the 'Tides of Innovation'.

David Graeber, in *Towards an Anthropology of Value*, notes that the word 'value' has been used in three ways in social theory: as appropriate moral standards (values); as the measure of an object's worth; and as a linguistic category that refers to meaningful difference (2001: 2). In this chapter, I will further explore the meaning of value in an ethnographic case study from Dobu Island, Papua New Guinea. In Dobu's 'gift economy', the three types of 'value' overlap and blend: moral standards (goodness, *bobo'ana*), economic value (heaviness, *mwau*) and linguistic categories of distinction (big versus small) are all used as strategies to deal with valuables.

In Dobu, the term *mwau* first of all refers to any kind of heaviness, weight, burden, difficulty, including pregnancy. 'Hard work' (*paisewa mwauna*) is the key to wealth, prestige and, ultimately, fame. The concept of 'work' (*paisewa*) includes notions of good moral conduct, of self-discipline, generosity and obedience (Kuehling 2005). The term 'heaviness' (*mwau*) has been further explored by Nancy Munn on Gawa Island. There, *mwaw* (a cognate of *mwau*) refers to a body that is heavy from excessive eating (1986: 75) or weakened due to a lack of food (86); it carries the undertone of grief (170), slow motion, illness, sleep (75–76) and food that cannot be eaten but must be shared (96). This strong connotation of hardship is evident on Dobu too; for example, in the concept that the mind/inside, *nua*, can be heavy (*nuamwau* means sadness, see Kuehling 2005: 288). In regard to value, this association seems surprising, but I believe that people imagine a person responsible for exchanging valuable objects is weighted down by the burden, slowed down in the attempt to take the right steps, needing to work hard in spite of feeling unwell, and constantly worried about the envy and criticism of others.

Value, as expressed in terms of heaviness, is an activity (working hard), an emotion (a 'heavy heart', as English speakers would say), as well as an unhealthy and endangered condition of the physical body. Objects that can create such a state are valuable, ambiguously desired and feared. A pregnant woman fears complications but values the baby that she is growing in a similar way as a lineage elder may fear sorcery attacks but nevertheless works hard to receive a precious *kula*[2] valuable. Large yams are the most valuable exchange item for women, yet space allows only a brief examination of this complex topic. For a similar reason, I will not engage in the complex debate on the value of *kula* shells here but focus instead on pigs, the other component of the category of *'une*, valuables that are 'worth dying for', as people say. The value of a pig is quite easily judged as its height is measured on one's body ('up to here', pointing at the knee or thigh) and its age according to the shape of its canines ('the teeth came out that far').

By reflecting on moral dilemmas in the reality of producing, distributing and consuming a pig in the Dobu region, I will show that people creatively blend old and new principles, mostly constructing their actions around forms of give-and-take that are morally accepted. The use of certain words appears as a prominent strategy to this end that I will explore here in some detail.

The social and economic value of 'expensive' words, as such vocabulary is referred to in Milne Bay English, has been described as closely linked to notions of secrecy, of magical formulas, occult names and powerful chants. Recent studies have pointed out the special role of powerful vocabulary for a number of non-Austronesian language groups (e.g. Crook 2007; Evans 2009; Goldman 1983; Keen 1994; Robbins 2012; Weiner 2001; Whitehouse 1994). I will here add an Austronesian perspective to this ongoing discussion. Annette Weiner has argued that in the Trobriand Islands:

> Words have their own power; in terms of conflict, words are more ominous and therefore ultimately more powerful than objects. Words, unlike objects, directly and immediately challenge the balance between control and personal autonomy' (Weiner 1976: 214).

Here, Weiner refers to spoken words of magic in the Trobriand Islands, but not only magical words are effective. In fact, words can be seen as more powerful than objects, especially when words alone are likely to be too emotional and potentially socially damaging. In such cases, it is more appropriate to veil feelings and words of anger in a gift. Weiner tells us that in Kiriwina, 'anger can always be expressed in yams' (1984: 172). In Dobu, likewise, there is a proverb, 'Who gives something of high value

---

2   *Kula* is a complex, ongoing gift exchange system that encompasses more than 30 islands and six distinct languages.

may speak out', referring to occasions of exchange where aggression and anger may be expressed while the donor literally throws a valuable towards the receiver. Typically, these gifts are combinations of precious shell ornaments (*bagi* and *mwali*), large yam tubers (*bebai*), and pork (*bawe*), and the terms for these valuable objects and the gifts they constitute together are 'expensive',[3] like 'pearl' would be an expensive word to most people in Milne Bay Province.

In my earlier work on ethics of exchange (Kuehling 2005), I argued that names for gifts are a useful starting point for social analysis because they provide a local charter for exchange behaviour. An approach to this complex subject through language seems appropriate in the light of local constructions of words as 'powerful, strong' (*waiwai-*), 'difficult to understand' (*mwau-*), 'big or long' (*sinabwa-*) or, in the islanders' use of Milne Bay English, 'expensive'. Some words for special objects receive their value from the object, like 'pearl', and these words adjust quickly to the needs and desires of the time. Another category of 'expensive' words refers to larger, more abstract concepts, like 'Amen' to prayer or 'degree' to education. These words need not be deeply understood but they are necessary to claim membership or display competence. The secret knowledge of names, objects and places, passed on as an honour, a repayment of services or as a sign of love are apt examples for this category. Other words are regarded as 'expensive' because they are long and only partially understood, clustered as modern formulas of power, replacing spells and memorised genealogies. These are political buzz words like 'development', 'infrastructure', 'sustainability' and 'global warming', 'shareholder' or 'capacity building'. Greek-based words like 'sophisticated', and Latin-based terms like 'descendants' are equally 'expensive' and seen as evidence for higher education (which is, quite literally, expensive, due to school fees and related costs). A third kind of term is 'expensive' because of its semantic link to 'hard work'. On Dobu Island, the villagers' local names for gifts are conceptualised in this way; such words are 'expensive' because they constitute exclusive knowledge that takes 'hard work' (social investment) to acquire.

In this chapter, I restrict myself to pigs and objects of the global economy as examples for this category. Focusing on words without their syntagmatic context may appear old-fashioned, but space does not permit such

---

3   In order to clarify that the word 'expensive' refers to the Milne Bay English expression, it will appear in italics.

analysis. The power of words ultimately hinges upon broader concepts of language use (see Brenneis and Myers 1984; Brison 1992; Watson-Gegeo and White 1990; Weiner 1984). Clearly, negotiations of value and the rhetorical skills employed deserve more attention, but I am not concerned with speech acts here and I focus on terms that carry value because they are constructed as part of the signified ('the same' in the Maussian sense, see Weiner 1976: 173). I will argue that such words have the capacity to exemplify local strategies of adjustment to new values that are washed ashore by the tides of change.

By telling the story of a pig that I bought for a feast in 1993, I will first demonstrate how today's economic needs can successfully build on principles from pre-capitalist days, providing both social profit and economic benefit. Elaborating on this case, I will move to a more general discussion of the economic, linguistic and social value of terms for gifts on Dobu Island. In contemporary Dobu, morals, gifts and obligations are challenged by family demands and the islanders' personal needs for modern goods and services. Strategies of value generation, from social capital to financial profit, provide a wider halo of context of local economies and they affect the handling of money and pigs on Dobu. Such strategies, encoded in language and audibly presented in face-to-face discourse, suggest more continuity in moral terms than my informants would have admitted to when they complained to me about 'money becoming too big'. While the growing importance of monetary exchanges is undeniable and obvious in my story, the happy ending shows how global and local valuables cannot be conceptualised as 'different' when they are ultimately used for the same purposes.

Vignette: The story of Skulfi, my fat sow

Pigs are an indispensable element of affinal exchanges. Most households raise one or two of them, which live in small pigsties and are fed by all family members with coconut, food scraps and leftovers. A pig has an individual owner and responds to its name; it is treated well until it is time to become an item of exchange. At that time, a senior member of the owner's matrilineage will request it to be returned in the form of pork when the opportunity arrives. Pigs are raised for the sole purpose of exchange because, as a rule, people do not eat their own pigs. 'It would be like eating a relative', people say. And yet, when pigs are killed the meat is redistributed so that all can eat the delicacy, causing my teenage 'brother' to sigh 'people shall die so that we can eat pork!' when he was tired of little bony fish and canned Spam.

Preparing for a feast involves searching for pigs—a difficult task if one's network of exchange partners is too loosely woven, as I learned in 1993 while trying to buy one as a contribution to my family's large mortuary (*sagali*) feast. In preparation for the feast, all adults were told to contribute a pig. Some families had raised piglets in anticipation of the event but others had to get them through their exchange networks. Of course, lacking the skills, networks and means for other forms of exchange, I was expected to pay money and I had not expected that it would be difficult to purchase a pig in a region where cash is always short. To my surprise, though, people were not willing to sell their pigs, explaining apologetically that their pig was raised for a specific purpose, such as a feast, or as a return gift. The term for such an exchange is *utua bawena*— to exchange a pig for a pig. Many times I was informed that so-and-so's pig was only for *utuwa bawena*. 'This pig is for my "fathers"'; 'This pig is already promised to my uncle for his *kula* partner'; 'This pig will be given to my in-laws'.

As time was running short it was with great relief that I learned about Skulfi, the fat sow, earmarked to raise school fees for the children of her owner. My Dobuan family was happy to have that pig and after I had purchased enough fuel we went by boat to meet the woman who had raised Skulfi. I was curious about the name and she told me that the name of the sow had prevented her from being exchanged in the old, non-profit, reciprocal ways in spite of the high demand for pigs. Now, she said, she was very pleased to sell the pig to me, in fact, she expressed her relief that she did not have to continue 'building a fence around' Skulfi by denying her relatives their right to use this pig in affinal exchanges. Not that she sold Skulfi to a stranger, though, because I was a 'child' of my 'mother's' husband Thomas and, as my classificatory 'fathers', the family was inclined to assist in the preparations for the feast and entitled to receive a share of the distributed food.

Skulfi, the woman proudly told me, had escaped numerous obligations of *utua bawena* (swapping pigs in a delayed manner) because she was classified by her name as reserved for *mani bawena* (to exchange a pig for money), a new term built on old principles. This pig was not under the authority of the elders, it was not used for affinal relationship-building but it was reconstructed as a valuable of individual ownership by using methods of the gift exchange practice. Skulfi, as I realised, was an investment to support the next generation to learn the skills needed to thrive in a global economy. Her owner was showing outstanding managerial skills and advertising strategies by using old principles for new contexts, waiting patiently for someone who had money and needed a pig.

At the *sagali* feast, after my brother had butchered Skulfi for me, I had to give pieces of meat and yam tubers to a large number of people. Since I was not familiar with the finer details of distribution (e.g. it was impolite to use most people's names), I had prepared a list of appropriate shouts, e.g. 'namesake, here is your gift—namesake from Mwemweyala!' but my voice did not carry far enough and while my 'mothers' helped me, their brother helped himself to some of the meat that I was clearly unable to distribute fast enough. Later, my 'mothers' joked about that incident and their brother's greed. The previous owner of Skulfi received a large gift from her brother's wife and a smaller gift from me. She could not eat Skulfi but it was easy to swap the pieces of meat and on that night many people had a sumptuous dinner with pork. I shared Skulfi's filet mignon (which is classified as 'intestines' and therefore not part of the distribution) with Patrick Glass, a British colleague who visited from the neighbouring island.

An economic dilemma, elegantly solved by naming a pig after a gift

Skulfi is an example for the creative adaptation of old principles of exchange. Naming an object classifies it as a gift for a certain purpose, for example in mortuary ritual and *kula* (see Kuehling 2005). The name Skulfi, in this sense, politely explained why this pig could only be sold for cash that would be given to the school's headmaster. It is a path (*eda*), a charter for the object that its owner has set up—a clever strategy for the typical situation of senior people's need for pigs for affinal exchanges. By making it well known that this pig was a school fee, the substance of the animal was metaphorically changed into cash, as names are felt to be deeply connected to their owners (Fortune 1963 [1932]: 100).

The case of Skulfi illustrates, I believe, how the islanders have merged the opposing forces of reciprocity and profit, of *kastom* and market, thereby creating new forms of exchange based on old principles. The desire for expensive objects and services, the need for cash and the conflicting pressures of sharing, keeping, investing and hiding have resulted in a series of rising and declining 'expensive' words. As schooling became free of fees for public schools in 2013, the word school fee (*skulfi*) will likely be evaluated differently in the near future. This leads us to the dynamics of value. I will next provide a wider context of 'expensive' words in Dobu, providing a historical frame that shows dynamics of inflation and revaluation. It is from this pool of knowledge that the owner of Skulfi had drawn the inspiration to try the strategy of naming the pig after its purpose (or imaginary substance).

Since pre-capitalist terms for gifts have clearly defined meanings that appear everlasting, they are valuable in their function as charter, a form of legal evidence. Terms for specific exchanges provide a clear definition of the correct return gift. When presenting their gift, people never fail to inform the audience of the term for it. Until today, the knowledge of a good number of these terms is a requisite for successful exchange, for a reliable network of exchange partners and, ultimately, for a 'big name'—for the right to speak out in public. In the past, affinal exchanges were the 'social glue' of the island, requiring complex ritual with various kinds of gifts (See Table 1). From the time a couple began to have sex until the year after the second partner had died, gifts were important markers of the relations between the two matrilineages that are connected by these affinal bonds. Today, only burial rites are deemed essential and even these are increasingly reduced to a 'small *kaikai*' (*masula gidalina*) (see Schram 2007 for such changes in a nearby Normanby Island community). Due to a lack of practise, some of the terms are losing significance and the repertoire of economic strategies shrinks.

The name of a gift clearly states the role of the giver in the exchange ritual and thereby defines the appropriate counter-gift, expressing the ongoing cooperation between groups. Typically spoken by old men who are the senior members of their matrilineage, terms like *utua bawena* (to swap pigs) stand for significant exchanges, synonymous with 'hard work' (*paisewa*), which may, for example, confer gardening rights and allow the giver a moment of superiority: the right to speak out. 'Expensive' words are powerful—they gain their special value by being restricted knowledge—available only to those who have earned it. The words change as new values and valuables appear and others fade.

In the past, 'expensive' words usually belonged to senior individuals' portfolios of myths and magic spells. The meaning of such words was partly orally transmitted and not 'understood', or further enriched and contextualised by the lived experiences of complex exchange events in various roles. These senior people worked hard to spread word of their capability, trying to achieve fame through complex exchange sequences that were continued over decades and embraced the wider region. The names of spirits, persons, places and *kula* valuables were not available for everybody to know. Being competent in local exchanges entailed the knowledge of ritual, including the order of gifts and the etiquette of reciprocity. Fame, social profit, as well as material benefits were the perks of 'expensive' knowledge; after all, who would dare to challenge you if it was widely known that you practise sorcery?

Personal names can be compared to names of gifts, especially those that explain land rights, like the names of ancestors and plots of garden land. In his analysis of Trobriand land litigation, Edwin Hutchins reports that 'a defense of rights in land is accomplished by presenting an account of the history of the land: a digest of its movement through social space. This movement is marked by events: exchanges of valuables, lifelong gardening relationship, deathbed proclamations, and the like' (1990: 413). Knowing the story of a piece of land gives land claims more plausibility and such 'expensive knowledge' may be kept by a lineage elder until the last moment of life as insurance for loving care by the relatives.

Unlike public names, nicknames, and terms for mundane, 'small' (*gidali-*) concepts and objects that are known and used by everybody, some personal names can only be used within the matrilineage and not at all during the time between death and the final mortuary feast for a person of that name (Kuehling 2005: 268). The secret names of spirits, plants and formulas are only passed on when the potential heir has demonstrated his or her eagerness, intelligence and subservience over many years by being helpful in all kinds of matters. Such names for gifts, land, spirits or ancestors are 'expensive' because they are clearly defined and closely linked to hard work, but value can also come from the unknown, exotic, desirable. In such cases, 'expensive' words do not need to have a meaning or to make sense. Magical formulas are an exchange item in this multilingual region, and there are many spells and special words that a Dobu speaker cannot understand. Magic seemingly 'works' on a phonetic rather than semantic level, as in 'Abracadabra'—an 'expensive' word to the audience of a circus magician who utters it as he produces the bunny from his top hat (Malinowski 1935: 213). Since such words are still regarded as a secret today, they will not be discussed here.[4]

The owner of Skulfi adjusted local strategies of respect and generosity to match the needs of today's requirements of the global economy.[5] In the early nineteenth century, change was marked by new 'expensive' objects that made life easier, especially for men, who were mostly in charge of dealing with Westerners (*dimdim*). Household articles, clothing, tools, beads and consumable goods began to trickle into the region, brought by *dimdim*, the term for westerners that may be a loan word from Tubetube and quickly became charged with notions of maleness, dominance, affluence, and emotions such as desire, fear and curiosity. Visiting ships exchanged goods such as iron tools for local resources such as yams; a number of traders tried to make a living in the area, a Marist mission came and left, and blackbirders abducted islanders as indentured labourers for mines and plantations (Lepowsky 1991; Macintyre 1983; Young 1983a, 1983b, 1983c). The latter learned Pidgin English and were introduced to objects of western wealth that they shared with their relatives at home—if they had the chance to see them again. Working hard to gain access to these new treasures that gave them a good head start in spite of their relative youth and lowly status, 'boys' from the D'Entrecasteaux Islands were praised as 'the best workmen in Papua' (Young 1983c). Captain John Moresby mentioned the use of Pidgin in the D'Entrecasteaux as early as 1876 (Mühlhäusler 1978: 1389); the first missionary used a Pidgin-speaking Ware Islander to explain his plans to the Dobu Islanders in 1891 (Bromilow 1929: 73–75, 116; Young 1977, 1980). The power of modern weapons, new diseases and new moral values was reflected in new words that must have been very 'expensive' to the islanders.

The British colonial administration did not attempt to overthrow old values. In the 1920s, government anthropologist F.E. Williams believed that for Papuans, 'ceremony had not only a social value, but also a psychological one directly related to depopulation: "Leave the native

---

4   Discourse about *kula* (*'ona 'une*) contains many 'expensive' words that are unintelligible without deeper knowledge of certain names (of partners, valuables, types of gifts and places).
5   For more detailed analyses of changes in village economics see also Foster (1995); Liep (2009); Thomas (1991); Schram (2007, 2011).

something worth living for, and he will live"' (Williams 1976 [1923]: 380, see also Young and Clark 2001: 16). In Williams' view, the mission schools, while not notably academic, assisted in the endeavour to bring the benefits of civilisation to Papuans (Young and Clark 2001: 26).

Governor Murray phrased the desired process of change as 'dovetailing existing customs into the new civilisation which we are introducing' (Murray 1924: ii; see also Young and Clark 2001: 23–24). Education became an 'expensive' word in the early years of the twentieth century, when the first generation of indigenous students was sent out into the wider world to work and the benefits of a paid job became more visible. Schooling, basic as it was and still is in many classrooms, was advertised as an alternative path to fame, a different kind of 'work' (*paisewa*). Acquiring some English and the principles of *dimdim* time was likely the greatest benefit of missionary schooling, and for over 100 years now, the vocabulary of Dobu has been incorporating English loan words (see Table 1).[6]

Table 1. Examples of Pidgin influence on Dobuan

baketi (bucket)	*masta* (white man)
butu (boots)	*naipi* (knife)
bwela (to boil)	*pelaipani* (frying pan, to fry)
foki (fork)	*peleti* (plate)
konin (quinine)	*sipun* (spoon)
kaikai (food)	*sopu* (soap)
kaliko (clothes)	*sosopani* (saucepan)
ketele (kettle)	*taim* (watch)
laplap (loincloth)	*talausisi* (trousers)
masisi (matches)	*tapwae* (tobacco)

Source. Compiled by Susanne Kuehling from word lists created during research on Dobu Island, July 1992 – January 1994, September 1997

While grammatical structures were scarcely affected, English terms for new objects, concepts of time and numbering, as well as for the new forms of governance were disseminated. Peter Mühlhäusler (1978) believes that a form of pidgin, Papuan Pidgin English (PPE), developed that dominated communication between Europeans and locals. Words like *gelasi* (glass), *masisi* (matches), *sospen* (pot), *sipun* (spoon), *tosi* (torch) are

---

6   Perhaps Dobu is particularly open to new words. As the lingua franca of *kula* exchange, it might have been spiced with more external influences then most other languages in the area. Bronisław Malinowski wrote: 'It is characteristic of the international position of the Dobuans that their language is spoken as a lingua franca all over the D'Entrecasteaux Archipelago, in the Amphletts and as far north as the Trobriands' (1922: 39).

likely to be of PPE origin (see Mühlhäusler 1978: 1426). Typically, such PPE nouns are in singular form without the English plural marker 's' but often combined with qualifying words (1405). At that period, numerals must have been introduced, although there is reference to the use of a knotted cord that indicated the length of any period of indentured labour (1433). The former use of specific terms for units or categories (like 'person' (*tomota*) = 20, yams counted in baskets, other objects being in bundles) was not abandoned but included into the numerical system (see also Thune 1978). Today's pronunciation of numerals on Dobu is consistent with PPE data (Mühlhäusler 1978: 1409) and it is likely that these terms were 'expensive' in the early days, even though the benefits of mathematics were still unknown to the islanders.

These changes did not destroy or even diminish the old principles of value, exemplified in the terms below that are based on an ethic of reciprocity (food for work, debts to be repaid) and of a clear definition of who gives which type of gift. This clarity is needed because people are multiply related and often have considerable choice of role during a feast (as a landowner, a 'father', a child of a man, an affine, etc.). By contributing to a *pegita* gift, for example, I identify myself as the child of a male member of the mourning matrilineage. I also know that I will receive a relatively small counter gift from my father's sisters (called *seudana*) while the largest part is given as an acknowledgement of all the love and care that my father has given me, a free gift (*esio daita*) to compensate his free gifts to me when I was small. In such decisions, emotions materialise in objects, and some of the terms below show how gifts can deal with love and friendship, fear and respect, envy and anger. These emotions coalesce in gifts (see Table 2).

Table 2. A selection of old words of value

'uma	yams cultivars, over 50 types are distinguished by taste, texture, scent, colour, and value
'une	the most valuable things: *kula* shells and pigs
aga / ula'ula	general: word for debit
asepara	general: to share received gifts from feasts
awabusayo	general: (mouth-shit-you) or *sinetaeyo* (mother-shit-you) or *nimasipwa* (hand-tied) All three used to be not insults but great compliments that required *tele'uwai*
bagi	*kula* valuable, a string of fine red shell disks cut from *Chama*
bawe	pig
bebai	the most valuable thing for a woman: large yams that constitute a major gift almost every exchange. Different cultivars (*'uma*)

deba'ose	general: used as a derogatory term for stingy people who do not share food
eguyai	general: to share, to give away food or things
emaisa	general: verb for finishing a debt
giyepweula	general: used as a derogatory term for someone who is 'too much asking', also '*sida alena*', mainly behind someone's back
gomana saune	general: share for owner of fishing net for its use
kitomwa	*kula*: personally owned *bagi* or *mwali* that are not promised as a counter-gift
lagwa	general: payment for a pig with a *kula* shell
lotau	general: return gift of equal size
mwali	*kula* valuable, a white slice of a *Conus* shell that roughly fits onto the arm of a man with a decoration of shells and beads
ni'aula	general: cooked food given to workers
oboboma	general: gift '*une* and food out of gratitude for help
paisewa	general: hard work, to be compensated, e.g. with cooked food (*ni'aula, loepa'ala*)
ta'ona	general: return/apology for mistake or humiliation
tele'uwai	general: return gift for a great compliment
bwabwale	**mortuary ritual sequence from death to the cleansing of the mourners**
basa	*bwabwale*: first gift after death – yams in bowl
e'e'ila	*bwabwale*: departure gifts for widow/er
ege'egelu	*bwabwale*: first gift after death – yams in hands
esio daita	*bwabwale*: part of *pegita* that is not repaid
e'talai	*bwabwale*: voluntary gift of '*une*
loeyawasina	*bwabwale*: cooked food for people who bring gifts
matabora	*bwabwale*: gift of pig and food as apology for absence
mwagula'ubu	*bwabwale*: cooked food given by widow/er before leaving
mwaie	*bwabwale*: exchange of yams to 'clean' a man's yam seeds ('*uma*) after his death
nimaloepala	*bwabwale*: cooked food for people who bring gifts
pegita	*bwabwale*: large gift to the mourning matrilineage by the children of its men
seudana	*bwabwale*: part of *pegita* that is repaid later
talo	*bwabwale*: first gift after death – yams in bowl, at *basa*
talo	*bwabwale*: payment of '*une* to undertakers for their work
yolova	*bwabwale*: gift for undertakers
sagali	**large mortuary feast, held every 10 years or so, to 'finish off' all deaths**
ari'ari	*sagali*: gift to clan fellows who help in burials

dagula lasa	*sagali*: gift to big men in *kula* by heir of big man
etogelasa	*sagali*: direct exchange of pigs between families before *sagali* distribution
etouyosa	*sagali*: repayment to those who gave a pig as *losusu*
e'une sebwagibwagilina	*sagali*: extra large basket of yams plus pork to shame a spouse (*bubuna to'umalina manuna*); or for spouse to thank for help and work (*oboboma manuna*); or for namesake of the deceased to free the name (*waliesa manuna*)
lema / bwaga	*sagali*: raw food given as a help to relatives
losusu	*sagali*: gift of food as a contribution by relatives of in-laws
talaboi	*sagali*: repayment of those who gave no pig as *losusu*
utua bawena	*sagali*: exchange of pigs with delayed repayment

Source. Kuehling 2005: Appendix 1, 287–89

PPE was used in early church services on Dobu (Bromilow 1929: 73), in Samarai and Port Moresby; it also emerged as prison/court language (Mühlhäusler 1978: 1384–386). The word *kalabus* (*calaboise*) for jail, still in use, is an example from 1891 (Bromilow 1929: 75), also the verb *lokapu-* (to lock up). As Dobu became the interisland language of Christianity within a large part of the Massim, and English the language of instruction at school, PPE was increasingly restricted to non-official contexts (see also Mühlhäusler 1978: 1383). Some 'expensive' words of old converted their value to adjust to the changes in spiritual life, and to the superficial decline of local myth and magic.

Terms for the classification of yam cultivars, for example, have clearly been devalued as there are now alternative means to feed a family (e.g. with purchased rice) and to fulfil exchange obligations (by purchasing any kind of large yams). Yam, in precolonial times, was owned by individuals in a more complex manner than today. The various cultivars (*'uma*) could only be planted and consumed by specific persons, but with the introduction of markets, these taboos lost their authority and, nowadays, people say that they plant their yams 'anyhow' in a 'careless' or 'unruly' fashion (*besobeso*).

The Wesleyans on Dobu appropriated (and re-interpreted) local words of value for their bible translation: the Last Supper was translated as *sagali*, the final, and largest mortuary feast that is supposed to 'finish it all', to stop the mourning and get on with life. The missionaries intervened directly in local exchanges by demanding valuable objects as church offerings and by engaging in exchanges on their own terms. Disregarding local ethics and introducing new needs, such as for clothing and smoking, they established new principles of value. Wesleyan hymns and prayers, names and time schedules clearly took hold as 'expensive' words, but not all practices were accepted and the islanders provided their own explanations that did not always accord with missionary doctrine. The annual offering called *ebwaea daita*, literally, to give for no reason, could well be seen as a compensatory gift (*pwaoli*) to God because he gave his son for our sins (see Kuehling 2005: 150).

Bronwen Douglas has argued that Christianity is not very individualistic in Vanuatu but rather it has been forced to 'negotiate the nexus of individual and community in locally appropriate ways' (1998: 6). My data from Dobu confirms Douglas's view that 'the essentialist conflation of modernity, individualism, consumption, and "the west," in opposition to tradition, communalism, antimaterialism, and "nonwest," is both ethically dubious and logically specious' (2002: 9). Given such complexity, the 'expensive words' of Christianity cannot be adequately discussed here (Table 3) (but see also Douglas 2001; Errington 2006; Syme 1985; Young 1977, 1980, 1989, 1997).

Table 3. Some 'expensive' words with a Christian interpretation

Buki tabu	Bible in Dobu language (Bromilow 1926)
Buki wali	United Church hymn book (Buki 1963)
Eaubada	God
ebwaea daita	annual, competitive collection of money
iine idi 5 Kina	annual collection of money for women's groups
Litigo ina bible	New Testament in Dobu language (Lithgow 1985)
sagali	the Last Supper
Sunday *tapwalolo*	weekly gift of 5–20 Toea at service (secret)
tapwalolo	Church service, to pray, Sunday (Bardsley 1892: 36)
Women's fellowship	weekly gift of 5–20 Toea at service (public and recorded)

Source. Compiled by Susanne Kuehling from word lists created during research on Dobu Island, July 1992 – January 1994, September 1997

Over the generations, the complex economic practice of gift exchange was enriched by new concepts of value. The names for gifts, the key objects of exchange and the rules that define their use retained their value, and my list of over 100 terms for gift categories, collected in the 1990s, is certainly incomplete. Skulfi is the result of the economic dilemma that grew during the 150 years of contact but was definitely not absent before, as sharing is always in danger of being corrupted by the desire to hide and to keep in 'the bittersweet life of intense sociality' (Young 1971: ix). Terms for greedy or stingy persons are not new, although some of the motivations for both characteristics have changed. Naming the pig, changing its 'substance' from gift to commodity by declaring it part of the cash economy was a successful strategy for insulating it from the various demands that arise with every death in the extended family and beyond. Skulfi's owner used a phrase that I have heard during *kula* negotiations: 'I built a fence around it' (*ali ya sa'una*), demonstrating that she must indeed have found the right words from a very 'expensive' context of old, to maintain her position that this pig was not *'une* but cash. The woman elegantly solved the economic dilemma of village solidarity versus individualistic needs and desires.

A moral dilemma, elegantly solved

Parents of young children are particularly vulnerable to requests from their own parents and uncles. When faced with the obligation to obey as a prime strategy for being granted secret knowledge later in life, middle-aged people are often compromised by conflicting needs. Denying a request in a respectful manner is essential to maintain social standing, and in the case of Skulfi, this was achieved by naming the pig after its utilitarian purpose.

Schooling is ambiguously constructed, as selfish and lazy, as a benefit or a sacrifice. Sending children to school means that they cannot help with chores around the house and garden, or taking care of younger siblings. The money needed for their fees, lunch boxes, clothing and so on usually tears a large hole into the fluctuating family budget. In the light of these sacrifices it is astonishing that parents sent their children to school during the first half of the last century, when the benefits of schooling must have been obscure to them. Students usually did not enjoy school and feared the corporal punishment (like brutally cleaning dirty fingernails with a broomstick and frequent lashings with a stick). Once they dropped out of school, most old people I met told me that they quickly forgot the painfully acquired literary and numeracy skills that they could not use for anything that mattered. Only a few went into further training off-island, and those *togelu* often did not come back. Even today, reading and writing are regarded as a waste of time, and in the evening, when I sat on my veranda with a book or fieldnotes, neighbours would often come and attempt to save me from the sorry state of being lonely and idle (see also Liep 1999).

During World War II, when the islanders hosted some American troops, the soldiers' incredible material wealth amazed the locals. To their understanding, these *dimdim* (black as well as white Americans) had infinitive access to canned food and hard biscuits, powerful weapons and means of transport. Globalising forces had finally reached the backwaters of Papua and prepared the grounds for a greater desire for new goods and more willingness to experiment with formal education and with cargo cults (fieldnotes, 12 December 1993; see also Lepowsky 1990). In the 1960s, I was told, changes in language accelerated, and items and practices of the global economy became available to villagers on a more regular basis. More children were induced to pursue secondary education, the first generation of university graduates emerged and a wider network of services, trade stores, schools and air and boat services were set up by the Australian administration.

As before, new 'expensive', exciting and desirable objects and their names were adapted to local usage and grammatically treated as Dobu words. Although in many cases there are also Dobu words that could be used (e.g. cash loan: either *buki* or *lowaga*), the 'expensive' market-economy context is more clearly expressed by using the terms derived directly from English (e.g. stock: *sitoki* and not *losa'uyamwana*, to put something on hold). English language skills increased and the first generation of bilingual children was raised while I conducted fieldwork.

The benefits of school education became more visible as remittances began to support single families, for example by sending supplies for a small trade store (*kentin*) that, if it worked out, could provide some food and maybe even a modest cash income. In spite of the best intentions, such plans routinely shatter on the cliffs of reciprocity, of demand sharing and the need to pay respect to senior relatives and affines. Stores run dry, store keepers feel threatened by witchcraft and sorcery, supplies are delayed and every exchange ritual in the larger community is likely to drain the small stock and cause financial ruin. Eventually, perhaps, a relative with an income will refill the *kentin*. While economically unsound, the effects of these ventures in capitalism are quite egalitarian. So far, there is no painful difference between those with money and those without.

Table 4 shows the new terms for household objects like curtains, locks and corrugated iron roofs with water tanks that found their way into the region after the war. New purchasing vocabulary has been developed, including the notorious *lowaga*, or *buki* (credit), which is probably based on the old practice of 'making a new payment' (*lo'aga*) but modified to a mere promise of repayment. The terms for ordering, making profit and for keeping supplies in stock, as well as those for writing a testament and sending mail, indicate that these concepts of the global economy were accommodated linguistically but such 'expensive' things were, and still are, luxuries.

Table 4. Examples of terms of new value

Nouns:	
bank notes: *notis*	letter: *leta*
biscuit: *biskit*	market (goods and place): *maketi*
block of land: *bloki*, *bwa'a*	order: *oda*, *bwau*
canned fish: *mekelel* and *samoni*	parcel: *pasolo*
cargo: *kago*	price: *maisa*
carton (of goods, beer): *katon*	profit: *polofiti/mani*
coins: *siliba* [i.e. silver]	rice: *laisi*
corrugated iron: *eion*	stamp: *sitempi*
credit: *buki*, *lowaga*	stock: *sitocki*
curtain: *keteni*	testament: *wilwil*
exchange of pig against money: *mani bawena*	boat ticket: *tiketi*
grease, cooking oil: *gilisi*	trade store: *kentin*
key: *ki*	water tank: *tenki*
Verbs:	
to be upset: *solagu i* out, my inside is out	
to buy: *gimwane*	
to bribe/grease/bargain: *geligelisi*	
to collect money: *loegogona*	
to mail s.th.(with pers. pron. infix): *posti-ya*	
to ring (telephone): *rinrin*	
to sell s.th.: *maketi*	
to sign: *saini*	

Source. Compiled by Susanne Kuehling from word lists created during research on Dobu Island, July 1992 – January 1994, September 1997

New practices, from bulk shopping at trade stores and chartering a boat to discreet nightly sprees to a trade store (in the hope that the neighbours will not notice) led to new forms of exchange that were based on established terminology. Selling pigs for cash, *mani bawena*, as we have seen in Skulfi's case, is a good example for such new constructions, but many things can be sold off one's veranda as *maketi*: pieces of meat, fish, second-hand clothing, pineapples, watermelons, sweet varieties of mangos, hair pins from town, photographs (like the ones that my messenger purloined and sold as his *maketi* to the Miadeba people whom I had intended to be the receivers of a free gift). Even the usually informal reciprocal sharing of betel nuts has been affected, as people have started to sell the desired drug to each other. Apologetically raising their eyebrows, shoulders and hands, people would say, 'Sorry, these betel nuts are my *maketi*'—and people would accept it (not without complaining behind their backs, however).

There are limits to such entrepreneurship, however, and being excluded when elders are looking for a pig may cause jealousy, open comments, less enthusiastic assistance, perhaps even magical retribution. Naming the pig Skulfi, and declaring it as *mani bawena* helped the woman to avoid being called selfish or greedy by her relatives and neighbours, integrating the deal in the overall principles of gift-giving in spite of the different outcome (investing in one's children rather than one's elders). The name Skulfi morally positioned its owner as a good woman who looks after her children, exercising positively valued self-discipline (*alamai'ita*) by securing funds for their benefit.

By integrating the cash transaction in the overall scheme of gift-giving, Skulfi's case illustrates a creative way of merging old and new, and one could ask if *mani bawena* is a local version of globalisation or rather a globalising of local principles. Is the pig raised to produce cash needed for school fees a product of western or of Dobuan ideologies of exchange? In short, is Ms Skulfi, the pig, a gift or a commodity, does she produce surplus or social relations? Could her value be expressed in purely economic terms or is it so deeply embedded in the local epistemology that one cannot comprehend it without taking into account the larger socioeconomic context? The case indicates, I believe, that our economic dichotomies do not apply universally, as *mani* can become a term of local value, just like *maketi* (for business).

Money is 'expensive' because chartering a boat to visit exchange partners, supporting school children, buying food, tobacco and kerosene to entertain guests, or paying for votes at elections are all accepted paths towards fame—after all, money can be used to buy pigs, shell valuables and large yam tubers; even land rights are not out of bounds for people with money. Old wealth is meant to be in flux, as pigs and yams travel between matrilineages, are distributed at *sagali* feasts and eventually returned at the next occasion. Western wealth is meant to remain with an individual—unfortunately for its owners, this principle does not work well in Dobu, where objects are neither gifts nor commodities and will constantly be redefined in multiple and sometimes contradictory ways. I cannot count the times when someone 'borrowed' my fuel to run an important errand by speed boat—I never even saw the container again. Marilyn Strathern has reported that the Highlanders of Mount Hagen remark on the 'speed' of money (1999), but I never heard this expression while on Dobu.

Don Kulick has pointed out that the new wealth can be a burden as it strains social relations (1992: 48), and indeed, junior people, store keepers, boat owners, receivers of remittances as well as those few islanders with an income as teachers, nurses or church staff are under pressure from all sides. Being praised for one's generosity is sometimes less satisfying than being filled to the brim with cookies and other store food, but the ethics of exchange promote scrupulous sharing. Beneath the surface of the principle of generosity (*oboboma*) there are elaborate strategies of hiding, of saving for later, of pretending to have nothing left. Handbags, for example, often have side pockets where tobacco and betel ingredients can be hidden. Of course, everybody knows about these devices but it is too intrusive to check another person's bag and the performance of asking and dissimulation is often elaborately played.

The tensions that arise from new 'expensive' things and practices indicate imperfect blending, when money is hidden in a bank account or in shares and effectively pulled out of local circulation, when store keepers feel threatened by witchcraft because they have refused 'the old lady' her sugar on credit, and when inflating mortuary feasts are draining cash resources so much that families decide to drop the *bwabwale* ritual and have a small dinner instead (Schram 2007). These difficulties in blending the global with the local are, of course, a widespread phenomenon (for other places in Melanesia see, for example, Akin and Robbins 1999).

Young, educated people, in particular high school drop-outs who return to the village, have difficulty accepting their junior status and, as they miss the relative luxury of their school dormitory and the relative freedom of high school life, they reject the system of authority and disappoint their elders who call them worthless, selfish and lazy. Caught between the requirements of a subsistence economy and the desire for global products, these younger people (mostly men) use their English language skills to indicate their worthiness, talking about 'education', 'infrastructure', 'development', 'reggae music', and 'regional members'—pretending a deep understanding of such new 'expensive' words that, sadly, appear as mere wrappings without content (see Kulick 1992: 250).

Older people also note and criticise an increased desire for fashion items (*stailo*) among teenagers. Such 'expensive' objects and practices are brought home to Dobu by visitors from urban areas. Teenage girls decorate their hair with fancy pins (*herpin*) and use deodorant (*spre*, *pefium*), boys like soccer boots (*sokabuti*), organise disco nights (*disko*), listen to string band music on tapes (*tepi*) and smoke pre-rolled cigarettes or 'Winfields'. The money for these 'expensive' prestige objects is mostly provided by their relatives in town, to whom they write requesting letters. I received many such letters, partly written in English and partly in the Dobu language. Usually, the request (*sida*) is phrased in Dobu while the greeting and closing formulas were in English. 'Expensive' words of the cryptic kind characteristic of magic are also reinvented and used by teenagers who have learned English to construct code words to 'talk dirty' without being reprimanded by their parents, for example, by writing the word SWIMMING (Sleep While I Move My Inter National Gear) on a wall, or tattooing ITALY (I Truly Always Love You) on their arm. This practice is consistent with the old value of keeping cross-sex relationships secret and it continues the genre of veiled talk, but now such words are used by people of low status who do not yet deserve, in terms of the egalitarian gerontocracy, to 'own' such words.

A dietary dilemma, elegantly solved by keeping, selling and eating

I have so far argued that the moral dilemma of dealing with money and other items that represent the global economy brings out new strategies of hiding, of keeping and of limited sharing that are derived from well-known exchange principles of pre-cash times. I have shown that these strategies can be successful while admitting that there are problematic zones of problematic overlap. I have also argued that tensions are not a new phenomenon in Massim exchanges and that elaborate strategies of hiding and keeping are a normal element of a gift economy. Conflicts about land rights were a reality before commodities were imported to the region; fights and hard words are not a result of the global economy and the state. Clearly, people try to make the best of their situation and it would be nice to have the pig, share the pig, and eat it as well. This is how Skulfi's owner excelled and inspired me to write about our encounter.

Reflecting on the deal, I realised that I was the perfect customer for Skulfi, because I was classified as an affine. Since it is impolite to refuse anything to a needy in-law, the woman could always explain to the senior members of her matrilineage that she had to show me due respect (*amayaba*) and help me to find a pig. Selling Skulfi to me could be interpreted as a gift to support affines (*losusu*) that, in the context of *sagali*, would require a counter gift called *etouyosa*, consisting of a large piece of pork and a basket of yams. Since I had paid, I did not give her *etouyosa*, but she nevertheless received a good portion of meat from me, which she could not eat herself but which she quickly swapped and, in the end, we all ate pork.

Skulfi had another 'expensive' effect: as I distributed her meat at a *sagali* feast, I became a landowner of my village and to this day I can go to Losina and ask for land to settle and make a garden. *Sagali* is one of the most 'expensive' terms in Dobu, as this large feast accumulates hundreds of pigs and tons of yams. Among all the pork there was Skulfi, the pig that was bought with cash, in a transaction named in line with ancient principles, and passed through affinal networks in order to be butchered and distributed in a mortuary ritual to a crowd who redistributed the pieces until almost everyone ate pork. Skulfi and the other pigs, according to pre-Christian beliefs, floated over to the mountain Bwebweso on Normanby Island, where the spirits of the dead live in their spirit villages and consume the spirit aspect of *sagali* gifts. So, in the end, Skulfi made everybody happy by feeding us all now and in the future, by providing a school fee and giving me land rights. The woman who raised Skulfi got the best possible deal.

'Expensive' words: A fruitful field of study

After more than 100 years of strong and direct influence of English, 'expensive' words from the realm of origin myths, ancestor stories and folk-tales are in decline. To my knowledge, storytelling evenings take place very rarely in Dobu. With the loss of such lore, verbal expressions and mythological connections between the landscape and its inhabitants are lost. Modern myths are passed on without the formalities of a storytelling night, although they seem to build on old motifs (as the mythical link between snakes and wealth is adduced in relation to a real bank robbery). So far, terms for exchange have persisted and I expect them to remain significant—at least among the senior people who represent and manage big gifts in the name of their matrilineage.

While young people are interested in urban life, its adventures and luxuries, most adults are more concerned with their fishing and gardening, exchange obligations and other activities that enable everyday subsistence and the achievement of higher status within the community. *Kula* exchanges and mortuary feasts are still significant and continue to maintain local relationships. These are the realms of magic and of truly 'expensive' words, of clever rhetoric and the avoidance of 'hard words' (see Weiner 1984). It seems as if the repertoire in this genre is shrinking, but this may also be due to senior people's pet peeve that 'in the past, everything was better'.

New words, like 'development', 'agriculture', 'infrastructure', 'profit', 'loan' or 'shares' are highly visible as they are deployed in government propaganda and appear on T-shirts and posters. But they are semantically blurry. A loan (*lowaga*), for example, is rarely paid back; 'profit' is seen as mutual benefit; 'shares' have been explained to me as 'we share'. These words are the repertoire of people with low status in the village who gain additional prestige through their networks with the outside world. They are used by politicians, and appear as magic formulae rather than as clearly defined exchange terms—they are supposed to attain a goal but they do not specify the details. Like magical formulae, they seem to lose their power when they become part of everyday usage. When they are employed in speeches they obscure rather than clarify an argument. Such words like *mani bawena* (to buy pigs) describe a transaction between individuals and refer to a singular event. Typically, younger people with higher education use them as strategic tools to further their personal interests, in spite of their inferior position in society. New 'expensive' words are powerful insofar as they represent the outside world. While socially less efficient on the village level, they can nevertheless open paths to land rights and wealth, and with money people can buy higher status. The entanglement of these old and new 'expensive' words, therefore, has a profound impact on power relations, emotions of anger and shame, local politics and globalisation.

Skulfi is a good example for the strategic use of 'expensive' words to facilitate profitable deals. The pig's name made clear that she was different from other pigs named Northwind or Fluffy, who were also loved and pampered until their time came to die, turning them into nameless pieces of meat. Those other pigs left behind a debt, a personal relationship and a story about family solidarity, but Skulfi left behind 200 Kina when she became my pig, and while she was also butchered and distributed, her death supported higher education and the deal was over once the sow was purchased. While I remember the name of the pig, and its price, I forgot the name of her owner. In this light, Skulfi was a very expensive name! She became a story or two.

We have so far concentrated on the rise of new 'expensive' words, but the demise of such terms, the devaluation of concepts, practices and objects, would be equally instructive. It seems that 'expensive' words become ordinary once they are used by everybody, especially people of low status. Their currency becomes worn. School activities, for example, are usually described with loanwords from English, the dominant language of the curriculum: *disdisturbi-* (v., with personal suffix, to disturb), *bailo* (ballpen), *buki* (book), *lain* (v., to fall in line), *netibol* (v., to play netball), *sekand* (v., to shake hands), *sokasoka* (v., to play soccer), *winwin* (v., to win), *woliwolibol* (v., to play volleyball).

These words nevertheless provide an interesting field of research, as they point to changes in lifestyle. It appears, for example, that the children's games of old have lost their appeal. Instead of playing games like *'enokonoki* (throwing spears against a rolling banana stem), or making cat cradles (*abi*), today's village kids play with marbles (*mabolo*) or, a favourite, with rubber bands (*rabaraba*, *figa 8*, and other games) (Table 5).

Table 5. Examples of English loan words in everyday use and in devaluation

ball: *bola*	to kiss: *kisi*
bleach: *sinowait*	to make a party: *patipati*
elastic: *rababen*	to make a picnic: *pikiniki*
friend: *peleni*	to scold: *kotukotu* (going to court)
marbles: *mabolo*	tombstone: *sementi*
slippers/flip-flops: *silipas*	towel: *towelo*
to be drunk: *sipak*	water tank: *tenki*
to be naughty: *bikhed*	Christmas: *kerisimasi*

Source. Compiled by Susanne Kuehling from word lists created during research on Dobu Island, July 1992 – January 1994, September 1997

I have heard many old men complain about the 'pidginisation' of Dobuan, although they also use the ordinary household words. These words are fully integrated into Dobuan grammar and accordingly linked with particles of various kinds; syllables are repeated in verbs and adjectives, and tenses are formed in the way typical for Austronesian languages (see Lithgow 1992: 46). Although there are usually alternatives of Dobuan origin, these words are part of the basic vocabulary of the islanders of today: 'Some people blamed the children and youth, but in most places they said, "We all do it", and I believe that is generally true' (47).

The dynamics of change are visible in terminology, especially in the rise and fall of 'expensive' words. I did consider including here a list of terms for affinal exchanges from courtship to death, but I decided against it as most of them are not performed any longer and the terms are not only devalued but doomed to die. Changes are negotiated by adjusting notions of value in everyday life, visible in language use, where structural principles are conservative. Often, as we have seen in the Skulfi example, older ideas are recycled and adjusted when new realities require new words, much like grammatical structures that persist more stubbornly than the lexemes of a language. New words are valued for the larger world they stand for, and not understanding their meaning renders them exotic and 'expensive'. Skulfi is the product of a 'structure of conjuncture' in Marshall Sahlins's sense, an example of how people transform culture in the act of reproducing it (see Kulick 1992: 19; Sahlins 1981: 14).

Today, a large exchange network may be replaced by a fat bank account—one accumulated by children who have been sent to secondary school in spite of the onerous fees. In this regard, Skulfi the sow was trotting on the path of market economy and individual profit but, in the long run, that path joined the larger road of reciprocity and mutual benefits. After a short stint of individualism, so to say, Skulfi returned to the realm of village solidarity. But I wonder whether she really ever left it. The opposition between gifts and goods is blurred when remittances provide future land rights, when pigs and yams can be bought with money and used for rituals. Remittances from, and visits by, urban relatives have a strong impact on exchanges on Dobu today, and they are a real challenge to the elasticity of the kinship system of mutual assistance. The power of new 'expensive' terms for exchanges is an indicator for this tendency, as it reflects on a shift of power relations away from respecting elders toward school graduates with cash incomes. People say that 'we cannot eat money'—but some have realised that, yes indeed, money feeds a family just fine if it is available.

Skulfi, the fat sow, created relations based on *mani*. One might hope that by now the children whose school fees were paid by me through the medium of Skulfi have found jobs and help to sustain their mother. *Mani* bought me land rights in Dobu, too, because I had killed Skulfi for a *sagali* feast. It is but a small step from *utua bawena* (swapping pigs) to *mani bawena*, from sharing (*oboboma*) to selling (*maketi*), from naming a spirit in a healing chant to naming a pig according to its purpose. The example confirms Maurice Bloch and Jonathan Parry's statement that money 'may mean different things within the same culture' (1989: 22).

As I have shown, it makes sense to compare 'old' and 'new' 'expensive' words with regard to their meaning. While most 'expensive' words of old were restricted to senior people who were in charge of organising exchanges, executing magic and telling mythological stories, the new 'expensive' words are far more often used by younger, usually male individuals with formal education and experience of the western world. These are words with blurry meanings—their value stemming from being long and complicated, for example, '100 per cent' (instead of 'totally'), and 'requesting' (instead of 'asking'). A sentence can be transformed from colloquial into 'expensive' English by simply using the thesaurus in MS Word. 'I see a red house', for example, can become 'I perceive a crimson domicile'. Very 'expensive', indeed a genre commonly found in official letters, instructions of products, political propaganda, bank and business correspondence, creating a world divided into those who can understand (or at least pretend to) and those who cannot.

The distinction between 'old' and 'new' does not paint a picture of polarity, however, as individuals creatively develop new ideas based on old and new 'expensive' words and principles. Ethnographic publications may disclose 'expensive' words to the uninitiated in the communities that we study (see e.g. Akin and Creely 2002: 92), or help to revalue such terms by giving them a prestigious place in a book. Morality and exchange are interwoven in a multilayered cloth that consists of threads of old and new materials. Some parts are threadbare and require darning, others have become brittle from disuse, but since this cloth is essential to everyday life, it is 'expensive'. Local understandings of value in semantic, moral and economic aspects are in flux as 'expensive' words need frequent updates to accommodate changes brought by global forces or by clever individuals, like the owner of Skulfi. Some patterns appear to be more persistent, supporting my argument that the cloth of value is woven with moral and economic principles of 'goodness' (*bobo'ana*) and 'hard work' (*paisewa*).

References

Akin, David and Kathryn Creely. 2002. 'A Kwaio case study from the Melanesian archive'. In *Handle with Care: Ownership and Control of Ethnographic Materials*, ed. Sjoerd Jaarsma, ASAO Monograph Series, pp. 81–93. Pittsburgh: University of Pittsburgh Press.

Akin, David and Joel Robbins (eds). 1999. *Money and Modernity: State and Local Currencies in Melanesia*. Pittsburgh: University of Pittsburgh Press.

Bardsley, George H. 1892. *Diary of George H. Bardsley, 8 May 1891–24 Jan. 1892*. Microfilm, Pacific Manuscripts Bureau, The Australian National University.

Bloch, Maurice and Jonathan Parry (eds). 1989. *Money and the Morality of Exchange*. Cambridge: Cambridge University Press.

Brenneis, Donald L. and Fred R. Myers (eds). 1984. *Dangerous Words. Language and Politics in the Pacific*. New York: New York University Press.

Brison, Karen J. 1992. *Just Talk: Gossip, Meetings, and Power in a Papua New Guinea Village*. Berkeley: University of California Press. doi.org/10.1525/california/9780520077003.001.0001.

Bromilow, William E. 1929. *Twenty Years Among Primitive Papuans*. London: Epworth Press.

——. 1926. *Buki tabu 'ena Dobu: The Bible in Dobu*. Port Moresby: The Bible Society PNG.

Buki, Tapwaroro. 1963. *Dobuan Catechism and Hymn Book*. Salamo: The United Church Printing Press.

Crook, Tony. 2007. *Exchanging Skin: Anthropological Knowledge, Secrecy and Bolivip, Papua New Guinea*. Oxford: Oxford University Press. doi. org/10.5871/bacad/9780197264003.001.0001.

Douglas, Bronwen. 2002. 'Christian citizens: Women and negotiations of modernity in Vanuatu'. *The Contemporary Pacific* 14(1): 1–38. doi. org/10.1353/cp.2002.0007.

——. 2001. 'Encounters with the enemy? Academic readings of missionary narratives on Melanesians'. *Comparative Studies in Society and History* 43(1): 37–64. doi.org/10.1017/S0010417501003577.

——. 1998. 'Traditional individuals? Gendered negotiations of identity, Christianity and citizenship in Vanuatu'. Discussion paper 98/6. State, Society and Governance in Melanesia. Canberra: The Australian National University.

Dousset, Laurent and Serge Tcherkézoff (eds). 2012. *The Scope of Anthropology: Maurice Godelier's Work in Context*. New York: Berghahn.

Dutton, Tom. 1992. *Culture Change, Language Change: Case Studies from Melanesia*. Canberra: The Australian National University.

Errington, Felicity. 2006. 'Two women in Dobu: An intimate exploration of the experiences of two single missionary women in 1890s New Guinea'. Honours thesis. Department of History, University of Sydney.

Evans, Nicholas. 2009. *Dying Words: Endangered Languages and What They Have to Tell Us*. London: Wiley-Blackwell. doi. org/10.1002/9781444310450.

Fortune, Reo F. 1963 [1932]. *Sorcerers of Dobu: The Social Anthropology of the Dobu Islanders of the Western Pacific*. London: Routledge and Kegan Paul.

Foster, Robert J. 1995. *Social Reproduction and History in Melanesia: Mortuary Ritual, Gift Exchange, and Custom in the Tanga Islands*. Cambridge: Cambridge University Press.

Goldman, Laurence. 1983. *Talk Never Dies: The Language of Huli Disputes*. New York: Tavistock Publications.

Graeber, David. 2001. *Toward an Anthropological Theory of Value: The False Coin of our own Dreams*. New York: Palgrave. doi. org/10.1057/9780312299064.

Hutchins, Edwin. 1990. 'Getting it straight in Trobriand Island land litigation'. In *Disentangling: Conflict Discourse in Pacific Societies*, ed. Karen Ann Watson-Gegeo and Geoffrey White, pp. 412–58. Stanford: Stanford University Press.

Jaarsma, Sjoerd (ed.). 2002. *Handle with Care. Ownership and Control of Ethnographic Materials*. Pittsburgh: University of Pittsburgh Press.

Jolly, Margaret and Martha Macintyre (eds). 1989. *Family and Gender in the Pacific: Domestic Contradictions and the Colonial Impact*. Cambridge: Cambridge University Press.

Keen, Ian. 1994. *Knowledge and Secrecy in an Aboriginal Religion*. Oxford: Clarendon Press.

Kuehling, Susanne. 2005. *Dobu: Ethics of Exchange on a Massim Island, Papua New Guinea*. Honolulu: University of Hawai'i Press.

Kulick, Don. 1992. *Language Shift and Cultural Reproduction: Socialization, Self, and Syncretism in a Papua New Guinean Village*. Cambridge: Cambridge University Press.

Lepowsky, Maria. 1991. 'The way of the ancestors: Customs, innovation, and resistance'. *Ethnology* 30(3): 217–35. doi.org/10.2307/3773632.

——. 1990. 'Soldiers and spirits: The impact of World War II on a Coral Sea island'. In *The Pacific Theater: Island Representations of World War II*, ed. Geoffrey Miles White and Lamont Lindstrom, pp. 205–230. Honolulu: University of Hawai'i Press.

Liep, John. 2009. *A Papuan Plutocracy: Ranked Exchange on Rossel Island*. Aarhus Universitetsforlag.

——. 1999. 'Pecuniary schismogenesis in the Massim'. In *Money and Modernity: State and Local Currencies in Melanesia*, ed. David Akin and Joel Robbins, pp. 131–50. Pittsburgh: University of Pittsburgh Press.

Lithgow, David. 1992. 'Language change on Fergusson and Normanby Islands, Milne Bay Province, Papua New Guinea'. In *Culture Change, Language Change: Case Studies from Melanesia*, ed. Tom Dutton. Pacific Linguistics Volume 120(C): 27–47. Canberra: The Australian National University.

——. 1985. *Loina tabu auwauna*. Ukarumpa: Summer Institute of Linguistics.

Macintyre, Martha. 1983. 'Changing paths. An historical ethnography of the traders of Tubetube'. PhD thesis. Canberra: The Australian National University.

Malinowski, Bronisław. 1935. *Coral Gardens and their Magic: A Study of the Methods of Tilling the Soil and of agricultural rites in the Trobriand Islands. Volume Two: The Language of Magic and Gardening*. London: George Allen & Unwin.

——. 1922. *Argonauts of the Western Pacific: An Account of Native Enterprise and Adventure in the Archipelagoes of Melanesian New Guinea*. London: Routledge & Kegan Paul.

Mühlhäusler, Peter. 1978. 'Papuan Pidgin English rediscovered'. Proceedings of the Second International Conference on Austronesian Linguistics. Canberra. Pacific Linguistics Series C 61: 1377–446.

Munn, Nancy D. 1986. *The Fame of Gawa: A Symbolic Study of Value Transformation in a Massim (PNG) Society*. Cambridge: Cambridge University Press.

Murray, J.H.P. 1924. 'Introduction to The Natives of the Purari Delta by F.E. Williams'. Territory of Papua, Anthropology Report No. 5. Port Moresby: Government Printer.

Otto, Ton and Nicholas Thomas (eds). 1997. *Narratives of Nation in the South Pacific*. Amsterdam: Harwood Academic Publishers.

Robbins, Joel. 2012. 'Some things you say, some things you dissimulate, and some things you keep to yourself: Linguistic, material and marital exchange in the construction of Melanesian societies'. In *The Scope of Anthropology: Maurice Godelier's Work in Context*, ed. Laurent Dousset and Serge Tcherkézoff, pp. 25–45. New York: Berghahn.

Sahlins, Marshall David. 1981. *Historical Metaphors and Mythical Realities: Structure in the Early History of the Sandwich Islands Kingdom.* Ann Arbor: University of Michigan Press. doi.org/10.3998/mpub.6773.

Schram, Ryan. 2011. 'Finding money: Business and charity in Auhelawa, Papua New Guinea'. *Ethnos* 75(4): 447–70. doi.org/10.1080/001418 44.2010.539703.

——. 2007. 'Sit, cook, eat, full stop: Religion and the rejection of ritual in Auhelawa (Papua New Guinea)'. *Oceania* 77(2): 172–90. doi. org/10.1002/j.1834-4461.2007.tb00011.x.

Strathern, Marilyn. 1999. *Property, Substance and Effect: Anthropological Essays on Persons and Things.* London: The Athlone Press.

Syme, Tony. 1985. 'Cultural Exchange on Dobu. An Exchange Perspective of Culture Contact on Dobu, Papua, in the 1890s'. Honours thesis, Melbourne: La Trobe University.

Thomas, Nicholas. 1991. *Entangled Objects: Exchange, Material Culture, and Objects in the Pacific.* Cambridge, MA: Harvard University Press.

Thune, Carl E. 1978. 'Numbers and counting in Loboda: an example of a non-numerically oriented culture'. *Papua New Guinea Journal of Education* 14 (Special Issue): 69–80.

Watson-Gegeo, Karen A. and Geoffrey White (eds). 1990. *Disentangling: Conflict Discourse in Pacific Societies.* Stanford: Stanford University Press.

Weiner, Annette B. 1984. 'From words to objects to magic: "Hard words" and the boundaries of social interaction'. In *Dangerous Words: Langauge and Politics in the Pacific,* ed. Donald L. Brenneis and Fred R. Myers, pp. 161–91. New York: New York University Press.

——. 1976. *Women of Value, Men of Renown. New Perspectives in Trobriand Exchange.* Austin: University of Texas Press.

Weiner, James. 2001. *Tree Leaf Talk: A Heideggerian Anthropology.* Oxford, New York: Berg.

White, Geoffrey Miles and Lamont Lindstrom (eds). 1990. *The Pacific Theater: Island Representations of World War II.* Honolulu: University of Hawai'i Press.

Whitehouse, Harvey. 1994. 'Strong words and forceful winds: Religious experience and political process in Melanesia'. *Oceania* 65(1): 40–58. doi.org/10.1002/j.1834-4461.1994.tb02487.x.

Williams, F.E. 1976 [1923]. 'The Vailala madness and the destruction of native ceremonies in the Gulf Division'. Territory of Papua, Anthropology Report No. 4, Port Moresby: Government Printer. Reprinted in *Francis Edgar Williams: The Vailala Madness and Other Essays*, ed. E. Schwimmer. St Lucia: Queensland University Press.

Young, Michael W. 1997. 'Commemorating missionary heroes: Local Christianity and narratives of nationalism'. In *Narratives of Nation in the South Pacific*, ed. Ton Otto and Nicholas Thomas, pp. 91–132. Amsterdam: Harwood Academic Publishers.

——. 1989. 'Suffer the children. Wesleyans in the D'Entrecasteaux'. In *Family and Gender in the Pacific: Domestic Contradictions and the Colonial Impact*, ed. Margaret Jolly and Martha Macintyre, pp. 108–34. Cambridge: Cambridge University Press. doi.org/10.1017/CBO9781139084864.007.

——. 1983a. *Magicians of Manumanua: Living Myth in Kalauna*. Berkeley: University of California Press.

——. 1983b. 'The Massim: An introduction'. *The Journal of Pacific History* 18(2): 4–10.

——. 1983c. 'The best workmen in Papua: Goodenough Islanders and the labour trade, 1900–1960'. *The Journal of Pacific History* 18(2): 74–95. doi.org/10.1080/00223348308572460.

——. 1980. 'A tropology of the Dobu Mission (In memory of Reo Fortune)'. *Canberra Anthropology* 3(1): 86–108. doi.org/10.1080/03149098009508619.

——. 1977. 'Doctor Bromilow and the Bwaidoka wars'. *The Journal of Pacific History* 12(3–5): 130–53.

——. 1971. *Fighting with Food: Leadership, Values and Social Control in a Massim Society*. Cambridge: Cambridge University Press.

Young, Michael W. and Julia Clark. 2001. *An Anthropologist in Papua: The Photography of F.E. Williams, 1922–39*. Hindmarsh: Crawford House.

7

Development, Tourism and Commodification of Cultures in Vanuatu

Marc Tabani

Introduction

Anthropology has long considered that the drastic social and cultural changes that affected the island societies of the Western Pacific now belong to the past. It was currently held that the definitive historical and societal break followed upon the global process of colonisation and Christianisation, and was achieved with a second great wave of western influences during and after World War II. These earlier massive, destructive and violent cultural impacts were not necessarily fatal, but nonetheless they had irrevocable consequences. However, a host of new exacerbating factors have contributed over the long term to the destabilisation of a precarious societal balance and to the weakening of cultural and religious syncretisms that Melanesian islanders succeeded in elaborating and maintaining in earlier colonial times, while periodically reshaping them up until the early period following independence.

Such cumulative ruptures seem at least to have deeply altered traditional capacities to change progressively (Sahlins 1992, 1999) when they have not also westernised many attempts at coping with 'indigenization of modernity' or 'develop-man' processes (see Robbins 2005; Babadzan 2009).

Former nationalist leaders envisioned the road to independence in Vanuatu as a process of 'modernization without Westernization' (Babadzan 1988: 222); however, successive governments to this day have not been able, in that country, to offer anything more, to many of their fellow citizens, than the prospect of resigning themselves to the idea of a creeping westernisation without the benefits of modernisation.

For two decades, neoliberal reforms along with a general political fragmentation in state governance (Hassall 2007; Morgan 2004) have been accelerating factors in the rapid social and cultural changes occurring in Vanuatu. *Divlopmen* is a notion that has been widely popularised by Bislama (Vanuatu's Creole language). Frequently understood only in a very abstract manner by most inhabitants of rural areas, nonetheless it is perceived, more or less, by many of them as an obstacle to the continuation of their *kastom*. The most tangible aspects of this powerful dynamic of economic and social transformation of societies of the so-called 'outer islands' are multiple: an increasing rural exodus, the intensive growth of foreign investment and land-grabbing, an ubiquitous tourism whose impact is seen as ambiguous, the generalised monetisation of rural communities and the emergence in them of new forms of social inequalities, the construction of a middle class of rural origins, as well as the rise of individualism and advanced forms of consumerism (comparatively with Papua New Guinea (PNG), see Errington and Gewertz 1999).

Very similar to the proletarianisation of peasantries elsewhere in the Third World, this phenomenon has not previously been experienced in Vanuatu, at least not on the same scale (Rodman 1987). One of its features is the spread of real poverty from its urban settings (Bryant-Tokalau 1995) to the more populous rural zones. The growing social dependence on manufactured imported food also increases the prospect that hunger will pose a serious threat for greater numbers of people in the case of natural disaster.[1] Eighty per cent of Vanuatu households now possess a mobile phone after its introduction in 2007, while 100 per cent of them are constantly increasing their consumption of imported rice. It is not at all surprising that, in order to guarantee national cohesion and state stability, after saving lives, the next priorities declared under the state

---

1   In considering the question of self-sufficiency as to food production in Vanuatu, a quantitative study has recently shown that among six village communities in six densely populated islands, imported processed food bought in retail shops constitutes close to 50 per cent of all food consumed by the average household (Lebot et al. 2014).

of emergency in the wake of cyclone Pam in March 2015 were urgent distributions of rice and the rapid repair of the Global System for Mobile Communications (GSM) network in the outer islands.

Vanuatu is typically characterised as a predominantly rural country, inhabited by a majority of peasants who are more or less dependent on subsistence farming. However, except for inefficient local bureaucracies or international organisations and NGOs in league with them, who could seriously claim that 75 per cent of the country's population is still rural (Vanuatu Millennium Development Goals Report 2010)? Migration— short- or long-term, circular or permanent, sometimes seasonal—between Port Vila and 'the islands' developed as a highly complex process in terms of spatial cultural continuities (Lindstrom 2011). Thousands of unqualified rural workers who are recruited in all regions of the country are being employed overseas on short-term (Recognised Seasonal Employers Scheme in New Zealand and Australia) or long-term contracts (employment on Taiwanese fishing boats). The strict delimitation between what could be defined in Vanuatu as 'urban', 'peri-urban' and 'rural' is obviously blurred on Efate (around Port Vila), as it is on the southeast coast of Santo (around Luganville). More and more people near Lenakel (Tanna), Lakatoro (Malekula) or Longana (Ambae) are adopting urban lifestyles and livelihoods. Local observers agree that the total urban population of Vanuatu can, on occasions, be doubled.[2] To be urbanised in Vanuatu today means first and foremost to have temporarily or permanently left behind the semi-cash economy inherited from the colonial era, and to remain in a zone of direct state intervention (see Rio 2011).

Vanuatu is listed among the least developed countries and receives regular funding for poverty reduction programs although, officially, poverty is seldom mentioned in the country's internal debates. Locally the word 'poverty' is sometimes considered as inappropriate in describing its socioeconomic realities. In an 'untouched island paradise', ranked highest according to alternative wellness indicators—the 'happiest country in the world'—people cannot really be considered to be poor, rather they should be seen as rich on account of their culture, environment and diversity.

---

2   During his visit to Vanuatu in 2013, Senator Bob Carr, then Australian Minister for Foreign Affairs, mentioned in his official speeches that Port Vila numbered 60,000 inhabitants ('Australia's Minister for Foreign Affairs visits Port Vila', *Vanuatu Times*, 15 February 2013). If one considers that in Vanuatu the usual process of 'circular migration' toward urban areas is overall becoming permanent and cumulative, then it would be quite plausible to claim that the real demographic divide between the 'urban' and 'rural' population is much closer to a ratio of 40 to 60 than to the official figure of 25 to 75.

Wealthy members of the ruling class would add that redistribution mechanisms inherent to *kastom ekonomi*[3] are sufficient to mitigate an unbalanced distribution of wealth. Despite the protests of Ephraïm Kalsakau, the national leader of the United Trade Unions and Vanuatu Labour Party, in Vanuatu the 'justice for the poor' program of the World Bank and AusAID has been renamed 'justice for everyone' (*jastis blong evriwan*) (JBE meeting, discussion notes, Port Vila, 4 February 2010). What neoliberal entrepreneurs now share with former Melanesian socialists is this ideological motivation to deny the capitalist process of class formation; while 'God never went on strike' (Lini quoted in Howard 1983: 198), *kastom* is also praised for making no divisions between rich and poor and it can even serve as pretext 'to "lock" many ... people into pre-capitalist forms of production, and as population pressure and the desire for cash increases, these people form a 'reserve army' of cheap labor for the bourgeoisie' (ibid.: 202).[4]

During my fieldwork research in Vanuatu,[5] I have always devoted a great deal of attention to the observation of the cultural impacts of ongoing socioeconomic development in different rural zones of the archipelago, and especially on the island of Tanna where I have spent most of my time. To assess whether the numerous and rapid changes that have occurred in the meantime are as profound, extensive and violent as the earlier significant historical disruptions is not an easy matter, but we might presume that they are at least as irrevocable in terms of their cultural consequences. But such powerful transformations have never before been so strongly influenced by the development of tourism as the country's main industry. Shortly after independence, tourism had already become the primary source of national income through directly or indirectly related activities, but its

---

3   The year of the *kastom ekonomi*, officially celebrated by the Republic of Vanuatu in 2007 and whose mission was extended to 2010, seems like a final resurgence of the idea of Melanesian socialism that saw *kastom* as a 'force for development' (see below). In the presentation of this program by the present minister of lands and former director of the Vanuatu Cultural Centre, Ralph Regenvanu, it is instructive to note that underdevelopment or poverty, which are never named, are attributed not to the incompatibility between two systems, but to the decline of customary chiefs who are no longer able to assume their role as mediators between the needs of the market and a domestic mode of production. In order to remedy this situation he proposes institutionalising neotribal chiefs, suggesting they should be called 'State Chiefs', so as not to confuse them with 'customary clan chiefs', their role somewhat resembling the function of the Assessors under colonial rule (Geismar and Regenvanu 2011: 43).

4   This still alarmist forecast in the 1980s has become a reality today.

5   From 1993 till 2009, I led a dozen fieldwork trips in Vanuatu, lasting from two to nine months each. From 2010 till 2014, I lived permanently in Port Vila and spent a large part of my time on Tanna Island for the management of several anthropological and cultural projects.

steady and continuous growth continues to be quite spectacular. Less than 10,000 people visited Vanuatu in 1987, visitors numbered 40,000 in 1995, 100,000 in 2002 and 300,000 in 2012. Tourist arrival figures are considered as 'amazing' and 'phenomenal' by the Vanuatu Hotels and Resorts Association (*The Independent of Vanuatu* no. 468, 16 February 2013). The record number of tourists is also attracting increasing foreign investment frequently motivated by the prospect of quick profits or easy land-grabbing.[6] Since its beginnings, tourism development has never followed any 'socialist way' in Vanuatu (see Douglas 1996: 245), it was always 'largely dominated by international intermediaries and expatriate owner-managers, mostly Australians and New Zealanders resident in Vanuatu' (Cheer 2015).

In Vanuatu, policymakers unanimously consider tourism to be the leading economic sector through which the country should strengthen its development. No matter the extent of damage caused by the monster tropical cyclone Pam in 2015 or warnings about the necessity for Vanuatu to diversify its economy, among Vanuatu's economic and political elites an unshakeable belief in the benefits of tourism seems to have become a matter of faith. Following an historical overview describing the conversion of Vanuatu to a cult of development, which for the tourism industry sometimes seems reminiscent of a new form of cargoist expectations,[7] in this chapter, I will highlight some aspects of the cultural price to pay for the extension to rural zones of the problematic economic sector of 'ethnic tourism'.

In this brief exposition I shall discuss two sets of data documenting local aspects of the process of the commodification of cultures, through which a commoditised *kastom* is turned into a mere tourist attraction. First, I shall provide a short historical survey of the ideological background

---

6   If land-grabbing in Vanuatu has been oriented toward tourist development for two decades (see De Burlo 1989), the pressures on coastlines is now driving islands like Efate and Santo toward a systematic process of land alienation.

7   It would take too long to look further into the question of the prophetic, indeed messianic, posture regularly adopted by numerous Vanuatan political figures, but I refer the reader to the large file on the speculative dealings of the former prime minister Moana Carcasse concerning the construction of a new airport on the island of Efate, which would bring in 'millions' of Asian tourists to Vanuatu, dealings that are directly linked to the fall of his government in March 2013. Of the same order are the murky plans supported by other public authorities to establish a new age 'artists' colony' on Tanna, driven by a New York hip hop prince known by the ghostly alias of DJ Spooky. The project had to be abandoned on Tanna but seems to be going ahead on Efate (Basic project info: Vanuatu Pacifica Foundation website. Online: www.the-vpf.org/ (accessed 12 September 2016)).

of the *kastom* and development rhetoric in Vanuatu. This issue will highlight some of the outcomes of mass tourism on Tanna, especially the increasing monetisation of rural economic systems and its influence on indigenous representations of traditional culture and social relationships. I shall add some brief comments about other problematic aspects of the commodification of *kastom*, when it is related to the organisation of huge traditional ceremonies. In this perspective I shall argue that mass tourism, as a factor of drastic change, does not act to strengthen *kastom*— whatever the alterations of cultural forms, values and practices that are precisely involved in this process. I shall leave analysis of issues such as the individual or national economic advantages of the development of tourism in Vanuatu to the field of tourism studies, which already boasts an impressive literature on this and related questions. The value of anthropology for analysing also the losses of values (see Paini and Gnecchi-Ruscone, Introduction, this volume) will lead me to make some concluding comments on the disturbing issue of the 'prostitution of culture' as a metaphor of some of the worst aspects of Melanesian or Pacific modernities.

Development and *kastom*

'Development', asserted a founding father of the Republic of Vanuatu on the eve of independence, is merely 'another word for change' (Lini 1980: 30). Traditional island cultures, in the view of a first generation of young, educated Melanesian nationalists, should no longer be seen as 'the most resistant to change'. If *kastom* (tradition) is continuously being transformed it must serve as 'a force for development' (ibid.), rather than presenting an obstacle. Together with Christian principles, Melanesian values were emphasised by the newly independent state to embody its imagined continuity with precolonial forms of sovereignty and development, and to promote the renewal of an idealised indigenous 'communal way' that had been undermined through 70 years of colonial rule and the imposition of a capitalist economy. Socialist policies were first presented by ni-Vanuatu nationalists as being more suitable for Melanesia in order to maintain a balance between national economic imperatives (globally driven modern changes) and the social and cultural requirements of *kastom* (locally inspired indigenous changes).

Socialism is not a 'dirty word' insisted another founding father, Barack Sope (1974: 53), but rather a modern notion that simply translates indigenous ideas about what he deemed to be the main characteristics of a timeless 'Melanesian village life': 'no hierarchical barriers and egalitarian principles [that] are evident in many aspects of social structures' that had been in existence for hundreds of years before the establishment of the New Hebrides Condominium (ibid.: 54). However, the influence of the 'myth of Melanesian Socialism' (Howard 1983) in framing national development plans in Vanuatu was of very short duration, and even more limited. In fact, since the beginning of Vanuatu's independence, the control over the formal economy by state institutions mostly inherited from the colonial system has been the 'least socialistic' among Pacific Island states (ibid.: 193; see also Premdas 1987; Miles 1998; Tabani 2002). The political elites of Vanuatu have never confirmed any real desire on their part to embrace socialist development. An international context, marked by the collapse of the Soviet empire, facilitated the 'Melanesian way' abandoning its initial 'socialist touch'. Since the official neoliberal turn taken by Vanuatu at the end of the 1980s, the encouragement of foreign investment and the strengthening of national capital held by an urban middle class have remained a constant theme in the country's economic guidelines and one that has continually been reaffirmed since then, most recently with the ratification in 2012 of Vanuatu's World Trade Organization (WTO) membership.

In comparison with socialism, the national rhetoric promoting *kastom* has become a real success story in Vanuatu. Even when not all groups praise the value of *kastom* (Taylor 2010: 282), it is still a major strategic notion in the national political arena, a main ideological prerequisite for maintaining the spirit of 'unity within diversity', one always brandished by state authorities in their quest for popular legitimacy and officially presented as the basis of national cohesion. *Kastom* not only became an *affaire d'état* (Miles 1998: 71; see also e.g. Babadzan 1988; Tabani 2002; Holtz 2010) but also a focal point for socioeconomic development. But neither before nor after the bankruptcy of the state in the 1990s, the severe reform program begun in 1997 (known as the Comprehensive Reform Program) or the Millennium Development Fund in 2004 has *kastom* succeeded in becoming clearly a 'force for development'. Instead, foreign powers started to become even more suspicious about some of the political uses and abuses of the concept that, in the post-Lini era, was sometimes suspected of concealing the growth of a massive system of corruption.

But more and more criticism is now targeting its economic dimension. Open access for international companies to local resources and to the national market has, in the views of foreign investors and development agencies, now become a main criterion for the acceptability of *kastom*, where *kastom* must be seen to be compatible with their interests. More than ever, in the present global context, the non-market-friendly aspects of *kastom* are assessed as 'obstacles to development' (Babadzan 2006).[8] Surviving premodern modes of production and neotraditional authorities serving as intermediaries with a modern colonial system are an inherited part of the older variant of capitalism that most Pacific Islands states perpetuated in their early phase of independence. Today this twofold system is under lethal threat from 'a more advanced form of capitalist penetration that no longer required chiefs or tradition (except to entice tourists)' (Howard 1983: 180).

Early history of tourism in Tanna

In the 1980s, tourism in the outer islands of Vanuatu was strictly restricted, mainly for reasons of cultural and social preservation but also, more prosaically, because of a lack of basic infrastructure. Outside the island of Efate and its capital Port Vila, only tourists who had their day trips organised by tour operators, yachtspeople and cruise ship operators were allowed to travel in isolated rural zones. This prohibition also applied to some other areas, for similar reasons. Before 1994, when the Vanuatu Cultural Centre (VKS Vanuatu Kaljoral Senta) lifted a moratorium on cultural research, foreign academic fieldworkers were also banned from rural zones. The measure was intended to preserve the stability of the structures of the newborn state of Vanuatu after various disturbances had occurred during the independence period, especially on the islands of Santo and Tanna, at present two of the main tourist destinations outside

---

8   During a political meeting in Tanna in June 2008, the late Edouard Natapei, then minister, campaigned on the theme of the necessity of giving up *kastom* when it appeared as an obstacle to *divlopmen*—a proposal that, for numerous participants, amounted shockingly to an appeal to dispense with Christian values, because in the collective imagination, just as in the constitution, custom and Christianity go together.

Efate. Today, the nation state's stability no longer seems to rely on such direct political control over foreign activities in the country. The main goal now is to develop the country, to encourage people and communities to engage in business and to earn income.

Predictions about the advent of tourism as a major industry in Vanuatu can be dated to the late 1960s (Douglas 1996: 239–41). The speculative projects of the 1970s that aimed to build residential homes for thousands of US Vietnam War veterans on Santo can also be related to cargo tourism expectations of this kind.[9] These economic predictions were not realised until quite recently, with developments that began less than 20 years ago and that are just starting to reveal all of their societal impacts. At the beginning of the 1990s, after more than a decade of independence, just one hotel, limited in capacity, was established on Santo, together with some other tourist bungalows on Tanna known as the Tanna Beach Resort[10] and formerly operated by an Australian expatriate, Bob Paul. Both establishments were in the upper medium price range, and tended to specialise in all-inclusive group tours. Bob Paul arrived on Tanna in 1946. He was in the vanguard of the island's tourism business when he launched Company Tours in 1960, founded the first private domestic airline company and initiated the construction on Tanna of the first airstrip (Dunn 1997). Regardless of how underdeveloped the island was in pre-independence days and how 'primitive' the living conditions of its people were deemed to be by the colonial society in Port Vila, its suitability for tourism was assured by the presence of Mt Yasur, one of the most accessible volcanoes in the world, together with other beautiful natural attractions.

According to Joël Bonnemaison, tourism was causing problems on Tanna and 'by 1970, incidents involving local villagers had become increasingly frequent. Bob Paul set up a profit-sharing scheme whereby he would give the people of Ipekel, a village that is the headquarters of his John Frum

---

9   In 1967, Jimmy Stevens, leader of the Santo-based Nagriamel indigenous movement, had contacted Eugene Peacock, an American land speculator wishing to invest in the New Hebrides. Peacock, whose commercial activities were based in Hawai'i, had acquired vast areas of land, on Santo in particular. His plan was to subdivide these properties into small plots in order to sell them on to American Vietnam veterans (see Beasant 1984: 45).

10   As a result of a conflict between local landowners and the resort owners, the lodge (renamed Tanna Lodge) was mostly burned to the ground in July 2015.

opponents,[11] two Australian dollars per tourist, an appreciable amount of money at the time' (1994: 307). As a consequence of that conflict, the John Frum people closed the volcano to tourists for nine months in 1977–1978, causing several violent incidents.[12] To explain their decision, John Frum leaders from Ipekel sent a letter to the French District Agent that ended with the words 'no tourist, no money, no problem'. Mweles, a leader of the millenarian John Frum movement in Sulphur Bay (southeast Tanna), added that 'he was weary of quarrels caused by money', and concluded with the motto 'kastom ino laekem mani' (custom does not like money) (ibid.). 'Such a philosophy was not always easy to understand. Disenchanted, the trader Bob Paul stated: My troubles began on the day I decided to share my profits and involve the John Frum in my business' (ibid.).

Similar incidents were reported by Lindstrom in the same period. Christian and kastom groups quarrelled about whether or not to accept money from Paul's tourists to allow them to participate in the great nakwiari ceremonies (sometimes mislabelled toka dances) (Lindstrom 1982: 326); other groups entered into conflicts about the control of kastom when some of them wanted to perform their dances in a secularised context in Port Vila (ibid.: 237). What is remarkable about these early conflicts is that even if they originated from the tension between kastom and money, namely exploiting kastom to make money, the amounts were too limited to have any serious large-scale socioeconomic impact. From the 1970s until today the number of tourists has increased a thousandfold (exceeding 15,000 a year in Tanna) and the charge for a visit to the volcano has increased from $US2.50 to $US50. Two questions quickly arose from this first period of tourism development: is kastom saleable as a spectacle and, more broadly, who has the right to use kastom for non-customary purposes not legitimated by kastom, whether political, commercial or scientific? Exploitation through

---

11   John Frum is the name of a famous millenarian politico-religious movement (and of its main cultic spirit) born at the end of the 1930s in Tanna. Western fascination with John Frum has contributed to making it one of Melanesia's most famous cargo cults. The cargo cult label applied to the John Frum myth became an essential selling point for Tanna in the tourism market (see Lindstrom 1993).

12   The conflicts that arise out of the exploitation of the volcano Yasur for tourism have been constant on Tanna since the 1970s. Here too, without going into detail, a thesis alone would not suffice, let me say simply that the main part of the profits (probably more than 90 per cent according to a report that appeared in the 'Mt Yasur Volcano Fees', Vanuatu Daily Post, 2 December 2014) has been pocketed by a private firm basing its legitimacy on 'customary land rights' (these same land rights being constantly contested by other groups). This profit, which could be in the vicinity of US$1 million per year, is only very marginally redistributed among the island's population. The maintenance of the road for a month yields a kompani of 10 men chosen in turn by a village the sum of $20 per person per month.

wage labour, humiliating wage-earning conditions, modern political uses of *kastom*, an understanding of the western world surrounding them as a huge accumulation of commodities: these are realities that have been experienced by people from Tanna for several decades. Nevertheless, the awareness of the possibility of also transforming *kastom* into a commodity was new. More surprising, at first glance, is the fact that Christian groups who were the first to reject their *kastom* have in certain local cases also been the initiators of its commodification.

Tanna Beach Resort was not one boasting luxury accommodation. But since it was expensive, it was dedicated to upmarket tourism. This elite tourism had contributed to creating problems on Tanna, but their real cause was still mainly political. Bob Paul was believed by the John Frum people and the *kastom* groups to be a strong supporter of the Vanuaaku Pati (VP), the nationalist party that led the country to independence. 'His store, house and tourist bungalows in Lenakel were located in the midst of Christian, predominantly VP, territory, therefore he was considered as the ally of VP partisans' (Bonnemaison 1994: 307). He was seen by these groups as perpetuating the pre-war dictatorial rule of the Presbyterian mission and the British colonial authorities, known in the history of the island as the 'Tanna Law' period. In contrast, Bob Paul's business did not create major social problems, nor was it a source of growing social inequalities. In that period (1970–1990), the number of tourists was limited (never more than a few hundred in a year), though a majority of children in the islands would still never have seen white foreigners face-to-face.[13]

Nevertheless, the lack of tourist infrastructure in this early period did not necessarily discourage overseas visitors. In fact it may have led to forms of tourism that were also a burden on local populations. The commodification of culture has been fostered by market forces, but these might often conflict with customary prescriptions about taking care of, and sharing with, foreign visitors. I remember guide books in the 1990s giving tips on how to sleep for free in ni-Vanuatu villages—in other

13 The island children of today, unlike those of 20 years ago, now ask for sweets or pens when they meet foreign visitors whom they used to call *Elobabae*. All those tourists and all those sweets, but the outsiders would often restrict their communication with island residents to elementary forms of politeness, that is, 'hello' immediately followed with 'bye-bye'.

words saving money by staying with people who have none. John Peck and Robert Gregory have highlighted that this was already the case in the 1970s on Tanna:

> Tourist grade housing is unavailable on the outer islands, but there are usually some sort of accommodations that can be used such as Government 'guesthouses' (usually an empty thatched roof hut with some sort of stove and beds) or occasionally travellers can stay in Mission facilities, if arrangements are made in advance. These more primitive facilities are beginning to attract small groups of campers and people who really want to 'rough it'. The hazards of the trip are sufficiently exciting so that everyone usually enjoys an authentic 'experience'. One problem with this sort of tourist activity, however, is that it places a difficult and often unrecognized burden on the local population. When a camper arrives in one of the outer islands, the local people have no option but to accept and take care of him or her, partially because custom requires them to share with a stranger, partially because there is nowhere to get rid of the stranger (2005: 274).

The quest for authenticity, which tourism has largely contributed to promoting from the very beginning of its local development, was not without consequence as regards the objectification of the Tannese cultural heritage. The ideological dimension of *kastom* and the state encouragement of ethnic tourism have meant that the islanders have become self-reflexive in relation to their own lifeways. *Lukluk vilej laef* (to observe villagers' everyday life), for example, is a formula used in former times to explain and justify rural tours and visits by colonial delegates, police, missionaries and anthropologists in exercising their control over the population. Today it is used to rationalise the perceived interest of tourists in villagers' traditional life. The tourists do not really know what to expect from such cultural experiences, but the villagers have been taught, even trained, how best to nourish their fantasies. The tourists' desire to experience *kastom* everyday life directly means that islanders have themselves incorporated exotic aspects valued by foreigners into their own lives. For the last 15 years, this has led to a multiplication of '*kastom* villages' on Tanna as elsewhere in the country.

These villages are ordinary living places, neither more nor less traditionalist than other places in Vanuatu. The only difference resides in the fact that they are intentionally marketed as 'traditional'. This means that it is the inhabitants themselves who have to select and emphasise the tangible aspects of their culture that they think will be of interest to tourists. One of the main options for tourists in Tanna is to choose between the different degrees of traditionality on offer: between a 'full *kastom*' cultural show and display enacted by performers in strictly traditional dress (the men wearing penis sheaths and the women appearing bare-breasted) or attired in neotraditional dress (*lava-lava*) for the men and coconut bras for the women) (Robinson and Connell 2008; see also Connell 2007). They no longer simply live their culture, they now perform it for the purpose of 'culturalist safaris'.[14] This does not mean that their performed culture is no longer authentic, but it is obviously dependent on a global market:

> The traditional/neo-traditional 'culture' that tourists consume is both real and manufactured in the sense that people nourish and protect traditions partly because these can be sold to visitors hungry for the sensation of difference. Islanders dance for reasons more important than money; dance still functions as it always has to bring together people from two regions. But tourism, too, promotes and motivates cultural performance and islanders have for touristic reasons become careful to husband and manage cultural resources whether these are dance, religious ceremony, art style, or a cuisine (Lindstrom 2015: 186).

The fast-growing mass tourism on Tanna

The harbinger of mass tourism in Vanuatu was the opening of a number of 'cabins' at the Port Resolution Nipikinamu Yacht Club in Tanna in 1994. In Port Resolution, adventurous tourists can experience a tropical paradise lying well off the beaten track. A tiny peninsula fringed with beautiful white sand beaches, a sheltered lagoon, an easily accessible active volcano and a significant historical and cultural heritage site where Captain Cook himself is the first western visitor now remembered. With none of the usual modern facilities—no electricity, no stores, no running water, no internet connections and, before 2008, no mobile phones—it is a fabulous world's end location. At the beginning of the 1990s, an income-earning project financially supported by foreign aid was launched to promote tourism in Port Resolution but in a way that respected its unique and fragile environment.

14　I borrowed this formula from Alain Babadzan, personal communication, 11 November 2012.

Local people, with the help of David Sharland, a British volunteer business development officer working for the Vanuatu Government, started with the building of a Robinson Crusoe-style yacht club. After its official opening in August 1992, the second phase of the project, the construction of local-style cabins where overseas short-term visitors can take part in village life as paying guests, was completed in December 1994. The whole community was involved in decision-making for the project. This was a key component in establishing and managing it. A project committee ran the day-to-day business, while the chiefs only stepped in if there were any serious problems. Each employee from the village (kitchen staff, house girls, guides, gardeners, etc.) received a small personal remuneration and the rest of the benefits were used for community needs. Local food and handicrafts were made available for sale. In this way the income earned from foreign visitors remained within the local community. Twenty years later, this project of small-scale or basic tourism, which had the hallmarks of becoming a success story when it began, has become very divisive for the local community.

The original stability of the project was based on a delicate political and economic balance between land owners, local chiefs and dominant families. But with the death of Chief Narua Sasaero, in 1999, this state of equilibrium was comprehensively broken. Narua's family was accused of excluding all the other families from the management of the yacht club, keeping the benefits for themselves exclusively and exploiting a piece of land that had been provided by other families. The breakdown of this community-managed business also coincided with the death of a highly esteemed sea-dweller of the Port Resolution Bay, a tame mature dugong. In the 1990s the dugong had become a major tourist attraction on Tanna. In the eyes of the local villagers, it was never just an ordinary sea mammal. The dugong was thought of as Kassara, the spirit of a local ancestor, belonging to the name-set group of a local chiefly family (Nowar) and even as an avatar of Mwatiktiki, the Tannese name for the well-known trans-Oceanic cultural hero.

The arrival of the dugong in Port Resolution was interpreted as a spiritual symbol, a gift made to the villagers by one of their mighty ancestors in order that people could share the benefits of the expected *divlopmen*. Fees paid by tourists so that they could swim with the dugong were at first allocated in a strictly communal way and only used for collective projects. With the ill-feeling and quarrels that arose in the wake of Chief Narua's death, this community income was no longer shared. From once being a symbol of good fortune, Kassara now represented a new pretext for divisions in the community. When the innocent animal finally died, Fred Nase, a new John Frum prophet (Tabani 2008, 2009), claimed that he was personally responsible for its death, which he had brought about in order to punish the villagers for their greed and for having used a local spirit for the purposes of profit. According to traditional beliefs, spirits have their own means of punishing those for whom the greed for money has overridden the rules and spirit of *kastom*, but of course no tour operator was ever worried about supernatural risks of that nature.[15]

The initial success of the yacht club in Port Resolution later prompted foreign investors to set up their own Melanesian-style guesthouses, but without any community management or sharing of benefits. Friendly Bungalow in White Sands and Relais de la Baie des Tortues in Turtle Bay, also located on the east coast near the volcano, entered into serious competition at the local level to attract backpackers and other ecofriendly tourists. In Port Resolution this has led to the original investment being divided up. Over a period of 10 years, six different bungalow guesthouses and restaurants have opened, all located in the tiny peninsula of Port Resolution.

This self-interested behaviour has resulted in many personal grievances being aired between the main families of the village. The loss of trust between all of these groups is so strong that still today they have not even reached agreement over the appointment of a new village chief following the death of Narua. Economic inequalities have also arisen between the families who own bungalows and those who rely solely on farming. Furthermore, in other parts of the island, close to Lenakel and especially in the area of the volcano, more than 30 guesthouses have opened their doors—even if a large minority of them host no more than a couple of tourists all year. Nevertheless, the setting up of these bungalows has aroused such envy and greed among nearby villagers that it is now one of the main sources of land conflict. Since then, several hectares in Port Resolution with beach frontages have been sold to foreign investors, awaiting the development of infrastructure to set up hotels as investments.

---

15 The frustrations and the feelings of powerlessness that have very frequently attended the birth of 'cargo cults' can also arise when the money from tourism is suddenly taken away from rural populations. Such a situation was observed by Eric Silverman (2013) in relation to the communities of the Sepik in a post-tourism context, with the end of the exploitation of cruise ships on the river.

Tourism, cash earning and social conflicts

Aside from persistent and extensive land-grabbing, with the beginning of colonisation and especially in the era of the labour trade in the Pacific in the second half of the nineteenth century, Melanesians have experienced some dramatic consequences of wage labour. Powerful tools used to establish the colonial order and maintain its domination over indigenous societies included the exploitation of indigenous labour, the alienation of their land and the introduction of money. Western uses of money—a supreme 'fetish' of fetishised goods and services, of commoditised products according to Karl Marx, or through its domination engendering a special case of alienation in the social and cultural realm, a dehumanisation defined as 'reification' following Georg Lukács—have been analysed in their own way by indigenous societies and frequently criticised as a characteristic component of colonial forms of oppression and domination.

The modern capitalist use of money (labelled 'state monies' by Akin and Robbins (1999); or 'exchange currencies' by Graeber (2012)) in former embedded economies of Melanesia did not succeed in reducing all aspects of social relationships to categories of exchange; traditional monies (respectively named 'local currencies' or 'social currencies' by the authors just quoted) continued to coexist or to combine with the former (Akin and Robbins 1999). In Vanuatu, state monies have more often been accepted and welcomed by Christianised groups (Protestants) than by pagan and later by Catholic and neotraditional groups, with the latter being more prone to reject or to keep separate white men's money, when attempts to control it have failed. However, with its spread into Melanesian societies, the most prized fetish of the White Man increasingly became a destabilising element.

The issue of money also commonly and symptomatically arose in the context of so-called 'cargo cults' or assimilated indigenous movements. On Santo Island, in the 1920s, the Rongoforo cult was categorised as a crisis of insanity, characterised by a special form of delirium on the part of its prophet and his supporters concerning the use of money (Raff 1928). In 1945, also on Santo, the Naked Cult had, as one of its priorities, the rejection of *money belong White Man* (Guiart 1958). The history of the famous John Frum movement offers numerous discourses about the power, but also the dangers, of money. John Frum's promises of money in plentiful amounts regularly alternated with incredible rushes on Tanna's stores by his supporters in order to spend all the money accumulated on the island—when the money was not thrown into the sea. Economic non-cooperation with strangers has also been clearly expressed through the expectation of the Tannese of obtaining their own money: '*By and by money blong me he come, but face blong your fella king, take'em e go back*', would threaten John Frum leaders (Guiart 1956: 155). On the new coins awaited by supporters, instead of the king there would be represented a coconut tree (ibid.).[16] The end of foreign money on the island was to coincide with the departure of foreigners. Prefiguring the slogan painted on walls in Paris in 1968, the Tannese motto in the 1950s was 'never work … for white men'.

The grey literature of the *John Frum Files* tells us that, in the 1940s, this rejection of state money was one of the main things of concern to the colonial authorities.[17] They worried about this problem in particular as it concerned them directly, while other problems more generally related to the power of the missions (Presbyterians and Seventh-day Adventists) over the population. In their materialist analysis, the administrators of the condominium suggested that behind the rise of *Johnfrumism* on Tanna there was a mismatch between commodity supply and demand. The fall of the price of copra and the global context of World War II had trapped people into a pattern of inactivity. When the stores were empty, attempting to earn money became pointless. In the views of colonial delegates and officers, the commodity market and the trade of manufactured goods should have been reactivated in order to put a stop to this indigenous movement. And indeed, *Johnfrumism* draws its energy from complete idleness: instead of working and consuming, people spend their days in uncontrolled kava-drinking sessions and erratic dancing flash mobs, outside of any traditional framework. Nevertheless, despite a later increase in the price of copra, nobody went back to work. A rising awareness of exploitation by foreign employers or traders was fuelled by memories of past experiences.

---

16   In a similar way the Nagriamel movement on Santo, when dissidence in relation to the future independent state was in full swing, established a bank and struck coins, with silver coins representing the emblematic crest of Nagramiel on one side and the portrait of Jimmy Stevens, founder of the movement, on the other. In September 2014, the Turaga nation movement on the island of Pentecost, which militates for the sovereignty of a first pan-Pacific nation, announced, via a campaign of public posters, its intention to adopt and strike its own money.
17   Administrative correspondence, New Hebrides British Service, Southern District 17/11/2 (Western Pacific Archives 1875–1978).

However, Tannese still have a reputation for being strong workers, if they want or need to work. Their capacity for what they used to call *had wok* (hard work) has been demonstrated on several occasions: in the cotton fields in Queensland at the end of the nineteenth century, on the docks at Port Vila to unload US army materials or building roads in Efate during World War II, and today in Vila as bus drivers, construction workers or night watchmen. Things are different on Tanna. Such activities as community work, subsistence farming, hunting, fishing or any other productive activity that does not necessitate a financial transaction— *mekem vatu*—are not considered as 'doing work'. Commercial or labour contracts made between Tannese people are always influenced by the social exchange network between *nieli* (allies or customary partners), even when, at first sight, in a monetised context, this may appear as pure exploitation.

To be one's own master, free to do whatever one likes, is still one of the most prized values in Tanna, and in other islands, regardless of whether it is more and more difficult to sustain that ideal. The opposite of 'hard work' or the 'way of money' is the way of life associated with what Marshall Sahlins (1974) used to describe as the 'domestic mode of production', and could be translated by the Bislama expression *stop nomo*:

> *Mi stap nomo* … 'I just live' or 'I just am' … If you want to eat, you just go to the beach and catch a fish. Otherwise, you go to your garden and grow vegetables. You don't need money, just a little to buy soap or kerosene. But if you want to, you can do without. *Mi stap nomo* … This simple, commonly used phrase, adds Miles, speaks volumes about the chasm between a self-subsistence worldview and a developmental one (Miles 1998: 178).

In the past, people in Tanna used to say that there was very little money on the island. But today, with tourism, there are small amounts of money in every neighbourhood and in every house; limited though these amounts certainly are, there is enough for people to think that money can transform their lives, and for them to be greedy to get more. That is why older Tannese regularly remind the younger generation that *kastom hemi bitem mani* (custom is more powerful than money) or likewise that *long kastom evrisamting hemi fri* (with custom you don't need money). In the past, ni-Vanuatu never needed large amounts of money. To get money for school fees or other big expenses they had to migrate and find work in Port Vila. Up until now most people would not have considered Tanna to be a place where it is legitimate to make profits. Chief Isak Wan, from Sulphur Bay, said to me in his own words: '*Mani hemi gud laef bat mani i mekem man i rabem brata mo sista blong hem*' (money can facilitate your life, but it can also lead you to hurt your brother and your sister) (Ipekel village, Tanna, April 2004).

The development of mass tourism in Tanna does not mean the arrival of tourists in vast numbers or a huge increase of money locally. But with around 15,000 tourists a year (to a population of around 30,000 inhabitants), tourism has become a local industry with all of the social and cultural consequences that it involves. Tourism has largely contributed to turning the monetisation of rural communities into a now well-established reality. Until recent times, Tannese people could have been considered to be self-sufficient producers and only marginally as consumers. Today they have become consumers on a much larger scale. Many households are buying an ever-increasing part of their food in shops, while subsistence agriculture and the traditional technological knowledge associated with it are declining (Lebot et al. 2014).

Many young Tannese try to find employment in Port Vila. There they are confronted with an urban economy run by expatriate managers who, in a couple of months or less, can earn what they could expect to earn over a lifetime.[18] Overseas seasonal working schemes in New Zealand or Australia offer employment conditions that, for many people, are sometimes reminiscent of the old blackbirding scheme, even if working on Taiwanese fishing boats is thought to be much worse. In Lenakel, Tanna's small capital, also called *blackmantown* since every storekeeper is Tannese while resident expatriates are virtually absent, a considerable amount of capital has already been accumulated, but it is kept hidden under pillows. To display wealth that is not of a traditional kind (except for trucks, which cannot be hidden) is not approved of and can even be dangerous. A route to wealth should be accompanied with secrecy (Rousseau 2015: 27). That is why the local branch of the Vanuatu National Bank is not able to observe any signs of the accumulation of personal wealth in personal accounts (as I was informed by the bank's director in Lenakel, March 2011).

---

18 Material wealth of 'Whites' is frequently explained in Vanuatu by supernatural means. They are sometimes suspected to individually own a *majin blong mekem mani* (a machine to make money, not to be confused with automatic cash dispensers like in Port Vila). Once, a group of informators mimed to me how such machine was working: 'Just push on the button and a banknote will appear'. Likewise, the Free Mason Lodge of Mele in Port Vila, locally called *Satanik*, is commonly considered by ni-Vanuatu as 'a church of white businessmen sacrificing young children to earn a lot of money'.

Tourism, too, through the monetisation of village communities, has contributed to a growing feeling of social inequality in a rural context. Local indigenous businessmen (storekeepers, tourist operators, truck owners, kava planters, now form a new group of capitalist entrepreneurs, even if they feel ashamed and deny that they belong to a new rural middle class, except when they are in Port Vila or overseas where they can enjoy their newly acquired privileges. In the past, people in Tanna used to say that there were no rich people and no poor people—these words once had no meaning. But today these categories have become real, and some Tannese will add that they feel closer to a poor person from another island than to the rich people from their own island. As one of its many consequences, this has led to a regular increase in the crime rate among the young people of Tanna, not only in Port Vila, but also in their home islands where once criminality was almost unknown.[19]

The commodification of *kastom* and the business of traditional ceremonies

The ancestors of the ni-Vanuatu created their own unique, and spectacular, ceremonies. These ritualised events were traditionally used to sustain both the cosmic and social orders, and at the same time to redistribute within the society the benefits of the abundance of food and well-being produced by them. The aesthetic and spiritual achievements of these events were part of people's symbolic investments and magical powers. These ceremonies belong exclusively to them, even if it seems impossible to attribute any specific 'copyright' to the whole ritual process as such. The move to change the spirit of these ceremonies—that is to aim at raising revenue instead of maintaining social relations, celebrated by food and other ritualised exchanges—has mainly come about because of the development of tourism. In Vanuatu, before a couple of decades ago, it never happened that a traditional ceremony was completely recast for exclusively economic purposes.

---

19   As a result of historically shared views by Christians and John Frum opponent groups against *nahak* (sorcery), violent reactions to the consequences of changing forms of social stratification did not lead on Tanna to the same increase of sorcery retaliation practices as in urban places or northern provinces of Vanuatu (Rodman 1993; Rio 2010; Taylor 2015; for a comparative insight with PNG about sorcery and modern inequalities see Eves 2000).

In a former article (Tabani 2010), I highlighted processes of contemporary aestheticisation and commodification of culture in certain important rituals held in Vanuatu. These customs, which have been elevated by different (local as well as foreign) agents to the rank of cultural identity symbols, are the same as those repeatedly shown in tourist brochures that encourage visitors to discover the 'real Vanuatu' via its dramatic and spectacular customs, even though *kastom*, or rather *kastoms* in the plural, cannot be reduced simply to the category of the 'performing arts'. The most famous of these regular events in Vanuatu include, notably, the *Nagol* land dive in the south of Pentecost Island, the *Rom* dances on Ambrym, the initiatory sand drawings in the northern central islands, the *Nakwiari* ceremonies and the annual cargoist celebrations of the followers of the John Frum movement on Tanna, every 15 February. Since the 1970s the organisation of 'festivals of traditional arts', held in all the Pacific states, has been added to these; on these occasions, a 'best-of' of national or regional neorituals, in abbreviated and folkoric form, will usually be performed. Through political, commercial and legal processes, the traditional referent of these updated ritualisations has been replaced by a celebration of the *kastom* theme itself. The valorisation at various levels of Vanuatu's cultural customary heritage appears to be a paradox. *Kastom* is more and more frequently invoked for political and commercial purposes. Nevertheless, *kastom* as an ongoing practice, coupled with an idealisation of the ancestral past, is seen by many ni-Vanuatu both as the focus of, and the cure for, the main ills brought by westernisation.

In that article I also pointed to the increasing monetisation of village communities through the global promotion of *kastom* performances by the media and for the purposes of tourism; at the local level, this monetisation is more and more frequently considered to be a factor of inequality or division. I based parts of my argument on the *Nagol* ceremonies in South Pentecost, and discussed the differing nature of its national and local political uses, and different aspects of its economic exploitation.[20]

---

20 The most severe statements about commercial exploitation of *Nagol* were made by Gratien Tiona, a local ni-Vanuatu journalist:

'The *Gaul* Land Dive [*Nagol*] has become a business, an opportunity for earning money ... Over the last few years, the number of dives has increased and the ritual has become a competition ... The members of a council responsible for the *Nagol* activities are said to have embezzled money brought by foreign visitors whose numbers increase every year ... This practice would have made money for the community of southern Pentecost if the rights had been paid for ... The spirit of collective work

I had the opportunity to summarise my views at several conferences in Vanuatu and provided a précis of my findings to national and regional newspapers and on radio. My interview for ABC Radio Australia (21 May 2010), followed by *The Independent of Vanuatu* (22 May 2010), was titled, without my approval, 'Vanuatu's *Nagol* season denounced as tourist trap'. Among the reactions that followed in Port Vila and Pentecost was that of *Nagol* ceremonial leaders who were prompted to give their own point of view on the current situation.

In a reply to ABC Radio Australia (28 May 2010), 'High chiefs of Pentecost want more tourists', Luc Fago, who has been in the vanguard of the tourist development of *Nagol* among the West Coast Christian communities, was not concerned about the dangers resulting from increasing the number of land dives in order to increase their financial benefits. He admitted that the ceremony earned considerable local income. On the occasion of a recent visit to South Pentecost by Serge Vohor, former infrastructure minister, Fago demanded new infrastructure in order that the island could host even more tourists for the event. In his speech for the opening of the *Nagol* season, he expressed the wish that the government build a wharf so that thousands of tourists from cruise ships would be able to attend the ceremony at each session.

In another response, 'Pentecost Chiefs in Vanuatu move to take control of *Nagol* ritual' (*Vanuatu Daily Post*, 9 February 2011), the chiefs of Pentecost Island declared that the tradition had become too commercialised and that they were seeking to regain full control of the ritual. A Vanuatu correspondent, Hilaire Bule, reported that with the ceremony being performed three times a week for tourists the South Pentecost Council of Chiefs, Malbangbang, resolved to take over the entire management of the ritual:

> They have to have the control and the good management of the ceremony because they say if they don't have the control, *Nagol* will lose its traditional value. If they organise three ceremonies per week it means that they have to cut more trees, more vines and it will have a negative impact on the environment of the people of South Pentecost ('Pentecost Chiefs in Vanuatu move to take control of *Nagol* ritual', *Vanuatu Daily Post*, 9 February 2011).

has deteriorated and each village has decided to take charge of the *Nagol* and to organize it as it wishes with a sole aim: to make money' ('Le saut du Gaul à Vaté, c'est l'argent qui compte', *Vanuatu Weekly*, 30 June 1998).

Bule also reported that the chiefs of South Pentecost were still to decide how frequently they would allow the ritual to take place, and what kind of commercial limits they wanted to impose on it:

> Chiefs from the southern part of the islands have described the decision of South Pentecost Tourism Committee as 'prostitution' of their tradition. They said that three ceremonies per week were putting their environment at risk because people have to cut down more trees and vines to build the tower for each ceremony.

> Chief Telkon said it was now time for tour operators to cooperate with chiefs to preserve the traditional values of *Nagol* which is linked with the harvest of yams. He warned that Malbangbang will not hesitate to take action against the government, National Tourism Office and other stakeholders if they don't cooperate with them. This action could include stopping tourists coming to Pentecost for the land diving (ibid.).

According to Miranda Forsyth, Chief Telkon's criticism of the prostitution of *Nagol* could 'appear to be an excellent example of "the community" exercising agency over its traditional knowledge' (Forsyth 2012: 15). However, pertinently, she observes that 'a different perspective is given' by an anthropologist who had devoted his PhD thesis to the traditional land dive ceremonies in Pentecost (see Lipp 2008):

> Telkon Watas was the very individual who re-introduced the *gol* on Pentecost's more easily accessible West coast to attract tourists in the seventies. The massive inflation of *gol* performances is thus to a large extent his work, or at least an outcome of his initial initiative. He has always benefitted immensely – and often – from it, while the people actually doing the performance, have not – or not much …

> Telkon Watas is a much feared man on Pentecost. He has been accused of mismanagement, betrayal, sorcery, and murder. I would say that all of these accusations are true. As far as I see it, this is yet another move by Telkon Watas, now a man in his seventies, to secure this '*kastom* as commodity' for himself and some of his sons. It has nothing to do with an interest in this outstanding and intricate performance itself. What would be much more needed, and would make more sense, is transparency with regards to what happens with the enormous influx of money that the gol tourism generates (Thorolf Lipp, Asaonet discussion list, 19 February 2011; also quoted in Forsyth 2012: 14–15).

Nevertheless, Thorolf Lipp fails to mention that he was himself in conflict with Chief Telkon, who refused to allow him to organise a huge cultural 'collaborative project' in Germany with friends from Pentecost. One of the team members died and Chief Telkon was suspected of having killed him by sorcery (Jacob Kapere, personal communication, April 2010). The so-called *Ursprung* project nevertheless went ahead and was very successful.[21] Lipp raises the questions: 'Who has benefitted from this venture? Who came in touch with it through which communication channels?' (Pigliasco and Lipp 2011: 401), but one might ask, too, to what extent 'collaborative work' also first and foremost benefits the personal career of anthropologists and other professionals in the cultural field—their personal success can thus also lead to *kastom*'s attractiveness for tourism development being reinforced.

The *Nagol* ceremony, which is practised only by the people of South Pentecost, is one of Vanuatu's most colourful events and attracts thousands of visitors each year during the season. In the 1990s, there was growing interest in the ceremony on the part of commercial film crews, production companies and travel agents. At the same time, the disruption caused to the inhabitants of Pentecost by the inflow of money and by the misappropriation involved in its distribution has increased continually. In 1995, the Vanuatu Government threatened to ban the *Nagol*. Since then, at the same time as the tradition was being turned into a commercial attraction, its cultural significance was being lost, while the image of the *Nagol*, the inhabitants of Pentecost and the people of Vanuatu in general were being distorted.

Finally, with the aim of controlling the situation, the VKS decided in January 2006 to place a 'moratorium' on material concerning the *Nagol* appearing in commercial films and other audiovisual productions organised by foreign firms on Pentecost. Thus, by taking this initiative, the VKS was attempting to convince all the parties involved to join it in:

> the elaboration of a coordinated plan for managing the *Nagol* ceremony in order to preserve its cultural meaning and guarantee the transmission of traditional knowledge to younger generations ... to ensure that the considerable cash revenues generated by the commercial activities related

---

21 'In Germany, the three exhibitions have so far been visited by approximately 5,000 people and the South Sea Collection in Obergünzburg continues to attract a growing number of visitors. Five radio broadcasts, between three and 30 minutes in length, have been aired, two by the national German cultural program *Deutschlandfunk*. A half-hour live television broadcast with our [ni-Vanuatu] guests was aired by the Bavarian Broadcasting Association. Seventeen newspaper articles were published, including a full-page article in Munich's largest newspaper, *Münchner Merkur*, and a half-page article in Germany's biggest tabloid, *Bild*' (Pigliasco and Lipp 2011: 401–402).

to the *Nagol* were properly channelled into sustainable development appropriate to the needs of the communities of this region ('Moratorium – ban – on commercial filming of *Nagol*', VKS, 1 January 2006).

Attempts to get round the moratorium have already led to one tragedy. The ban did not apply to ni-Vanuatu professionals and, in April 2008, the Australian production company Beyond Productions, acting for the National Geographic Society, is said to have bribed a young cameraman, Hardy Bill Ligo, who worked for the national television channel, to film the ceremonies for them. Excessive risk-taking seems to have destabilised the tower, which collapsed, killing the cameraman instantly ('TV cameraman dies in film shoot', *Vanuatu Daily Post*, 17 April 2008). The chiefs of South Pentecost claimed that the incident happened as a result of lack of respect for its traditional values. The chiefs said that the ceremony was held outside the appropriate season. In both cases, the main criticism only targets the question of benefits, whether these are increasing or not, and who is authorised to control the performance. Nobody is prepared to address the main issue: are the *Nagol* divers still ritual performers or are they now merely paid workers, entertainment industry employees? Who is responsible when divers die during a *Nagol* performance—the spirits of ancestors, *kastom* chiefs or tour operators and media companies?

The instrumentalisation or the exploitation of these rituals, which are significant religious expressions stemming from an established common cultural heritage, but which nowadays are performed principally to indulge the fantasies of foreign tourists for the profit of outside speculators, is a reality of which most ni-Vanuatu are well aware. The participants in these ceremonies do not see them as false rituals but as rituals that have been diverted from the meaning and purpose they once had. Their commercialisation is on the one hand presented by the state authorities as an aid for local *divlopmen* and on the other it is experienced by those directly concerned as a growing threat to social cohesion. The most recent episode involving the vicissitudes of the *Nagol* ceremony occurred in the season of 2015, it shows how the social tensions arising from it are now being expressed in a violent way:

> Tourists and visitors watched in disbelief as around 150 people of the Wawan Area on South Pentecost cut down a *Nagol* tower on the side of Lonoror Airport in the Central part of the island around 11 o'clock Saturday [April 15] in the morning as the performers of the customary or Pentecost jump was about to get underway …

> Chief [Peter] Watas, who has succeeded chief Telkon Watas who died last
> year, explained that a resolution from a Malbangbang council of chiefs
> meeting stipulates that all Wawan custom must only be performed in the
> South Pentecost area (*Vanuatu Daily Post*, 17 April 2015).

Chief Watas further explains that in the eight years that the Nagol was
staged at Lonoror, the people of South Pentecost have not earned a single
vatu from their custom. 'This is because tour agents, who pay money to
the Lonoror people, bring tourists to Lonoror Airport by plane. They walk
one minute to the *Nagol* tower and after watching the show they board the
plane and head back to Port Vila. Road and sea transports, bungalows and
guest houses in Pangi and artefacts vendors from the South Pentecost earn
nothing from their custom' ('Lonoror Nagol tower cut down by Wawan
people', *Vanuatu Daily Post*, 17 April 2015).

In Tanna, I regularly asked local participants if it was a good thing that more
and more tourists and film crews were coming to watch the performance
of the John Frum 15 February ceremonies. Their answers generally fall into
two categories. On the one hand, many Tannese think that it is good to
use ceremonies to promote the island in order to attract more tourists. But
they do not want too many visitors either. And they are scared that they
could one day lose control over their own ritual events. On the other hand,
villagers who protest against the rise in the number of journalists and film
crews, accused of exploiting *kastom* for personal profit, are, however, often
the same as those who hope that there will be a rise in tourist numbers as
well. Even if visitors do not pay any direct fee to the villagers, the business
generated by such an event outside of the island is widely seen as already
having reached the level of the commercial exploitation of the *Nagol* in
Pentecost. A cultural policy is presently endorsed by the Tannese branch
(Tafea Kaljoral Senta or TKS) of the Vanuatu Cultural Centre in order
to prevent problems arising. Nevertheless, Jacob Kapere, Director of the
TKS, provides a realistic statement as to the limits of his agency:

> I have regularly attended these John Frum ceremonies for many years.
> Before, very few tourists and journalists attended this event. Sometimes
> there were no foreign visitors at all. But today we have the feeling that
> their number is close to exceeding that of local participants. In order
> that the situation does not become a problem in Tanna as it already is
> in Pentecost, the Tafea Kaljoral Senta encourages the communities not
> to demand money from those who attend the local ceremonial events or
> who want to film them. We try to assess the needs of local communities
> in order to provide some material support. The danger lies in dealing with

money and giving it just to some particular chiefs without then having any
control over its collective redistribution. If our policy proves inadequate
for maintaining that control, we could ban film crews and journalists
from coming, but we could not ban tourists, since we cannot stop the
ceremonies themselves (Jacob Kapere, interview, 15 February 2008).

Conclusion

Knocking down the *Nagol* tower of a rival group that no longer respects
customary copyright and denouncing the unbridled exploitation of
the ceremony as 'cultural prostitution' are mostly desperate attempts
or admissions of failures. The rural communities of the archipelago no
longer have the power to stop the influx of tourists on their lands, as was
still possible in the 1970s, nor to prevent them attending cultural events.
Massive attendance of tourists to local ceremonies affects their original
purpose as inevitably as the growth of tourism remains a major threat for
indigenous land. The frequent local conflicts generated by the marketing
of elements of traditional cultures could at best bring them to an end, with
the risk of destabilising even more the rural communities (comparatively
with Fiji see Pigliasco, Chapter 9, this volume). To find solutions to
these concerns, tourism projects beneficial to the poor (*pro-poor tourism*)
(Trau 2012) are actually being conceived in Vanuatu. But this type of
developmental approach is itself criticised by experts in tourism studies
who stress, in relation to these projects, that they are no less capitalist and
cannot only be of exclusive benefit to the poor (Harrison 2008).

However, in this context the sensitive subject of cultural prostitution
cannot simply be discarded as an expression of a vain even if radical
critique. Such sense of humiliation shall be characterised as an allegory
of modernity, similar to how it was expressed by Walter Benjamin, when
he proposed that 'prostitution can lay claim to being considered "work"
the moment work becomes prostitution' (Benjamin 1999: 348). The dual
aspect of the fetishism of the merchandise embodied by the figure of the
prostitute, both worker and product, is realised in this global context
where 'capitalist society creates and enforces a massive and universal
commodification, which means prostitution of everything and everybody'
(Salzani 2007: 152). Some authors observe that the most virulent criticisms
of the marketing of the *Nagol* have come from anthropology and cultural

studies (Cheer, Reeves and Laing 2013: 441), an observation that might be extended to ethnic tourism in general. How can we forget, in the Pacific context, the hard-hitting words of someone like Roger Keesing?

> Mass tourism and the media have created a new Pacific in which what is left or reconstructed from the ruins of cultural destruction of earlier decades is commoditized and packaged as exoticism for the tourists … The commoditization of their cultures has left tens of thousands of Pacific Islanders as aliens in their own lands, reduced to tawdry commercialized representations of their ancestors, histories and cultures. Beneath the veneer of fantasy, the Islanders are pauperized in village hinterlands or themselves commoditized as menial employees … The elites seeking to attract foreign investment and tourist dollars inevitably become complicit in this process of reification and commoditization, the pimps of cultural prostitution (Keesing 1996: 174).

Or those of Christopher Tilley, just as explicit in relation to the Small Nambas of Malekula:

> Western influence having successfully destroyed traditional culture is now having the effect, through tourism, of picking over its bones in a show which heartlessly reduces it to an exoticized spectacle for entertainment. The relationship between the dominant and the dominated is simply being reproduced in the post-colonial context in a new virulent form, a prostitution of culture. The exploitation involved substitutes the physical violence and land alienation of colonialism for a more subtle and insidious symbolic violence in which people sell themselves as part of a pan-Pacific human zoo, and thereby their souls (Tilley 1997: 85).

However, anthropologists were not the first to stress the pauperisation and humiliation of rural communities in the Pacific, facilitated by the surge in tourism and the practices that go with it. Early accusations of 'cultural prostitution' were made in 1975, on the occasion of the Festival of Melanesia 2000, the first celebration of a Kanak identity turned into a spectacle (see the tract posted in the streets of Noumea in 1975 by some Kanak revolutionary militants, reproduced in the newspaper *Les Calédoniens*, no. 4, 1 March 1975: 12–13; see also Graille 2015). Next it was the turn of militant nationalists in Hawai'i to denounce the prostitution of their culture for the benefit of tourism and colonial domination over this state of the Union (Trask 1991). Likewise, Frederick Errington and Deborah Gewertz (1996) commented on insistent complaints in the 1990s by Chambri peoples in PNG against the prostitution of their customs. Next it was the turn of militant nationalists in Hawai'i to denounce the prostitution of their culture for the benefit of tourism and colonial domination over this state of the Union (Trask 1991).

It is scarcely surprising that 10 years later, in Vanuatu, the same causes produce the same effects and bring about the same reactions on the part of the local populations. Just after the archipelago had been struck by the most destructive cyclone in living memory, and the ni-Vanuatu were left with only the clothes on their backs as they lamented the extent of the damage, the national office of tourism rushed to launch an advertising campaign with the slogan 'Vanuatu still smiles'. Stuck in an ideological representation of an idealised precolonial past, exploited for their human, cultural, land, mineral, fishing and environmental resources, the rural communities of Vanuatu now see themselves being offered no other choice by their rulers than that of being 'constrained to smile and "be happy", because that is part of their symbolic image' (Keesing 1996: 174). Anthropologists could sometimes help to imagine the conditions of a 'sustainable tourism' but it is also their role to warn people that cultural prostitution is not a force for *kastom*, but rather a sign of 'consuming cultures' (Linnekin 1997) of those for whom *kastom* is, at least partially, a lived culture.

References

Akin, David, and Joel Robbins. 1999. 'An introduction to Melanesian currencies: Agency, identity, and social reproduction'. In *Money and Modernity: State, and Local Currencies in Melanesia*, ed. David Akin and Joel Robbins, pp. 1–40. Pittsburgh: University of Pittsburgh Press.

Akin, David and Joel Robbins (eds). 1999. *Money and Modernity: State, and Local Currencies in Melanesia*. Pittsburgh: University of Pittsburgh Press.

Babadzan, Alain. 2009. 'L'indigénisation de la modernité: La permanence culturelle selon Marshall Sahlins'. *L'Homme* 190: 105–28. doi. org/10.4000/lhomme.22118.

———. 2006. 'Culturalism, neo-liberalism and the State: The rise and fall of neo-traditionalist ideologies in the South Pacific'. In *Public Policy and Ethnicity: The Politics of Ethnic Boundary Making*, ed. Elizabeth Rata and Roger Openshaw, pp. 54–65. New York: Palgrave Macmillan.

———. 1988. 'Kastom and nation-building in the South Pacific'. In *Ethnicities and Nations: Processes of Interethnic Relations in Latin America, Southeast Asia, and the Pacific*, ed. Remo Guidieri, Francesco Pellizzi and Stanley J. Tambiah, pp. 199–228. Austin: University of Texas Press.

Beasant, John. 1984. *The Santo Rebellion: An Imperial Reckoning*. Honolulu: University of Hawai'i Press.

Benjamin, Walter. 1999. *The Arcades Project*, trans. Howard Eiland and Kevin McLaughlin. Cambridge, MA and London: Belknap Press of Harvard University Press.

Bonnemaison, Joël. 1994. *The Tree and the Canoe: History and Ethnography of Tanna*, trans. Josée Pénot-Demetry. Honolulu: University of Hawai'i Press.

Brown, Anne M. (ed.). 2007. *Security and Development in the Pacific Islands: Social Resilience in Emerging States*. London: Lynne Rienner Publishers.

Bryant-Tokalau, Jenny J. 1995. 'The myth exploded: Urban poverty in the Pacific'. *Environment and Urbanization* 7(2): 109–30. doi. org/10.1177/095624789500700205.

Cheer, Joseph M. 2015. 'After the cyclone: Why relying on tourism isn't in Vanuatu's interests'. *The Conversation* 15 April. Online: theconversation.com/after-the-cyclone-why-relying-on-tourism-isnt-in-vanuatus-interests-39874 (accessed 6 September 2016).

Cheer, Joseph M., Keir J. Reeves and Jennifer H. Laing. 2013. 'Tourism and traditional culture: Land diving in Vanuatu'. *Annals of Tourism Research* 43: 435–55. doi.org/10.1016/j.annals.2013.06.005.

Connell, John. 2007. 'The continuity of custom? Tourist perceptions of authenticity in Yakel Village, Tanna, Vanuatu'. *Journal of Tourism and Cultural Change* 5(2): 71–86. doi.org/10.2167/jtcc084.0.

Connell, John and Barbara Rugendyke (eds). 2008. *Tourism at the Grassroots: Villagers and Visitors in the Pacific*. London and New York: Routledge.

De Burlo, Charles. 1989. 'Land alienation, land tenure, and tourism in Vanuatu, a Melanesian island nation'. *GeoJournal* 19(3): 317–21. doi.org/10.1007/BF00454578.

Douglas, Ngaire. 1996. *They Came for Savages: 100 Years of Tourism in Melanesia*. Alstonville: Southern Cross University Press.

Dunn, Marney. 1997. *Pandemonium or Paradise. Kath and Bob Paul in the New Hebrides 1946–1980*. Bathurst: Crawford House Publishing.

Errington, Frederick and Deborah Gewertz. 1996. 'The individuation of tradition in a Papua New Guinean modernity'. *American Anthropologist* 98(1): 114–26. doi.org/10.1525/aa.1996.98.1.02a00100.

Errington, Frederick K. and Deborah B. Gewertz. 1999. *Emerging Class in Papua New Guinea: The Telling of Difference*. Cambridge: Cambridge University Press.

Eves, Richard. 2000. 'Sorcery's the curse: Modernity, envy and the flow of sociality in Melanesian society'. *Journal of the Royal Anthropological Institute* 6(3): 453–68. doi.org/10.1111/1467-9655.00026.

Forsyth, Miranda. 2012. 'Lifting the lid on "the community": Who has the right to control access to traditional knowledge and expressions of culture?' *International Journal of Cultural Property* 19: 1–31. doi.org/10.1017/S0940739112000021.

Friedman, Jonathan and James G. Carrier (eds). 1996. *Melanesian Modernities*. Lund: Lund University Press.

Geismar, Haidy and Ralph Regenvanu. 2011. 'Re-imagining the economy in Vanuatu: An interview with Ralph Regenvanu'. In *Made in Oceania: Social Movements, Cultural Heritage and the State in the Pacific*, ed. Edvard Hviding and Knut M. Rio, pp. 31–50. Wantage: Sean Kingston Publishing.

Graeber, David. 2012. 'On social currencies and human economies: Some notes on the violence of equivalence'. *Social Anthropology* 20(4): 411–28. doi.org/10.1111/j.1469-8676.2012.00228.x.

Graille, Caroline. 2015. 'Des militants aux professionnels de la culture: les représentation de l'identité kanak en Nouvelle-Calédonie (1975–2015)'. PhD thesis. Univeristé Paul-Valery Montpellier-III.

Guiart, Jean. 1958. *Espiritu Santo (Nouvelles-Hébrides)*. Paris: Plon.

———. 1956. *Un siècle et demi de contacts culturels à Tanna (Nouvelles-Hébrides)*. Paris: Musée de l'Homme.

Harrison, David. 2008. 'Pro-poor tourism: A critique'. *Third World Quarterly* 29(5): 851–68. doi.org/10.1080/01436590802105983.

Hassall, Graham. 2007. 'Elite conflict in Vanuatu'. In *Security and Development in the Pacific Islands: Social Resilience in Emerging States*, ed. Anne M. Brown, pp. 225–47. London: Lynne Rienner Publishers.

Holtz, Andreas. 2010. 'Culture as a political function in the Pacific: Vanuatu and Tonga compared'. *Pacific News* 34: 24–27.

Howard, Michael C. 1983. 'Vanuatu: The myth of Melanesian socialism'. *Labour, Capital and Society* 16(2): 176–203.

Hviding, Edvard and Knut M. Rio (eds). 2011. *Made in Oceania: Social Movements, Cultural Heritage and the State in the Pacific*. Wantage: Sean Kingston Publishing.

Keesing, Roger. 1996. 'Class, culture, custom'. In *Melanesian Modernities*, ed. Jonathan Friedman and James G. Carrier, pp. 162–78. Lund: Lund University Press.

Lebot, Vincent, Laurent Legendre, Stéphanie Carrière, Laurence Pascal and Marc Tabani. 2014. *Végéculture: Ecosystèmes, territoires, ressources vivantes et agricultures 2010*. Compte-rendu de fin de projet, programme Agence Nationale de la Recherche (ANR-10-STRA-0011).

Lindstrom, Lamont. 2015. 'Cultural heritage, tradition and tourism on Tanna'. In *Pacific Alternatives: Politics of Culture in Oceania*, ed. Edvard Hviding and Geoffrey White, pp. 180–99. Oxford: Sean Kingston Publishing.

———. 2011. 'Urbane Tannese: Local perspectives on settlement life in Port Vila'. In *Trentenaire de l'indépendance du Vanuatu*, ed. Marc Tabani, pp. 255–66. Special issue of the *Journal de la Société des Océanistes* 133.

——. 1993. *Cargo Cult. Strange Stories of Desire from Melanesia and Beyond*. Honolulu: University of Hawai'i Press.

——. 1982. 'Leftmap kastom: The political history of tradition on Tanna, Vanuatu'. *Mankind* 13(4): 316–28.

Linnekin, Jocelyn. 1997. 'Consuming cultures: Tourism and the Commoditization of cultural identity in the island Pacific'. In *Tourism, Ethnicity, and the State in Asian and Pacific Societies*, ed. Robert E. Wood and Michel Picard, pp. 215–250. Honolulu: University of Hawai'i Press.

Lini, Walter Hadye. 1980. *Beyond Pandemonium: From the New Hebrides to Vanuatu*. Suva: University of the South Pacific.

Lipp, Thorolf. 2008. *Gol: Das Turmspringen auf der Insel Pentecost in Vanuatu. Beschreibung und Analyse eines riskanten Spektakel*. Berlin: LitVerlag.

Miles, William F.S. 1998. *Bridging Mental Boundaries in a Postcolonial Microcosm: Identity and Development in Vanuatu*. Honolulu: University of Hawai'i Press.

Morgan, Michael G. 2004. 'Political fragmentation and the policy environment in Vanuatu, 1980–2004'. *Pacific Economic Bulletin* 19(3): 40–48.

Peck, John G. and Robert J. Gregory. 2005. 'A brief overview of the old New Hebrides'. *American Anthropologist* 7(4): 269–82.

Pigliasco, Guido Carlo and Thorolf Lipp. 2011. 'The islands have memory: reflections on two collaborative projects in contemporary Oceania'. *The Contemporary Pacific* 23(2): 371–410. doi.org/10.1353/cp.2011.0045.

Premdas, Ralph. 1987. 'Melanesian socialism: Vanuatu's quest for self-definition'. *Journal of Commonwealth and Comparative Politics* 25(2): 141–60. doi.org/10.1080/14662048708447514.

Raff, E. 1928. 'Extract from a letter from Rev. E. Raff, Vila, New Hebrides, 10 January 1924'. In *Orokaiva Magic*, ed. Francis. E. Williams, pp. 100–101. Oxford: Clarendon Press.

Rata, Elizabeth and Roger Openshaw (eds). 2006. *Public Policy and Ethnicity: The Politics of Ethnic Boundary Making*. New York: Palgrave Macmillan.

Rio, Knut. 2011. 'Policing the Holy Nation: The state and righteous violence in Vanuatu'. *Oceania* 81(1): 51–72. doi.org/10.1002/j.1834-4461.2011.tb00093.x.

——. 2010. 'Handling sorcery in a state system of law: Magic, violence and *kastom* in Vanuatu'. *Oceania* 80(2): 182–97. doi.org/10.1002/j.1834-4461.2010.tb00079.x.

Robbins, Joel. 2005. 'Humiliation and transformation: Marshall Sahlins and the study of cultural change in Melanesia'. In *The Making of Global and Local Modernities in Melanesia: Humiliation, Transformation and the Nature of Cultural Change*, ed. Joel Robbins and Holly Wardlow, pp. 3–22. Aldershot and Burlington: Ashgate.

Robbins, Joel and Holly Wardlow (eds). 2005. *The Making of Global and Local Modernities in Melanesia. Humiliation, Transformation and the Nature of Cultural Change*. Aldershot and Burlington: Ashgate.

Robinson, Prue and John Connell. 2008. 'Everything is truthful here. Custom village tourism in Tanna (Vanuatu)'. In *Tourism at the Grassroots: Villagers and Visitors in the Pacific*, ed. John Connell and Barbara Rugendyke, pp. 77–97. London and New York: Routledge.

Rodman, Margaret C. 1987. *Masters of Tradition: Consequences of Customary Land Tenure in Longana, Vanuatu*. Vancouver: University of British Columbia Press.

Rodman, William. 1993. 'Sorcery and the silencing of chiefs: "Words on the wind" in postindependence Ambae'. *Journal of Anthropological Research* 49(3): 217–35. doi.org/10.1086/jar.49.3.3630495.

Rousseau, Benedicta. 2015. 'Finding the diamond: Prosperity, secrecy, and labour in Vanuatu'. *Oceania* 85(1): 24–37. doi.org/10.1002/ocea.5071.

Sahlins, Marshall. 1999. 'Two or three things that I know about culture'. *Journal of the Royal Anthropological Institute* 5(3): 399–421. doi.org/10.2307/2661275.

——. 1992. 'The economics of develop-man in the Pacific'. *Res* 21: 12–25.

——. 1974. *Stone Age Economics*. London: Tavistock.

Salzani, Carlo. 2007. *Constellations of Reading: Walter Benjamin in Figures of Actuality*. Oxford and New York: Peter Lang.

Silverman, Eric K. 2013. 'After cannibal tours: Cargoism and marginality in a post-touristic Sepik River society'. *The Contemporary Pacific* 25(2): 221–57. doi.org/10.1353/cp.2013.0031.

Sope, Barak. 1974. *Land and Politics in the New Hebrides*. Suva: South Pacific Social Sciences Association.

Tabani, Marc. 2010. 'The carnival of custom: Land dives, millenarian parades and other spectacular ritualizations in Vanuatu'. *Oceania* 80(3): 329–28. doi.org/10.1002/j.1834-4461.2010.tb00088.x.

——. 2009. 'Dreams of unity, processes of divisions and indigenous movements: Inter-manipulations as cultural heritage in Tanna (Vanuatu)'. *Païdeuma Mitteilungen zur Kulturkunde* 55: 27–47.

——. 2008. *Une pirogue pour le Paradis: le culte de John Frum à Tanna (Vanuatu)*. Paris: Éditions de la Maison des Sciences de l'Homme.

——. 2002. *Les pouvoirs de la coutume à Vanuatu: traditionalisme et édification nationale*. Paris: L'Harmattan.

Taylor, John P. 2015. 'Sorcery and the moral economy of agency: An ethnographic account'. *Oceania* 80(1): 38–50. doi.org/10.1002/ocea.5072.

——. 2010. 'Janus and the siren's call : Kava and modernity in Vanuatu'. *Journal of the Royal Anthropological Institute* 16(2): 279–96. doi.org/10.1111/j.1467-9655.2010.01625.x.

Tilley, Christopher. 1997. 'Performing culture in the global village'. *Critique of Anthropology* 17(1): 67–89. doi.org/10.1177/0308275X9701700105.

Trask, Haunani Kay. 1991. 'Lovely hula hands: Corporate tourism and the prostitution of Hawaiian culture'. *Contours* 5(1): 8–14.

Trau, Adam M. 2012. 'Beyond pro-poor tourism: (Re)interpreting tourism-based approaches to poverty alleviation in Vanuatu'. *Tourism Planning and Development* 9(2): 149–64. doi.org/10.1080/21568316 .2011.630750.

Vanuatu Millennium Development Goals Report. 2010. Port Vila: Office of the Prime Minister.

Wood, Robert E. and Michel Picard (eds). 1997. *Tourism, Ethnicity, and the State in Asian and Pacific Societies*. Honolulu: University of Hawai'i Press.

8

Diversification of Foods and their Values: Pacific Foodscapes

Nancy J. Pollock

Diversification of foods and gastronomic habits has been an ongoing process for Pacific settlers. Following the World Summit on Sustainable Development (2002), authors of a recent study of dietary diversity have proposed that understanding the relationship between biodiversity and dietary diversity is vital to assessing ways of sustaining health in both developed and developing countries (Johns and Sthapit 2004). A reconstruction of such dietary diversity across the Pacific can contribute to understanding how Pacific communities have maintained their well-being within challenging island environments. But a variety of food choices can have a downside, if the necessary cash to buy food is scarce. In this chapter, I provide an overview of how Pacific communities have managed plant diversity in the face of 'tides of innovation' that added commercial foods to the inventory.

The first settlers brought some food plants as they journeyed from the west out into the Pacific; these constituted their idea of 'good food'. Some 6,000 years later a new group of settlers, mainly missionaries and colonialists from Europe and America, introduced their own ideas of 'good foods' that dismissed local foods as 'uncivilised'. The third innovation occurred after World War II when ideas of 'good food' arrived from both the west and the east of the Pacific. Each set of concepts of good food expanded the gastronomy by adding new values to foodways. The range of choices has been vastly increased as have the moral precepts of 'good food'.

Choice between familiar and unfamiliar introduced foods has marked the history of humanity as omnivorous, as Claude Fischler (2001) has developed the concept. Though humans have been designated as biologically able to eat anything, cultural precepts handed down from the ancestors have dominated choices. Cultural heritages include gastronomic developments of both food plants and foodways that have long necessitated a balance between finding 'familiar' foods known to be healthy and acceptable, while also tasting 'unfamiliar' foods that may not be acceptable, or considered dangerous to consumers (Fischler 2001: 61). Reconstructed Pacific Island gastronomies illustrate Fischler's model of drawing on historical data for European, mainly French, settlement societies. He demonstrates how human societies have expanded their reliance on familiar foods by adding new food resources and new ways of processing after they have been tested and tried. The dynamics of 'good food' selection is under constant management to meet new cultural and environmental limitations.

Early voyagers across the Pacific were seeking islands where they could establish a community (Kirch 2002; Matisoo-Smith 2015). Finding familiar foods necessitated adapting food plants brought with them from Southeast Asia that survived and reproduced in island environments. But islands, whether low or high, did not produce the familiar starch foods, rice or millet, that early voyagers were used to, so they had to rely on root and tree crops that they carried with them and suited the new island environments (Barrau 2012 [1961]; Lebot 2009). Subsequent 'tides' of arrivals brought new species, new varieties of taros, yams, etc., from the west over a period of some 500 or more years; they gradually increased the established array to include some 10 different root and tree starchy foods for their security (Pollock 1992). The second 'wave' of visitors, mainly European maritime explorers, whalers, missionaries and colonisers who all arrived from the east of the Pacific, brought new demands for European-type plant foods, such as wheat products, for bread and beer, cabbages, potatoes, turnips, that constituted their 'familiar' foods (Burnett 1968). Captain Cook found that the foods he encountered in Tahiti and elsewhere in 1769 differed markedly from the foods he needed to feed his (mainly British) crew; a meeting of tastes resulted (Pollock 2013). Some introduced food plants, such as potatoes in New Zealand, survived, to be added to the food resource inventory, while many were lost. In the mid-twentieth century, new food concepts stressed the importance of meat in the diet among the introduced gastronomic variations (Smil 2013). After World War II, a third tide (almost a tsunami) has overwhelmed local Pacific food resources with a diversity of global foods, mostly prepackaged, not planted. The main value of this increasing diversity is that it can provide food security in the face of threats (typhoons, tsunamis) to crops and other local supplies. But it also introduces a new dimension—the need for cash to buy the new diversity (Simatupang and Fleming 2001). We consider the paradox that modern diets based on purchased food systems are of necessity less diverse than early subsistence diets.

Changes in the choices among food resources and early gastronomies can be reconstructed for Pacific Island settlers from a range of analytical approaches from archaeology and prehistory to ethnobotany and social ecology. We can expand Arjun Appadurai's discussion of modernity addressed through 'ethnoscapes' as anthropological reconstructions of societal concepts across time and space (1996: 65) by referring specifically to 'foodscapes' as they too emerge with globalisation in our third 'tide of innovation'. Ethnoscapes refer specifically to social patterns of food use and beliefs over time, as these have been impacted by 'global flows' essential to cultural life (ibid.: 33).

A previous example of a foodscape, that has close parallels with Pacific foodscapes, was constructed by Sidney Mintz for slaves transported from Africa to a new Caribbean island environment where they planted familiar root crops from their African homeland. Maintaining a familiar diet during enslavement, Mintz argues, provided the vital step towards 'tasting freedom' post-slavery abolition (Mintz 1996: 36–49). For Pacific communities, similar root crop staples have provided local resilience as a management strategy in the face of threats to food security from outsider innovations.

Foodscapes include stress on non-material values (as well as material values) of desirable foodstuffs that enable an interface between genealogy and history to be formulated. Prehistorians' reconstructions and early ethnographic and other reports provide a framework through which anthropologists can formulate how diversified diets, transported over vast spaces and time, have added a dynamic resilience to gastronomic innovations (Appadurai 1996: 65).

Reconstructions of foodways are embedded in analysts' own values. The language of food has many dimensions, based on varying theoretical persuasions (Pollock 2011a). A multitude of histories of food is emerging in the new millennium, either of specific foods such as sugar, potato or salt (Kurlansky 2010; Mintz 1985; Zuckerman 1998) or general overviews (e.g. Flandrin and Montanari 1999; Freedman 2007; or Mennell 1985). Among these overviews, four modes of presentation of 'the language of food' are outstanding (Pollock 2011a). Food has been seen as an economic component, a material good to be produced and traded for profit and wealth; early ethnographers placed food concerns in a chapter on economics (e.g. Weiner 1988 in the Holt Rinehart Case Studies in Cultural Anthropology Series; Firth 1959), but more recently have contrasted local values with introduced capitalist values (e.g. McCormack and Barclay 2013). Pacific governments' annual returns to international bodies such as the Food and Agriculture Organization of the United Nations (FAO), the International Monetry Fund (IMF) and the World Health Organization (WHO), and most recently the Millennium Development Goals (MDG), while addressing internal concerns such as 'Building Resilience to Food and Nutrition Security' (Secretariat of the Pacific Commission 2014), also consider contributions of food imports to sustainable development and health (Johns and Sthapit 2004). A second language, that of politics of traded foods, exports and imports, is addressed in food policies. A third language, that of nutrition, has provided a paradigm that has expanded exponentially since World War II (e.g. Coyne, Badcock and Taylor 1984); dietary practices have been evaluated for their contributions to biological health, and specifically to a range of non-communicable diseases (NCDs), such as diabetes (Ohtsuka and Ulijaszek 2007; Toledo and Burlingame 2006). A fourth language, that of the social ecology of food diversity, to which this chapter contributes, is also phrased in various linguistic forms; Luisa Maffi's (2001) edited volume contains papers that link language, knowledge and the environment within her argument for 'the moral imperative of diversity' for which local knowledge is a capital resource (Harmon 2001). 'Good food' is multivariant.

When we consider selections of resources for foodstuffs, traditional ecological knowledge comes under scrutiny for its contributions to a sustainable future. By addressing the question posed by Aldo Leopold and taken up by Maffi, 'How can we humanly occupy the Earth without rendering it dysfunctional? (2008: 267), it becomes apparent that the place of biocultural diversity is being addressed from a variety of viewpoints

(Pretty et al. 2009). In this chapter, I extend consideration of biodiversity in the Pacific as a strategy that integrates traditional knowledge with cultural diversity to increase both quality and quantity of food concepts in order to sustain a healthy future (Johns and Sthapit 2004: 155).

Drawing on Marshall Sahlins's (1985) emphasis on the significance of history for understanding cultural diversity in the Pacific, I trace three 'tides of innovation' in Pacific foodscapes. Earliest settlers gradually expanded their food inventories to include several species and varieties of taros, yams and breadfruit, both seedless and seeded, by selecting planting material that best suited familiar tastes, and plants that grew well in the new island environments (Lebot 2002). In more recent times, from mid-eighteenth to mid-twentieth century, that diversification process has expanded rapidly to incorporate foods and food concepts introduced by colonists and missionaries from further afield, who also wished to replicate their familiar foods whether from European or American homelands, or from China, India and Southeast Asia. In the last 60 years, diversification has extended to include selected 'globalised' foodstuffs that have intruded into both plantations and market places. They come together with new interpretations of the concepts of 'good foods' as promoted in the media and elsewhere. These three 'tides of innovation' through reconstructed foodscapes provide a perspective on how Pacific peoples have maintained their notions of food security while also 'updating' them with new ways of thinking about food, new food concepts and new moral values to suit the modern environment. *Me'a kai* chef Robert Oliver depicts today's varied Pacific 'foodways' as they fit today's lifestyles, with elaborately illustrated recipes from Fiji, Samoa and Tonga and other parts of the Pacific designed to tempt new food uses for modern contexts, especially tourism (Oliver, Berno and Ram 2010); these variations constitute his training of Pacific Island chefs to extend their repertoire of uses of island foods (Oliver 2013).

Seeking islands, seeking foods

Early settlers had to establish their food resources based on their cultural and environmental knowledge. Peopling the Pacific, whether by Austronesian speakers or earlier groups, has been much debated by prehistorians from many perspectives. Analyses of material artefacts that archaeologists have exposed has led to the construction of 'Lapita culture', a thesis constructed around evidence of pottery sherds from sites in Vanuatu to Samoa (Kirch 2002). Dating such finds, linked with reconstructions of historical linguistic data for such artefacts, has led to an association between Lapita culture and the Austronesian family of languages, widespread across Oceania and beyond (Kirch and Hunt 1988). Prehistorians suggest that Lapita voyagers sailed from Taiwan or Southeast Asia to settle western islands (Near Oceania/Melanesia), thence further eastward to the islands of the eastern Pacific (Remote Oceania/Polynesia and Micronesia) (Kirch 2002). As they crossed the Pacific these voyagers introduced what prehistorians call 'transported landscapes' to refer to the modes of planting food resources, together with animals, such as rats and dogs, that accompanied them (Kirch and Hunt 1988). Familiar planting techniques, namely vegetal reproduction or irrigation, that were transferred from the homeland had the greatest success, based on hindsight. Cultural knowledge that these settlers used to select particular plants and their mode of reproduction provides a base from which to reconstruct Pacific foodscapes.

Plant foods featured prominently in early Pacific foodways, inasmuch as we can reconstruct them from recent reports of cultural practices. Plant foods constituted some 83 per cent of the diet (Barrau 2012 [1961]), with fish as the main accompaniment. Pigs featured at feasts, and celebrations, or as gifts to visitors, but were not regularly eaten by Pacific communities. Early visitors such as Joseph Banks, James Cook and missionaries noted the heavy reliance on an array of plants that featured in the everyday diet of Tahitians or Tongans; they also received these, both as direct gifts or dined on them at feasts (Banks, cited in Beaglehole 1955). Plant foods, eaten with a small accompanying piece of fish or coconut, constituted the familiar 'good food'. That consideration marked a major difference from the visitors' food values, as Cook noted during his first encounter in the Pacific in 1769 (Pollock 2013). For their tastes, meat constituted the main item in their daily diet, eaten with potatoes and other vegetables. This 'meeting of tastes' highlighted the marked difference between familiar food values that Pacific settlers had brought with them from their Southeast Asian homelands, and the familiar food values that Cook and other European visitors brought from their homeland. Root and tree foods were considered to be the 'good foods' in the Pacific, but they must be accompanied by a small piece of fish or coconut to satisfy the eaters.

As prehistorians draw on new techniques, such as DNA analysis, to reconstruct the place of plants and animals in early lifeways, considerations of forms of taros, yams and other food and useful plants are linked to recent ethnographic evidence recorded by early visitors in the nineteenth and twentieth centuries; botanists and ethnographers provide a glimpse of earlier foodways of Polynesians, Fijians, Hawaiian and Māori (e.g. Barrau 2012 [1961]; Best 1925; Handy, Handy and Pukui 1972; Joseph Banks and Captain Cook in Beaglehole 1955; Seemann 1862). In the absence of 'hard' material from archaeological remains, other than fish and bird bones, new modes of reconstruction rely on findings from DNA and cytogenic testing of taros, yams, paper mulberry, etc., to give us 'phylogeographic analyses of plants and animals, [that] can serve as proxies for reconstructing the pathway of colonizing canoes' (Matisoo-Smith 2015: 2). When we consider the cultural values in which those food concepts are embedded, we raise questions about the 'moral imperative of diversity' (Harmon 2001) as it contributes to food security as sustainable community support.

Each canoeload of settlers brought cultural concepts of food usages that had become familiar in their homelands in Asia (Pollock 1992; Tan 2011). But they had to be innovative. Islands posed particular challenges due to the absence of familiar plant resources, particularly rice, that could be used as food, and the presence of poor soils, salt laden moisture and other climatic exposures. New arrivals had to find new ways to avoid extreme hunger while attempting to meet familiar dietary needs and tastes. Subsequent visitors were welcomed as they brought new food plants and new varieties of familiar plants. Each community had to derive ways to render those plants into edible and tasty foods. Pounding, drying, fermenting and transforming by heat were all practices they had used in their homeland that could be adapted to the root and tree starches (Pollock 2011b).

The early inventory of plant foods included Colocasia taro, Dioscorea yams, breadfruit, bananas (*musa*) and coconuts (Barrau 2012 [1961]; Pollock 1992). As far as we can reconstruct these all originated in Southeast Asia or New Guinea. All of these plants could be transported by canoe over short distances without undue loss. All were reproduced by vegetal propagation, allowing Pacific residents to choose to propagate those plants that suited their tastes and the environment. Planting calendars were developed as part of that inherited ecological knowledge (Pollock 1992). Crops were rotated, using shifting agriculture techniques to maintain a steady food supply on islands with poor soils, such as atolls and raised reefs, for example, Niue (fieldnotes July 1996: 9). Residents drew on observations of climate, storm and drought changes, and knowledge of plant growth patterns (see Colenso 1880 for Māori planting knowledge). When food sources were destroyed by cyclones, saltwater inundations, or other climatic events, social controls such as *rahui* were imposed, as Captain Cook experienced (Pollock 2013). Communities developed these controls to placate the gods, and thus to ensure an ongoing food supply.

From those first plantings, several species and many varieties of those food plants became the major components of Pacific diets (Barrau 2012 [1961]; Pollock 1992). Four species of taro/dalo were introduced of which *Colocasia esculenta* and *Alocasia* species were the earliest, followed by the large-leafed *Cyrtosperma* species that have been the hallmark of Kiribati foodways. Xanthosoma taros were introduced much later, perhaps in the eighteenth century, and from central America; they are particularly favoured by Tongans, though produce smaller corms. Various varieties of each of these species of taro have been selectively added to island communities' foodways—some 72 varieties were recorded as used by Hawaiians in the early twentieth century (Handy, Handy and Pukui 1972). Similarly, several species of yams were added to the Dioscorea plantings, with several varieties being selectively chosen over time.

Breadfruit (*Artocarpus var.*), bananas (*Musa var.*) and pandanus (*P. odoratissimus*) and coconuts (*Cocos nucifera*) have also provided edible fruits for Pacific residents over several hundred years. They are seasonal, so root cuttings were selected to extend the seasons of fruiting, as well as for increased fruit size and taste, plus suitability for storage by fermentation. In her research reports Diane Ragone (2006) not only differentiates the distributions of seedless breadfruit from seeded breadfruit, but lists the names of the many varieties of these trees found in Tahiti and the eastern Pacific. Similarly, many species and varieties of bananas have provided a highly valued starchy component of the diet—especially noteworthy is the recent work of the late Lois Englberger and colleagues on the 'red' banana, known as karat in Pohnpei, which provides a vital source of Vitamin A where this variety is used (Englberger 2011). Pandanus trees have provided another source of Vitamin A, particularly on atolls with poor soils; again varieties were selected that suited local tastes and climatic environments. I recorded 26 named varieties of pandanus on Namu atoll in the northern Marshalls in 1967; some varieties were preferred for their sweet fruit 'keys', while other varieties were planted for their leaves used in thatching (fieldnotes, May–September 1967). On the raised reef of Nauru, pandanus was the only starchy food, and the only source of food, that would grow on the limestone soils hit by periodic droughts; these plants were all removed during phosphate mining during the twentieth century (Pollock 2015). Current residents must buy all their food, imported largely from Australia.

Sweet potatoes (*Ipomoea var.*), cassava (*Manihot esculenta*) and (from the seventeenth century) potatoes (*Solanum var.*) are all later adoptions that enhanced the Pacific Island food inventory. Many scientists agree that sweet potatoes entered the Pacific from South America, initially, but the pathways by which species spread across the Pacific have been the subject of enquiry by botanists, prehistorians and others (Ballard, Brown, Bourke and Harwood 2005; Jacomb et al. 2014; Yen 1974). Distinctions between *kumara*, *camote* and *batatas*, all terms for sweet potatoes in languages across the Pacific, indicate that many varieties of the plant were selectively chosen for local attributes, including taste, local environmental suitability, a range of colours of the starch and of the skin (Ballard, Brown, Bourke and Harwood 2005). Sweet potatoes have made a major contribution to modern Pacific diets, but their provenance is proving challenging.

Coconuts (*Cocos nucifera*) have been an additional mainstay of Pacific diets, both on atolls and on high islands (Barrau 2012 [1961]). They are among 'the staples we eat', (Malolo, Matenga-Smith and Hughes 1999). The much quoted '101 uses' of coconuts include both the fresh 'meat' or dried as copra for cash sales, and the very pure juice, or coconut water. Coconut cream derived from pressing the meat of mature nuts has made a major contribution as an accompaniment to the starchy root and tree fruits, and more recently to boiled rice and other recipes (Oliver, Berno and Ram 2010). Varieties of palms have been selected for the size of the fruit, their regular bearing of fruits, as well as their suitability to particular Pacific environments.

Add to these nine different species used as food plants, seasonal tubers such as arrowroot, amaranth and sago in the southwestern Pacific, and the fish they caught to accompany such base foods, it is clear that Pacific communities have developed a broad basis for their food security that is both culturally and environmentally significant.

Sharing food has been a key principle that maintained diversification that has dominated both Asian and Pacific foodways into current times (Pollock 2013; Tan 2011). Generosity is a core value by which communities support one another; it has enabled neighbours and kin groups to provide both material and moral assistance to those who have lost crops, and homes, through typhoons or tsunamis and other environmental events. Marshallese gave me a phrase, an aphorism—'When we go down, we go down together'—as key to their thinking about living on atolls. Any visitor passing by a house, whether on the high island of Futuna, or in a rural Fijian village, is invited to 'Come and drink tea', which may mean literally sharing tea, or a bowl of rice with fish. During my stay of 15 months, my personal small stock of food was rapidly depleted as I tried to return the plates of food gifts, whether breadfruit, or pancakes, that my neighbours on Namu atoll sent me. Following local custom, I tried to send the plate back with something from my food stores (fieldnotes, February–December 1967).

Figure 30. 'Good foods' at Talamahu market (breadfruit, *kape*, coconuts, green banana, taro leaves)

Source. Photographed by Nancy Pollock, Tonga, 1990

Feasts, as formalised means of sharing. differ with various degrees of elaboration. Those that mark yearly cycles, such as First Fruits, as recorded in detail by Captain Cook during his visit to Tonga (Beaglehole 1955), or in Fiji, include many types of plant foods, as well as pigs and fish (see Figure 30). Missionaries considered these feasts as extravagant, a waste of food that seemed to them to be in excess of 'biological' needs, as William Ellis (2012 [1830]) remarks for Tahiti. They did not appreciate the local values, or the extent of redistribution of foods from such events, and the social enjoyment of such occasions when everyone had 'more than enough' to eat. The capacity to eat large amounts of food when available, but also to not eat for several days when food was scarce marked a difference in ideologies between Pacific communities and the new arrivals. It also marked yet another disjuncture in attitudes to diversification.

Local ecological knowledge includes various forms of processing local starch foods to make them edible, and to extend their availability. All of the crops (except coconuts) had to be cooked to make them edible. The earth oven has proved to be the most efficient way of cooking (e.g. Marshall 1985; Nojima 2008), though cooking with hot stones, or in bamboo stems, or grilling breadfruit or fish in the embers are used to alter small amounts of raw roots or fruits. But the earth oven was the most widespread mode of cooking across the Pacific, whether in pits, or surface fires. Both small and large amounts of food could be well cooked using the least amount of fuel, scarce on atolls. Pottery used in parts of Southeast Asia was used to boil some foods (Guiart 1982: 82), but the earth oven was more universal (Marshall 1985). Now that prehistorians have established that Lapita pottery was used for ceremonial burial purposes rather than cooking (Sand 2014), it is clear that the earth oven was the preferred mode of cooking root vegetables.

Processing necessitated peeling and pounding to remove toxicities, especially when trying out new foods (Fischler 2001) or providing a new taste, or extending the availability of seasonal crops such as breadfruit fermentation (Pollock 1984). Fermentation practices, such as soy from tofu, or fish pastes, were carried from Southeast Asia to be transformed for use with local foods such as *poi* from taro in Hawai'i or pit breadfruit— *mahi, masi, bwiru* across the eastern Pacific (Pollock 1984). The fermented product not only provided a means of storage of excess, but even more importantly provided an alternative taste to the fresh fruit, an additional diversification.

Pounding local roots released the starchy pith from the fibres, as Māori obtained a starch from roots of the Pteridium fern, *aruhe*, to make cakes baked in the earth oven, or Hawaiians produced *poi* from taro roots. Selected roots of the ti tree (Fankhauser 1992) were also pounded after baking in ovens in Marquesas, Tonga and New Zealand and elsewhere to release the sugary sap, which was added to other foodstuffs. Pounding kava plant roots has gradually replaced the earlier practise of chewing the roots to release the starchy sap, mixed with water that has been a major beverage across the Pacific (Pollock 2009b). Pounding tools remain in museums and other collections as evidence of the cultural importance of pounding to change the natural product into a useful form. Pounding the paper mulberry/Broussenetia plant for use in tapa cloth as under recent scrutiny by plant geneticists (e.g. Matisoo-Smith 2015), is an example of the wide applications by local residents to create cultural capital (Pigliasco, Chapter 9, this volume), particularly for wearable woven cloth (Paini, Chapter 4, this volume).

Processing foods was part of the 'transported landscape'. Ancestors had transferred practices used in their homelands to add value to plant foodstuffs. Not only were plant foods part of the 'transported landscape' but they were part of the transformation of those plants to provide alternative food tastes, and thus variety. These transformation processes have made a major contribution to sustainable development in Pacific societies.

Early foodscapes illustrate how island settlers established a broad range of plant foodstuffs and processing techniques to provide a strong base to the variety of familiar foods, 'the staples we eat' (Malolo, Matenga-Smith and Hughes 1999). Reliance on a starch accompanied by a small side dish of fish or coconut formed the basis of gastronomic principles brought from the west, but gradually further diversified by the addition of new plant foods such as sweet potato and cassava, introduced from South America in the east. We don't know about introductions that either failed to thrive, or were not acceptable to local tastes. A great diversity of foodways was established over some 500 years to provide security for well-being. To this familiar base other innovations have been added, with alternative values and tastes.

New foods for new tastes

In the eighteenth century, new arrivals from both the east of the Pacific and the west were seeking their own familiar foods, but could not satisfy their tastes readily with the foods that Pacific communities offered. They found that their food concepts and gastronomic satisfactions differed markedly from those utilised in Pacific host communities (e.g. Cook's searches to revictual his ships, see Pollock 2013). Newcomers introduced new foods and ways of eating that Pacific residents added gradually to their existing gastronomies. A new form of omnivores' dilemma (Pollan 2006 for the US) resulting from these dual gastronomies persisted and increased biodiversity. But it also threatened traditional forms of food security.

With the arrival of European ships circumnavigating the Pacific and missionary colonists from Europe and America in the early 1800s came new ideas for 'good foods' and how and when they should be served. Since Captain Cook and other European ships' captains had left behind in the Pacific seeds of useful foods and animals to revictual future ships and for subsequent settlers, their Pacific Island hosts became exposed to an array of unfamiliar foods, and new ways of thinking about 'good foods' (Pollock 2013). William Dampier named the tree that bore fruits 'as big as a boy's head' (*Artocarpus sp.*) the 'breadfruit' tree after the bread he was seeking, while other scientists such as Banks, Georg Forster and Jules Dumont D'Urville recorded names of local foods as botanical specimens. But sources of meat, particularly beef, were the most missed food item, to eat with grains such as flour from which to make 'proper' bread and beer. This dearth, as they considered it, could only be rectified, they considered, by planting seeds of food plants that were familiar to their European tastes. However, as Forster records of Cook's second visit to Queen Charlotte Sound, New Zealand, in 1773, local Māori had not nurtured the seeds that Cook's crew had planted so that 'the radishes and turnips had shot to seed, but cabbages and carrots still grew well, but were not harvested, and there was an abundance of parsley and onions, but the peas and beans were lost; probably destroyed by rats, and the potatoes had probably been removed by the local Maori people' (Forster in Colenso 1880: 4). These seed plants did not fit Māori concepts of food (for whom roots provided the main food), though they had discovered that visitors were keen to take potatoes and pigs in exchange for iron, knives, gunpowder and other desirables (Best 1925; Duyker 2014). As noted of New Zealand Māori in the 1850s, 'Maori were in transition from their own to European ideas' (Forster cited in Colenso 1880: 5). Forster referred to Māori as 'great cultivators', but other European writers were less charitable. Missionaries such as Thomas Williams writing about Fiji and Fijians in the 1850s emphasised the need to change local food habits in order to 'civilise' the people (Williams 1858).

European foodways were considered vital to civilising these Pacific societies (Williams 1858). While missionary households across the Pacific Islands relied at first on gifts from their hosts of taros, yams and breadfruit in season, they were keen to introduce their ideas of 'good food' and how it should be served, and associated values. But in 1850, as Williams, a missionary in Fiji, notes, new arrivals eagerly awaited the twice yearly visits of their missionary ships to bring 'good food', such as flour, dried meat and seeds to plant their familiar foods in their gardens. Missionary wives demonstrated their gastronomic principles to local women each Sunday after church when local Fijian women were invited to share an elaborate meal, European-style, with the pastor's family. These newcomers believed that Fijian women should replace the plentiful supplies of taros, yams and other local starchy foods, with wheat flour products to make bread and cakes, but the wheat and jam, etc. had to be imported, and thus was often scarce (and full of weevils), and required people to pay with cash, which was very limited (Pollock 1989; Williams 1858). Attempts to replace readily available local starch foods by irregular supplies of imported foods established the counter positioning of subsistence reliance with cash dependency.

Throughout the nineteenth century, Pacific Island communities were increasingly exposed to imported foods, and new associated gastronomic practices and values. For the next 100 years, Fijians, ni-Vanuatu and other Pacific communities were bombarded with an ever-increasing range of imported foods, particularly rice and tinned meats, and fish, while maintaining a strong reliance on subsistence foods, particularly in rural areas and outer islands (Regenvanu 2009). Choices between making a meal from one of the various root crops growing in the gardens and local fish, or cooking some rice with a small taste of tinned meat or fish, introduced both social and economic dilemmas, as well as major clashes between cultural values (Pollock 1992). Purchasing food stood in contrast to Pacific concepts of food sharing.

Contrasts between food concepts became further elaborated by the development of plantations. Whether of coconuts for copra oil, as in Samoa and elsewhere, or of extensive fields of sugar cane in Fiji, or timber, Pacific residents lost their land and were forced to rely on buying imported foods, such as rice, with any scarce cash (see Jourdan 2012 for the Solomons). Plantation workers brought in as immigrants from India in the case of Fiji, and Indonesia in New Caledonia, brought their own food concepts; rice was their mainstay, complemented by the necessary vegetables. If they could plant their desirable foodstuffs in small gardens around their plantation accommodation, they added to the local biodiversity.

Meat as a major component of any meal, as Williams (1858) and other missionaries noted, also introduced a new set of concepts, as well as having an environmental impact. Cattle were introduced, adding new stresses on farmers' lands, and on their meagre cash incomes. Many families in Fiji, for example, could afford only one cow, or, as in the case of Western Samoa, the company managing the coconut plantations introduced cows to browse under the palm trees. Finding cattle breeds that survived in tropical environments and produced good meat was a slow process, supplemented by tinned and preserved meats imported from Australia and New Zealand. As shipments of frozen meat mainly to Europe became accessible in some Pacific communities from the 1880s onward, so demand increased. Food import bills rose dramatically in the late nineteenth century, as the Fiji Blue Books records show (Knapman 1987), but mainly to meet colonisers' needs. Since the islands had few commodities to export, other than plantation produce, balance of trade figures for small islands showed increasing reliance on imported foods, with exported goods unable to maintain a balance. With higher priority given to European introduced foods over the plentiful and varied supply of local subsistence foods, the conflict between local and imported concepts of food increased, and has continued to present times. Distinct differences between the values (social and economic) of local foods in contrast to imported foods, as material goods, has had ever-increasing significance for the well-being of Pacific communities throughout the twentieth century. Increasing variety has come at a cost to family lifestyles including health, as well as to government policies for agriculture, health and financial independence.

Market places became intermediary sites where local producers sold their food produce to the new settlers for small amounts of cash. A diverse range of produce was displayed with cabbages, tomatoes, squash and eggplants joining the taros, yams and cooking bananas, as per demand in Suva, Nuku'alofa or Tahiti (Hardaker and Fleming 1984). Sales of such foods along with any fish or shellfish families had caught, brought small cash returns, while also increasing the variety for purchasers of foods to be served at household meals. Market places in Tahiti, Suva and Apia became meeting places for both social as well as economic exchanges (ibid.). Small stores in each rural community brought a small income to the village owners.

Biodiversity increased with the arrival of newcomers from the west and east who introduced new food plants and new ways of eating, that is meals that fitted their concepts of 'good food' and derogated local Pacific concepts. Newcomers established an infrastructure of purchased foods that included both market places and supermarkets, and the beginnings of overseas trade, particularly food imports. Pacific Island governments and communities faced a new perspective on their food culture, with local foods such as taro and yams devalued as 'uncivilised' while purchased foods though scarce were promoted as more desirable. But local foods that continued to provide diversity that underpinned security were not easily supplanted.

Increasing options – glocalisations

Globalisation has been challenged at a theoretical level as it implies universal ideologies are paramount over local heterogeneities (Robertson 1995). The neologism 'glocal' reasserts the importance of heterogeneity, as George Ritzer suggests, as it includes traditional values in their ecological setting alongside introduced worldwide values. Local values can be seen to interpenetrate alongside new global values (Ritzer 2003; Robertson 1995). The concept of glocal reasserts the importance of maintaining local values as appropriate in globalising contexts.

Globalisation as linked to the spread of industrialised systems, including food, has been widely re-examined in the new millennium. Joseph Stiglitz' assessment of 'development that works', for example, while recognising that multinational corporations can be blamed for the 'ills of globalisation' as well as for its achievements, suggests that the 'democratic deficit', that relates to inequalities, and alternative values has to be overcome if security, including food security, is to become a major alternative value to economic globalisation (2006: 289). Lack of cash is a major feature of what he calls the 'democratic deficit'.

Multinational corporations, such as McDonald's, Kentucky Fried Chicken (KFC), and canned soft drink companies, such as Coca-Cola (see Foster 2008) have contributed to our understanding of the diversity of food choices, particularly in urban areas of Pacific Island economies. Turkey tails and lamb flaps (Gewertz and Errington 2010), overflowing from US, New Zealand and Australian meat industries, have filled the freezers of Pacific urban supermarkets to offer tasty, highly desirable, and affordable meat products; they have become new indicators of the cash economy and status. While increased demand by customers in urban areas is welcomed by retailers, it is decried by medical experts for the negative health effects associated with these excessively fatty foods; when agencies such as the Fiji National Food and Nutrition Committee, and similar agencies in other Pacific Islands, advise governments to resist these imports, the economic rationale of profits and growth is found to be dominant over health concerns.

Whether globalised distributions of food complexes have benefited island societies' food security is the subject of many perspectives. At the island community level the range of foods available has been increasing at a rapid rate since World War II. But whether introduced food and foodways are less reliable than local foodways is debatable. As island communities experience threats of cost increases and irregular transportation links, as well as environmental devastation by cyclones, they are faced with changing perspectives of 'good foods' that necessitate juxtaposing new values against old ones. Resiliency assessment, whether at household and/ or community levels, indicates that island communities have devised their own actions and reactions to managing biodiversity when threatened by extra-Pacific intrusions (Feeney 2014).

After the dramatic impacts of World War II in the Pacific on both the people and the environment, colonial economic development plans focused on agricultural production for commercial markets, while political management plans focused on the viability of various regional interactions. The Pacific Forum and Secretariat of the Pacific Community (SPC, formerly South Pacific Commission) have become intermediary to FAO and WHO recommendations (Herr 1994) as well as the Millennium

Development Goals, especially Target 1, which relates to food. Health issues were addressed by managing transitions from infectious diseases to the newly emerging occurrences of NCDs, such as coronary heart disease (CHD), type 2 diabetes and obesity (Ohtsuka and Ulijaszek 2007). The moral principles that underpinned these changes were based on differing ideologies and moral values. For Pacific Island security, resilience necessitated integrating the 'old' familiar ways with selected aspects of new ideas.

Five-year development plans, drawn up by economists contracted to Australian, British and New Zealand governments in the 1960s, recommended ways to extend cash cropping beyond copra, sugar cane and timber plantations in Fiji, Papua New Guinea and even on small islands such as Niue. Cash cropping was seen as the major development tool that would lift Pacific economies from their (strong) subsistence base into the modern trading world. Subsistence crops were not included in the initial plans of the new agricultural department policies (e.g. see Chandra and Sivan 1981). Plantation crops such as coffee and cacao, as well as copra, were promoted as better land management techniques to overcome smallholdings, and as the means for Pacific farmers to gain access to the cash needed to spur on local economies (Ward and Proctor 1980).

Rapid urbanisation, begun in the 1880s, but accelerating in the 1960s, increased the divergence between local food sufficiencies and the needs of urban settlers. Calls for support from relatives still based in the rural sector were met by extending gifting networks, and also by increasing dependency on food markets in urban areas. The Talamahu market in Tongatapu, and city markets in Suva and Papeete, provided the interface between rural producers looking for a cash return for their taros and watermelons, and their urban kin who longed for the 'familiar' foods from the land. Subsistence economies co-existed with the new superettes and market stores full of imported foodstuffs. Local food provisioning was merging with new food options sitting temptingly on store shelves.

The dietary consequences of urbanisation began to manifest in a range of NCDs, such as diabetes (e.g. Zimmet 2000). Zimmet's paper, titled 'Globalization, coca-colonization and the chronic disease epidemic', laid the blame for the increased rates of NCDs on the new (imported) foods that Pacific Islanders were consuming. This issue has escalated through to 2016 when the question of whether soft drinks should be subject to legislation or taxation is high on the health policy agenda across the

Pacific, and in New Zealand. Nutritionists' assessments of whether Pacific Island urban diets are a main contributing factor to NCDs and obesity (Coyne, Badcock and Taylor 1984) indicates the dangers attributed to health of increasing choices when limited cash is the only means of access to foods.

Migration, both internal and international, has introduced a new dimension to the effects of many choices, but it has reduced means to obtain selected foods based on health outcomes. Population movements, whether to find new lifeways, including jobs, reunification of families or education, have led to extended food transactions with overseas relatives. Tuamotuans provided their Papeete-based relatives with fresh fish in return for lettuces and some meat sent by chilly bin on the flights across French Polynesian waters (fieldnotes, June 1976). Similarly, Rarotongans welcomed the chilly bins of Kentucky Fried Chicken and chips that arrive with relatives flying in from New Zealand; in return they might send an *umu*, earth oven of cooked Pacific foods including taro, and breadfruit and fish, to their relatives based in Auckland. Such transactions serve to reinforce Pacific values of sharing food as expressions of ties to identity through tastes of foods from home (Pollock 2009a).

Regional networks designed to enhance economic and political growth through supporting linkages between island nations, such as Pacific Forum, and Forum Shipping and Forum Fisheries have provided a bridge between the colonial inputs of Australia, Britain and New Zealand in the south Pacific, and America in northern Micronesia—a bridge that was designed to bring the newly independent nations into close liaison for what was considered, by outsiders, to be similar needs (Herr 1994). In 1970, Ratu Sir Kamisese Mara, first Prime Minister of Fiji, and spokesperson on new regional concerns voiced a new regional view, the Pacific Way, that espoused alternative values based in an ideological cohesion of Pacific ideas in the face of the major tide of westernisation (Mara 2015). Regionalism has remained as a background ideology to provide mutual support between like organisations such as the Melanesian Spearhead Group formed in 1988 to provide food support after major cyclones, such as Pam in Vanuatu 2013, and Winston in Fiji 2016. International support for local food accessibility is welcomed as in FAO's root crops program.

Issues of sustainability are under the spotlight as climate change becomes a major point of discussion for Pacific nations. Anote Tong, former President of Kiribati, an atoll nation under threat, is providing leadership to awaken European and American leaders to the imminent plight of Pacific nations (Tong 2016). Sustainability of food access at both national and community levels is a major concern for Pacific Forum leaders. But that access is heavily reliant on both jobs to access cash as well as maintenance of healthy dietary choices. That some Pacific nations are recording an inability to meet the MDG target of sufficient food at $1 per day is an indication of an alarming trend towards food poverty.

Health concerns have been identified for Pacific communities by postcolonial programs established by WHO on an international scale, and the Secretariat of the Pacific Community on a local scale. Establishment of a nutrition sector of SPC in 1946 supported enquiries into dietary practices that had previously been deemed insignificant. Findings from dietary reports for many Pacific Islands, particularly with growing urban populations, documented the dietary options that were leading to the health transition towards increasing rates of heart disease, diabetes and cancers, particularly obesity (Coyne, Badcock and Taylor 1984). Compilations of data have extended the medical paradigm to include cultural factors (Brewis 2011). Awareness of amounts of sugar consumed in many forms, such as soft drinks, biscuits and cakes, largely hidden in 'processed foods', is highlighted in discussions of whether education or legislation is the best way for governments to control sugar intake (e.g. Egger and Swinburn 2010).

There are two very different conceptualisations of 'good food', the one that emphasises local produce such as root and tree starches is very distinct from the second, the outsiders' views of good food based in grains, meat, vegetables and sweet foods. Collaborations have benefited from a strengthening 'binary' approach, as Pacific dieticians present in *Pacific Foods: The Staples We Eat* (Malolo, Matenga-Smith and Hughes 1999). Projects that encourage households to combine root crops together with some imported foods such as rice, meat and vegetables in their food selections are gaining recognition for what they can contribute to improving a healthy diet in today's glocal world.

The persistence of food concepts in which the starch food is dominant, rather than protein and vegetables, challenges the options available for 'modern' consumers' views of 'good food'. From another view of globalisation, Eugene Eoyang's (2007) image of two-way mirrors, reflecting eastern and western poetics as they co-occur in the modern world, suggests that alternative views of food should be seen as complementary rather than as opposites. Asian concepts, as early settlers transported them into the Pacific, have established particular views of food that differ from but are today mixed with a number of introduced European/western concepts. The emergence of a glocal approach embeds the food component of traditional economic knowledge as it contributes to emerging gastronomic ideology; rice and fast foods and meat have been added, as the price allows. Choices between global and local are based on several complex moral principles that must be juggled by consumers, depending on modes of accessibility and desired outcomes.

Moral concerns

Biodiversity has generally been evaluated as beneficial to the societies involved (Maffi 2008). But negative outcomes must be considered. The wide range of foodstuffs and foodways that has offered Pacific Island residents food security is under challenge in the new millennium by the range of imported foods and foodways, including processed foods and takeaways. Europeans introduced plantation agriculture in the nineteenth century, which in part replaced household food crops. More recently, the diversity of foods appearing on supermarket shelves and takeaways in Suva or Tahiti teases local consumers who don't have the means of access, namely cash. A fried chicken takeaway, or even a soda drink has become highly desirable, with strong moral concerns.

The concept of 'good food' as established in cultural values has many layers. Globalisation subsumes a universal set of values, for example, MDG Target 1 that sets a target of $1 per day as a worldwide measure of improved food access, that is the dollar value of foods. An approach that values heterogeneity, as discussed here, contrasts Asian-based values for Pacific communities with European/American values. When we add rapid environmental changes as they affect biocultural diversity, we are faced with a range of alternative views as to how sustainability should be addressed (Maffi 2008). Food security, as the moral concern addressed here for Pacific Island communities, has become based on an integration of local and global food values.

Key moral values that have developed in the Pacific over time stress food as an integral part of cosmology and social beliefs, over and above its material elements. The cultural elements of gastronomy outweigh the biological, Claude Fischler (2001) indicates, but global thinking has placed more stress on the biological impacts of good and bad food on health as the key to future population sustainability; while Alexandra Brewis (2011) argues obesity is a biocultural issue. Pacific communities are asserting their resilience to imposed moral concerns by choosing foods according to their own cultural heritage as it is interpreted in the modern world, as well as listening to outside advice.

Purchasing food has further increased the diversity of options alongside access to local starch staples. Where taros are more expensive than rice then urban households face difficult choices; taro and yams have become the feature of Sunday after church lunches in Tonga (Tevita Ka'ili, personal communication, 24 June 2006). As a special treat, local foods are offered to the wider social group as a taste of heritage, but at a price. Attempts to earmark the importance of local rather than imported foods, as in Fiji's 1990s overstamp 'Eat More Local Foods', are fraught by the expense of local staples. Householders have to make many choices when daily provisioning, whether from the gardens or from the stores. Deciding which is 'better' has become very complex, as messages come from many directions, whether family, media or health professionals.

New messages have been added to long-held gastronomic beliefs and practices. As missionaries and colonialists advocated replacement of local root crops by grain-based foods, and meat as more 'civilised', so outsiders' ideas about good food have continued to infiltrate Pacific societies at all levels. Healthy foods, affordable foods and tasty foods compete with the array of fast foods, processed foods, snacks and imported meats, such as turkey tails and lamb flaps, all requiring cash. Where can householders turn for the best advice? Are the major concerns economic or well-being? The range of foods available today highlights the dilemmas of diversity.

If glocalisation is 'the interpenetration of global and local, resulting in unique outcomes in different geographic settings' (Ritzer 2003: 2), then understanding gastronomic values provides a tool for consideration of such interpenetrations, in this case in Pacific societies. New values are becoming integrated with old ways, as in the promotion of breadfruit or cassava chips in snack packets. Marketers such as McDonald's in Asia have adapted their standard hamburger product to offer Asians an alternative of meat between rice patties instead of a bun (as in Hong Kong, fieldnotes, August 2009). And chefs in Pacific resort hotels are being trained to present local dishes, such as taro gnocchi, to their guests whether visitors or locals (Oliver 2013). The added value marks a 'meeting of tastes'.

Glocalisation has come to the fore as a form of resilience to socioeconomic shocks from environmental upheavals, as in Vanuatu after cyclone Pam, and now in Fiji after cyclone Winston (February 2016). Rice is the inevitable relief food, but aid to assist with rebuilding local crops and infrastructure (RNZI radio broadcast, 13 March 2016) recognises values beyond the purely material aspects of rebuilding lives, both social and material. Generosity with food still continues as a basic principle in many Pacific communities, both in the islands and in cosmopolitan settings; it transcends dollar values, but households have to constantly re-evaluate their personal situations as to what they can afford to contribute.

Those promoting biocultural diversity as an approach that incorporates human values within an environmental approach to nature (rather than as a major agent of economic growth) include a range of moral considerations (Maffi 2008). When sustainability was phrased in terms of balancing environment, society and economy, as advocated at the Rio Summit (Brundtland and WCED 1987), it strengthened a positive view of biocultural diversity. But at the same time it also addressed 'Leopold's challenging question: how can we humanly occupy the Earth without rendering it dysfunctional?' (Maffi 2008: 267). Whether the diversification of foodways can continue is a key consideration. A degree of dysfunction already exists when households, communities and nations are faced with difficult decisions. Food imports, whether necessary or expedient, remain a concern for Pacific nations striving to control their own economies. Dumping foods and soft drinks by international companies, though they may be customer favourites but judged unhealthy, highlights the dysfunctionality of many options.

Traditional ecological knowledge has gained its standing as a glocal response to sustainability. By interweaving local dietary principles for well-being with outsider economic pressures, including nutritionists' principles, emphasis on the glocal is incorporating new demands, as from climate change, while also providing the continuity of food security practices and thinking. Biodiversity-focused strategies are being formulated that build on both traditional food systems within their ecological contexts and new ventures as the main pathway to a sustainable future (Johns and Sthapit 2004). For example, research on salt-resistant taros is being undertaken by the Secretariat of the Pacific Regional Environment Programme (SPREP) to meet the impact of rising sea levels, while also having acceptable tastes and textures.

Food accessibility remains the core value. Biodiversity presents apparent options, but monetary values have intruded into dietary choices. Choices abound, but they give rise to many new moral gastronomic dilemmas. While agencies such as MDG set a target to reduce poverty by increasing food access with $1 per day as their number 1 priority worldwide, that raises concerns such as the importance of local foods being more than their dollar value.

Moral obligations to support biodiversity in the Pacific have been taken up by various agencies addressing sustainable Pacific futures. In particular, SPREP supports national agricultural programs, while also coordinating a regionally integrated approach to international demands such as FAO. The Pacific Forum continues to adjust its role in mediating between the demands of major international organisations such as FAO, WHO and the United Nations Economic and Social Commission for Asia and the Pacific (ESCAP) where local values confront international standardising values. The Forum Fisheries agency's two-fold emphasis to promote local fishery developments while also supporting local national efforts to control international fisheries' exploitation of Pacific fish stocks, provides an example of complementary approaches. Epeli Hau'ofa's oft-cited (2008) declaration of an alternative approach to the Pacific as 'a sea of islands' rather than islands in the Pacific Ocean promotes a more inclusive view of the islands' own priorities, the Pacific Way, that underlines the glocal. The values associated with local knowledge are precious *taonga* that have been threatened over the years by outsider impositions, but have resulted in strengthened local resilient responses, that is, maintaining biodiversity.

Maintaining local integrity, based on self-sufficient principles and local food concepts is basic to any glocal approach. Foodscapes can provide the cultural dimensions of changes, whether economic or 'nutrition transitions', on both gastronomic ideology and practices. Measuring food poverty by a yardstick of $1 per day (MDG Target 1) provides only one dimension of biodiversity—foods that people can buy—but it devalues the contribution of local foods to well-being and the economy. A glocal measure is needed.

Conclusions

Diversity of foodstuffs increases gastronomic choices. But those have both positive and negative values when cash economies intervene. Waves of innovation have increased food security in the Pacific Islands over some 500 years, marked by new arrivals introducing plants that fit local gastronomic principles as well as the environment. The resulting 10 species of plant foods marked a gastronomic system transferred out of Asia, which has been adapted over time by residents to meet the challenges of varied island environments. Certain foods have been prioritised as 'good food' over others; the significance of a starch food eaten with a small accompaniment of coconut meat or fish has endured despite 200 years of alternative priorities.

An alternative foodway introduced a disjuncture, a moral dilemma, that opposes local cultural values, with the many moral concerns that abound with international assessments of foods and their uses. Even more problematic is the devaluation of local foods in favour of introduced foods and the associated gastronomies. The foodscape discussed here indicates the impact of new sets of values associated with foods and their uses as they contribute to a glocal form of food security. A secure future has become problematic in the face of globalisation, where householders must choose between a range of moral concerns every time they provide for their families. Cash does not necessarily increase the range of foods accessible to those households, or simplify moral concerns.

Biodiversity has been considered here to extend beyond the food plant resources, expanded over time and space, to include new ideologies such as economic and nutritional analyses. What is considered good food is highly variable. Some communities have chosen to include new processed foods in their diets, when they can afford them, while others struggle to offer their families more than rice eaten with a small piece of fish or coconut meat when breadfruit is out of season. Support for development of a glocal food economy is apparent in the local Fiji Food and Nutrition Committee attempts to ensure that the diversity of local foods can be sustained in the onslaught of market-oriented, multinational food intrusions, supported by outside agencies such as the root crops programmes of SPC (Malolo, Matenga-Smith and Hughes 1999). Choices between the familiar and new, less familiar food products form a continuum with the past; the glocal combination offers greater resiliencies to future shocks, whether social or environmental, and materialist views of food. Fiji's adage to encourage its people to 'Eat More Local Foods' has Pacific-wide relevance.

References

Appadurai, Arjun. 1996. *Modernity at Large: Cultural Dimensions of Globalization.* Minneapolis: University of Minnesota Press.

Ballard, Chris, Paula Brown, R. Michael Bourke and Tracy Harwood (eds). 2005. *The Sweet Potato in Oceania: A Reappraisal.* Pittsburgh: University of Pittsburgh and Sydney: University of Sydney.

Barrau, Jacques (ed.). 2012 [1961]. *Plants and the Migrations of Pacific Peoples: A Symposium.* Papers from a symposium held at the Tenth Pacific Science Congress of the Pacific Science Association. Honolulu: University of Hawai'i.

Beaglehole, John. 1955. *The Journals of Captain James Cook. Vol. 1, The Voyage of the Endeavour 1768–1771.* Cambridge: Cambridge University Press for the Hakluyt Society.

Best, Elsdon. 1925. *Maori Agriculture: The cultivated food plants of the natives of New Zealand, with some account of native methods of agriculture, its ritual and origin myths.* Wellington: Dominion Museum.

Brewis, Alexandra. 2011. *Obesity: Cultural and Biocultural Perspectives.* London: Rutgers University Press.

Brundtland, Gro Harlem and World Commission on Environment and Development (WCED). 1987. *Our Common Future: World Commission on Environment and Development.* Oxford: Oxford University Press.

Burnett, John. 1968. *Plenty and Want: A Social History of Food in England from 1815 to the Present Day.* Harmondsworth: Penguin.

Chandra, Satish and Param Sivan. 1981. 'Taro production systems studies in Fiji'. Regional Meeting on Edible Aroids, Suva, Fiji. Provisional Report, no. 11, pp. 181–93. Stockholm: International Foundation for Science.

Colenso, William. 1880. 'On the vegetable food plants of the ancient New Zealanders before Cook's visit'. *Transactions and Proceedings of the Royal Society of New Zealand 1868–1961* 13: 3–38. Online: rsnz. natlib.govt.nz/volume/rsnz_13/rsnz_13_00_000420.html (accessed 3 October 2016).

Coyne, Terry, Jacqui Badcock and Richard Taylor. 1984. *The Effect of Urbanisation and Western Diet on the Health of Pacific Island Populations.* Technical Paper. no. 186. Noumea: South Pacific Commission.

Duyker, Edward. 2014. *Dumont d'Urville: Explorer and Polymath.* Dunedin: Otago University Press.

Egger, Garry and Boyd Swinburn. 2010. *Planet Obesity: How we're Eating Ourselves and the Planet to Death.* Crows Nest, NSW: Allen & Unwin.

Ellis, William. 2001 [1830]. *Polynesian Researches: During a Residence of Nearly Eight Years in the Society and Sandwich Islands.* 4 vols. London: Fisher, Son and Jackson.

Englberger, Lois. 2011. *Let's Go Local: Guidelines Promoting Pacific Island Foods.* Rome: Food and Agriculture Organization of the United Nations.

Eoyang, Eugene. 2007. *Two-way Mirrors: Cross-cultural Studies in Glocalization.* Lanham MD: Lexington Books.

Fankhauser, Barry. 1992. 'Radio-carbon dates for Umu Ti from South Canterbury'. *New Zealand Archaeological Association – Archaeology in New Zealand* 35(1): 27–39.

Feeny, Simon (ed). 2014. *Household Vulnerability and Resilience to Economic Shocks: Findings from Melanesia.* Farnham: Ashgate.

Firth, Raymond. 1959. *Economics of the New Zealand Maori.* Christchurch: Whitcoulls.

Fischler, Claude. 2001. *L'Omnivore.* Paris: Odile Jacob.

Flandrin, Jean-Louis and Massimo Montanari (eds). 1999. *Food: A Culinary History,* trans. Albert Sonnenfeld. New York: Columbia University Press.

Foster, Robert. 2008. *Coca-Globalization: Following Soft Drinks from New York to New Guinea*. New York: Palgrave Macmillan. doi. org/10.1057/9780230610170.

Freedman, Paul (ed). 2007. *Food: The History of Taste*. Berkeley: University of California Press.

Gewertz, Deborah and Frederick Errington. 2010. *Cheap Meat: Flap Food Nations in the Pacific Islands*. Berkeley: University of California Press.

Guiart, Jean. 1982. 'A Polynesian myth and the invention of Melanesia'. *Journal of the Polynesian Society* 91(1): 139–44.

Handy, E.S. Craighill, Elizabeth Green Handy and Mary Kawena Pukuʻi. 1972. *Native Planters in Old Hawaii: Their Life, Lore, and Environment*. Honolulu: Bishop Museum Press.

Hardaker, J. Brian and Euan Fleming. 1984. 'Smallholder modes of agricultural production in the South Pacific'. *Pacific Viewpoint* 25(2): 196–211.

Harmon, David. 2001. 'On the meaning and moral imperative of diversity'. In *On Biocultural Diversity Linking Language, Knowledge and the Environment*, ed. Luisa Maffi, pp. 53–70. Washington, DC: Smithsonian Institution Press.

Hauʻofa, Epeli. 2008. 'Our sea of islands'. In *We Are the Ocean: Selected Works*, ed. Epeli Hauʻofa, pp. 27–40. Honolulu: University of Hawaiʻi Press.

Herr, Richard. 1994. 'The United Nations, regionalism and the South Pacific'. *The Pacific Review* 7(3): 261–69. doi. org/10.1080/09512749408719096.

Jacomb, Chris, Richard Holdaway, Morten E. Allentoft and Emma Brooks. 2014. 'High precision dating and ancient DNA profiling of moa (Aves: Dinornithiformes) eggshell documents a complex feature at Wairau Bar and refines the chronology of New Zealand settlement by Polynesians'. *Journal of Archaeology Science* 50: 24–30. doi. org/10.1016/j.jas.2014.05.023.

Johns, Timothy and Bhuwon Sthapit. 2004. 'Biocultural diversity in the sustainability of developing country food systems'. *Food and Nutrition Bulletin* 25(2): 143–57. doi.org/10.1177/156482650402500207.

Jourdan, Christine. 2012. 'The cultural localization of rice in the Solomon Islands'. *Ethnology* 49(4): 263–82.

Kirch, Patrick Vinton. 2002. *On the Road of the Winds: An Archaeological History of the Pacific Islands before European Contact*. Berkeley: University California Press.

Kirch, Patrick Vinton and Terry L. Hunt (eds). 1988. *Archaeology of the Lapita Cultural Complex: A Critical Review*. Seattle: Burke Museum.

Knapman, Bruce. 1987. *Fiji's Economic History, 1874–1939: Studies of Capitalist Colonial Development*. Canberra: National Centre for Development Studies, Research School of Pacific Studies, The Australian National University.

Kurlansky, Mark. 2010. *Cod: A Biography of the Fish that Changed the World*. New York: Random House.

Lebot, Vincent. 2009. *Tropical Root and Tuber Crops*. Montpellier, France: Centre de Coopération Internationale en Recherche Agronomique pour le Développement (CIRAD).

——. 2002. 'La domestication des plantes en Océanie et les contraintes de la voie asexuée'. *Journal de la Société des Océanistes* 1(2): 114–17.

McCormack, Fiona and Kate Barclay (eds). 2013. *Engaging with Capitalism: Cases from Oceania*. Research in Economic Anthropology. Bingley: Emerald Group Publishing Ltd.

Maffi, Luisa. 2008. 'Biocultural diversity and sustainability'. In *The Sage Handbook of Environment and Society*, ed. Jules Pretty, Andy Ball, Ted Benton, Julia Guivant, David R. Lee, David Orr, Max Pfeffer and Professor Hugh Ward, pp. 267–77. London: Sage.

—— (ed.). 2001. *On Biocultural Diversity: Linking Language, Knowledge and the Environment*. Washington, DC: Smithsonian Institution Press.

Malolo, Mele'ofa, Taiora Matenga-Smith and Robert Hughes. 1999. *Pacific Foods: The Staples we Eat*. Noumea: Secretariat of the Pacific Community.

Mara, Ratu Sir Kamisese. 2015. *The Pacific Way: A Memoir*. Honolulu: University of Hawai'i Press.

Marshall, Yvonne. 1985. 'Who made the Lapita pots?' *Journal of the Polynesian Society* 94: 205–33.

Matisoo-Smith, Lisa. 2015. 'Ancient DNA and human settlement of the Pacific: A review'. *Ancient DNA and Human Evolution*. Special issue of *Journal of Human Evolution* 79: 93–104.

Mennell, Stephen. 1985. *All Manners of Food: Eating and Taste in England and France from the Middle Ages to the Present*. Chicago and Urbana: University of Illinois Press.

Mintz, Sidney. 1996. *Tasting Food, Tasting Freedom: Excursions into Eating, Power, and the Past*. Boston: Beacon Press.

——. 1985. *Sweetness and Power: The Place of Sugar in Modern History*. New York: Viking, Penguin.

Nojima, Yoko. 2008. 'Cooking with stones: An ethnoarchaeological study of stone oven cooking strategies in Island Melanesia'. PhD dissertation, Honolulu: University of Hawai'i at Mānoa.

Ohtsuka, Ryutaro and Stanley Ulijaszek (eds). 2007. *Health Change in the Asia-Pacific Region*. Cambridge: Cambridge University Press.

Oliver, Robert. 2013. *Real Pasifik: Food Culture of the South Pacific*. NZTV, April–June 2016 (six weekly programmes).

Oliver, Robert, Tracy Berno and Shiri Ram. 2010. *Me'a Kai: The Food and Flavours of the South Pacific*. Auckland: Random House.

Pollan, Michael. 2006. *The Omnivores' Dilemma: A Natural History of Four Meals*. New York: Penguin Random House.

Pollock, Nancy J. 2015. 'Nauru phosphate history and the natural resource curse narrative'. *Journal de la Société des Océanistes* 138–39: 107–20.

——. 2013. *Meeting of Tastes: Captain Cook's Gastronomic Experiences in Tahiti and New Zealand, in Fish and Ships – Food on the Voyages of Captain Cook*. Catalogue of exihibition. Whitby: Captain Cook Memorial Museum.

——. 2011a. 'Language of food'. In *The Oxford Handbook of Linguistic Fieldwork*, ed. Nicholas Thieberger, pp. 235–49. New York: Oxford University Press.

——. 2011b. 'Gastronomic influences on the Pacific from China and Southeast Asia'. In *Chinese Food and Foodways in Southeast Asia and Beyond*, ed. Tan Chee-Beng, pp. 47–74. Singapore: National University of Singapore Press.

——. 2009a. 'Food and transnationalism: Reassertions of Pacific identity'. In *Migration and Transnationalism: Pacific Perspectives*, ed. Helen Lee and Steve Tupai Francis, pp. 103–14. Canberra: ANU E Press. Online: press.anu.edu.au/publications/migration-and-transnationalism (accessed 9 September 2016).

——. 2009b. 'Sustainability of the kava trade'. *The Contemporary Pacific* 21(2): 265–96. doi.org/10.1353/cp.0.0070.

——. 1992. *These Roots Remain: Food Habits in Islands of the Central and Eastern Pacific since Western Contact*. Honolulu: University of Hawai'i Press.

——. 1989. 'The early development of housekeeping and imports in Fiji'. *Pacific Studies* 12(2): 53–82.

——. 1984. 'Breadfruit fermentation practices in Oceania'. *Journal de la Société des Océanistes* 40(79): 151–64. doi.org/10.3406/jso.1984.2544.

Pretty, Jules, Bill Adams, Fikret Berkes, Simone Ferreira de Athayde, Nigel Dudley, Eugene Hunn, Luisa Maffi, Kay Milton, David Rapport, Paul Robbins, Eleanor Sterling, Sue Stolton, Anna Tsing, Erin Vintinnerk and Sarah Pilgrim. 2009. 'The intersections of biocultural diversity and cultural diversity'. *Conservation and Society* 7(2): 100–12. doi.org/10.4103/0972-4923.58642.

Ragone, Diane. 2006. '*Artocarpus altilis* (breadfruit)'. In *Traditional Trees of Pacific Islands: Their Culture, Environment and Use*, ed. Craig R. Elevitch, pp. 85–100. Hōlualoa, Hawai'i: Permanent Agriculture Resources (PAR).

Regenvanu, Ralph. 2009. 'The traditional economy as the source of resilience in Melanesia'. Paper presented at the Lowy Institute conference, The Pacific Islands and the World: The Global Economic Crisis, 3 August 2009, Brisbane, Australia. Online: www.aidwatch.org.au/sites/aidwatch.org.au/files/Ralph-Brisbane2009LowyInstitute.pdf (accessed 9 September 2016).

Ritzer, George. 2003. 'Rethinking global, glocalization/grobalization and something/nothing'. *Sociological Theory* 21(3): 193–209.

Robertson, Roland. 1995. 'Time-space and homogeneity-heterogeneity'. In *Global Modernities*, ed. Mike Featherstone, Scott Lash, and Roland Robertson pp. 24–44. London: Sage. doi. org/10.4135/9781446250563.n2.

Sahlins, Marshall. 1985. *Islands of History*. Chicago: University of Chicago Press.

Sand, Christophe 2014. 'Ritually breaking Lapita pots: Or, can we get into the minds of Oceanic first settlers? A discussion'. *Archaeology in Oceania* 48(1): 2–12. doi.org/10.1002/arco.5006.

Secretariat of the Pacific Commission (SPC). 2014. *Building Resilience to Food and Nutrition Security*. Online: IFPRI.info/tag/resilience (accessed 9 September 2016).

Seemann, Berthold C. 1862. *Viti: An Account of a Government Mission to the Vitian or Fijian Islands in the Years 1860–61*. Cambridge: Macmillan & Co.

Simatupang, Pantjar and Euan Fleming. 2001. *Integrated Report: Food Security Strategies for Selected South Pacific Island Countries*. Bangkok: United Nations Centre for Alleviation of Poverty Through Secondary Crops' Development in Asia and the Pacific (CAPSA) Working Paper #59. Online: purl.umn.edu/32661 (accessed 16 September 2016).

Smil, Vaclav. 2013. *Should We Eat Meat? Evolution and Consequences of Modern Carnivory*. Oxford: Wiley-Blackwell. doi. org/10.1002/9781118278710.

Stiglitz, Joseph. 2006. *Making Globalization Work*. New York: W.W. Norton & Co.

Tan, Chee-Beng. 2011. 'Cultural reproduction, local invention and globalization of Southeast Asian Chinese food'. In *Chinese Food and Foodways in Southeast Asia and Beyond*, ed. Chee-Beng Tan, pp. 21–46. Singapore: National University of Singapore Press.

Toledo, Alvaro and Barbara Burlingame. 2006. 'Biodiversity and nutrition: A common path toward global food security and sustainable development'. *Journal of Food Composition and Analysis* 19: 477–83. doi.org/10.1016/j.jfca.2006.05.001.

Tong, Anote. 2016. 'Current crises and future trajectories'. Keynote speech, Pacific Wave Conference, February, Wellington.

Ward, R. Gerard and Andrew Proctor. 1980. *South Pacific Agriculture Choices and Constraints: South Pacific Agricultural Survey 1979*. Canberra: The Australian National University and Asian Development Bank.

Weiner, Annette B. 1988. *The Trobrianders of Papua New Guinea*. New York: Holt Rinehart and Winston.

Williams, Thomas. 1858. *Fiji and the Fijians: The Islands and their Inhabitants*. London: A. Heylin.

Yen, Douglas. 1974. *The Sweet Potato and Oceania: An Essay in Ethnobotany*. Honolulu: Bishop Museum Press.

Zimmet, Paul. 2000. 'Globalization, coca-colonization and the chronic disease epidemic: Can the Doomsday scenario be averted?' *Journal of Internal Medicine* 247(3): 301–10. doi.org/10.1046/j.1365-2796.2000.00625.x.

Zuckerman, Larry. 1998. *The Potato: How the Humble Spud Rescued the Western World*. New York: Farrar, Straus and Giroux.

9

The Innovation of Tradition: Reflections on the Ebb and Flow of Heritage Regimes in Fiji

Guido Carlo Pigliasco

Background

Back in July 2008, the session on Cultural Heritage and Political Innovation at the European Society for Oceanists (ESfO) meeting in Verona was slowly moving towards the lunch break. Edvard Hviding, chairing the session, had just finished introducing the last paper of the morning, mine, when a latecomer's steps echoed on the marbled floor of the Sala Farinati in the old civic library. When I looked up, Marshall Sahlins was taking a seat just in front of me, in the front row. After delivering my paper on cultural heritage policymaking in Fiji, I took the first question. That was when Sahlins, half chuckling, spoke up to say that all these efforts to safeguard cultural heritage were quite otiose, for while traditional symbols, medicinal plants and other such elements of cultural heritage might eventually be safeguarded by the law, in the meantime local genealogies representing the most treasured possessions belonging to the very custodians of that cultural heritage were being lost.

I asked him to be more specific, and Sahlins told a little story: a few years earlier, he had begun to research a particular genealogy at the National Archives of Fiji. However, when he returned to Suva a couple of years later the material was gone, and he was never able to complete his study. His conclusion? The same might just as easily happen to the tangible or intangible cultural heritage material they are trying to protect now. To me it seemed we were at an impasse. I argued that it is precisely cases like that of the lost genealogy that demand 'cultural mapping' programs, traditional knowledge databases and *sui generis* legislations. I could tell that Sahlins was genuinely perplexed, as well as unconvinced, but he indulgently allowed the session to come to an end, and we all proceeded to a nearby pizzeria to have lunch.

Anna Paini and Elisabetta Gnecchi-Ruscone (Introduction, this volume) emphasise how this collection of essays, originally arising out of discussions at our ESfO 'Putting People First' themed meeting in Verona, was inspired by the 1993 Suva Declaration. Echoing such a theme, two decades after the Suva Declaration, a Facebook group called NA NODA MASI—Do not TM our Cultural Heritage (hereafter Na Noda Masi), with a couple of thousand Fijian and Pacific Islander followers 'who share a passion for cultural heritage', objected to a trademark application by Fiji Airways to own several *masi* (bark cloth) *kesakesa* (designs).[1] One of the first comments was posted on Facebook by Millie Vulaca Tukana on 14 January 2013:

> Sorry Fiji Airways, u can't buy this or put a price tag on it, this was inherited, it is ours, lets all put up *masi* prints of these as cover photos on our FB & tell them, this is mine not yours. God bless the Fijian people, God Bless Fiji. Lets cover our profile pic with *masi* too.

Soon, Na Noda Masi posted a new headline on Facebook: 'The Women of Cakaudrove speak out'.[2] The Fijian province of Cakaudrove is on the northern island of Vanua Levu. Interviewed by the *Fiji Times*, Dimitimiti Lewenilovo, president of the Cakaudrove chapter of the Soqosoqo Vakamarama, an organisation devoted to fostering women's crafts, said that the airline's new logo includes designs that are sacred to the *vanua*

---

1   *Kesa* is a liquid dye extracted from the root of the elaeocarpus tree. It is used by renowned Moce Island women artists to stencil cloth made from the bark of the paper mulberry tree with family owned designs (*kesakesa*) (see Kooijman 1977: 37). In Fiji known as *masi*, and across the Pacific often as tapa, such cloth can be made in large sheets highly prized for their decorative value, exchanged as valuable gifts, and often still worn on formal occasions such as weddings.
2   Na Noda Masi, 'The women of Cakaudrove speak out', Facebook posting, 10 February 2013. Online: www.facebook.com/photo.php?fbid=659520247407633&set=a.652745184751806.157522 .647830625243262&type=1&theater (accessed 30 January 2013).

of Cakaudrove.[3] The designs are also known as *masi bola ni Cakaudrove*, and they are used by women in the province to identify the *masi* they make as being from Cakaudrove. In the interview, Lewenilovo explained:

> We have seen it on the newly designed logo of the airline company and this is a concern since these are designs that are ours alone, something that has been part of our identity and we have never been approached or consulted by the company that now lays claim over it (Rawalai 2013).

Sahlins's trenchant comment at Verona, *mutatis mutandis*, turns out to have been clairvoyant. Fijians, like many other indigenous communities in the Pacific, are in danger of losing control of their most treasured possessions, which have been passed on generation after generation and are now floating in the public domain and in danger of being trademarked by anyone, including, as in the *masi* case, other Fijians. After all, Sahlins (Chapter 1, this volume) concluded more recently that European imperialism has not been the only source of desire for alterity and quests for potency. As this volume goes to print, it is not even clear if and what kind of settlement is on the table—or perhaps under the table to avoid igniting new clamor—to accommodate the Fiji Airways *masi* case.[4] Sadly, the Fiji Airways *masi* artist Makereta Matemosi, who passed away at her Namuka-i-Lau settlement home outside Lami in late April 2014, will not be able to see its end, or what is perhaps the beginning of such an inconvenient Fijian quarrel.[5]

---

3   Tomlinson defines the *vanua*: 'A complex domain encompassing chiefs, their people, land, and tradition' (2009: 6). However, he recently observed that 'the term has become polarized by being defined in one direction as the inherently good foundation of indigenous Fijians' collective identity, and in the other direction as the inherently bad location of demonic influence which thwarts their efforts and holds them back' (Tomlinson 2014: 121).

4   On 19 January 2015, Fijilive reports that Fiji Airways has declined to comment on claims by the people of Moce saying their trademark application was still with authorities. According to the same news however, Ministry of iTukei Affairs Permanent Secretary Savenaca Kaunisela would have indicated 'that it would be hard for Fiji Airways to patent the design because it was not unique, but rather had designs which belong to an iTaukei group'. Online: www.pireport.org/articles/2015/01/20/fiji-airways-no-comment-over-masi-motif-trademark-allegations (accessed 5 March 2017).

5   In the frequently asked questions section of their petition, the Na Noda Masi group explains that the artist Makereta Matemosi, an emigree in Suva from Moce Island, did not create unique *masi* motifs for Fiji Airways:

> she used *masi* motifs that have been handed down over the generations in her community. She is not the creator or the only user of those motifs—there are hundreds more *masi* makers in Fiji who use some or all of these motifs too. So in short: she doesn't own the TM to the motifs since she didn't create it from scratch; since she doesn't own the motifs, the motifs are therefore not hers to give to Fiji Airways for a price; many people commission *masi* pieces for weddings, significant occasions, but they do not consider that they can then reproduce the *masi* motifs just because they've paid for one piece (Na Noda Masi, 21 February 2013. Online: www.change.org/petitions/prime-minister-voreqe-bainimarama-appeal-to-stop-air-pacific-trademarking-15-distinct-masi-motifs (accessed 21 February 2013)).

Drawing on a decade of direct observations of cultural mapping and policymaking regarding Fiji's cultural heritage (Pigliasco 2007, 2009a, 2009b, 2011, 2012a), in this chapter I offer a commentary on the work-in-progress efforts, challenges and paradoxes encountered by Fiji policymakers and their consultants in the process of turning thick lore into soft law, inventorying both the materiality and intangibility of *iTaukei* (indigenous Fijian) cultural heritage and estimating its socially and emotionally ascribed value—one of the most elusive concepts encountered by legal scholars, for questions of 'value as morality' cannot be avoided (see Otto and Willerslev 2013: 15).[6]

Heritage or trademark regimes?

The 'heritage regime' has recently become a powerful, 'increasingly neoliberal' (Coombe 2012: 378) notion, replacing odd technocratic acronyms and paternalistic definitions of tangible and intangible cultural heritage. Envisioning a set of principles, guidelines and procedures that regulate and valuate cultural resources and human capital with an increasing emphasis on governance priorities, market ideology and global tourism, the idea of heritage regimes is inescapably linked to the gradual UNESCOisation[7] and bureaucratisation, or 'managerialist gaze' (Coombe and Weiss 2015: 46), of Pacific Island heritage, making visible and tangible the intangible.

I actually can't help but view this chapter as a fated sequel to my timid concerns expressed five years ago in 'Are the grassroots growing?' (Pigliasco 2011). The risk of UNESCOisation triggering friction and conflict between the different scales and actors involved, as in the Fiji Airways case, is now a doomed reality. Chiara De Cesari (2012: 407) and others stress 'the diverse understandings of and stakes in heritage' occurring between international and local experts—the grassroots—

6   As several of my colleagues (see Blake 2014) have pointed out, it is unfortunate that very few international lawyers and legal scholars have engaged with heritage regimes and related topics, leaving a gap in the legal literature and room for non-legal scholar commentators to advance unseemly and unfruitful critical theory of law arguments.
7   Advanced (and feared) by Richard Merritt and Elizabeth Hanson back in 1989, this derisive term was recently revamped by David Berliner (2012) in his work on an ancient royal town of northern Laos designated by United Nations Educational, Scientific and Cultural Organization (UNESCO) as a World Heritage site.

and also between the state and the grassroots.[8] In other words, 'heritage is a new language of political currency for seeking investment, but it has also assumed enhanced value in advancing the political agendas of grassroots, minority and indigenous actors' (Coombe and Weiss 2015: 56; see also Schofield 2014; Geismar 2015).

Legal scholar Rosemary Coombe's words of wisdom on cultural properties and their politics have never sounded more appropriate: 'attempts to construct new regimes of state-based property rights lag far behind traditional customs, contemporary mores, and, particularly, the new practices, protocols, ethics, and relationships of mutual respect and recognition that have been provoked by cultural property claims' (2009: 407).

In an official press release, Na Noda Masi clearly implies how in Fijian and Pacific Islander epistemology, the infringement takes place by trying to own something, versus simply using it:

> We support and applaud Air Pacific for choosing to use *masi* motifs on the new Fiji Airways fleet. We are proud that our culture is being showcased to the world. But we don't support Air Pacific's application to trademark these motifs. These cultural motifs are used in *masi* making, mat-weaving, wood-carving and by other artisans and craftspeople. These motifs were not created by Air Pacific and have been handed down over the generations. The trademark means that *masi* makers, carvers, weavers and our craftspeople will have to ask permission from Air Pacific if they want to use these *masi* motifs or *draudrau* in future. We advocate that cultural art should remain in the public domain for all to enjoy. We agree there is a need for legislation which protects our intellectual property but we strongly advocate against any corporation owning cultural practices. We offer our collective support, advice and help in working with the state to find legislation which protects our intellectual property but which does not compromise its integrity.[9]

Na Noda Masi's petition created a real momentum on the Internet and was endorsed by various indigenous organisations calling on the Fiji authorities to put in place:

---

8   See the chapters by Ballacchino, Broccolini, Graezer Bideau, Kockel, and Leblon in *Heritage Regimes and the State*, ed. Bendix, Eggert and Peselmann (2012).
9   Na Noda Masi, Facebook posting, 6 February 2013. Online: www.facebook.com/fijimasiforeveryone (accessed 6 February 2013).

laws to protect these motifs and all forms of cultural expression and traditional knowledge. We hope in future that our culture will continue to be strengthened by being encouraged in schools, that it be celebrated with festivals and continues to be manifested freely by the craftspeople, artisans, designers and people of Fiji.[10]

Na Noda Masi recognises the wider repercussions:

A flash in the pan or long-term change? As many have pointed out, this discussion is much bigger than one company and fifteen designs … How are we going to protect the many unique aspects of our culture while keeping things fair, dynamic, and authentic into the future?[11]

Clearly, this local incident is becoming a regional and international affair and reflects both the impasse that Fiji and Pacific Island countries are facing and the demand for a policy informing domestic legislations to support the protection of their tangible and intangible heritage sites at the national, regional and international levels. Almost at the same time as the *masi* case, a pair of Samoan-inspired patterned women's leggings caused significant trouble over at Nike. Nike's tattoo-like, printed 'Tattoo Tech Tights' sparked ire among the transnational Samoan communities in Australia and New Zealand for the design's similarity to the *pe'a*, the traditional male tattoo in Samoa, forcing the company to pull the product and issue an apology. It is foreseeable that more similar cases will emerge in Fiji and other Pacific Island nations working on strategies to protect their tangible and intangible cultural heritage. Scholars of cultural property have neglected a fundamental tenet of legal anthropology, Coombe argues, namely that identities do not exist before the law but are forged in relation to the law and the subject positions afforded by legal regimes and policy negotiations (Coombe 2011b: 115).

Max Planck Institutes' intellectual property (IP) expert, Silke von Lewinski, observes that developing countries are now showing 'their muscles in different international fora' (2009: 125). On the other hand, she recognises that the international, regional and even national instruments inspiring this renaissance in the field of IP rights are still too far away from rules with which the local communities could feel comfortable, or they are too

---

10   Na Noda Masi, Facebook posting, 8 February 2013. Online: www.facebook.com/photo.php ?fbid=659574510735540&set=a.659449237414734.158457.647830625243262&type=1&theater (accessed 8 February 2013).
11   Na Noda Masi, Facebook posting, 10 February 2013. Online: www.facebook.com/ fijimasiforeveryone (accessed 10 February 2013).

abstract (von Lewinski 2009: 124; Nand 2012). The language employed by the policymakers becomes 'neither "familiar" nor "unfamiliar"', an artefact neither of local culture, nor of regional or international institutions (Jolly 1996: 185; see also Riles 1998: 397). In Anthony Seeger's words, such a language looks at 'art' but not much at those who produce that art (personal communication, 12 March 2012).

Several legal commentators have been trying to engineer alternative proprietary paths and recommendations to bypass the perceived weaknesses and potential sites of conflict inherent in the development of *sui generis* legislation. Ownership of traditional knowledge in the sense used by *sui generis* legislation is not a customary concept. Well cognisant of the fragility of many customary institutions around the region, Miranda Forsyth has been evaluating a series of constructive alternative approaches, from a practical toolbox of regulatory strategies in place of the current proprietary rights approach (Forsyth 2013a) to cultural sustainability strategies urging a consideration of existing customary mechanisms (Forsyth 2015). In particular, after David Throsby (2010), she stresses that regulatory structures need to balance the objectives of supporting the interests of artists and custodians of cultural heritage today, and ensuring the continuation and evolution of local knowledge systems and traditional expressions of culture as a body of inspiration for future generations (Forsyth and Farran 2015: 13–14).

In the last decade, theoretical writing by several legal anthropologists has demonstrated the relevance of the social sciences and, in particular, anthropology to the articulation of the complexity of property relations (see Busse and Strang 2011: 2). Both legal anthropology and interdisciplinary scholarship on intellectual property have illustrated the law and society tenet that 'identities are forged in accommodation and in resistance to law, and that communities and localities are forged in relation to legal representations and their interpretations' (Coombe 2011a: 80–81).

As I examine in the following sections, it is in this climate of constraint on one side and innovation on the other that Fiji is continuing its journey to protect Indigenous Fijian (*iTaukei*) IP rights in their tangible and intangible cultural heritage via an ad hoc statutory law (Draft Legislation), and a National Cultural Policy (Draft Cultural Policy) designed to inform the Draft Legislation itself. More recently, anthropological analysis of policy and lawmaking, like its older sister legal anthropology, is allowing us to observe under which conditions fragments of culture and society are brought into new alignments with each other to create new social and semantic terrains and provide the rationale for 'regime change' (see Shore, Wright and Però 2016: 2).

Have we been narrowing 'property' to mean 'ownership'?

Pacific Island countries' demand for a policy informing domestic legislations to support the protection of their traditional knowledge and expressions of culture emerged in Fiji in April 1995 with the Suva Declaration, issued at the time the South Pacific Regional Consultation on Indigenous Peoples, Knowledge and Intellectual Property Rights was held in Suva. The Suva Declaration declared 'the right of indigenous peoples of the Pacific to self governance and independence of our lands, territories and resources as the basis for the preservation of indigenous peoples' knowledge' (Preamble). In addition to a hoary, at this point, criticism of the current IP protection system, the Suva Declaration also contains a plan that, although essentially concerned with the protection of local biological resources and calling for a moratorium on bioprospecting in the Pacific, is also designed to 'encourage chiefs, elders and community leaders to play a leadership role in the protection of indigenous peoples' knowledge and resources' (Suva Declaration 3.1), and 'strengthen the capacities of indigenous peoples to maintain their oral traditions, and encourage initiatives by indigenous peoples to record their knowledge in a permanent form according to their customary access procedures' (Suva Declaration 8.0).

As a result, four years later, in February 1999, UNESCO and the Secretariat of the Pacific Community (SPC) convened a 'Symposium on the Protection of Traditional Knowledge and Expressions of Traditional and Popular Indigenous Cultures in the Pacific Islands' in Noumea. The symposium brought together the representatives of 21 states and territories of the South Pacific region. It took stock of the different aspects of the protection of traditional knowledge and expressions of popular indigenous cultures in the Pacific Islands, and adopted a Final Declaration. The next year, the Pacific Island Economic Ministers supported the Pacific Islands Forum Secretariat (PIFS) in its work with the SPC in developing an integrated regional policy framework and model legislation for the protection of traditional knowledge in its relation to biodiversity, agriculture, ecological, medicinal and traditional expressions of culture, encouraging guidelines from the regional members.

The 2002 Regional Framework for the Protection of Traditional Knowledge and Expressions of Culture contains the Model Law for the Protection of Traditional Knowledge and Expressions of Culture (Model Law). The Model Law, an IP-based *sui generis* system creating new IP-like rights for intangible cultural heritage, is designed to legislate traditional and moral rights over traditional knowledge and expressions of culture that previously might have been regarded as part of the public domain. The Model Law is not an indigenous declaration. It provides a hybrid national and regional approach including enforceable sanctions. It establishes a regional legislative framework, but leaves matters of implementation to policymakers in accordance with their national laws and systems. The Model Law encourages the inclusion of customary law and traditional governance systems in national legislation over cultural property rights. It recognises that the traditional custodians should remain the primary decision makers regarding the use of their traditional knowledge and expressions of culture in accordance with their customary forms of protection.

In October 2003, the 32nd Session of the General Conference of UNESCO, 'considering the importance of the intangible cultural heritage as a mainspring of cultural diversity and a guarantee of sustainable development' (UNESCO 2003), adopted the Convention for the Safeguarding of the Intangible Cultural Heritage (Convention). Clearly, Article 12 (Inventories) and Article 13 (Other measures for safeguarding) of the Convention triggered a revival of tradition, leaving Pacific Island policymakers 'in between', in a sort of a chicken-and-egg paradox involving envisioning inventories, adopting a general policy aimed at promoting the function of the intangible cultural heritage in society, and eventually adopting appropriate legal, technical, administrative and financial measures aimed at establishing documentation institutions for the intangible cultural heritage.

The biggest problem both the Model Law and the Convention face is that the rhetoric of cultural ownership may give rise to 'absurd claims' (Comaroff and Comaroff 2009, cited in Coombe 2009: 406), particularly when contemporary social categories are deployed to make possessive assertions with respect to historical objects that long predate the identities of those claiming them (Appiah 2006, cited in Coombe 2009: 406). We are fundamentally misunderstanding the very concept of property if we focus primarily upon a western model of exclusive individual or corporate ownership. As Coombe and other legal scholars (see Carpenter, Katyal and Riley 2009) suggest, critics of cultural property wrongly conflate property with a narrow and fundamentalist paradigm of property that emphasises alienation, exclusivity and commodification.

In this direction, over the past two decades, we have witnessed a new and vital field of cultural rights norms and practices emerging in the shadows of cultural properties yet to be validated by formal systems of western law (Coombe 2009: 407). Cultural heritage policies, in particular on intangibles, have acquired a new social and political value in Fiji and Oceania. Undoubtedly, since the time of the 'Study on the Protection of the Cultural and Intellectual Property of Indigenous Peoples' (the Daes Report),[12] a more nuanced international understanding of cultural property has developed. If 'cultural property can be distinguished from intellectual property by comparing the type of relationship that exists between a person and a commodity' (Attar, Aylwin and Coombe 2009: 318–19), then it often translates more into 'custodianship' than 'ownership'.

Elsewhere (Pigliasco 2009a, 2010, 2015), I have explained how in the case of Fijian firewalking (*vilavilairevo*)—today a signature brand statement of Fijian national culture 'owned' by the Naivilaqata *bete* (priestly clan) of the Sawau people of Beqa Island—custodianship operates outside the logic of 'possessive individualism' (Harrison 2000: 676).[13] In other words, whereas western IP seeks to define products of human creativity that can be alienated from their creators, in Beqa among the Sawau, like in other traditional communities across the Pacific, the ownership of intangibles does not include the possibility of alienation, for 'property is actually a form of sociality' (Harrison 2000: 676; see also Miller 2001; Weiner 1992).

---

12   Erica-Irene Daes, academic, diplomat and United Nations expert, is best known for her almost 20 years of work with the United Nations Working Group on Indigenous Populations promoting the cause of the world's indigenous peoples. The report, produced in consultation with indigenous organisations, representatives of the First Peoples/First Nations and a wide variety of NGOs, was submitted to the United Nations Commission on Human Rights, Sub-Commission on Prevention of Discrimination and Protection of Minorities in 1993.
13   Harrison is borrowing the idea of 'possessive individualism' from Crawford Macpherson (1962).

Hence, instead of narrowing property to mean ownership, Marilyn Strathern suggests we 'disappear' property, focusing our analysis without worrying about the meaning of property or whether the events we are investigating are really about property (Strathern 1984, cited in Verdery and Humphrey 2004: 11; see also Strathern 1999: 203). For a long time, the western idea of property rested on the establishment of a series of expectations. As Jeremy Bentham argued, 'Property is nothing but a basis of expectation ... It is not material, it is metaphysical; it is a mere conception of the mind' (1876: 111–12). Bentham also warns us that from the beginning any possession is very precarious, thus that property and law 'are born together, and die together' (ibid.: 113).

Eliesa Tuiloma was the principal legal officer with the Attorney General's Office in charge of the revisions of the Draft Legislation when I interviewed him in Suva in 2008. In the early version of the Draft Legislation that was sitting on his desk then, ideas of possessions, moral rights, caveats and redress were already embedded and inextricable, as became clear from our discussion. A prospective user of traditional knowledge or expressions of culture who wants to obtain the traditional owners' consent for a non-customary use, Tuiloma explained to me, must first file an application specifying the ways in which a specific traditional knowledge (TK) or expression of culture (EC) will be used. The application will be published in a national newspaper, and will include instructions to interested persons as to how they may obtain a copy of it. Now, if a *mataqali* claims to be a traditional owner of the TK or EC in question, it has 28 days to advise the Cultural Authority.[14] The traditional owners have certain 'moral rights', which include the right of attribution of authorship; the right not to have TK and EC falsely attributed to them; the right not to have their TK and EC used in insulting, derogatory or culturally or spiritually offensive ways; and the right to its divulgation and retraction. So, if the non-traditional user fails to make an application or uses the TK and EC in a way not described in the application or inconsistent with the traditional owners' moral rights, the traditional owners have a basis for a legal claim against that person—although, as Tuiloma pointed out,

---

14 *Mataqali*, often referred to as a 'subclan' (see Arno 1993: 9), is one of the most significant kin groups in Fiji and a major unit of social organisation throughout Fiji. It is equivalent to a landholding entity where all members have proprietary rights to an area of the land (ibid.; Nayacakalou 1975: 165; Ravuvu 1987: 17; Tomlinson 2009: 34).

nothing would keep the traditional owners from attempting to resolve a dispute through alternative procedures, or customary law and practices (Eliesa Tuiloma interview, 5 June 2008).

From more recent interviews I had with Fiji policymakers in March 2013, it seems these ideas will reappear, elaborated even further, in the Cultural Policy. Fiji's Cultural Policy is in the process of redrafting its norms, in particular engineering proprietary rights to be vested in the community, individuals or the Cultural Authority, envisioned by the Model Law as a mediator between prospective users of Fijian TK and EC and traditional knowledge holders. The ambiguous term 'community', often seen as a 'convenient conceptual haven' (Forsyth 2013a: 1; see also Coombe and Weiss 2015),[15] has been gradually expanded to include various legal entities, such as an association, a legal representative, a trustee, a corporation or a government body established by the community on behalf of the community and in whom the exercise of communal rights in traditional knowledge and expressions of culture would be vested; it can even refer to an individual who meets specific criteria, such as an indigenous person who is connected to a local community and who has received knowledge through intergenerational means. Lastly, the Cultural Authority—an entity stipulated in the Model Law and promptly inserted in the early resolutions of the Draft Legislation—would assume ownership of orphaned or unidentifiable traditional knowledge and expressions of culture.[16]

15 'Community is important because it is typically seen as a locus of *knowledge*; a site of *regulation* and management; a source of *identity* and a repository of *tradition*; the embodiment of various *institutions* (say, property rights), which necessarily turn on questions of representation, power, authority, governance, and accountability; an object of *state control*; and a theatre of *resistance* and struggle (of social movements and potentially of *alternative visions of development*)' (Watts 2000: 37).
16 The 5th Draft of the Legislation of September 2005 introduced the idea of a Cultural Authority consisting of a chairperson and four other members, appointed for a term of up to three years and eligible for reappointment. The originally drafted functions of the Cultural Authority were to receive and process applications; to monitor compliance with authorised user agreements and to advise traditional owners of any breaches of such agreements; to develop standard terms and conditions for authorised user agreements; to provide training and education programs for traditional owners and users of traditional knowledge or expressions of culture; to develop a code of ethics in relation to use of traditional knowledge and expressions of culture; to maintain a record of traditional owners of knowledge and expressions of culture (Pigliasco 2007: 392).

The UNESCO's Intangible Heritage Convention, adopted in 2003, entered 'into force' in 2006.[17] Recently, Janet Blake commented that the Convention broke new ground, introducing new terminology and new definitions of existing terms, and requiring a reexamination of some approaches to international and national lawmaking and policymaking by creating a new paradigm for identifying and safeguarding intangible cultural heritage that shifted the focus of significance (2014: 291). Other commentators like Chiara Bortolotto instead juxtapose the domestication of the UNESCO Convention—and in particular its inventorial section from state members—to the quintessential symbol of cultural homogenisation, McDonald's, and its highly standardised procedures (2012: 277).

Fijian policymakers realised that a total reliance on both the Model Law and the Convention would be insufficient and inconvenient for resolving core issues of identification of ownership, benefit sharing and compensation, to name a few. Instead of allowing lawyer consultants and policymakers to decide these issues through debates based on hot air, achieving what Annelise Riles (2006: 194) would call the '"infinity" of consultations', the policymakers introduced the idea of first having in place an ad hoc, Fijian language database of Traditional Knowledge and Expressions of Culture, shifting the focus from economy to social capital. In 2004, the Institute of Fijian Language and Culture (recently renamed *iTaukei* Institute of Language and Culture)[18] launched the ambitious *Na ituvatuva ni kilaka itaukei kei na kena matanataki*, the national inventory of indigenous Fijian traditional knowledge and expressions of culture currently referred to as the Cultural Mapping Programme. From its inception, cultural mapping

---

17   According to Article 34 of the Convention, it entered into force on 20 April 2006 for those States that had deposited their respective instruments of ratification, acceptance, approval or accession on or before 20 January 2006. It shall enter into force with respect to any other State three months after the deposit by that State of its instrument of ratification, acceptance, approval or accession. Currently, the Convention lists 165 State members, including Fiji, which ratified it on 19 January 2010.
18   On 30 June 2010, the Cabinet approved a Ministry of Fijian Affairs Decree that replaced the words 'Fijian' or 'indigenous' or 'indigenous Fijian' with the word 'iTaukei' in all written laws and all official documentation and public offices when referring to the original and native settlers of Fiji.

in Fiji promised to be more than just creating an inventory of cultural sites, cultural rituals and traditional knowledge, as its process involves consultation, assessment and information gathering.[19]

As in the case of the Solomon Islands, as presented by Lawrence Foanaʻota and Geoffrey White, the project obviously had to face and challenge 'the continuing influence of European visions of culture as premodern "tradition" signified by objects and activities to be collected and preserved' (2011: 291; see also Pigliasco and Lipp 2011). Designed as a collaborative process involving face-to-face, culturally protocolled dialogues and interviews between stakeholders and trained indigenous Fijian researchers, the project, regardless of Fiji's political turmoil, remained on track. With over 1,700 villages visited, and all but one of Fiji's 14 provinces culturally mapped, the *iTaukei* Institute of Language and Culture research teams are now in the process of returning to the first province mapped, Namosi, to update information gathered in the last 10 years.

Carried out in three phases—'pilot tests', 'focal collection of cultural data' and the 'assessment and input of final data'—the Cultural Mapping Programme initially planned to complete the project in three years (2004–2007). In the meantime, according to the Institute's former director, Pita Tagicakirewa, nine more years have been added for the 'refinement of data collection methodologies, the improvement in digital equipment use and storage of data, the digitisation of archived materials, the recruitment of additional field officers, the refresher training programs and the improvement of the Fijian language database of Traditional

<hr/>

19   Paragraph 5.2.3 'Nature and Objectives of National Inventory' of the training manual for the 'May 2005 Training Workshop on Field Research Methodology Designed for Cultural Mapping Field Officers' specifies that:

Designated in Fijian as *na ituvatuva ni kilaka itaukei kei na kena matanataki*, the national inventory project envisages the diverse traditional knowledge and cultural expressions that explicitly exists within the culture of the *iTaukei* (native Fijians). For the 14 provinces that compose Fiji, each has its own distinct local knowledge and cultural system, which characterise their uniqueness. However, with globalisation and rapid development in information technology, traditional expressions in Fiji are continually being exploited for commercial purposes, and on the verge of being replaced completely by a massive culture of modernism. Hence, the inventory is/was established with the following issues in mind: (i) the preservation and safeguarding of tangible and intangible cultural heritage; (ii) the promotion of cultural diversity; (iii) the respect for cultural rights; and (iv) the promotion of tradition-based creativity and innovation as ingredients of sustainable economic development.

Knowledge and Expressions of Culture housed at the *iTaukei* Institute of Language and Culture' (Pita Tagicakirewa, personal communication, 28 March 2013).[20]

Cultural policy and cultural industries: An oxymoron?

Recently, both Palau and the Cook Islands have completed their national cultural policies and enacted traditional knowledge and expressions of culture laws, while in Kiribati, Solomon Islands, Papua New Guinea and Vanuatu cultural policies and statutory laws have been submitted for peer reviewing and comments are getting incorporated in the final drafts. In the case of the Solomon Islands, Foana'ota and White observe how national cultural practices from the colonial period to the present 'have taken place in an isolated, fragmented environment with few connections to governmental institutions that might sustain them. Hence, the urgent need for some form of cultural policy' (2011: 291). Clive Gray would probably identify the motives behind the Solomon Islands and other Pacific Island governments' involvement with cultural policy as ranging from the promotion of 'national glory' to the maintenance of 'order and control' (2007: 204).

In Fiji, the situation is that after 19 drafts of the Draft Legislation, the acquired language mediated by international policies, recommendations, workshops, guidelines and action plans induced the working group to make a legislative U-turn in order to first draft a policy to serve as a guideline *for* the Draft Legislation. The urgency of this move was also underlined in June 2014 by Sipiriano Nemani, Director of the Fiji Museum, and former Principal Policy Convention Officer at the Department of Heritage and Arts, in an interview on Fiji One Television, 'Because our activities in the culture sector in Fiji is spread all over the place, there are often duplication of functions and some of our legislation are very archaic and old and need to be revised' (see Datt 2014).

---

20 The choice of adopting only the standard Fijian language (*Na Vosa Vakaviti*) in such an overtly multiethnic Pacific Island nation as Fiji has been enforced and defended since 2004 to ensure maximum confidentiality of the information stored. Vanuatu, the first Pacific Island nation to complete its 'cultural mapping', adopted a trilingual database for the Vanuatu Kaljoral Senta (Vanuatu Cultural Centre) (see Geismar and Mohns 2011).

Warning us against being taken in by 'surface appearances', Gray emphasises how cultural policy does not operate in splendid isolation from broader societal pressures (2007: 205). Cultural policies are the result of conscious choices made by political actors. Andrew Arno observes that 'policy and rule are a linked discursive pair, and neither makes sense without the other' (2009: 153). Fijian policymakers realised the necessity of a policy to inform the legislative drafting process after setting up a body of self-contained rules and formulating some amendments based on the suggestions of international consultants, the Secretariat of the Pacific Community's guidelines, Panama's legislation on collective rights of indigenous communities and the Peruvian laws protecting the collective knowledge of indigenous peoples.[21] Last but not least, they also considered the work and suggestions of Unaisi Nabobo-Baba (2006) on developing a policy to ensure that *iTaukei* knowledge and epistemology receives greater recognition.

Ten years after its inception, and with a conspicuous number of policy practitioners and consultants involved, Fiji's National Cultural Policy is in the process of being rewritten and reframed.[22]

Applying additional intellectual pressure, the 2011 Melanesian Spearhead Group (MSG) Framework Treaty on Traditional Knowledge and Expressions of Culture is trying to get some attention through a different angle and political force. The Treaty was initially envisioned as a Melanesian strategy to bypass the complexities surrounding national legislations and to strengthen trade, cooperation and the exchange of Melanesian cultures and Melanesian traditions and values among its member countries of Fiji, Papua New Guinea, New Caledonia, Solomon Islands and Vanuatu. The MSG legislative intent appears, however, to be one size fits all—and

---

21　The working group initially outlining Fiji's National Cultural Policy was composed of members from the *iTaukei* Institute of Language and Culture, the Department of Culture and Heritage, the Attorney General's Office and the Ministry of Fijian Affairs, assisted by Eliesa Tuiloma, former Principal Legal Officer and drafter of the legislation, and Gail Olsson, an independent consultant for the TradeCom Programme financed by the European Development Fund, which is currently financially supporting the legislation.

22　As this chapter goes to print, there is clear indication of an imminent motion coming from Fiji's Parliament of the Republic of Fiji to accelerate the approval process of the Draft Legislation and proceed to sign and promulgate the bill protecting Indigenous Fijian traditional knowledge and expressions of culture, while the Draft Policy's approval necessitates a swifter pre-legislative scrutiny at Cabinet level.

only Melanesian—when we have MSG member states like Fiji developing a National Cultural Policy first in the effort to establish relationships at both regional and international levels in the cultural heritage sector.

Fiji's Draft Cultural Policy appears to have been more concerned with reviving Fiji's economies and, more recently, redirecting its support of the cultural industries by supporting the so called MSME (micro, small and medium enterprise) sector, as well as emphasising economic empowerment of *iTaukei*, youth in general and young women in particular. The Draft Cultural Policy is basically designed to allow the creation of new opportunities for income and employment while supporting artistic and cultural creativity. For example, the Draft Cultural Policy includes recommendations for developing and making available micro-credit, advisory services and training for developing products and services that involve traditional knowledge and expressions of culture. Clearly emerging from the spirit of the policy are the vital role of customary law and protocols and their complex relationship with intellectual property rights and existing regulations (i.e. copyrights, trademarks, patents, designs and geographical indications) and, ultimately, with the Cultural Mapping Programme and related database, which are aimed at identifying the small communities that may be the holders of traditional knowledge or stewards of heritage sites (Pigliasco 2011).

Meeting all the goals that are proposed in the Draft Cultural Policy, in particular those aimed at establishing a viable framework for the use of traditional knowledge and expressions of culture in Fiji, will be, obviously, quite challenging. As of 2013, the Draft Cultural Policy indicated a mandatory connection with customary law and protocols as well as national policies and laws on copyright and related matters. As noted earlier in this chapter, the Draft Cultural Policy is in the process of being rewritten to meet some new objectives: foremost, raising awareness of the importance of respecting, understanding and protecting *iTaukei* values, language, cultural expressions and traditional knowledge through educational curricula and media;[23] next, paying particular attention to youth, including assistance and training to support *iTaukei* cultural practitioners in the tourism industries and in local, regional

---

23 In its 2013 draft, the Cultural Policy explicitly promised to have been developed in consultation with Fiji's *iTaukei* communities across its 14 provinces since the very inception of the cultural heritage awareness movement in 2004, reflecting the commitment of both the policymakers and *iTaukei* to safeguard, protect and promote their traditional knowledge and expressions of culture. The respect for the moral and spiritual integrity of *iTaukei* traditional knowledge and expressions of culture includes

and international festivals; and, lastly, rebuilding confidence around the creation of a label of authenticity and a system to mark products made by *iTaukei* artists and craftspeople, a sort of 'Brand Fiji', with the support of the Ministry of Tourism to provide new markets for *iTaukei* cultural products.

The Fijian policymakers I interviewed pointed out that the *iTaukei* must be ready to negotiate both traditional and non-traditional ways of living and knowing. Increasing contact with other cultures has brought alternative ideas and philosophies of life, and this has affected traditional value systems. The results include pressure to adopt individualistic ideals over communal ones, growing migration from villages to cities for education and work, weakening social structures and loss of cultural knowledge and information.[24]

Several questions mediated through workshops and regional meetings and in particular the 2006 SPC Guidelines[25] seem also to be addressed by the Draft Cultural Policy: the subject matter of protection, the criteria for protection, determination of ownership and of the beneficiaries, exceptions and limitations regarding rights, how rights will be managed, how rights will be enforced, what processes can be used for dispute resolution, what the relationship is with existing IP protection and how international and regional protection will be addressed.

The Draft Cultural Policy appears to find additional inspiration in the Revised Draft Provisions for the Protection of Traditional Cultural Expressions: Policy and Objectives and Core Principles (Draft Provisions) elaborated in 2006 by WIPO (World Intellectual Property Organization) (WIPO 2006). Overall, the Draft Cultural Policy is quite ambitious in its approach and reach, and in particular in its understanding of the

---

censuring the collection and publication of traditional stories without consent or proper attribution, or in a culturally offensive manner, as for example in the frequent appropriations of the *itukuni* and *italanoa* of Dakuwaqa, the Fijian ancestral shark god, and other legends as marketing tools on tourist websites.

24   In its 2013 draft, the policy was still finding the wording for *iTaukei's* cultural systems and *iTaukei's* understanding of the world based on three kinds of knowledge: *kila ni vuravura* (knowledge of the empirical world), *kila ni bula vakaveiwekani kei naitovo* (knowledge of the social order and sociocultural relationships) and *kila ni bula vakayalo* (knowledge of the cosmos).

25   On 28 April 2009, the Secretariat of the Pacific Community made available on its website the 2006 guidelines designed to assist policymakers in Pacific communities in the development of national legislation for the protection of traditional knowledge and expressions of culture based on the Pacific Model Law 2002. Online: www.spc.int/hdp/index.php?option=com_docman&task=cat_view&gid=37&Itemid=44 (accessed 28 January 2016).

role of intellectual property rights (IPRs) in mediating between local knowledge and the global marketplace, in its effort to recognise possible misappropriations and misuses. Most notably, the Draft Cultural Policy recognises that the term 'owners' is not necessarily useful or appropriate to refer to *iTaukei* communities when the goal is to focus on the group's cultural capital and its sustenance rather than its potential exploitation in the marketplace. As discussed earlier, 'ownership' may trigger strife and conflict within communities.

The Draft Cultural Policy's most innovative approach in establishing guidelines regulating the integrity of Fijian traditional knowledge and expressions of culture is perhaps the inclusion of documentation of past misuse and misappropriation. Among the examples of misuse and misappropriation, the Draft Cultural Policy mentions the unauthorised reproduction of traditional *masi* designs, as well as the misappropriation and misuse of images commonly available in the public domain of 'sacred rituals' like the *vilavilairevo* (firewalking ceremony).[26]

In this sense, the Fijian language database of Traditional Knowledge and Expressions of Culture becomes an arm of the Draft Cultural Policy and subsequent Draft Legislation. The database's information will be needed to enforce and expand the protection of intellectual property rights, arrange benefit-sharing among the traditional custodian communities, and control access to the traditional knowledge and expressions of culture in the cultural database itself by both research and educational institutions, as well as by private sector entities.

While the Database of Traditional Knowledge and Expressions of Culture and the application of customary law and practices remains a priority of the Draft Cultural Policy, the development of a *sui generis* legislation to protect traditional knowledge and expressions of culture still represents one of its major objectives and obstacles. A delicate point will be the relationship of the Draft Legislation with existing intellectual property

---

26 In January 2005, the *iTaukei* Institute of Language and Culture (formerly, Institute of Fijian Language and Culture) supported the *A ituvatuva ni vakadidike e sawau* (the Sawau Project), a multimedia DVD project narrated by the Sawau people of Beqa (Hennessy 2009; Pigliasco 2009a; Pigliasco and Colatanavanua 2005), within the pilot project's part of Fiji's Cultural Mapping Programme, and Cultural Mapping Traditional Knowledge Database and Server, which was officially launched in May 2005.

rights to ensure consistency and complementarity with them.[27] According to von Lewinski, commenting about the Model Law, this is 'nothing new'. These overlaps are expected:

> where an existing intellectual property right applies in an individual case, the specific folklore protection may apply cumulatively. Such an overlap of protection is justified on the grounds that both the purposes of protection and the conditions thereof differ in the case of each IP or specific folklore right. Accordingly, these systems of protection remain consistent in themselves (von Lewinski 2009: 123).

Another delicate point, the solution of which is yet undisclosed, appears from early drafts of the legislation: the establishment of a Cultural Authority, which may be integrated into an existing institution, and whose core responsibilities would include implementing and coordinating policy and prospective legislation, monitoring infringements and administering rights and eventual disputes. The initial idea was to replace the too broad institution of a Cultural Authority with an Indigenous Intellectual Property Rights Authority. Back in 2008, Tuiloma thought that any 'authority' in charge of cross-checking and pursuing the relevant traditional knowledge and expressions of culture should not be working in isolation from Fiji's copyright and patenting office copyright structure, which may be able to provide support for recognising their existence or previous registration (Eliesa Tuiloma, interview, 5 June 2008). This idea of centralising the various functions of intellectual property in Fiji reappeared when the Draft Cultural Policy was moving towards completion, with the creation in 2011 of a new entity, the Fiji Intellectual Property Office (FIPO), capable of patenting and putting to better use intellectual property or traditional knowledge.

Believing that Fiji's intellectual property laws continue to be a relic of the colonial era, Fiji's Attorney General Aiyaz Sayed-Khaiyum argues that for these reasons Fiji's present intellectual property regime does not fully comply with international treaty obligations. Because of the lack of effective coordination among various government departments, Sayed-Khaiyum believes that laws, policies and practices with respect to

---

27   These include the *Copyright Act 1999*, *Trademarks Act 1933*, *Patents Act 1879*, *Merchandise Marks Act 1933*, *Industry Emblem Act 1973* and the *United Kingdom Design Protection Act 1936*. According to Salvin Nand (2012: 56), the relationships will be quite difficult to ascertain, for with the exception of the *Copyright Act* these legislations were formulated and enacted without any policy consideration given to traditional knowledge and expressions of culture.

intellectual property are not effectively enforced. FIPO is thus becoming a one-stop shop for anything related to copyright and other related rights, trademarks, patents, designs, merchandise marks, geographical indications and also traditional knowledge and expressions of culture. A concern is that, with the prospective development of a label of authenticity and the creation of 'Brand Fiji' by the Ministry of Tourism, along with the associated marketing of *iTaukei* culture, FIPO may become a cul-de-sac, clogging the office of the solicitor-general and permanent secretary for justice, which, with WIPO, is responsible for FIPO's administration.[28]

For example, in the Fiji Airways *masi* case, in the absence of legislation to protect the *masi* makers, it will be very interesting to see how the case will be evaluated, and by whom. Na Noda Masi's e-petition[29] against the trademarking of the 15 *masi* motifs was submitted to the Registrar of Trademarks office at Suvavou House in Suva—where FIPO is also housed—accompanied by an independent legal opinion drafted by legal scholar Miranda Forsyth (2013b), a brief on anthropological evidence on the 15 motifs compiled by Cresantia Frances Koya Vaka'uta (2013) and a list of recommended consultants who would provide testimony against the trademarking of these *kesakesa* and any other form of indigenous collective knowledge.[30] The *masi* case also has a potential intersection with the

---

28   The global IP treaties that Fiji is party to include the Berne Convention for the Protection of Literary and Artistic Works, the Rome Convention for the Protection of Performers, Producers of Phonograms and Broadcasting Organizations and the Trade-Related Aspects of Intellectual Property Rights Agreement. Fiji is also party to a range of traditional knowledge and expressions of culture related treaties such as the UNESCO World Heritage Convention, the UNESCO Convention for the Safeguarding of the Intangible Cultural Heritage, ILO 169 on Indigenous and Tribal Peoples, the Convention on Biological Diversity and the International Undertaking for Plant Genetic Resources. At the regional level, Fiji is a member of the Pacific Islands Forum Secretariat (PIFS), the Secretariat of the Pacific Community (SPC) and the Secretariat of the Pacific Regional Environment Programme (SPREP), which have assisted in the development of norm-setting guidelines for traditional knowledge and expressions of culture that have influenced the Cultural Policy, while at the subregional level, it is a member of the Melanesian Spearhead Group, which promotes cultural solidarity within the countries of Melanesia.

29   See 'Petition to Appeal to stop Air Pacific trademarking 15 distinct masi motifs', *Change.org*. Online: www.change.org/petitions/prime-minister-voreqe-bainimarama-appeal-to-stop-air-pacific-trademarking-15-distinct-masi-motifs (accessed 28 January 2016).

30   Upon an extension granted by the Registrar (Solicitor General) of Trademarks Office, on 24 September 2013, Fiji Airways lawyers filed counter statements to the opposition presented by the *iTaukei* Trust Fund Board, the Fiji Museum, Cresantia Frances Koya Vaka'uta, Seini Nabou, Akaninsi Kedravate and the Institute of Indigenous Studies against the airline company. On the same day, Na Noda Masi posted on Facebook the following statement:

According to Mr. Seeto from the Registrar of Trademarks office, all five objectors will then be invited by the Registrar (Solicitor General) to respond to the counter statement before the Registrar decides whether to grant the trademark application to Fiji Airways, or to reject

recent emphasis on culture industries. On this topic, the instrumentality of both the Draft Cultural Policy and the Draft Legislation are even more straightforward.

Several policy scholars and commentators believe that both 'culture' and the 'arts' are instrumental tools for the attainment of non-cultural goals (Gray 2007).[31] According to Andy C. Pratt, culture industries and cultural policy are 'oxymorons': 'One reason for the ambivalent position that the cultural industries occupy is that they are commercially oriented and commonly regarded as mass or low culture. Yet, they are situated under the umbrella of "cultural policy"' (Pratt 2005: 31). Coombe observes that 'there is little doubt that many new cultural collectivities making possessive claims do so as market actors for economic purposes' (Coombe 2011a: 80; see also Comaroff and Comaroff 2009). In *The Economics of Cultural Policy*, Throsby observes that, over recent years, the evolution of cultural policy has at times been characterised as a 'transformation into an arm of economic policy', which 'may appear somewhat far-fetched, seeming to subordinate the lofty purposes of culture to the sordid demands of the marketplace, a final realisation of the Adorno/Horkheimer nightmare of the commodification of culture' (2010: 6).

David Hesmondhalgh and Andy C. Pratt observe that the boom in interest in the idea of the 'cultural industries' (or creative industries) in academic and policymaking circles raises poignant questions about shifting boundaries between culture and economics, and between art and commerce. They ask a straightforward question: 'What lies behind such policies?' (Hesmondhalgh and Pratt 2005: 1). The 2012 Secretariat of the Pacific Community's *Regional Culture Strategy: Investing in Pacific Cultures, 2010–2020*, which is focused on investing in Pacific cultures in the period of 2010–2020, promotes Pacific cultural industries as tools for development and to create opportunities for the Pacific Island nations: 'cultural industries offer potential to address issues of poverty

---

it. Once the Registrar decides, that decision can be appealed to the Fiji High Court. So we are still at the exchanging paper stage folks, not yet at courtroom stage smile emoticon hang in there, we're following the legal process set out in the Trademarks Act with our objection.

The day after, 25 September 2013, Na Noda Masi posted on Facebook its last update so far: 'The counter statement does not specifically answer the assertions we have made that these motifs are ancient and existed long before Air Pacific and Fiji Airways and that they were documented, proving that they were not created by Fiji Airways in the last year alone'.

31   A Regional Consultation on the Cultural Industries, held in Fiji in 2010, was jointly organised by the Secretariat of the Pacific Community and the Pacific Islands Forum Secretariat, and funded by the European Union (see Huffer 2010).

and sustainability through increased income generation by communities, cultural practitioners and entrepreneurs. They are recognised internationally as a growth area, one that enables people to express themselves creatively, with dignity and on their own terms' (Council of Pacific Arts and Culture and the Secretariat of the Pacific Community 2012: 14).

In *Weaving Intellectual Property Policy in Small Island Developing States*, Miranda Forsyth and Sue Farran (2015) challenge the assumption that intellectual property rights will automatically promote 'cultural industries', and caution that they may have 'unanticipated negative consequences' (Forsyth and Farran 2015; see also Forsyth 2015).[32] The point becomes even more clear in regard to the recent overemphasis on culture industries in policy talks at local and regional levels (among others see Huffer 2010; Teaiwa 2012; Teaiwa and Mercer 2011; Tuiloma 2012). Cultural industries without adequate customary support may risk ignoring indigenous epistemologies and following the spiral path, as mentioned by Throsby (2010), where enlightenment conflates with mass deception satisfied only by the products of capitalism.

This shift and expansion in cultural industries' focus has actually been made possible by, among other developments, the European Union agreement that granted €713,474 (the equivalent of about FJ$2 million) to the Secretariat of the Pacific Community for a project to strengthen the cultural sector in six Pacific Island countries: the Federated States of Micronesia, Palau, Solomon Islands, Tonga, Tuvalu and Vanuatu.[33] The project targets four specific but complementary and mutually supporting areas of the cultural sector: policy development, cultural industries promotion, cultural heritage preservation and exchanges between Pacific and Caribbean museums.

---

32 The recent and enigmatic UNESCO 'Florence Declaration' of 4 October 2014 recognises that:

The full potential of the cultural industries at the core of the creative economy must be harnessed to stimulate innovation for economic growth, full and productive employment and decent work for all. When cultural and creative industries become part of overall growth and development strategies, they have proven to contribute to the revitalization of national economies, generate green employment, stimulate local development and foster creativity. Evidence shows that they provide new local development pathways that build on existing skills and knowledge (UNESCO 2014).

33 This SPC project is called 'Structuring the cultural sector in the Pacific for improved human development' and resulted from a call for proposals for projects under the 'Investing in People' Thematic Programme. Online: www.spc.int/hdp/index.php?option=com_content&task=view&id=89&lang=french (accessed 28 January 2016).

The way Fiji and other Pacific Island nations have, in Sahlins's (2005: 6) and also Jolly's (2005: 138) words, 'indigenized the power of the foreign' in their policies, as well, the ways that they have envisioned innovations in their traditions and customs, is quite remarkable. However, it's nothing actually new from a legal historical perspective. The 'indigefication' of legal concepts is well known in western jurisprudence since the incorporation of Roman law into German folk law. The Tongan *kato alu* (traditional Tongan basket) becomes, for instance, a framework for outlining the important domains of Tongan culture, showing how indigenous epistemology, domains of tangible and intangible cultural heritage and cultural industries could be evoked and wrapped together in the different layers of the basket (Fua, Tuita, Kanongata'a and Fuko 2011: 10).

Nevertheless, and not to underestimate China's and other Pacific Rim countries' considerable and growing influence and economic competition in Oceania, behind these remarkably culturally sensitive policies may actually lie the negotiation of exclusive/joint fishing and deep-sea mineral and energy exploration rights, among others, of far greater value to the EU than the millions donated to the Pacific region.[34] These recent neocolonial forms of control over the trade routes, and political-financial alliances in Fiji and other Pacific Island nations, suggest that policymakers have to carefully evaluate and balance the power differentials existing in the field of cultural policymaking and the regulation of the cultural industries (see Hesmondhalgh and Pratt 2005: 11). While cultural policies and cultural industries might stress local priorities, needs and place-based cultural values, their activities are shaped by the activities of external actors, including states, corporations, NGOs, UN bodies and development aid institutions. All have particular interests in 'empowering communities as entrepreneurs, owners, stewards, or custodians of what are perceived to be scarce and endangered forms of knowledge' (Coombe 2011a: 79, 93).

---

34 The European Union is a major donor to Pacific ACP countries. The African, Caribbean and Pacific Group of States (ACP) was created by the Georgetown Agreement in 1975. Since 1975, the EU has provided the Pacific ACP with a total of €194 million for regional projects. This is in addition to over €2 billion provided to Pacific ACP countries bilaterally over the same period. Currently, there are 15 members of the Pacific ACP Group. The eight original signatories are: Fiji, Tonga, Samoa, Tuvalu, Kiribati, Vanuatu, Papua New Guinea and Solomon Islands. In 2000, six new members joined: Cook Islands, Federated States of Micronesia, Republic of the Marshall Islands, Nauru, Niue and Palau. Finally, in May 2003, Timor Leste became the 15th member to join. See Pacific Islands Regional Secretariat n.d.

An update on cultural industries in Fiji, ironically clairvoyant of the recent Fiji Airways *masi* case, was offered at a talk given at the Conference on Creativity, Innovation, Access to Knowledge and Development at The Australian National University in Canberra in 2012 by Eliesa Tuiloma, the former legal officer and one of the architects of both the Draft Cultural Policy and Draft Legislation, 'emigree consultant' in the Republic of Nauru, and more recently on the staff of the Permanent Mission of the Republic of Fiji to the United Nations in New York.

Tuiloma well recognises the opportunities and limits of the creative industry. While creativity and innovation emerging from traditional knowledge and expressions of culture are the raw materials for the creative industry in Oceanic countries, among the current constraints he recognises are uncertainty about Fiji's political and social stability; current policy and legislative deficiencies on traditional knowledge and expressions of culture; inadequate intellectual property legislation, registration systems and enforcement; institutional bureaucracy; high operational costs; and insufficient access to venture capital, low-interest financing, grant funding and markets.[35] His thoughts easily translate from legalese into something like 'don't count your chickens before they're hatched'. How can we promote cultural industries if we are unable to protect our cultural rights in our own country first?

Conclusion: And the *vanua*?

Echoing education scholar Unaisi Nabobo-Baba's statement that 'individualism for its own sake is abhorred' (2006: 44), the energetic late Fijian intellectual Ropate Qalo claims that the whole idea of 'ownership' in Pacific Island society is repulsive. Somebody, however, is clearly taking advantage of this. Qalo argue:

> the lack of a coherent voice to promote Pacific epistemology means that it is discounted, particularly when it comes to policymaking. Although there are many local institutions that are (partially) derived from local customs, they have so far failed to adequately promote Pacific life principles (Huffer and Qalo 2004: 108).

---

35 PowerPoint presentation given at the Conference on Creativity, Innovation, Access to Knowledge and Development, held at The Australian National University, Canberra, 22–23 September 2012.

A decade after Qalo's statement, it is yet to be verified if Pacific Island policymakers will be able to respectfully indigenise the legislative approach to putting intellectual property regimes to work and rendering autochthonous cultural identities and epistemologies in the language of copyrights, trademarks, patents, industrial design rights and cultural and creative industries (see Comaroff and Comaroff 2009: 56). In the meantime, more cultural policies are emerging in Fiji, in Melanesia and beyond, and more glossy pamphlets and 'handbooks' are generated in workshops, meetings and conferences by regional intergovernmental organisations and agencies. At the same time, more economic resources related to the very social and cultural capital that both policies and regional and international intergovernmental organisations are trying to safeguard and implement are traded quid pro quo and exploited in exchange.

I have elsewhere described the strenuous forward-thinking work of Fijian cultural heritage connoisseur and policymaker Sipiriano Nemani. He has been emphasising for years that while both the Draft Legislation and its Draft Cultural Policy are instruments designed to bring awareness to the grassroots, the heritage custodians:

> no government policy, no organised workshop, no financial assistance can help the indigenous community in Fiji elevate its traditional values and identity. All is vested with the *vanua* and those at the helm of traditional leadership to proactively pursue and reinforce to members of the *vanua* the importance of maintaining key customs (Nemani cited in Pigliasco 2011: 325).

In other words, it is the *vanua* that is expected to take up the initiative to ensure that their intangible heritage is safeguarded and continues to evolve. It is the *vanua* that inevitably should emerge as a pivotal element in both the Draft Legislation and the Draft Cultural Policy.

Matt Tomlinson (2014: 122) explains that the *vanua*, considered a divine gift that God gave exclusively to indigenous Fijians, became the political emblem that mobilised popular support for the coups of 1987 and 2000. In the wake of Fiji's coups, which have brought ethnic tensions, fiscal deficit, deregulation and displacement of Fijian people, Tomlinson and many non-Fijian anthropologists have felt it necessary to analyse transformations in understandings of the *vanua* (Brison 2007; Kaplan 2011; Ryle 2010; Tomlinson 2014: 142).

Before I left Suva in March 2013, Ropate Qalo shared some thoughts about the Fiji Airways *masi* case with me. Qalo firmly believes that all Fijians have to do is go back to their *vanua*, while legislators should keep conducting theoretical and pragmatic research into Pacific customary laws, values and worldviews to articulate the contemporary complexity of property relations of the *vanua* and within the *vanua* (Ropate Qalo, personal communication, 25 March 2013). In a sagacious commentary that appeared in the *Fiji Times Online* exactly one year before he passed away, Qalo places Fiji Airways in his 'eponymous power elite of Fiji' list, eponymous power referring to 'the interlocking interests of elites from three key aspects of society—politics, corporations (or economy), and the military—and how they had coalesced into one tightly knit power centre that worked to reinforce and steward their political and economic interests' (Qalo 2015).

Sadly, it is too late to ask Ropate Qalo to shed some light on the transformations in understandings of the role of the *vanua* in Fiji's contemporary nomenclature. The risk I see is that heritage regimes and related instruments may be mystifying or misrepresenting the social dynamics of the *vanua*, neglecting actual differences in the interests and internal relations of power. In these heritage regimes and transnational processes of legal and political articulation, communities, as in the case of the Fijian *vanua*, are in important ways 'imagined', and traditions are often invented as innovative and generative foundations for investment, planning and development (see Coombe 2011a: 79, 2011b: 106; Coombe and Weiss 2015: 48). Legal scholar Rosemary Coombe has clearly exemplified in her corpus of work how these communities empowered as heritage regimes through the recognition of their traditional knowledge and cultural expressions are often situated at the intersection of the old regimes of power and attachment, emerging forms of governmentality and new imaginaries of social justice. Despite the emphasis placed on grassroots priorities, their activities are shaped by the activities of external factors, foreign institutions, global networks of influence and transnationally circulating policy instruments that have incorporated heritage norms into their own agendas (see Coombe 2011a: 79; Coombe and Baird 2015).

While perhaps more than just a sparkle of innovative thinking is permeating Fijian and Pacific Island epistemologies, as I have expressed before (Pigliasco 2012a), the path crossing the fields of ethics, politics and cultural policy appears yet slippery and tortuous in Fiji. It is possible in fact that the Fiji Airways *masi* case is one of those situations in which, echoing Strathern (2011), it is not appropriate to talk about property regimes, nor of heritage regimes, but of sharing, stealing and borrowing simultaneously, not forgetting the different genre the Fijian practice of *kerekere* has evolved into in the era of globalisation. From a 'begging system' as described in Hocart's (1929: 99–101) classic ethnography of the Lau Islands to the less pejorative '*demander une chose*' (Hazelwood 1850 cited in Sahlins 1993: 855), to a wider mechanism permitting the soliciting of goods, services, resources and use rights, a sort of entreaty that cannot respectfully be denied.[36] I wonder to what extent the 'tenets of the orthodoxy conceived and propagated by Fiji's protectionist colonial administration have become ineradicably absorbed into the Fijian national consciousness' (France 1969: 174), and 'culturally mediated by the indigenous people' (Sahlins 1993: 864), will be ingeminated or perhaps *indigeficated* in the new legal instruments designed to safeguard Fijian tradition.

References

Appiah, Kwame Anthony. 2006. *Cosmopolitanism: Ethics in a World of Strangers*. New York: W.W. Norton & Co.

Arno, Andrew. 2009. *Alarming Reports: Communicating Conflict in the Daily News*. New York: Berghahn Books.

——. 1993. *The World of Talk on a Fijian Island: An Ethnography of Law and Communicative Causation*. Norwood, NJ: Ablex.

Attar, Mohsen al, Nicole Aylwin and Rosemary J. Coombe. 2009. 'Indigenous cultural heritage rights in international human rights law'. In *Protection of First Nations' Cultural Heritage: Laws, Policy, and Reform*, ed. Catherine Bell and Robert Paterson, pp. 311–42. Vancouver: University of British Columbia Press.

---

36   While Thomas (1992, 1993) observes that in the first decade of colonial rule, several regulations and resolutions recommended the suppression of *kerekere*, Sahlins (1993: 854) observes that *kerekere* was so ubiquitous, multiform and commonly practised, as a cornerstone of Fijian life, that to attempt to legally interdict it was absurd.

Ballacchino, Katia. 2012. 'Unity makes … intangible heritage: Italy and network nomination'. In *Heritage Regimes and the State*, ed. Regina F. Bendix, Aditya Eggert and Arnika Peselmann, pp. 121–140. Göttingen Studies in Cultural Property Series 6. Göttingen: Universitätsverlag Göttingen.

Bell, Catherine and Robert Paterson (eds). 2008. *Protection of First Nations Cultural Heritage: Laws, Policy, and Reform.* Vancouver: University of British Columbia Press.

Bendix, Regina F., Aditya Eggert and Arnika Peselmann (eds). 2012. *Heritage Regimes and the State*. Göttingen Studies in Cultural Property Series 6. Göttingen: Universitatsverlag Göttingen.

Bentham, Jeremy. 1876. *Theory of Legislation*, translated from the French of É. Dumont by R. Hildreth. London: Trübner & Co.

Berliner, David. 2012. 'The politics of nostalgia and loss in Luang Prabang (Lao PDR)'. In *Routledge Handbook of Heritage in Asia*, ed. Patrick Daly and Tim Winter, pp. 234–46. London: Routledge.

Blake, Janet. 2014. 'Seven years of implementing UNESCO's 2003 intangible heritage convention—honeymoon period or the "seven-year itch"?' *International Journal of Cultural Property* 21(3): 291–304. doi.org/10.1017/S0940739114000113.

Bortolotto, Chiara. 2012. 'The French inventory of intangible cultural heritage: Domesticating a global paradigm into French heritage regime'. In *Heritage Regimes and the State*, ed. Regina F. Bendix, Aditya Eggert and Arnika Peselmann, pp. 265–82. Göttingen Studies in Cultural Property Series 6. Göttingen: Universitätsverlag Göttingen.

Brison, Karen J. 2007. *Our Wealth Is Loving Each Other: Self and Society in Fiji*. Lanham MD: Lexington Books.

Broccolini, Alessandra. 2012. 'Intangible cultural heritage scenarios within the bureaucratic Italian state'. In *Heritage Regimes and the State*, ed. Regina F. Bendix, Aditya Eggert and Arnika Peselmann, pp. 283–302. Göttingen Series in Cultural Property 6. Göttingen: Universitätsverlag Göttingen.

Busse, Mark and Veronica Strang. 2011. 'Introduction: ownership and appropriation'. In *Ownership and Appropriation*, ed. Veronica Strang and Mark Busse, pp. 1–19. Oxford: Berg. doi.org/10.1484/m.mcs-eb.4.3002.

Carpenter, Kristen, Sonia Katyal and Angela Riley. 2009. 'In defence of property'. *Yale Law Journal* 118: 1022–125.

Comaroff, John L. and Jean Comaroff. 2009. *Ethnicity, Inc.* Chicago: University of Chicago Press. doi.org/10.7208/chicago/9780226114736.001.0001.

Coombe, Rosemary J. 2012. 'Managing cultural heritage as neoliberal governmentality'. In *Heritage Regimes and the State*, ed. Regina F. Bendix, Aditya Eggert and Arnika Peselmann, pp. 375–87. Göttingen Studies in Cultural Property Series 6. Göttingen: Universitätsverlag Göttingen.

———. 2011a. 'Cultural agencies: the legal construction of community subjects and their properties'. In *Making and Unmaking Intellectual Property: Creative Production in Legal and Cultural Perspective*, ed. M. Biagioli, P. Jaszi, and M. Woodmansee, pp. 79–98. Chicago: University of Chicago Press.

———. 2011b. 'Possessing culture: political economies of community subjects and their properties'. In *Ownership and Appropriation*, ed. V. Strang and M. Busse, pp. 105–27. Oxford: Berg.

———. 2009. 'The expanding purview of cultural properties and their politics'. *Annual Review of Law and Social Science* 5: 393–412. doi.org/10.1146/annurev.lawsocsci.093008.131448.

Coombe, Rosemary J. and M. Baird. 2015. 'The limits of heritage: corporate interests and cultural rights on resource frontiers'. In *A Companion to Heritage Studies*, ed. William Logan, Máiread Nic Craith and Ullrich Kockel, pp. 337–54. Hoboken: Wiley-Blackwell. doi.org/10.1002/9781118486634.ch24.

Coombe, Rosemary J. and L. Weiss. 2015. 'Neoliberalism, heritage regimes, and cultural rights'. In *Global Heritage: A Reader*, ed. L. Meskell, pp. 43–69. Hoboken: Wiley-Blackwell. doi.org/10.2139/ssrn.2644495. ·

Council of Pacific Arts and Culture and the Secretariat of the Pacific Community. 2012. *Regional Culture Strategy Investing in Pacific Cultures 2010–2020*. Suva, Fiji: Secretariat of the Pacific Community. Online: www.spc.int/hdp/index2.php?option=com_docman&task=doc_view&gid=386&Itemid=44 (accessed 28 January 2016).

Datt, Halitesh. 2014. 'Fiji soon to have a cultural policy'. *Fiji TV Headlines*, 1 June. Online: fijione.tv/fiji-soon-to-have-a-cultural-policy/ (accessed 14 September 2016).

De Cesari, Chiara. 2012. 'Thinking through heritage regimes'. In *Heritage Regimes and the State*, ed. Regina F. Bendix, Aditya Eggert and Arnika Peselmann, pp. 399–413. Göttingen Studies in Cultural Property Series 6. Göttingen: Universitätsverlag Göttingen.

Foana'ota, Lawrence and Geoffrey White. 2011. 'Solomon Islands cultural policy? A brief history of practice'. In *Made in Oceania: Social Movements, Cultural Heritage and the State in the Pacific*, ed. Edvard Hviding and Knut Rio, pp. 273–99. Wantage: Sean Kingston.

Forsyth, Miranda. 2015. 'Cultural economics and intellectual property: tensions and challenges for the region'. *Asia and the Pacific Policy Studies* 2(2): 356–69. doi.org/10.1002/app5.77.

——. 2013a. 'How can traditional knowledge best be regulated? Comparing a proprietary rights approach with a regulatory toolbox approach'. *The Contemporary Pacific* 25(1): 1–31. doi.org/10.1353/cp.2013.0004.

——. 2013b. 'How can the theory of legal pluralism assist the traditional knowledge debate?' *Intersections: Gender and Sexuality in Asia and the Pacific* 33 (December). Online: intersections.anu.edu.au/issue33/forsyth.htm (accessed 28 January 2016).

Forsyth, Miranda and Sue Farran. 2015. *Weaving Intellectual Property Policy in Small Island Developing States*. Cambridge: Intersentia.

France, Peter. 1969. *The Charter of the Land: Custom and Colonization in Fiji*. Melbourne: Oxford University Press.

Fua, Seu'ula Johansson, Tu'ilokamana Tuita, Siosiua Lotaki Kanongata'a and Koliniasi Fuko. 2011. *Cultural Mapping, Planning and Policy: Tonga*. Nuku'alofa: Secretariat of the Pacific Community.

Geismar, Haidy. 2015. 'Anthropology and heritage regimes'. *Annual Review of Anthropology* 44: 71–85.

Geismar, Haidy and William Mohns. 2011. 'Database relations: Rethinking the database in the Vanuatu cultural centre and national museum'. *Journal of the Royal Anthropological Institute* (n.s.): 133–55. doi.org/10.1146/annurev-anthro-102214-014217.

Graezer Bideau, Florence. 2012. 'Identifying living traditions in Switzerland: Re-enacting federalism through the UNESCO Convention fopr the safeguarding of intangible cultural heritage'. In *Heritage Regimes and the State*, ed. Regina F. Bendix, Aditya Eggert and Arnika Peselmann, pp. 303–326. Göttingen Studies in Cultural Property Series 6. Göttingen: Universitätsverlag Göttingen.

Gray, Clive. 2007. 'Commodification and instrumentality in cultural policy'. *International Journal of Cultural Policy* 13(2): 203–15. doi.org/10.1080/10286630701342899.

Harrison, Simon. 2000. 'From prestige goods to legacies: Property and the objectification of culture in Melanesia'. *Comparative Study of Society and History* 42(3): 662–79. doi.org/10.1017/S0010417500002978.

Hazelwood, David. 1850. *A Feejeean & English and an English and Feejeean Dictionary*. Viwa, Fiji: Wesleyan Mission Press.

Hennessy, Kate. 2009. '*A ituvatuva ni vakadidike e Sawau*: The Sawau Project DVD'. *Visual Anthropology Review* 25(1): 90–92. doi.org/10.1111/j.1548-7458.2009.01025.x.

Hesmondhalgh, David and Andy C. Pratt. 2005. 'Cultural industries and cultural policy'. *International Journal of Cultural Policy* 11(1): 1–14. doi.org/10.1080/10286630500067598.

Hocart, Arthur Maurice. 1929. *Lau Islands, Fiji*. Bernice. P. Bishop Museum Bulletin, 62. Honolulu: Bishop Museum.

Huffer, Elise. 2010. 'Culture offers opportunities for economic development'. *International Network for Arts and Business*. Online: www.artsmanagement.net/index.php?module=News&func=display&sid=1330 (accessed 12 September 2016).

Huffer, Elise and Ropate Qalo. 2004. 'Have we been thinking upside-down? The contemporary emergence of Pacific theoretical thought'. *The Contemporary Pacific* 16(1): 87–116. doi.org/10.1353/cp.2004.0011.

Jolly, Margaret. 2005. 'Beyond the horizon? Nationalisms, feminisms, and globalization in the Pacific'. *Ethnohistory* 52(1): 137–66. doi.org/10.1215/00141801-52-1-137.

——. 1996. '*Woman ikat raet long human raet o no?* Women's rights, human rights, and domestic violence in Vanuatu'. *Feminist Review* 52 (Spring): 169–90.

Kaplan, Martha. 2011. 'Alienation and appropriation: Fijian water and the Pacific romance in Fiji and New York'. In *Changing Contexts, Shifting Meanings: Transformations of Cultural Traditions in Oceania*, ed. Elfriede Hermann, pp. 221–34. Honolulu: University of Hawai'i Press. doi.org/10.21313/hawaii/9780824833664.003.0014.

Kockel, Ullrich. 2012. 'Borders, European integration and UNESCO heritage: A case study of the Curonian Spit'. In *Heritage Regimes and the State*, ed. Regina F. Bendix, Aditya Eggert and Arnika Peselmann, pp. 227–246. Göttingen Studies in Cultural Property Series 6. Göttingen: Universitätsverlag Göttingen.

Kooijman, Simon. 1977. *Tapa on Moce Island, Fiji*. Leiden: E.J. Brill.

Koya Vaka'uta, Cresantia Frances. 2013. 'Anthropological evidence of the 15 intended iTaukei Tapa cloth (masi) motifs pre-dating the creation of the Air Pacific/Fiji Airways logo'. Online: works.bepress.com/cf_koyavakauta/18/ (accessed 1 February 2016).

Leblon, Anaïs. 2012. 'A policy of intangible cultural heritage between local constraints and international standards: "The cultural space of the *yaaral* and *degal*"'. In *Heritage Regimes and the State*, ed. Regina F. Bendix, Aditya Eggert and Arnika Peselmann, pp. 97–118. Göttingen Studies in Cultural Property Series 6. Göttingen: Universitätsverlag Göttingen.

Macpherson, Crawford Brough. 1962. *The Political Theory of Possessive Individualism: Hobbes to Locke*. Oxford: Clarendon Press.

Merritt, Richard L. and Elizabeth C. Hanson. 1989. *Science, Politics, and International Conferences: A Functional Analysis of the Moscow Political Science Congress*. London: Lynne Rienner.

Miller, Daniel. 2001. 'Alienable gifts and inalienable commodities'. In *The Empire of Things: Regimes of Value and Material Culture*, ed. Fred R. Myers, pp. 91–115. Santa Fe, NM: School of American Research Press.

Nabobo-Baba, U. 2006. *Knowing and Learning: An Indigenous Fijian Approach*. Suva: Institute of Pacific Studies, University of the South Pacific.

Nand, Salvin S. 2012. 'Protecting and revitalizing traditional knowledge and expressions of culture: For an equitable future in Fiji'. In research papers from *The WIPO-WTO Colloquium for Teachers of Intellectual Property Law - Geneva, 2011*, ed. A. Mendes-Walsh and S. Meghana, pp. 55–73. Geneva: World Intellectual Property Organization.

Nayacakalou, R.R. 1975. *Leadership in Fiji*. Melbourne: Oxford University Press.

Otto, Ton and Rane Willerslev. 2013. 'Introduction: Value as theory: Comparison, cultural critique, and guerilla ethnographic theory'. *HAU: Journal of Ethnographic Theory* 3(1): 1–20. doi.org/10.14318/hau3.1.002.

Pacific Islands Regional Secretariat. n.d. 'European Development Fund'. Online: www.forumsec.org/pages.cfm/strategic-partnerships-coordination/european-development-fund/ (accessed 28 January 2016).

Pigliasco, Guido Carlo. 2015. 'From colonial pomp to tourism reality: Commodification and cannibalization of the Fijian firewalking ceremony'. In *From Romance to Reality: Representations of Pacific Islands and Islanders*, ed. J. Schachter and Nancy Lutkehaus. *Pacific Studies* 38(1–2): 140–81.

———. 2012a. 'A tortuous path: From law to policy in Fiji'. Paper presented at the invited session Policy Talk: Processes and Rationales at the International Conference on Sociolegal Conversations across a Sea of Islands, joint Annual Meetings of the Law and Society Association and the Research Committee on Sociology of Law (ISA), co-sponsored by the Canadian Law and Society Association (CLSA), the Japanese Association of Sociology of Law (JASL), and the British Socio-Legal Studies Association (SLSA), Honolulu, HI, 5–8 June.

——. 2012b. '"Are they evil?": Denominational competition and cultural demonization on a Fijian island'. *People and Culture in Oceania* 28: 45–68.

——. 2011. 'Are the grassroots growing? Intangible cultural heritage lawmaking in Fiji and Oceania'. In *Made in Oceania: Social Movements, Cultural Heritage and the State in the Pacific*, ed. Edvard Hviding and Knut Mikjel Rio, pp. 273–99. Wantage: Sean Kingston Publishing.

——. 2010. 'We branded ourselves long ago: Intangible cultural property and commodification of Fijian firewalking'. *Oceania* 80(2): 237–57.

——. 2009a. 'Intangible cultural property, tangible databases, visible debates: The Sawau Project'. *International Journal of Cultural Property* 16: 255–69. doi.org/10.1017/S0940739109990233.

——. 2009b. 'Local voices, transnational echoes: Protecting intangible cultural heritage in Oceania'. In *Sharing Cultures 2009: International Conference on Intangible Heritage*, ed. Sérgio Lira, Rogério Amoêda, Cristina Pinheiro, João Pinheiro and Fernando Oliveira, pp. 121–27. Barcelos: Green Lines Instituto para o Desenvolvimento Sustentável.

——. 2007. 'The custodians of the gift: Intangible cultural property and commodification of the Fijian firewalking ceremony'. PhD dissertation. Honolulu: University of Hawai'i at Mānoa.

Pigliasco, Guido Carlo and F. Colatanavanua. 2005. *A ituvatuva i vakadidike e Sawau* (The Sawau Project). Suva: Institute of Fijian Language and Culture.

Pigliasco, Guido Carlo and Thorolf Lipp. 2011. 'The islands have memory: Reflections on two collaborative projects in contemporary Oceania'. *The Contemporary Pacific* 23(2): 371–410. doi.org/10.1353/cp.2011.0045.

Pratt, Andy C. 2005. 'Cultural industries and public policy: an oxymoron?' *International Journal of Cultural Policy* 11(1): 31–44. doi.org/10.1080/10286630500067739.

Qalo, Ropate. 2015. 'The new power elite'. *Fiji Times Online*, 11 April. Online: www.fijitimes.com/story.aspx?id=301577 (accessed 28 January 2016).

Ravuvu, Asesela. 1987. *The Fijian Ethos*. Suva: Institute of Pacific Studies, University of the South Pacific.

Rawalai, Luke. 2013. 'Masi design concerns'. *Fiji Times*, 10 February, p. 14.

Riles, Annelise. 2006. *Documents: Artifacts of Modern Knowledge*. Ann Arbor: University of Michigan Press. doi.org/10.3998/mpub.185485.

———. 1998. 'Infinity within the brackets'. *American Ethnologist* 25(3): 378–98. doi.org/10.1525/ae.1998.25.3.378.

Ryle, Jacqueline. 2010. *My God, My Land: Interwoven paths of Christianity and Tradition in Fiji*. Farnham: Ashgate.

Sahlins, Marshall. 2005. 'Preface'. *Ethnohistory* 52(1): 3–6. doi.org/10.1215/00141801-52-1-3.

———. 1993. 'Cery cery fuckabede'. *American Ethnologist* 20(4): 848–67. doi.org/10.1525/ae.1993.20.4.02a00100.

Schofield, John. 2014. *Who Needs Experts? Counter-Mapping Cultural Heritage*. Farnham: Ashgate.

Shore, Cris, Susan Wright and Davide Però (eds). 2016. *Policy Worlds: Anthropology and the Analysis of Contemporary Power*, New York: Berghahn.

Strathern, Marilyn. 2011. 'Sharing, stealing and borrowing simultaneously'. In *Ownership and Appropriation*, ed. V. Strang and M. Busse, pp. 23–41. Oxford: Berg.

———. 1999. *Property, Substance and Effect: Anthropological Essays on Persons and Things*. London: Athlone Press.

———. 1984. 'Subject or object: Women and the circulation of valuables'. In *Women and Property: Women as Property*, ed. R. Hirschon, pp. 158–75. New York: St Martin's Press.

Tapaleao Vaimoana. 2013. 'Nike pulls Pacific-style tattoo gear'. *New Zealand Herald*, 15 August. Online: www.nzherald.co.nz/lifestyle/news/article.cfm?c_id=6&objectid=10912467 (accessed January 28 2016).

Teaiwa, Katerina. 2012. 'Structuring the culture sector across the Pacific: The work of the Human Development Programme of the Secretariat of the Pacific Community'. Paper presented at the Conference on Innovation, Creativity, Access to Knowledge and Development in Pacific Island Countries, College of Asia and the Pacific, The Australian National University, 24–25 September.

Teaiwa, Katerina and Colin Mercer. 2011. *Pacific Cultural Mapping, Planning and Policy Toolkit*. Noumea: Secretariat of the Pacific Community.

Thomas, Nicholas. 1993. 'Beggars can be choosers.' *American Ethnologist* 20(4): 868–876. doi.org.10.1525/ae.1993.20.4.02a00110.

——. 1992. 'The inversion of tradition'. *American Ethnologist* 19(2): 213–32. doi.org/10.1525/ae.1992.19.2.02a00020.

Throsby, David. 2010. *The Economics of Cultural Policy*. Cambridge: Cambridge University Press. doi.org/10.1017/CBO9780511845253.

Tomlinson, Matt. 2014. *Ritual Textuality: Pattern and Motion in Performance*. Oxford: Oxford University Press. doi.org/10.1093/acprof:oso/9780199341139.001.0001.

——. 2009. *In God's Image: The Metaculture of Fijian Christianity*. Berkeley: University of California Press.

Tuiloma, Eliesa. 2012. 'The potential of cultural industries for development'. Paper presented at the Conference on Innovation, Creativity, Access to Knowledge and Development in Pacific Island Countries, College of Asia and the Pacific, The Australian National University, 24–25 September.

UNESCO. 2014. *Culture, Creativity and Sustainable Development: Research, Innovation, Opportunities*. Third UNESCO World Forum on Culture and Cultural Industries, Florence, 2–4 October. Online: www.unesco.org/new/fileadmin/MULTIMEDIA/HQ/CLT/pdf/FINAL_FlorenceDeclaration_1December_EN.pdf (accessed 14 September 2016

———. 2003. 'Convention for the Safeguarding of the Intangible Cultural Heritage 2003'. Paris. Online: portal.unesco.org/en/ev.php-URL_ID=17716&URL_DO=DO_TOPIC&URL_SECTION=201.html (accessed 13 September 2016).

Verdery, Katherine and Caroline Humphrey. 2004. *Property in Question: Value Transformation in the Global Economy*. Oxford: Berg.

von Lewinski, Silke. 2009. 'An analysis of WIPO's latest proposal and the Model Law 2002 of the Pacific Community for the Protection of Traditional Cultural Expressions'. In *Traditional Knowledge, Traditional Cultural Expressions, and Intellectual Property Law in the Asia-Pacific Region*, ed. Anton Christoph, pp. 109–25. The Netherlands: Kluwer Law International.

Watts, Michael J. 2000. 'Contested communities, malignant markets, and gilded governance: Justice, resource extraction, and conservation in the tropics'. In *People, Plants, and Justice: The Politics of Nature Conservation*, ed. Charles Zerner, pp. 21–51. New York: Columbia University Press. doi.org/10.7312/zern10810-003.

Weiner, Annette B. 1992. *Inalienable Possessions: The Paradox of Keeping-While-Giving*. Berkeley: University of California Press. doi.org/10.1525/california/9780520076037.001.0001.

World Intellectual Property Organization (WIPO). 2006. 'Intergovernmental Committee on Intellectual Property and Genetic Resources, Traditional Knowledge and Folklore'. Tenth Session, Geneva, 30 November – 8 December. Online: www.wipo.int/edocs/mdocs/tk/en/wipo_grtkf_ic_10/wipo_grtkf_ic_10_4.pdf (accessed 28 January 2016).

Epilogue

Christian Kaufmann

While the present volume might appear to the non-specialist reader as resulting from accidental mixing, the opposite becomes evident after thorough reading. In hindsight, a series of debates helped to push people forward in their thinking, at the Verona conference as much as ever since. The underlying logic went well beyond the truth in the popular slogan 'Think global, act local'. With 'Putting People First', the conference conveners encouraged anthropologists to read the slogan backwards, as through a mirror. Only from knowing how people think locally can we learn how they act globally. To act responsibly requires us to reflect on our own doing. Thus, turning the anthropological perspective around by 180 degrees means to query first the authors, and then, through them, to ask readers some uncomfortable questions. Good intentions are not good enough. Andrew Moutu is quite right in reminding anthropologists that they need first of all to ask themselves.

The texts assembled here stress the agency of people, their power to find ways to act according to their own ideas and needs, to innovate—notwithstanding the deadlock situations described in anthropological theories based on incomplete analysis. The authors provide us with some answers by demonstrating what anthropologists could achieve by 'Putting People First', that is, before their own discipline. These answers, as tentative as they may be, should help us to redefine the potential of our discipline in a forward perspective. Let us try to trace some lines of reflecting upon the texts as a help for a deeper appreciation of where we stand at present. In the following, I shall concentrate on issues I want to highlight, which does not mean that the contributions or ideas that I do not cite explicitly were of a lesser importance. Others shall read the texts differently as anthropology is evolving.

Perhaps surprisingly for conference-goers, the most immediate response to Moutu's appeal took the form of being asked whether indeed we knew who we were by way of questioning our eating (and drinking) habits. Do we really know what we are eating and thus who we are? How we relate ourselves to what we eat locally provides, literally, food for thought on how to act globally. At the closing event in Verona slow food offered from local sources in the Veneto combined with an input by the Kanak delegation challenged traditional views about the conference dinner as a social event. The food helped us in our search for an update to our identity as anthropologists, very much as the texts still do. Reflecting on people's evaluation of their own foodscape—that is the food they produce or obtain, the ways they prepare it or have it prepared by others, and the gusto with which they eat and share it—might prove a very basic and hands-on approach to local agency. It will immediately also provide a test field for anthropologists, allowing them to position themselves in relation to the people with whom they intend to work. If you abhor sago grubs, you might never fully grasp what sago means. But there is more to it.

Re-thinking anthropological questions and mind-sets in manifold social and therefore diverse cultural contexts is challenging. Yet, applying anthropological approaches to the width and depth of biodiversity will probably test our endurance to its limits. What seems so simple in its basics, that is to relate each society under study, including our own, to its natural environment, animated by a characteristic mix of live species and dead rocks, becomes quickly a site for entanglement. Is the idea to achieve symbiotic changes in society, cultural behaviour and the natural settings viable at all? Or, the other way around, are there ways to reduce the rate of disappearance of natural species, especially when and where the latter represent the environmental potential for future generations? If the grandparents of those who suffer most from the loss in biodiversity were among those who introduced changes to fishing or hunting or cultivating techniques in order to obtain higher returns, how to implement a protective strategy, and in whose people's name? Nancy Pollock shows how foodscapes, even when remaining bound by traditions, adapt quite speedily to changes in techniques of production and distribution. Where researchers are rehearsing the evidence for locally induced changes, Pacific Islanders appear to have been animated by their own curiosity to try new methods and to make choices in favour of adapting and integrating the new. They are practitioners, not scientists. A gap is widening. And when it comes to the extraction of minerals, locals (and with them also anthropologists) become dwarfs, too tiny to be taken seriously by Big Business and Governments alike (see e.g. Golub 2014; Rumsey and Weiner 2004; and Teaiwa 2014).

What foreigners have brought to peoples in the Pacific, for a few centuries across the sea, were often received as a welcome addition to the local life. Ever since the arrival of the first airplane in New Guinea almost 100 years ago, the way of entrance shifted radically from over the sea to across the sky. Why and how the foreign has often been appropriated through transformation, this we can learn from Marshall Sahlins's text. He puts the mark really high up by asking questions we had forgotten to ask. His 2008 Raymond Firth lecture, much easier to read than to listen to, is certainly the most radical appeal to reinvigorate informed anthropological debating about societies of wider Oceania by putting a concept basically on its head. By showing how in many Austronesian societies otherness or alterity was again and again defined as playing an integrative part in constituting chiefly or royal authority, we are getting ready to clean some old lenses or to even replace them.

Sahlins makes his point from a thorough analysis of local thinking in historically defined contexts. He provides some unexpected answers to the basic question of how to reconcile the need to validate a princely chief's or king's power in a way that people subjected to the acts of the very same authority do indeed accept their fate. For a social order to be set up as well as to get recognised from the bottom-up, the Austronesian model works in a double-step. First a stranger has to be accepted as a member of a given society, and in a second step that member needs to become these people's chief or king. Raymond Firth provides Sahlins with a guiding insight, based on local thinking: chiefs and kings are marked for becoming chiefs because they are said to be descended from foreigners who had arrived across the water or down from heaven—which on an isolated island surrounded by a reef almost look the same. These foreigners often married an important woman whose child would later become the new leader. On the other hand, the land and many basic rituals would remain under the control of the people native to the land. Sahlins underlines the aspect that this foreign origin of authority sparked again and again a local quest for things as well as for manifestations associated with the ultimate and always foreign source of power over the locals.

In a brilliant sidestep, we learn to read the reverence given among the Toradja of Sulawesi, or the Ifugao of Luzon or the Iban of Borneo to a head brought back from a headhunting trip as parallel to the reverence reserved for the chief of external origin. The head coming from an outsider becomes part of the group's own pride, and thus becomes an acknowledgement of how important external sources of life are for the well-being of a group. Hence the intense welcome for the returning successful headhunter by his mother. But the two segments remain in constant competition. Of course, here, Gregory Bateson is just around the corner. His analytical insights came from a non-Austronesian society without chiefs, however. Sahlins points to Bateson's model of Schismogenesis (Bateson 1958: 171–97, 265–98) as the most convincing way to analyse and unravel the underlying competition between conflicting positions. Schismogenesis helps to describe opposing poles of thinking that may consciously or subconsciously assist people in structuring their acts. Even ideals of behaviour or of orientation that seem to be mutually exclusive may thus lead to coherent acting whenever people either want to achieve power over people or sovereignty from other people, says Sahlins. For sure, not all stranger kings or chiefs of whom we know basic parts of their history fit exactly Sahlins's pattern of resolving an internal conflict, even if he can provide telling examples of congenial adaptations, such as the merger of the Islamic topos of Iksander (or Alexander the Great) with the Austronesian model of the stranger king for the princely houses of sultans on the island of Borneo and beyond. Sahlins's text makes inspiring reading because we can add new aspects from our own experiences and reading, thus formulating test cases for applying a formula such as 'Putting the Other' first in order to understand who the People are. To understand why and how consistently legitimating strangers as the source of authority and power, as much political as religious, is such a successful strategy in Austronesian societies of different eras makes a stunning contribution to our understanding of innovations in historical time. Because the Other, in life praxis the stranger, had for generations already provided the recognised source of legitimate power and even of wealth, Austronesian social order could not be implemented without strangers.

Let us assume that Marshall Sahlins's analysis explains a fundamental aspect of how in Pacific societies at large insiders deal with what outsiders have provided materially and immaterially, then local agency can only be appreciated, described or analysed in its relation to the agency of outsiders. This relationship may be seen as one of cooperation or of rejection, or most likely of cool interpretation—by which I mean a combination of overtly shown disinterest or even critique and of determined incorporation. The study and discussion of values under different aspects so prominent in this volume provide us ample evidence. It is very telling that the idea of parents having to pay a school fee for each child, an idea introduced by colonial powers betraying their democratic ideal that basic education would only reach everyone as long as it was for free, made a woman name her pig after this obligation, Skulfi in Dobuan (but also in Tok Pisin). From Susanne Kuehling's text we learn to appreciate how this mother booked her naming on the assumption that the agency of an outsider would lead to the result she intended, that is to provide her children with a chance for education without having to rely on traditional family bonds. On the other hand, the anthropologist acting in response to her local family's expectations would become the anticipated partner to the owner of the pig when buying the pig for money. In this case a symmetrical pattern of agency between the local and the foreign prevailed.

The problem with agency is that anticipating when and how the other is going to act becomes hazardous. Even with the best of intentions, the balance between local agency and outside input is hard to strike in anticipation. Not every test can be successful. Margaret Jolly tells the story, well described and analysed, of how the well-intended project of exhibiting the Forster collection from the voyages of James Cook located at the Göttingen Anthropological Institute (literally the Institut für Ethnologie) at venues closer to the Pacific Islands and Pacific Islanders developed its own dynamic. From what we read, the immediate agency of the objects that were shown at different sites was not strong enough to calm down local debates and to overcome sentiments of rejection (by Hawaiians) or of indifference (by the Australian audience). This clearly shows that the agency inherent in objects of historical importance as well as in art works, to which European museum-goers are geared and thus quite open, is different from the agency these same objects might be credited with by an audience that is socially or geographically closer to the people who originally made and used the objects shown.

At the Canberra venue the project was ideally meant to help open up mind-sets from past visions of European impact to a new model of looking with priority at the effective and efficient cooperation between local populations and the strangers from Europe. Surprisingly, though, the non-result arrived despite the effort of the exhibition organisers to stress the cooperative model in the texts and in the presentation of the objects. While the objects were moving, too many minds were staying put. Somehow, perhaps, the effort was not radical enough in form and content. Margaret Jolly's thoughtful presentation should be read widely in order to learn from it. Changing the public audience's perceptions through an exhibition requires more than just telling the basic story of observation and collecting as research methods. We should add here that the exhibition project on James Cook and the expedition scientists, with a series of three interconnected exhibitions held from 2009 to 2011 in Bonn, Vienna and Berne respectively, partly ran up against the same obstacles. Only its last version, the show in Berne, brought the visitors closer to a perspective wherein Pacific Islanders if not put first, were at least positioned very prominently. Using Tupaia's observations as an observer's (and museum visitor's) intellectual keyhole, so to speak, helped to display the objects made and used by Pacific Islanders in meaningful contexts, with an excellent response from the public. Tupaia's historically documented agency as successful mediator between the Europeans and local populations, especially Māori groups visited in New Zealand, opened a way to show Tupaia on an equal footing in contributing to the success of the voyage of the *Endeavour*.

Let's move our perspective over to the other side. Can local actors better anticipate the effects of their agency? The answer is probably yes and no. Yes, if they perform a series of formalised or ritualised acts for which the result is roughly predictable; no, whenever other actors and contingent situations come into play that in turn may either induce people to come up with new solutions or end in fatal conflict. Finding new ways might become visible or at least traceable in the form of new images, new words, new messages, new attitudes, new practices. Anthropology has entered this field, which is wide open, from different points of access. Not always has an orientation prevailed that privileged a view that, focusing on the agency of local actors or participants, was essential for obtaining results worth the effort of investigating. Only by 'Putting People First' can anthropology join in with a contribution that might help to open a window through which local actors could gain a view onto the consequences of their own doing for their own people.

Marc Tabani's essay is a step in this direction. It shows, hopefully not the least to the actors themselves, how well-intended innovations or adaptations can produce effects harming the foundations of one's own life. For Europeans, at least for those still familiar with their own history, including the history of tourism as well as of folklore, this does not come as a surprise. The examples from two regions of Vanuatu showing the side effects of a growing tourism trade announce in one respect an even more serious problematic: whenever the alienation of land comes into play conflicts are sure to arise, and there seems no easy way out. To reconcile social and economic drives that aim at goals that are incompatible and therefore lead to a clash of interests asks for an effort to coordinate the agency of insiders with that of the Other, the outsider. As long as tourists are guided by their curiosity and performers of a ceremony use the presence of the Outsider to accomplish their performance, symmetry of insider and outsider agency seems warranted. However, as soon as both— the travel agent drawing the tourist to the event and the performer—want to earn money for their input, a basic imbalance of agencies is established. Who will be able to redress the balance? The locals or the outsiders?

Local initiatives for protecting vital natural resources are hard up in competing against commercial strategies propagated both by local peers and by external experts at home in economical disciplines. The strategies of the latter are oriented towards high yield, that is in the domains of ore mining, agricultural mass production, ocean-wide fishing, and, of course, international trade. The supra-national actors all claim abidance by rules of international law. These rules basically stem from a delicate balance between European philosophical values developed since the age of Enlightenment and the practise of ex-colonial powers in dealing with each other as well as with smaller nations and their citizens abroad. Only slowly does the codification of internationally recognised law take place. Moving from European intellectual concepts to local concepts as they are being developed and discussed nowadays can be challenging indeed. How to reconcile local notions of ownership—or rather custodianship—with guidelines that should become valid globally? An interesting case is made by Guido Carlo Pigliasco, showing for Fiji to what extent a combined input is needed where reflecting on local ideas is based on a disinterested anthropological approach. There can be no doubt that dealing with the material as well as intangible cultural heritage in the context of nation states in the Pacific is a very serious matter. The confrontation over questions of rights in rituals once led easily to war, well before the arrival of the envoys of European colonial powers. Mutual recognition of intellectual property rights, that is formalising local concepts of how intangible heritage can be defined, by whom it is thought to be looked after or, within limits, owned, and who could be authorised to represent it, may help to resolve at least some of the conflicts.

Conflicting ideas are being voiced when it comes to marketing salient aspects of cultural heritage for tourism or even to consumers of local products. Intangible property rights may often have a very tangible aspect, too; they are often linked to land rights in a detailed way by referring to elements of worldview. Landownership in the Pacific and beyond always has a spiritual connotation, even more so today, as the authority of well-endorsed chiefs and kings is challenged by other powers. Not an easy lesson to learn for the drivers of economic forces. It may be equally worrying for those who wake up hearing that their national government has decided to assume a say on artistic or intellectual ownership on their behalf, as a way of protecting a national good; this could well stretch their belief in the good faith of Government tutorship to the outmost. Striking a balance between the agencies of local actors, of external and often anonymous actors, and of Government initiatives will continue to be a serious task, not only for law makers.

From an anthropological view point, of particular interest is what and how members of the scientific community from and on Pacific Islands think about these issues, and also how local agency does further evolve among themselves. With the text of the late Marie-Claire Beboko-Beccalossi as a guide, we get the feeling for just how much intellectual energy and social responsibility it took, over the years, for Kanak women to earn again an appropriate voice and place in contemporary society, a place as respected or even more so than in a distant past. Marie-Claire's and her network's long battle reflects indirectly, and perhaps not surprisingly, the extent to which traditional gender roles were completely transformed by the early generations of teachers, colonial administrators and missionaries who all came from male-dominated sections of European society. Their dominance took away from women a lot of the potential of social agency.

For Kanak women, the *robe mission* has become a key element in claiming their own identity, as much as individuals as when acting in a peer group. By analysing this model case of materiality, Anna Paini illustrates how difficult the reading of local agency can get depending on the perspective chosen. Europeans, even anthropologists would easily misread the old-fashioned European-style garments so popular among Kanak women as proof of the colonial power's efficient transformation of the locals' identity, whereas the opposite is the case. It is striking that in this development no marked difference between an urban background and communities in more remote island situations appears. Paini shows how at present both contexts merge into one, thus allowing tradition and traditional forms to gain a dynamic potential. In putting peoples first we need to question again and again our own discipline's viewing habits in the light of what people and peoples have to tell us.

Another aspect of materiality is illustrated by the case of the bamboo tubes engraved by Kanak storytellers and artists. Kanak society, especially on the Grande Terre of New Caledonia, where France installed in 1853 a penitentiary regime was much earlier exposed to forced colonisation with a numerically strong European presence. Local agency soon found a way to record pictures of the interaction between the traditional lifestyle and visiting colonial personnel by drawing on bamboo tubes. Roberta Colombo Dougoud took engraved bamboos, the focus of an exhibition in Geneva, back to Nouméa. This offered an opportunity to contrast the engraved bamboos of the nineteenth century with the work of a contemporary Kanak artist, Micheline Néporon, who reinvented the drawing on bamboo tubes with the aim of addressing a Kanak audience of today, confronting it with glimpses of problematic behaviour such us the abuse of alcohol leading to an incredibly high number of fatal car accidents. Here contemporary local agency responds to what outsiders had once contributed by collecting the old engraved bamboo tubes as well as by studying them, albeit under a hypothesis that aimed in the wrong direction. We would like to hear more about how Kanak society and their fellow inhabitants on the islands react to what artists of Micheline's generation have to tell them.

May the tide of innovations bring forth a rising force of fruitful contributions to help peoples of the Pacific maintain their potential to flourish. By 'Putting People First', anthropology could surely assist by developing its own potential of reflecting on how to match agencies, especially those that risk constraining each other. It's high time for cooperative efforts to aim beyond the limits of any separate discipline. In order to get there, scientists, social leaders, economists, politicians, food producers, cooks and—why not—artists need to share their forces, in the Pacific as much as elsewhere.

References

Bateson, Gregory. 1958 [1936]. *Naven, A Survey of the Problems Suggested by a Composite Picture of the Culture of a New Guinea Tribe Drawn from Three Points of View.* 2nd edition. with Epilogue. Stanford: Stanford University Press.

Golub, Alex. 2014. *Leviathans at the Gold Mine: Creating Indigenous and Corporate Actors in Papua New Guinea.* Durham: Duke University Press.

Rumsey, Alan, and James F. Weiner (eds). 2004. *Mining and Indigenous Lifeworlds in Australia and Papua New Guinea.* Wantage: Sean Kingston Publishing.

Teaiwa, Katerina Martina. 2014. *Consuming Ocean Island: Stories of People and Phosphate from Banaba.* Bloomington: Indiana University Press.

Contributors

Marie-Claire Beboko-Beccalossi (1942–2009) devoted her life to social justice and women's rights in the Pacific area. She had a lifelong commitment to give Kanak women a voice, a face and political representation. Marie-Claire was a founder member in 1983 of the Council of Melanesian Women of New Caledonia, head of the first Bureau Technique des Femmes at the former South Pacific Commission (SPC), president of the Federation of Melanesian Women's Associations, and delegate for Women's Rights for New Caledonia. In her work she always combined an attention to personal, institutional and 'field' dimensions, creating a vast network of relations in the Pacific region and beyond. She represented New Caledonia at the Pontifical Council for Justice and Peace in the Vatican. She died on 28 March 2009 and, according to her wishes, rests in peace in the forest near the village where she grew up (Petit Couli).

Roberta Colombo Dougoud studied sociology at the University of Urbino (Italy), after which she worked in the Social Anthropology Institute of the University of Fribourg, earning her PhD with the thesis 'Le storyboards di Kambot. Arte del Sepik tra tradizione e modernità'. Since 1999 she has been in charge of the Oceanic collection at the Musée d'ethnographie de Genève (MEG). She has carried out fieldwork in Papua New Guinea, Morocco and Italy. Her writings and research have focused on changes in traditional art, history of collections, contemporary Oceanic art, art and identity, tourism, intercultural communication and museography. She curated several exhibitions on Oceanic art, including *Bambous kanak. Une passion de Marguerite Lobsiger-Dellenbach* and *Traces de rêves. Peintures sur écorce des Aborigènes d'Australie*.

Elisabetta Gnecchi-Ruscone is an independent scholar who specialised in the anthropology of Oceania, in particular Papua New Guinea, where she did fieldwork in Tufi, Oro Province (1987–88 and 2013). Since 2003 she has been a lecturer on societies and cultures of the Pacific at the Università di Milano Bicocca, and has collaborated with the Museo delle Culture del Mondo Castello D'Albertis in Genova and with the Museo delle Culture in Lugano. Currently she is involved with projects at the new MUDEC (Museum of Cultures in Milano). A founding member of the ESfO board, she organised with Anna Paini the society's 2008 conference in Verona. Among her publications are *Dizionari delle Civiltà: Oceania* (2010 Electa, French edition, Hazan, 2011); *Antropologia dell'Oceania* with Anna Paini (Cortina, 2009); 'Parallel journeys in Korafe women's laments (Papua New Guinea)' in *Journal de la Société des Océanistes* 124, 2007; *Putting People First. Dialogo interculturale immaginando il futuro in Oceania*, ed. with Anna Paini (2011); '"Alla Nuova Guinea" Gli oggetti e le storie della collezione D'Albertis, Museo Castello di Genova', in *La densità delle cose*, ed. Anna Paini e Matteo Aria (Pacini Editore, 2014).

Margaret Jolly was an Australian Research Council Laureate Fellow from 2010–2015 and is a Professor in the School of Culture, History and Language in the College of Asia and the Pacific at The Australian National University. She is a historical anthropologist who has written extensively on gender in the Pacific, on exploratory voyages and travel writing, missions and contemporary Christianity, maternity and sexuality, cinema and art. Her books include *Women of the Place: Kastom, Colonialism and Gender in Vanuatu* (Harwood Academic Publishers, 1994); *Sites of Desire, Economies of Pleasure: Sexualities in Asia and the Pacific*, ed. with Lenore Manderson (University of Chicago Press, 1997); *Maternities and Modernities: Colonial and Postcolonial Experiences in Asia and the Pacific*, ed. with Kalpana Ram (Cambridge University Press, 1998); *Borders of Being: Citizenship, Fertility and Sexuality in Asia and the Pacific*, ed. with Kalpana Ram (University of Michigan Press, 2001); *Oceanic Encounters: Exchange, Desire, Violence*, ed. with Serge Tcherkézoff and Darrell Tryon (ANU E Press, 2009); *Engendering Violence in Papua New Guinea*, ed. with Christine Stewart and Carolyn Brewer (ANU E Press 2012); *Divine Domesticities: Christian Paradoxes in Asia and the Pacific*, ed. with Hyaeweol Choi (ANU Press, 2014); and *Gender Violence and Human Rights: Seeking Justice in Fiji, Papua New Guinea and Vanuatu*, ed. with Aletta Biersack and Martha Macintyre (ANU Press 2016).

Christian Kaufmann, obtained a PhD in cultural anthropology in 1969. He has done extensive field research in Papua New Guinea in 1966–1967, 1972–1973, 1983, as well as in Vanuatu in 1983, 1991, 1993, and field visits to New Caledonia and Arnhem Land, Northern Territory. From 1970 to 2005, he was curator at the Museum der Kulturen in Basel, responsible for the Oceania department. He joined curatorial and editorial teams in international exhibition projects, among them in 1996–97 on the Arts of Vanuatu, *Vanuatu. Océanie. Arts des îles de cendre et de corail/ Arts of Vanuatu*, ed. Joël Bonnemaison et al. (Paris, RMN and Bathurst, 1996); in 2005 on Australian paintings: *«rarrk» John Mawurndjul: Journey Through Time in Northern Australia*, with Bernhard Lüthi and Guido Magnaguagno (Museum Tinguely, Basel); and, in 2015, on Sepik art, *Arts du Sepik/Tanz der Ahnen – Kunst aus Papua-Neuguinea* in Berlin, Zurich, and Paris, with Philippe Peltier and Markus Schindlbeck on behalf of the Musée du quai Branly, Paris. From 1998 to 2005 he taught courses on Melanesian art at the University of Basel and later at the Sainsbury Research Unit (SRU), University of East Anglia, Norwich, UK, where he is a Research Associate. He is a founding member of the Pacific Arts Association.

Susanne Kuehling, a German anthropologist, is Associate Professor at the University of Regina in Canada. She received her MA from Göttingen University. For her doctoral research she conducted 18 months of fieldwork on Dobu Island, Papua New Guinea. Her PhD thesis, submitted at The Australian National University in 1999, was titled 'The name of the gift: ethics of exchange on Dobu Island'. She has published a book, *Dobu: Ethics of Exchange on a Massim Island* (University of Hawai'i Press, 2005), and journal articles on *kula* exchange, value, personhood, morality, gender, emplacement, and teaching methods. Her current project on the revitalisation of *kula* exchange, funded by the Canadian Social Sciences and Humanities Research Council (SSHRC), was developed during a number of visits to Dobu Island (2009, 2012, 2015). She taught for five years at Heidelberg University before moving to Canada in 2008.

Andrew Moutu studied philosophy and anthropology at the University of Papua New Guinea (1991–1996) before undertaking his master's and doctoral degrees in social anthropology from the University of Cambridge (1998–2003). He was British Academy Postdoctoral Fellow at the University of Cambridge (2004–2007), and Leach/Royal Anthropological Institute Postdoctoral Fellow at the National University of Ireland (2007–2008). He lectured in anthropology at the University of Adelaide (2009–2010) before returning home to Port Moresby to rebuild the National Museum and Art Gallery. His academic interests range from philosophical anthropology, legal anthropology and intellectual property rights, museums and material culture, Melanesian systems of knowledge, to holographic imagination and the anthropology of perception.

His monograph, *Names Are Thicker Than Blood,* was published by Oxford University Press in 2013. More recently he has taken up an interest in Papua New Guinea's modern history and with the ongoing concerns about the intersection between sorcery, witchcraft and the law in Papua New Guinea.

Anna Paini is Associate Professor in Cultural Anthropology at the University of Verona. Former chair (2005–2008) of the European Society for Oceanists, she is currently an ESfO board member. Since 1989 she has done extensive fieldwork in Lifou (Loyalty Islands). Her main research topics include anthropology and colonial history in New Caledonia; Kanak women's knowledge, practices and forms of sociality; cultural heritage and material culture. An ongoing research interest is the *robe mission*; she was invited to lecture on her field research at the Textiles Extraordinaires Festival in Manila (2015). She has published articles in English, French and Italian. Among her books are *La terra dei miei sogni. Esperienze di ricerca sul campo in Oceania,* ed. with Lorenzo Brutti (2002); *Il filo e l'aquilone. I confini della differenza in una società kanak della Nuova Caledonia* (2007), translated into French by the Université de la Nouvelle-Calédonie (forthcoming); *Antropologia dell'Oceania,* ed. with Elisabetta Gnecchi-Ruscone (2009); *La densità delle cose. Oggetti ambasciatori tra Oceania e Europa,* ed. with Matteo Aria (2014).

Guido Carlo Pigliasco is Affiliate Professor of Anthropology at the University of Hawai'i, a Fellow of the Explorers Club, a Foreign Law Consultant at the Supreme Court of the State of Hawai'i, and serves on the Board of Hawai'i European Cinema. He has practised international law, written 10 documentary films on contemporary Oceania for Italian television, published the ethnographic novel *Paradisi inquieti,* and directed 'The Sawau project' (*A ituvatuva ni vakadidike e Sawau*), a multimedia digital storytelling pilot on Pacific Islanders' rights in intangible cultural heritage supported by a grant from the Ministry of Fijian Affairs. Notable among his peer-reviewed publications is his co-edited book *At Home and in the Field: Ethnographic Encounters in Asia and the Pacific Islands,* examining the predicaments and politics of undisciplining ethnography in twenty-first-century productions of knowledge, moral economies, ontologies, place and temporalities. His anthology *Storie straordinarie di italiani nel Pacifico* (2016) portrays the narratives and memoirs of unhonoured, enigmatic, buried in oblivion Italian pioneers in fin-de-siècle Oceania.

Nancy J. Pollock continues to work on food security, with particular reference to the Pacific. She has taught anthropology and Pacific studies at Victoria University in Wellington, New Zealand, promoting awareness of New Zealand's relations with its neighbouring countries. Ongoing research in the central Pacific with Marshallese, Wallis and Futunan, Nauruan and Fijian and French Polynesian colleagues has enabled her to trace the links between Pacific gastronomies and those of China and Asia over time and space. Among her publications are 'The language of food' in Thieberger, *The Oxford Handbook of Linguistic Fieldwork* (2011), *A Meeting of Tastes: Captain Cook's Gastronomic Experiences in Tahiti and New Zealand* (2012), 'Nauru phosphate history', in *Journal de la Société des Océanistes* (2014), follow from an earlier publication on food security *These Roots Remain* (1992). She continues to write and publish while enjoying retirement.

Marshall Sahlins has spent most of his academic life at the University of Chicago, where he is currently the Charles F. Grey Distinguished Service Professor Emeritus of Anthropology. He is the executive publisher of Prickly Paradigm Press and the author of numerous articles and books on anthropological theory and in particular the Pacific; many of his books have been translated into several languages. Among them, *Stone Age Economics* (1972); *Islands of History* (1985); *How 'Natives' Think: About Captain Cook, for example* (1995); *Apologies to Thucydides* (2004), and *What Kinship is—and is not* (2013). Another book, provisionally titled *The Stranger-King; or, the Powers of Otherness*, is currently in preparation.

Marc Tabani is Senior Research Fellow at the Centre National de la Recherche Scientifique (CNRS) and affiliated to the Centre de Recherche et de Documentation sur l'Océanie (CREDO). He has conducted his research in Vanuatu, especially in the island of Tanna, since 1993. His main interests are the politics of identity and tradition, cultural change or indigenous movements and millenarianism. He has published several articles in French and English and edited two volumes: *Les pouvoirs de la coutume à Vanuatu: traditionalisme et édification nationale* (2002); and *Une pirogue pour le paradis : le culte de John Frum à Tanna* (2008). He is also editor and co-author of the French version of *Histri blong yumi: An history of Vanuatu* in four volumes (2010–2012) and editor of a special issue of the *Journal de la Société des Océanistes* dedicated to the 30 years of Vanuatu's independence (2011) and an Association for Social Anthropology in Oceania (ASAO) monograph, *Kago, Kastom and Kalja: The Study of Indigenous Movements in Melanesia Today*.

www.ingramcontent.com/pod-product-compliance
Lightning Source LLC
Chambersburg PA
CBHW050806270326
41926CB00026B/4580